Service Drive Revolution
Volume 1

Chris Collins

ChrisCollinsInc.com

Table of Contents

Episode #1: How To Increase Dealership CSI And Other Service Drive Secret Weapons

Chris: Welcome to Fixed Ops Evolution. This is Chris and my sidekick G Man, Gary

Gary: Welcome.

Chris: We have a fun agenda here for you today. We're going to talk about the silver bullet, the secret weapon to increasing everything, basically, it's squared so it increases closing ratios, CSI, how the customers feel about you on a deeper level, the love the customers have for you. Your customers are going to love you more.

Gary: That might be a little deep, I think, I don't know if we want to go that far.

Chris: Then, we're going to talk about a book that we highly suggest that everybody reads and enjoys. This is happy hour here.

Gary: End of the day, happy hour.

Chris: Do you feel guilty at all that we skipped to June?

Gary: A little bit but I was happy that you let me off the hook, actually

Chris: You liked that text?

Gary: I was like "Oh sleep, yes, I get to sleep."

Chris: We skipped the gym today, we didn't go, which isn't good. Dr. Lau is not going to be happy. I have a theory about Gary's health problems that we'll address in a later podcast, I think.

Gary: I don't know if that theory holds water.

Chris: We're going to get deep into that but, more importantly, this is the worse time of the year possible. I know some of you in other parts of the country where it's cold and you're like "Oh man, it was a great day, it's 50 degrees today because it's not -6." You guys are thinking this is the best time of the year but, to me, this is the worst time of the year because there's no football and who's going to go to a baseball game.

Gary: I don't know.

Chris: Have you thought about going to a baseball game?

Gary: I have thought about it, yes, especially moving to LA and the Dodgers are here and I thought about it.

Chris: Dodger dog. Do you want to have a Dodger dog?

Gary: I don't know. I'll put up with traffic and parking and all that for football but not for baseball.

Chris: My experience with Dodger Stadium is that it's quicker to walk than to drive.

Gary: And you're 10 miles away.

Chris: No, we're like three miles away, it's right there. It's right over that little hill right there. That's the fun part of being in downtown LA. Right now, this time of day - we're doing this in late afternoon - there are no good choices if you needed to go anywhere.

Gary: No, zero.

Chris: It's funny, when people are like "Where do you live?" And we're like "Oh Los Angeles" and they're like "Isn't there a lot of traffic?"

Gary: Yes, there's a lot of traffic. We were just talking about that earlier that you're screwed both ways because there's traffic in every direction. You're commuting in, there's traffic commuting out, it just doesn't matter. You're going to be in it except for 9:00 last night, it was good.

Chris: There can be traffic at 9:00.

Gary: I flew home.

Chris: Did you smoke a cigar on your way home?

Gary: I did not, no, not at 9:00.

Chris: We have all these cigars left over from NADA from our cigar party. We way over bought but we knew when we did it, we said "We'll buy more than we need but we know we can smoke them." I have had three cigar days.

Gary: I know for sure Dr. Lau is not listening to this so I can go on record and say I'm at least one to two a day right now.

Chris: I don't know what Dr. Lau told you but I'm supposed to have one a month.

Gary: I just don't engage him in that conversation. He thinks I don't smoke them so I want to keep it that way.

Chris: That's a good note.

Gary: Ignorance is bliss.

Chris: I won't ever mention that. He knows I smoke them because I've been to his fancy cigar thing in Beverly Hills with him.

Gary: He doesn't want us to smoke cigars but invites us to the Havana Room.

Chris: Right. SO, worse time of the year, no football. I wish football would come back. There's nothing. Pete Carroll is doing nothing, they're all like on vacation with their family. It's boring. To our topic today, the silver bullet, I think we have to set it up first with how we got to the point we did with instant inspection and the story of my friend Richard

Fish.

Gary: And the Evolution.

Chris: When I was running BMW, we had this weird deal at the
body shop that Carbea BMW, we had this weird deal with
the body shop that most dealerships have where they pay
you an amount of money to then get all your business,
because we didn't have our own body shop and it was a
weird deal. It had been a deal for a long time with the family
and this body shop owner, who had a bunch of body shops.
They really didn't do great work but they brought in a
new CEO, who was my friend, Rich Fish, one of the
greatest guys.
Do you know how I knew he was great? Right up front
when I met him, the first thing he does is come around to
the big client, wants to take you to lunch and the whole
thing. Him and I hit it off.

Gary: That's a stand up act.

Chris: Many nights and lots of fun situations with Fish but the first
thing he told me up front was, I should back up. I wanted
to up our deal. I think we were getting 10 grand a month
and I thought it was over 20. I'm like "Here comes this new
guy, I'm going to tell him we're going to take our business
somewhere else if we don't get 20."

Gary: Set the frame.

Chris: Clear as day, he just looks me right in the eye and he says
"You know these deals with dealerships will re-pay you
money for your business. I'm not a fan."

Gary: He did the take away right out of the gate.

Chris: Yeah. "I'm not a fan. They don't work for anybody." We're
like taking short cuts to try to pay you and BMW's are a
huge pain to work on.So it ends up, he's an amazing

4

operator and he ended up starting his own body shops, he has quite a few but in our friendship and in him sharing things and mentoring, one of the things that he went down the path with his own body shop years later was, he wanted to improve his turn time and just run a better business. He's always constantly trying to improve and he's just one of those guys that's on the forefront. He's telling me about the system in the body shop world and the basis of it was theory of constraints, which brings us to the book that we would recommend everybody to read. Every time we do one of these, we'll try to have a book because we read a lot of books around here and we'll try to pass it along. Whenever anybody comes here to the office they always are asking what books they should read so we're going to try to highlight one every podcast we do.

This one is called *The Goal, A Process of Ongoing Improvement*. It's by Eliyahu M. Goldratt. Take a shot at that.

Gary: No, I'm out.

Chris: Eliyahu - and it's the best selling business novel that introduced the theory of constraints and changed how America does business, over six million copies sold. I think on the back here it says it's one of the books that they use at Harvard Business School. The things that we learned from this book, this book basically is narrated in a very funny way because; if you listen to the audio of the book, they hired actors and it really is a novel. There's Trish, the guys wife hates how much he works all the time and she leaves him, she goes and stays with her parents, takes the kids.

Gary: No, she leaves him with the kids. She leaves him with all his problems and the kids.

Even better.

Gary: It was awesome.

Chris: In the beginning of the book, the guy finds himself in the situation where he's been promoted to factory manager and they make some sort of widget for something and he pulls in the first day and his boss's car is parked in his parking spot.

Gary: That's right.

Chris: Then he walks in and the boss has blown up the union over some order that's been back ordered and isn't happening. Then it comes to a pretty quick head where the boss closes the door and sits him down and says "I'm closing your plant in 90 days if you can't make it profitable." Something to that effect.

Gary: That's exactly right.

Chris: The guy goes on this journey and some of my favorite highlights from the book, the one that's the funniest to me is, they bought some automated machine, a robot, and everybody's excited about the robot. They're like "We got the new MX blah, blah, blah, robot." It reminds me a lot of when everybody was going to MPI.

Gary: This will fix everything, we've got the solution.

Chris: That reminds me too, what was the thing we used to have to do at BMW dealerships, called QMS?

Gary: QMS, Quality, Management Systems, yes.

Chris: Same situation where I'm sitting there with a bunch of dealers at the LA Auto Show, actually. I won't name the dealers but one of them has a huge ego. The factory guys are sitting at the table too and he's like "You've got to get QMS, it's the greatest, we're certified." I said "Did your CSI go up?" "No." I'm like "Are you making more money?" "No, no." But you documented all your processes? Flavor of the month, right?

Gary: We had rooms of binders of all this information that nobody looked at.

Chris: Everybody's signing up for these digital inspections but every time they'd put them in, the hours per would go down, sales would go down and I used to always tell those guys when they'd come around. I'm like "I'll tell you how to fix your software if you want" because it was the process, the system wasn't really taking into consideration that a technician - it just wasn't user friendly. Every time we'd unhook that, our hours per our own sales would go up, which is paper, right?

Same premise in this book is everybody's like "We got the new robot." "Wow, you got the new robot, that's cool." This guy is trying to figure out how to turn his factory around and he's in some meeting and his old college professor happens to be there. They're leaving, in passing his college professor is like "How's it going?" He says "We got the new robot." The guys says "Are your profits up?" He's like "No." He says "Are the overall efficiencies up?" He's like "No, the efficiencies are not part of the factor of 30% but no, our overall efficiencies are flat." He's like "Okay, well don't tell me about the robot."

Gary: He's like "Well your robot really isn't working then, is it?"

Chris: We've found that a paper inspection sheet works pretty good if you do it right. I'm not saying that technology isn't good but that was the thing in this book that just really hit home because the first time I read the book was when I was getting a lot of pressure from manufacturers to put in the digital ones. But every time we did it, the sales would go down and it was super expensive too. I'm like how am I going to tell a client; "You're going to spend five grand a month and watch your sales go down because you got the new software?"

Gary: It's fancy and you get a lot of good data but you can't sell anything more, in fact, you sell less. It's just not a good equation.

Chris: I'm thinking of one. Hopefully you'll say it but, what was the biggest take away in the book for you?

Gary: I don't know. I just think, honestly for them, they were locked into an old way of thinking and they're just like "This is how everything's always been done." I think, as they went through the process, they learned to look at things from a different viewpoint and kind of look at things as a whole and everything related to the goal, which is the title of the book, and if it didn't improve the goal, which was making money, selling products, then they abandoned it and they went on to try to find something better. That was my takeaway.

Chris: Even in the part about the robot, they ended up getting their old machines back.

Gary: Yeah, they brought them back in.

Chris: The old machines that they ditched for the robot, they ended up bringing them back in, which is so true to life, right?

Gary: Yes.

Chris: What about the fat kid?

Gary: What about the fat kid?

Chris: That's a great part of the book. That was a huge ah-ha moment.

Gary: I thought it was funny. I thought it was a little edgy using the fat kid as the example of the constraint in this day and age.

Chris: Evidently, Eliyahu Goldratt isn't interested in your HR department.

Gary: He doesn't play politically correct, I can tell you that for sure.

Chris: What's the politically correct way to say fat kid?

Gary: The less than agile young man.

Chris: Above average weight?

Gary: Yes. The slower than normal young man.

Chris: I'm going to say the fat kid and the funny thing about that was, he's like taking a boy scout troop out or something?

Gary: Yes, it was a boy scout troop.

Chris: In the - what they call the business novel - he's taking a boy scout troop out and they're hiking and he makes a parallel between his factory and these kids marching up the hill and I think the fat kid's in the middle.

Gary: He starts out towards the back.

Chris: Towards the back?

Gary: Yes, he still has some people behind him but he's towards the back of the line.

Chris: A huge gap?

Gary: A huge gap, yes. He's got to wait because he's in the middle and the fast kids are getting out in front of him too far and then you've got the fat kid holding the kids behind him back and so he's kind of stuck in this spot where he's trying to manage the whole line and he just can't, the way it's set up.

Chris: They end up putting him at the front.

Gary: Right.

Chris: It sets the pace for everybody and then there's no gaps and nobody's lost and you would never think to do that.

Gary: That's the opposite of what you would - if you're going for maximum speed and efficiency - that's not what you would do. You wouldn't put him out front.

Chris: The other one is, I think we've talked about this before, the part where it's okay for people to stand around.

Gary: Yes.

Chris: It's a hard one to swallow.

Gary: That's a hard one.

Chris: We're tracking efficiency. We want people working. We're trying to figure out ways that parts come on. I'm waiting for you to figure out a way for parts to be delivered by drones.

Gary: I think too, service managers, and I commend them all and I felt this way too when I was a tech, they care about their technicians, they want to keep them busy and so having them stand around and not turn hours; not only do they feel like they're hurting production but they also feel like they're hurting their incomer. It's this whole battle, this internal battle, that they go through every day to try to keep these guys busy.

Chris: It's hilarious. I mean, I think about the things that I've done in my career to keep technicians efficient and two that stand out really is putting parts guys in the shop.

Gary: Yes, we've done that one.

Chris: It didn't increase production at all.

Gary: Not a lick.

Chris: But it was a cool thing to say at a 20 group meeting, maybe one dollar at a time at a 20 group meeting and then the other one was having the cars delivered to the techs and that actually made efficiency go down because the techs were standing around waiting and they weren't very good managers of time that way to know to get a car coming before the car was done. It was an added layer of expense that actually efficiency went down. The thing you learn is that technicians that are going to be productive... like when you were a tech, you wouldn't have wanted runners, I don't think.

I remember, you just had cars stacked and so it wouldn't have mattered. You were going to figure out a way. We could have put a river through the middle of the shop and you would have figured out a way to get a ferry to get them to your bay to get them done, it wasn't going to matter. You had a number in your head that you were going to flag.

Gary: They think we want to layer in a process and a system to help these guys become efficient and what we're not thinking about is, we're just not involving them in that and so we're putting this process in front of them and all it's going to do is, it just clogs it up. It puts an extra wheel or cog or geer in the machine that doesn't need to be there and it just gums up the works and I've never seen any of those things make a headway at all.

Chris: No and you've tried them all with open mind.

Gary: Yes, I tried everything. To go back to your digital tablet multi-point thing, I did that twice and it failed both times.

Chris: You were nice enough. One of those was a pilot I was doing with one of those companies, it was going to be my signature thing and it just was a paperweight.

Gary: I want it to work, I really want it to work.

Chris: In the words of the great Scott Simpson, "It was a paperweight." Then the story about the goal and the inspiration from my friend Mr. Fish was that we started thinking "Why do we do things the way we do them in service because it's so inefficient?" Right?

Gary: Yes.

Chris: You write up the car and then it gets parked and then a tech goes and gets it and then they look at it, then they tell the advisor, then the advisor calls or texts and then does the tech pull it out? Especially nowadays when there's less and less diagnosis. The times I've done a warranty on how much diagnosis is actually done anymore, it's below 10% where a car comes in and needs diagnosis, like run ability or electrical. That varies by brand but there isn't a lot of diagnosis. A car is made so well anymore that really, why do we do all that?

Why don't we just inspect the car right upfront with the customer and take out all the steps and then what we found from it is, the closing ratios increase because customers love seeing their car with the technician and they like going behind the curtain and our sales per RO more than double just about every time, right?

Gary: Yes, I mean more than double in almost every occurrence and the closing ratios are just through the roof. I mean, we knew it was going to be good when we were testing it but it was better than we ever thought it would be.

Chris: It's easy to do and it all comes from that little thing, the theory of constraints, trying to figure out where the bottlenecks are in the business and how to improve the customer experience and the staff that just blows me away. When I was doing my research for my talk for NEDA, the workshop, I looked at that number Gary, I don't even know how many times. I could not believe that 82% of our customers go to independent shops or you lose them to techs.

Gary: That's crazy. It's insane.

Chris: If that isn't failure, I don't know what is.

Gary: I don't know. If you've been to some of those shops, and I've worked at some of those shops, there are no amenities there and so they're sacrificing a lot. There's definitely something driving them away from us and I can tell you one thing, from being on the other side of the fence, it's not price.

Chris: No, it's not price. I remember that when I was an advisor in Seattle. The independent shop was $20 higher than us and they were booked out weeks but people trusted them and they liked them and they were pulling right in the shop. It wasn't all the layers and bureaucracy that we have at dealerships. We know, with working with other service facilities, that customers actually will pay for their own warranty work sometimes because they don't want to deal with the dealership and that's just embarrassing.

Gary: Yes. I mean, I experienced that first hand. Most of the customers I had at the shop I worked at, they wouldn't want to pay. It didn't matter; maintenance, repairs, they wanted us to do everything for them because they had a relationship with us and they'd come and hang out in the shop and talk with the techs and sometimes they'd take us to lunch. They wanted us to work on their car unless they absolutely, like if they needed a transmission and it was outside of the scope of what they were willing to pay, then they'd take it for warranty repair but outside of that, they wanted us to do everything.

Chris: Those two things, they hurt my heart, they really do, that we lose that much in retention. The idea of instant inspection and changing the process and making it easy and building trust with the customer and breaking down that wall of "The technician's the guy in the back and you can't talk to them but we'll call you and let you know" and them feeling like "They're selling me stuff I don't need." It fixes all of that and it's the future for sure, it's catching on like wildfire and it's the future.

Gary: I know a lot of places are talking about doing pictures and video and I just think that there's this trend that's going back to service and this touch or this connection that you're going to make with the customers. I think that's what customers want. They don't want to be disconnected. I mean, we have the internet and we're constantly on the web and we're constantly disconnected from things. I think, when they're coming in and they have the opportunity, they want that service, they want that touch. They want to be close to that.

Chris: In just about every aspect of consumer purchasing, there's somebody that's starting to lead the hand made boutique. You can buy a set of knives for your wife that are like $2,000 hand made by some guy in a shop in like Maine and everything is going to that more crafty hand made, they really care about it, they make it the hard way, not the easy way. It's not automated and I think, in our industry, it's the same thing. The customers just want to pull right in the shop and talk to the guy. They don't want all the layers.

Gary: Right, exactly.

Chris: They don't want to mistrust us. They just want to go right to it and so that's really where it's headed. That's our food for thought for this podcast. How do you think we did with our first podcast here?

Gary: I'd say, being your first one, it's good!

Chris: We didn't fix your cholesterol.

Gary: No, we didn't even talk about my cholesterol, which is good. The more we talk about it, the more it goes up.

Chris: Did we talk about the Dallas Cowboys?

Gary: No, we didn't talk about the Cowboys either. That makes my blood pressure go up so we don't want that. I'm already medicated for that.

Chris: You're a walking time bomb for that.

Gary: Between blood pressure, estrogen and my cholesterol, I think I've got enough worries. I don't need the Cowboys in there.

Chris: I hope you got something out of this and we have the best service advisor training service manager training in the world, Gary, guaranteed.

Gary: Agreed.

Chris: For results.

Gary: The only technician training on the market right now.

Chris: That Gary did himself.

Gary: Yes.

Chris: You honestly look like you should have your own TV show. I don't know what you're doing in the TV show but you look like you should have your own TV show.

Gary: The TV show is x-rated as far as I can tell.

Chris: Not that part, just when you're at the car doing your inspection. You know how to inspect a car and all that. You look like you should be on one of those classic cars, rebuilding them or something.

Gary: I'm going to give all the credit to Lucas doing the editing. He made me look good in post-production.

Chris: Way to go Lucas. Well thanks everybody and we will see you next time.

Gary: Cheers.

Episode #2: Becoming A Champion In Service, The Magic Behind Customer Retention

Chris: Welcome to Service Drive Revolution, the podcast made with love for service managers, dealers, and anybody working on repairing or maintaining cars for customers. How you doing G-man?

Gary: Not so good today, bro. Not good at all.

Chris: Why?

Gary: A couple things-

Chris: I regret asking.

Gary: Yeah, right? That's one of those things-

Chris: Come right at me, "Doing not so good." Oh boy.

Gary: You're passing body in the hall, that's the passing people in the hall question is, "How are you doing?" You just hope that they say, "Good." And walk by.

Chris: Any puppies die? Geez Louis.

Gary: I don't know man, I have had a rough afternoon.

Chris: Let's table that. The podcast today is about how Magic Johnson would be a great service manager.

Gary: Yep.

Chris: And we're going to talk about that. The title might confuse you, but we do a lot of stupid stuff.

Gary: Absolutely and that's part of my issue today and why I'm not doing so hot right now. I'm sure I'll share that story with us.

Chris: Okay, get it out. Let's hear it. No what's wrong.

Gary: No, no, no, I want to start talking will go for the ... First of all, I have a cocktail in front of me. I already broke my vow not to drink for the next 30 days, but it's a sip, so I'm giving myself a pass.

Chris: Yeah, you're fine bro. You're 21, you're going to be okay.

Gary: I'm not in the 12 step program or anything.

Chris: Yeah, you're doing good, no but what's really wrong?

Gary: Well, try to get my car in for service.

Chris: Oh, yeah. No that story fits-

Gary: That's that one that-

Chris: That's inspiring us today, right?

Gary: That's the one that's got me feeling a little miffed actually, you know?

Chris: Okay, so let's talk about that. We just had coaching meetings so for anybody who doesn't know, we have coaching groups for service managers and we just had one in Boston, and then we had leet meeting here in the office, and then our West Coast coaching meeting. Before that, I spoke to two 20 groups. So I went to Nashville and where was the other one? Pittsburgh.

Gary: Pittsburgh, yeah.

Chris: We had a boot camp for new coaching members and then ... The one thing everybody says that just drives me crazy is,

"That won't work here, my market's different," And you're like, "Okay." Now what?

Gary: You know. Well I'm with customers every day or you know, potential clients for us every day and that's the one thing I hear. That's the most common objection is, "That won't work here, my market's different, you don't know my market." That's the common thing.

Chris: We're going to kick the shit out of that today with what we're going to talk about. That leads us to your story, some good friends of ours, and we love the family, and in no way are we picking on them whatsoever. We come to the coaching meeting and the service manager for this dealership's texting all the time, complaining, and traffic's downing and unapplied labor's up and everything sucks, and blah, blah, blah, my market. Meanwhile, the market is Southern California, luxury cars; like there's more luxury cars than Hondas or Toyotas here, right?

Gary: Yep. Especially in that neighborhood.

Chris: When we were number one and new car sales were Crevier. I'd be like, "No, we should be number one." You got Palm Beach, Florida-

Gary: Newport.

Chris: Manhattan here and maybe Dallas. There's just no reason why you can sell luxury cars. Now granted, in Orange County, there's four or five BMW stores and none of them are number one anymore so it's all mental but you should be. I don't know what is that dude, six months old?

Gary: Yeah, about six, maybe little better.

Chris: You bought SO, an F&I and you did the honorable thing. You bought everything in F&I.

Gary: Yeah.

Chris: So when you bought the car, you bought some package that guarantees that any dents or whatever, basically anybody cosmetic stuff smaller than what, a quarter?

Gary: Basically, twice a year, they'll touch up your bumpers because the bumpers gets scuffed, they'll pull out any dents that a PDR could pull out, painless dent repair. They'll take that out and then they do a detail and cleaning on it, so twice you get that done, it's called total image and is supposed to keep your car you looking new for the life of the lease. I thought, "Hey that's a cool idea, I really like it, so I bought it."

Chris: Done. Doing it.

Gary: I said, "Okay."

Chris: Because you walk around your car with like power tools and you can't be trusted.

Gary: Yeah, like week one without a ding.

Chris: Week one without a ding. Yeah, right out of the gate. Then, I don't know, what's wrong with the car? Some type of window won't close.

Gary: Yeah, the window is hitting the anti-traps kick, so the window won't roll up half the time.

Chris: They can fix that?

Gary: Yep.

Chris: Mine does that all the time.

Gary: Yeah, it needs to be fixed.

Chris: Gary, basically that same car or is yours a little newer?

Gary: Yeah, we have the same car.

Chris: So service manager's sitting in our meeting saying traffics down, right?

Gary: Yeah.

Chris: Unapplied labor's up, everything sucks, my market.

Gary: Life is not good.

Chris: You adventure yourself to make a service appointment, and take it from there.

Gary: I'm going to take a drink. I wanted to bring my car in and I'm pretty flexible, on time, it's like, "Okay I'll wait, whatever it's going to take to get it done." We call in and we give them the list of things that we want to do and the first thing they say is, "Okay well, first of all if you want this total image thing done, you've got a call total image first." It's like an insurance policy, so you have to put in a claim, so I'm like, "Eh, okay. All right." And then-

Chris: They're almost hoping you don't?

Gary: Yeah, right? An extra step but, I'm a good soldier so I'm going to do it. So I call the total image place and they're like, "Where you taking your car?" And I let them know where it was going to be, and they're like, "Oh, yeah they don't do very many of those, usually takes three or four weeks for you to get in." Right away I'm like, "Whoa, that's way too long but you know I'll take your advice and I'll call him back and see if I can get in." Put the claim in, that's done. Now, I go on to step two and I call the dealership and we-

Chris: Three calls?

Gary: Yep. Three calls now. I call the dealership back and say, "Okay we're ready now, we want to get our appointment done, and here's our list of stuff." Then again the person on the other end of the phone says, "Oh, you want to get a total image? Oh."

Chris: You suck.

Gary: Automatically I'm like-

Chris: You're one of them.

Gary: But now I'm starting to really regret-

Chris: Asshole that bought that.

Gary: Right?

Chris: They were so excited in finance.

Gary: They really wanted me to buy it. I really thought it was a great ... it had a lot of value.

Chris: You're stupid for buying it evidently.

Gary: I'm just going, "Man, why did I buy this thing, I just bought a chore? I could take it down to my local place and get it detailed." So right away they put me on guard and then they say, "We can't get you in until August for that. August 1st, to frame it, just depending upon when you're listening to it, right now it's June 1." We're talking about August 1 which is-

Chris: Couple months.

Gary: Ridiculous two months out. That's the longest service appointment I've have ever heard of, but the most shocking thing was this development.

Chris: There's two, two shocking things.

Gary: You'll have to remind me on the second one, but number one was that they wanted me to hold off on all my repair work until he came in for the total image in August and I thought, "Okay you guys are slow, your traffic's slow, and you've got your people telling me that they don't want me to bring my car in?" I was like, God bless her and she's trying to do her job and I guess what she was trained, but I told her, "Look, I'll just bring my car in to get the repair work done, because I'm tired of the window thing, and I know it needs service, and I know it needs a variety of other things so and then I'll just keep the August appointment for the total image."

Chris: Yeah, because by the way, my car only does that when it rains.

Gary: Mine does it at the worst possible time, like in the supermarket parking lot.

Chris: That's great, that's great you know booking by the BDC and awesome. But then you did say, "Okay but I want to bring it in anyways." They're booked out until next week but they're running out of work everyday.

Gary: Yeah.

Chris: What?

Gary: I'm still coming in next week.

Chris: Makes no sense.

Gary: Yeah, I don't get it and now-

Chris: I'm sure there's a little more to the story but it's all opportunity versus attitude and it's everywhere.

Gary: Well, yeah and we've had this conversation before and I mean this is a product, it's sold by finance, and service department's not thrilled about it, but I will say that the dealership is about 45 minutes from my house and I'm going to pass two on the way there. Like you said, we like the family and we think they're great, and so I wanted to give them the business which is why I bought my car there, and why making this really concentrated effort to have my car serviced there and I got this total image thing. I'm like, it's making me come back. I'm coming back and I'm driving a long distance to do it in LA. You might as well be driving to Colorado - it's a hike.

Chris: Oh, it's a commitment. Yeah, I went there yesterday,

Gary: It's working for them and it's giving them opportunity. My car's coming in, they have an opportunity to upsell me. I'm a buyer, I like to buy stuff when people try to sell it to me. They're missing the boat somewhere and it's somewhere in their mentality that's causing-

Chris: Yeah, it's all mental.

Gary: Yeah, it's all mental.

Chris: Then it's in the execution, but the mindset leads to the execution. If you're saying my market's different, if you're convincing yourself that everything sucks, then it'll suck.

Gary: Right. Exactly.

Chris: You can do it. You can do it. If you want it to suck, you can do it.

Gary: If every up is an opportunity, you know just to use a baseball analogy, you're going to get up to the plate and strike out more time than you're going to hit the ball, statistically. If you want to use a baseball analogy this is an up, you have the bat and you have an opportunity to hit the ball. You're not going to hit the ball, but you have an opportunity and you got take it when you have an up. You got to do it.

Chris: I agree. Then we saw this video and we actually played it at the coaching meetings just because it's so great. It's a Stanford business school interview of Magic Johnson. It's on You Tube and we'll put the link everywhere so you can easily get to it, but it's Magic Johnson Stanford University and it'll come up on You Tube. It's unbelievable, so if Magic Johnson was service manager, everything that he does comes down to mindset, it's unbelievable.

Gary: If he's a service manager, I'd have an appointment tomorrow.

Chris: He'd be selling you hotdogs.

Gary: Right.

Chris: You'd pull in the drive, and he'd be like, "What do you want on your hotdog?" You would just assume the sale.

Gary: Right, yeah, exactly.

Chris: It's crazy. A couple things from this video that were highlights for me, and jump in at anytime, but the idea that he knew he was going to be in the business world when he played for the Lakers, he asked the owner of the Lakers to let him understand the business. He opened the books to him.

Gary: Is his name Jerry?

Chris: I forget the name of the owner of the Lakers. I think he's passed away now, but he opened the books to Magic, and in that Magic asked the PR department, he said, "Hey, do me a favor, give me the names of everybody seated on the floor." The high rollers, right?

Gary: Mm-hmm (affirmative).

Chris: Then he asked 20 of them ... So he found out who is good in business and he asked them out to lunch. Here he is, calling him like he's the star of the Lakers, and he's like, "Hey you want to go to lunch?" And he asked them about business, while he was still with the Lakers. Planning way ahead.

Gary: I thought it was funny too, he used to cold call. "I cold called them all."

Chris: He gets it.

Gary: Not that cold it's a little warm, let's be honest.

Chris: One of the questions asks him in there is, "What surprised you about business?" and he said, "I thought the fact that I was Magic would've meant something." Everywhere he turned, he got his balls kicked in, nobody wanted to help him and nobody took him seriously. Even to one point when he was going up to Silicon Valley trying to get access to a fund to use the money, and he was trying to flip and buy investment properties in South-Central and one of the questions they asked him after they turned him down seven times is: "Well why hasn't anybody else ever come up here and asked to buy land in South-Central?" He said, "I can't answer that." He finally did get the money, he bought some shopping center that was 40% occupied. He bought it for like, is the number 24 million. Filled it up, got it 100% occupied and then flipped and sold it for 40, and they're like, "Oh, okay, here we go."

Gary: They're like, "Okay, you know what you're doing." How many banks did he say, what is it, 55 or something like that? He went to the plate 55 times, to 55 different organizations.

Chris: One thing he says here in my notes that I love about Banks. I know when I was trying to buy the Chrysler dealership, I got turned down 60 times, I think. He said that he got turned down 10 times by banks and then he said, "If 10 banks turn me down, then I'm going to make them all turn me down."

Gary: He just didn't give up.

Chris: There was the 11th one that gave him a little bit of a shot. The moral of that is it just isn't easy. Being Magic Johnson trying to do what he was doing, and very well connected to his community here in LA ... So one of his ideas from research, he's very well researched and versed on the marketing business, was that the urban community will drive out of their community to watch movies, the main-

Gary: What did he say? He did the research and said that, "They're the the number one movie audience." I guess you would say.

Chris: Yeah.

Gary: Movie ticket buyer.

Chris: They go to the movies. He went to Sony and he said, "Hey, look at this. Shouldn't we put a movie theater in South-Central?" And they're like, "Whoa."

Gary: We're the ones buying the tickets, let's put them where they are.

Chris: What about graffiti and gangs and the whole thing? So he partnered with Sony and he went in 50/50 with them and he opened them up and ended up being top 10 in the country and number one for food and concessions.

Gary: Yeah, he calls it per caps, so it's per caps, so per person that goes to the movies, he was collecting more money out of each person than any other movie theater in the area.

Chris: Because in that market, they don't go to dinner and then the movies, the movies is dinner.

Gary: The fascinating part of that is he matched the experience to the market, instead of coming in and saying a one-size-fits-all approach or saying that, "Well, it's an inner-city market so they're not going to want to spend money so why even have concessions? They're not going to buy a $15 bucket of popcorn." He didn't say that, he just went in and said, "Okay well, what do they want? If they want to eat, let's just provide them food." And he did that and-

Chris: He changed the menu. He said in that community it's grape soda, they wanted jalapenos on the hotdogs. Basically when Sony came in they gave him a two month supply of hotdogs.

Gary: That's right.

Chris: And he sold out the first night, which is amazing. He led the industry in per cap and so then he had the idea of: "Well, why don't we have a Starbucks here?"

Gary: Right.

Chris: He went up to Starbucks, I think he said he went up there four, five times and presented to the board. They're like, "What? What?"

Gary: So they were avoiding that, those areas because they don't think you can sell a five dollar cup of coffee in that neck of the woods, they just didn't think he could.

Chris: Charles from Starbucks said, "Okay, well, let me come down and see your movie theaters." And he said he got lucky when that happened because a Whitney Houston movie was opening or something, it was packed. Charles was blown away by his operation and how he did it. They're like, "Let's try three Starbucks." Then same thing. The one thing about that stuck out to me more than anything is we have clients in the worst part of Texas where there's nobody there but they're very profitable. You'll get somebody like, in the city, that's like, "Oh, you can't do that here." You'll have somebody in Columbus, Ohio that has an American domestic dealership that will have an ELR of 116, or 17. What's Glen's ELR, like 117?

Gary: Yeah, 117.

Chris: We have a bunch of clients all around him and better markets than him, and they're like, "They're 90." And they're like, "It's my market." You're like, "No it's your head, because it's not your market." The thing with him was when he has a way of wording things in a mindset about things. The thing that really stuck out to me was that he said to Starbucks, "People in South-Central, don't really know what a scone is. It's not their thing. So we're going to change." This really stuck out to me, "We're going to change the menu a little bit." He didn't change the menu a little bit, he blew up the menu. He's like, "We're going to have peach cobbler, we're going to have ... " He did a menu for the snacks that fit that market and then said, "Oh.-

Gary: Give the people what they want.

Chris: And one other thing that I don't want is to listen to elevator music." We played Prince and Motown. Basically he had a completely different menu, the only thing they were serving really was coffee and then playing different music. I was in one of those Starbucks because one of our clients down there in south-central is right by one of his first ones - it was one of the first three. It feels different but the way he sold it is, "I'm going to change a couple little things."

Gary: Yeah.

Chris: He's changing big things but it's all in the approach and the way he worded it. A lot of times with- We even do this with some of the manufacturers with their quick lead programs that are a joke. I always say like, "We're doing your quick lead programs, we're just doing a couple things different." Really, we're not doing any of that because it doesn't work. We know three months later they're not going to support it anymore, but the one thing with Magic, is he just has a really nice way about saying, "Oh, we're changing a couple things." But same thing. His Starbucks lead the country in per caps.

Gary: I guess this is mindset too, right? In his mind, he doesn't see them as big monumental things like we're just gonna make some tiny change, some tiny tweaks to the menu. For him it's like it's all attainable, it's not Mount Everest. He's gonna be able to get over that hill.

Chris: Yeah, the themes that he says, and I'm not gonna give away all of it because the video's too good now and I want everybody to, if you have the time to watch it. But the basis of it is over deliver and he always come back to "Opportunities happen when you succeed." You have to drive ROI, you have to drive results in then opportunity happens, but he, for a billionaire, he's the least entitled guy you'd ever imagine. He's not walking around thinking anybody owes him anything.

Gary: He had just as hard of a time as anybody else with getting into that. I mean, granted probably with his name got more meetings, but that didn't mean they were giving him money. He's a basketball player, they're not handing him 50 million dollars to go make an investment. He had a struggle and he had to go get it. I know in the video he talks about, getting down using some of his own money and getting to point where he was concerned that he didn't have enough.

Chris: He was leverage and he had big goals.

Gary: Yeah, but he would keep driving forward and he wasn't going to let that stop him. I can't even get my car in for service, it's ridiculous like this doesn't line up to me-

Chris: Maybe if you were Magic, bro.

Gary: I don't have a big enough name? Probably for that market.

Chris: Can you image to him what a pain in the ass it is if you were Magic and the guy's telling you he won't give you the loan, but, "Hey, would you take a picture with my kid." Because he's such a legend.

Gary: In Los Angeles, how many, especially in that neighborhood, how many movie stars are buying a driving BMWs and Mercedes and high-end cars and if you can't get your car in for service like I don't understand how that competes? I just can't imagine them with that amount of cloud, driving high-end vehicles that they would, that the would want to wait at all.

Chris: I know in Orange County, we would come up and pick them up because it was easier for them to let us do that than to deal with the dealerships here. They're booked out two weeks and we would just send somebody to pick it up.

Gary: Right, and guys like that. You want that influence you want them driving your cars.

Chris: I don't know but when you have celebrities come in and take pictures and it's good for the internet - it's good for all kind of stuff.

Gary: You want them talking about it. I remember there was a local celeb up in San Francisco that drove a high end car and all he would do is talk about it all the time, every time he got on camera and it's good for them, it's good business for them, you know?

Chris: Are you talking about the baseball player?

Gary: No.

Chris: He had a baseball player too. That was pretty cool. Man, it just drives me crazy. Can't do it here, my market's different. I think the key to success and the one thing I guess everybody listening to this that I'd like you to ask yourself is, if your market's different and it won't work there, then what are you going to do? Give up? I mean you've got to do something. You're only going to get somewhere by trying to do something. Then the next thing that happens in our industry, and this is the next layer, (we're constantly in part of the elite group) is a different kind of experience, is just to take ideas from other industries. If you think your market's different and you can't run as good as the other service centers in the country, or service departments, then you're really not going to be able to steal anything from a department store, or a restaurant, because you're way closed off to that and it's all hospitality. Really, we're in the hospitality business.

Gary: Right. Yeah, exactly.

Chris: It's all the same, it's making people feel comfortable and wanted and then putting them through a process.

Gary: For sure, and I don't think it's any different, I remember reading a book by Carl Sewell, and he was talking about that he didn't want his dealership ... I think he had a Cadillac store at the time. He didn't want it to be a car dealership, he wanted it to be a high-end retail department store, basically. He wanted to have that feel and that atmosphere to it, and he wasn't looking out and saying, "Well, my market's different because it's a car dealership." I think he partnered with Stanley Marcus, if I remember the book from Neiman Marcus, and he taught him how to be a high-end retailer and not how to run a car dealership.I think that to me, that's the magic. Magic Johnson going out and saying, "I'm going to open up a Starbucks in a place where they say it can't be done." I'm going to go do that because to him, that market's no different than any other market in the country. You just got to figure out what the tweaks are, as he put it, what are the tiny changes you have to make, and then match that to his consumers and he went and did that.

Chris: Most people in our industry are sitting back and going, "I'm not a basketball player, I could never do business." Meanwhile, he's way past that.

Gary: He doesn't have an MBA from anywhere, he's not a Stanford or a Harvard MBA grad, he just went out and made it work. He just wanted to learn, and he found some people that would teach him something, and he listened very intently to them and took their advice and then went and executed at a very high level.

Chris: To bring this full circle, everything we're talking about so far basically is about mindset, but the next part is about execution. One thing we do sometimes in our coaching meetings is we collect everybody's cell phones and then we make everybody call and make an appointment at their service department.

Gary: I had that done to me once.

Chris: It never works out like everybody thinks. I'll put a pile of cash and I'll be like, if it's the perfect phone call and they ask for everything and confirm it, you can have 100 bucks.

Gary: Right.

Chris: My money's usually pretty safe from guys that are running pretty good departments, but it's just the blocking and tackling in the execution. I know that this conversation is a surprise to the service manager that's running the dealership that you couldn't get into. It's all not known, but one big part of success is you that you've got to test the front door. You've got to walk in the front door every once and awhile and you've got to call and try to make an appointment and see. I think a lot of times we take for granted that our people are saying the right thing, that they're booking, that they're loading the shop and they're not.

Gary: I think too, the mindset has to be, you have a customer that wants to come in to your establishment, which is why it's there, it's why you open the doors, and they want to come in and they want to do business with you and they want to hand you money. And we're telling them, "Well, we don't really want your money right now, you're not really that important to us." It's just not the right way to do business.

Chris: Meanwhile there's a service manager in the back in his office going, "I don't know why my numbers are down, my traffic's down."

Gary: "Give me some marketing ideas, I need to increase my traffic."

Chris: Yeah.

Gary: I had a conversation yesterday, literally, and I had a service manager ask me for some marketing ideas to increase the traffic. I asked him, "Well, how far booked out are you?" And he goes, "A week." I said, "Well, what you need more customers for? Let's start moving ... Tell me when you're a day out and then ...

Chris: That's the biggest mistake is that traffic is profitability. You've got to focus on the customer experience and your average per ticket. Don't worry about traffic, it's in your per caps. You could sell more stuff if you took better care of people and wowed them a little bit, their wallets will fall out the back.

Gary: It starts the whole experience, right? If you feel good and you're there. To circle back to Magic's example, they walk into a Starbucks, and it doesn't feel like they're in some foreign place where it's not matched to them and their demographic. They walk in and they see things that are familiar for them, whatever's in the pastry case, and it makes them feel comfortable and want to spend money. They feel comfortable there, and it's the same thing for us. When we go to a car dealership or invite our customers in, we start off on the wrong foot. "Oh, well. Oh, you need that? Well, you know that's going to take six hours, sir and so ... "

Chris: "You shouldn't do it."

Gary: "Yeah, you probably, waste your time here." To me, it's like hey-

Chris: "You're an asshole for buying that in finance."

Gary: "Wow, your car needs help? We're here to help your car, bring it to us."

Chris: "You're one of those."

Gary: I think the mindset's got to be changed, we want customers. I don't care why they're there, I don't care what they're doing there. I don't care, I want them in the drive. I want a chance just to meet them and say hi, because then the next time they need something, they're going to come back to the friendly guy that said hi.

Chris: Oh yeah. I mean, imagine if we were doing inspections on all those details that were two months out. I mean, let alone, 800 bucks, 1,000 bucks a car?

Gary: Right, right.

Chris: It's all about your average per car. I don't know how many times we've seen dealerships where customers are bountiful. They're lined up, they're trying to get in, and the service department's losing money but they're busy, busy, busy, because they don't have a system and they haven't thought out the average per.

Gary: Right.

Chris: The average per is driven by customer experience and feeling good.

Gary: I see it all the time. I see ads, whenever we're paying money to run ads with loss leaders and they got so many cars in the drive, they can't get them all done.

Chris: Makes sense.

Gary: It doesn't, really doesn't.

Chris: Okay, can I ... For everybody, we're not a book report this week because the video was our book report and we love that video, and we encourage everybody to watch it.

Gary: Yeah, it's only about an hour. I mean, it's an hour long, so it's a decently long one, but it's worth the hour.

Chris: I'm going to sing a little song to you and then I want you to tell me the first thing that comes to mind, unless it's dirty or pornographic.

Gary: Okay, this is getting sprung on me, by the way, so I don't know what I'm going to say.

Chris: Are you ready?

Gary: Yeah.

Chris: I'm still Jenny from the block, I used to have a little, but I have a lot. I'm still Jenny from the block.

Gary: That reminds me of a wild time I had in Vegas not that long ago.

Chris: Oh?

Gary: A couple days ago.

Chris: Gary comes back from J-Lo in Vegas. He took his wife to J-Lo in Vegas and he's like, "I'm not drinking anymore. I'm detoxing."

Gary: That's what you feel like when you come back from Vegas.

Chris: It lasted like a week.

Gary: You just feel like you've got to detox. Three days in Vegas and I just felt like I needed to dry up.

Chris: So funny. We're too old for that bro.

Gary: Yeah.

Chris: The last couple times I've done that, it's not like when I was younger. When I was the general manager at Crevier, I would go out for three days at the beginning of the month. Like you know, close the month, print the financial, and I'd go on a Friday, come back Sunday, and I wouldn't sleep the whole time.

Gary: Yeah, I can't.

Chris: It would be fine now if I stayed up, just one night. If I stayed up 24 hours, it would take me two days to recover.

Gary: Yeah.

Chris: I'm too old for that.

Gary: We were getting back ... The other thing in Vegas though where you just don't feel like you need to sleep.

Chris: Until you get home.

Gary: Yeah, and then you get home and you're like, "Oh my God." I'm dead. Four in the morning, getting back, but yeah we're too old for that. It was fun anyways. My wife and I had a really good time.

Chris: I'm still Jenny on the block, used to have a little, but I have a lot. Pretty fun. We thank everybody for listening to this, we want to remind you that we are here to help you live your service department dreams. Whether it be training, advice, whatever we can do to serve you and also to remind everybody the $50,000 service manager challenge for this year is coming up. We're going to announce pretty soon the top dog event and who's attending, which is going to be fun, who are speakers are. We've got some big speakers.

Gary: We got some big names coming up.

Chris: We're going to give away $50,000.

Gary: Yeah. Should be a really fun event. It's always fun, but I think this year, we've got some over the top stuff planned. I'm pretty excited about it, it's going to be a lot of fun.

Chris: Is J-Lo going to be there?

Gary: J-Lo will not be there. She was wearing drop crotch by the way, it wasn't Y3, but it was drop crotch.

Chris: That's the style right now. Well, here in New York.

Gary: Right, yeah.

Chris: They make fun of my pants in Vermont. That's okay, Jeff.

Gary: You can't wear those through the airport in Columbus, Ohio, that doesn't work.

Chris: They don't like that.

Gary: No.

Chris: Nashville, either.

Gary: Yep.

Chris: You're from California.

Gary: Yeah.

Chris: You want some biscuits? That was the thing in Nashville, bro. Everything comes with biscuits and gravy.

Gary: I don't know how you stay skinner there.

Chris: Not that we're skinny here.

Gary: Right, yeah. It would be even harder here.

Chris: We're not missing any meals, it's fun. Cool, well thanks everybody. We hope you have a good start here to the month, and we will be back with a book report and a lot of fun next time.

Gary: Thank you.

Chris: All right, bye.

Episode #3: Using The Parts Department To Increase Service Efficiency

Chris: Welcome to Service Drive Revolution, how you doing G-Man?

Gary: Doing well.

Chris: How's your cholesterol?

Gary: Not where I want it to be, let's just say that. Not where I want it - not where Dr. Lau wants it to be.

Chris: You need to smoke more cigars, that's the key. That's what Dr. Lau always tells me, "Smoke some more cigars."

Gary: Yeah, yeah. Again, I just want to reiterate from the last several podcasts, Dr. Lau still does not know that I smoke cigars.

Chris: He'll never it.

Gary: We try keep that under wraps, yeah.

Chris: Until he's in a Service Drive wanting a revolution, he'll never hear this.

Gary: He'll never hear it, yeah. We're good, private.

Chris: We've done a string of coaching group events, meetings, parties. We're kind of at the end, but we're on our West Coast and Donnie's here.

Donnie: Hi.

Chris: Say hi Donnie.

Donnie: How are you doing?

Chris: How is your cholesterol?

Donnie: High.

Chris: It's terrible right?

Donnie: It's-

Chris: You're on a pill?

Donnie: I'm high, it's high and it's very high. Yes, I'm on a pill.

Chris: You should eat more red meat.

Donnie: No, not if you want more-

Chris: No, that's the key right? Cigars and red meat?

Gary: I'm on the ice cream, red meat diet right now.

Donnie: That's why it's the highest he's ever seen.

Gary: That's right. I did the veggie, veggie juice. My wife gets up at four in the morning and juicing fresh vegetables.

Chris: That's the funny thing. When Gary started working in the office, he'd come everyday and his wife, God bless her, she's so sweet, he would come with these jars, like the Mason jars, of this juice she would make every morning for him and some of it smelled like ass.

Donnie: Was it green?

Chris: He would drink it-

Gary: Every color in the rainbow.

Chris: I would be like "You like that?" He's like "Yeah, it's good!" He's like digging in just like "Yeah." Then, at some point

he got his blood test back and he gave up on the juice. I haven't seen the juice since because it didn't work.

Donnie: His iron content was way high, but is cholesterol was still way high?

Gary: I don't know about iron. He didn't say anything, but he ... I didn't actually see him, I talked to him on the phone. He has my results and I'm sitting there talking to him on the phone and he says "What I hear, what I'm looking at on your test results, what I believe is on the other side of the line is a guy that weighs 300 pounds and eats Carl's Junior for lunch everyday." I'm like "Bro! I'm salads and juice!" I haven't had Carl's Junior in 15 years. If that's what my test results are saying, that's what I'm going to eat from now on. That's why I shifted and I went ice cream and meat and I just gave up. I'm done.

Chris: Let's segway into what are we going to talk about on this podcast. We have a book. The book is called "You Are a Badass: How to stop doubting your greatness and start living an awesome life." Then we're going to talk about loving our parts department.

Gary: Yep, how to make your parts department an ally and help increase tech production.

Chris: You're taking over our parts department pretty soon, right?

Donnie: I am.

Chris: How do we make parts an ally?

Donnie: There's lots of ways I'm looking at.

Chris: Give us the top 100.

Donnie: The top 100. Well, the top one I'm trying to figure out right now is trying to get the parts faster to the technician, especially our quick lube area.

Chris: Roller skates.

Donnie: That and carts, I figured carts are good.

Chris: Roller skates are safer.

Donnie: Roller blades maybe?

Chris: No, skates. Old school.

Donnie: Old school. It's like you got a key, brand new set of roller skates or pair key or whatever, that Janis Joplin song is or whatever it is.

Chris: I don't know, you lost me with that one.

Donnie: Lost you on that one! No, we're trying to increase the productivity of our lube techs by putting air filters in a cabinet nearby.

Chris: Like in a cabinet right there?

Donnie: Putting a cabinet right there, putting it all up there. Just trying to make that happen, put it all in.

Chris: That's automatic, they shouldn't have to go to parts for that.

Donnie: No, but they are right now. They're having to spend a long time.

Chris: What you need to do is you need to do that and then you need to give them a faster lift.

Donnie: Yes, that is in the mix.

Chris: You'll double your oil change times like instantly. No, you're going to have parts runners in a golf cart?

Gary: What are you going to do?

Donnie: No, I'm actually going to have ... Sort of the idea I got from you with my used car team is where the used car team, as soon as they got the inspection done, of putting the parts in the car.

Chris: Yeah.

Donnie: As the ROS come along, I actually want to put a parts person on the drive. When the parts department, so as the car rolls through, they kind of get an idea of what's wrong with it. They can already start doing the parts request and then putting the puts on a cart and then rolling them out to the technician.

Chris: Okay. I have one idea and Gary did this before. It's a little different, so don't put them on the drive. There's two things and this is a great conversation actually. There's two things in parts that's happened in the last 15 years. The first one is when you have runners, you need less qualified, experienced parts guys, right?

Donnie: Correct.

Chris: The second thing is you can, whatever your DMS is, you can turn it on so the ROS print in parts.

Donnie: Already do.

Chris: They don't have to be out on the drive. They see it come out, they can give it to a runner. A runner picks it and can either put it there staged or if your guys are on teams, they can deliver it to the teams depending on the advisors. On the drive, I haven't had a lot of luck with that one, I don't know. I've tried it, for sure. I've put them out in the shop too, but it hasn't worked.

Gary: Yeah. When I had them in the shop in the stall with the technician. We separated the shop into teams and each team got a parts guy and they were in their stall. I felt like it slowed everything down. The techs got slower.

Chris: Yeah.

Gary: The parts guys just didn't like it.

Chris: Basically any mistake you can make, we've done.

Gary: Yeah.

Donnie: We started with our used car team, we separated out and we actually put a used car parts guy out there with my used car advisor. The advisors and the parts guy and his team are all out in one area. As the techs do the quote, they bring it to the advisor and then he can look up the parts right there. It's kind of sped up a little bit of his time there, having that used car parts guy there. Plus, he's looking for the good, better, best. If he's got to go to eBay to find something or if he's going through Rock Auto or somewhere to find a cheaper part, he's doing it from right there as the techs give it to him.

Chris: Yeah, that makes a little more sense just because you're doing off makes, but if it's a Chevy coming through the drive and have runners? But try it and let us know. I'd be curious.

Donnie: See we were trying to ... Since that scenario was working so well with our used car team, we were trying to flip that and see how we could use it on the customer pay side.

Chris: Hey, you know what works just like the used car team like that?

Donnie: What's that?

Chris: Instant inspection.

Donnie: Gary, now we're talking about parts.

Chris: You can put the parts in the car there too and it goes in.

Donnie: We're opening up a new store. The processes I want working in the new store I want working in my store currently. We were trying to get that instant inspection.

Chris: That thing with your fingers where you're like "Hit me," but you're at a blackjack table.

Donnie: Yeah, kind of doing something like that.

Chris: We played blackjack earlier, did you see that?

Gary: No, I missed the blackjack.

Donnie: I broke out even.

Chris: It was a long thing and I was ahead and it ended up even at the end.

Gary: Uh-huh.

Donnie: I was hoping to win, but I lost.

Gary: He normally wins. I usually don't play with him because he normally wins.

Donnie: You cut him thin to win.

Gary: Is that ... Oh, okay.

Chris: He didn't win.

Gary: Okay.

Donnie: I broke even.

Chris: Well, I guess that's winning. That's where we set the bar!

Gary: It's not losing!

Chris: The bar is so low that breaking even is winning.

Gary: Wasn't losing.

Chris: That's funny. No, but I remember coming back from a 20 group and we put all the parts guys, and you probably did the same thing because we were in the same 20 group. People come back from 20 groups and they're like "We're going to pay all of our advisors on gross because, you know, let's pay them all on hours."

Gary: What the hell, yeah.

Chris: Our ELR will go to four or less!

Donnie: Why are you looking at me like that? I just changed it to your pay plan.

Gary: Let's give them chairs.

Chris: I'm looking at you because we're talking, but if you have a guilty conscience it's a good time to get it out.

Donnie: I'm just feeling guilty because you were looking at me before my pay plans.

Chris: Everybody listening to this wants to hear about that. No, you go to a 20 group and we all did it, right? I think that's why we did it because some guy's like "Oh yeah, you increased my shop efficiency." I put kiosks out in my shop and granted, we had 70 techs. I think I had four guys out there, qualified parts guys banging the keyboard. Most of the time, they sat there. When it was all said and done, I did the efficiency, 90 days. Efficiency went down 5%. We put them back at the counter.

Gary: It's a distraction. Parts guys like to talk and that's not good for technicians. They don't want to talk. They don't want to talk about the movie they saw. They don't want to talk about the baseball game. They want to spin wrenches and when your air ratchet's going and you're trying to focus on a repair, the last thing you want is some guy over talking Star Wars in your ear, right? It just doesn't work that way and that's what was happening in our shop and it slowed everything down. Our shop production went down like 25%, it was bad. We had to pull the plug on it, it just didn't work. I think the model that works really well, and you were touching on it earlier, you want to keep your parts guys at the terminal. The number one complaint for technicians is when they come up to counter and they need help, nobody's there to help them, right? What's happening? The parts guy looked up a part for somebody else and he's off in the inventory and he's looking for the part. He's trying to figure it out or maybe it's not there and now he's talking to the manager. He's not where he needs to be, which is at the counter helping guys processing orders. By adding a runner, right away your dealer's going to look at you cross eyed because you're going to put a head, especially in parts, they hate heads.

Donnie: That was I already going to say, adding somebody that needs not to be there.

Gary: Yeah. We tucked it in service, it was a shop cleanup guy or something like that. We slid it under the rug. We had a guy, that's his only job was taking the part from the counter to the tech, every single time. The guys could just sit, literally sit at their counter and talk about Star Wars until somebody came up and then they'd process an order and then they'd go back to talking about Star Wars again. They weren't interrupting the production flow of the shop. The guys in the shop were getting their parts really fast. We saw a production tick up because of that.

Chris: Yeah, same.

Donnie: Same.

Chris: Bad.

Donnie: I just think that-

Chris: Quit the 20 group.

Donnie: Quit the 20 group. I just keep looking back at Gary like going ... If I go to my dealer and ask that, you know what I'm going to get? I'm going to get that look.

Gary: Hm-mm-hmm (affirmative).

Donnie: That look like you want to spend more money look.

Chris: Yeah, well that's a legitimate look! Did you know he's engaged?

Gary: I didn't, no.

Chris: Tell him how you proposed.

Donnie: I proposed at a basketball game. I actually had planned for years. It was February 12th and that happened to land on a basketball game. I kind of hinted around of "Do I do it on the big jumbo tron? Do I do it at halftime?" Actually it was kind of funny because rolling into that, a couple other proposals happened before that and I said "Hey, what do you think of that?" She's like "If you ever did that, I would hate you because I don't want that much attention."

Chris: Which means do that!

Donnie: Well, which I thought. I waited and actually my internal advisor worked for our dealership for 32 years, he's kind of one my to-go-to guys. I asked him, I said "Hey, will you help me out with this?" He said, "Yeah." I said "So how should we do this?" He's like "Well, we'll wait until the end of the game. Then, I'll distract her and then you can get down on one knee and then you can propose to her and do all this." I thought it would be great to do it with a Ring

Pop. I get to the game, we get all this. I had the Ring Pop in my pocket, but I had it in the wrapper and throughout the game, it got kind of warm in there. If you've ever had a Ring Pop and you're trying to open it up at that time that you need it, it's stuck to the wrapper. Everybody's filing out and he's got her attention and I'm trying to fumble with this Ring Pop and I'm messing up. Finally, I get it out of its package and I'm on one knee and I look at her and I said "So, would you marry me?" She looks at me like "Where in the hell did you find a Ring Pop?" She looks at me, she's like "Are you serious?" I'm like "Yeah."

Chris:　Kinda!

Donnie:　I'm on my knee here with a Ring Pop. I even made sure it was her favorite color, purple. I made sure everything was good. I actually had the real ring with me so I pulled it out and I said, "If this one doesn't work, would this one?" Then it sunk in and I realized I still had about 10,000 people watching.

Gary:　Ah.

Chris:　But you weren't on the jumbo tron?

Donnie:　No, we weren't.

Gary:　Watching the awkward exchange.

Donnie:　As they were leaving , everybody was kind of just watching us.

Chris:　What does she think about the car business?

Donnie:　It's kind of mixed. She likes it because she knows it makes good money, but she doesn't like the hours.

Gary:　Hm-mm-hmm (affirmative).

Chris: She's normal.

Donnie: She's normal, yeah.

Chris: Right?

Donnie: She understands, though. She gets it.

Chris: Does she know how to calculate hours?

Donnie: No.

Chris: No?

Donnie: No. We don't talk business at home. She hates talking business at home. Even though I do a lot of business from home.

Chris: How can you not?

Donnie: Yeah.

Chris: But I mean, it's part of life.

Donnie: My kitchen table right now is my laptop and about four folders full of ROs and up codes I'm changing. Yeah, fun stuff.

Gary: Not only do you have to work late hours, but you've got to bring it home with you too.

Donnie: Yeah.

Gary: Yeah, it's always fun.

Donnie: Thanks for reminding me.

Gary: You're right!

Chris: But will you marry me?

Donnie: But will you marry me?

Gary: Did I ever tell you my proposal story?

Chris: No.

Gary: It's similar. I didn't use a Ring Pop. I had been dating my wife for like six years and I finally that it's time. After six years I figured, "Okay, we're good." I bought a ring for her. I have no idea what I'm doing. I think I was 23, 24 something like that. I think I was 23, way too young. I planned this whole thing. I dressed up in a suit, completely opposite of what I would have done normally. Everything I wouldn't have done, that's what I did. I planted the ring at the restaurant, they put it in a glass of champagne. I did all of this crazy stuff. It all went down at the restaurant and so I said "Katya, will you marry me?" She said, "Hmmm, marriage huh?" I'm like, "Yeah!"

Chris: So, herpes!

Gary: Yeah! She's like, "Hmmm, well you know? I'm going to have to think about that. Like what? What is going on?

Donnie: You're waiting for the answer and you're like...?

Gary: Yeah until the waitress walks up and because I had set it all up ahead of time, she was just giddy. She's like "Oh my God. Here show me the ring! What's happening?"

Chris: "I wish my boyfriend would propose to me this way!"

Gary: I'm looking at her. I'm going "She hasn't said yes yet." We're still in the exchange, we're negotiating apparently over this deal. We're trying to close her. It wasn't until the

51

drive home before ... It was the most awkward probably two hours finishing dinner and dessert and then drive home before she finally agreed to marry me. 22, 23 years later, whatever it's all history.

Chris: He's got a great story about the first kiss too, but we should talk about parts a little more before we get to that.

Gary: Maybe more parts.

Chris: Okay. One thing that I hear a lot from guys is when they implement our system and they're playing games and they're having fun, the parts department's left out. Have you ever had success doing any kind of competition with the parts guys?

Gary: Yeah. You have to think differently because the parts department's a little bit different. You can't go in with the same thing that you're thinking about with service. If you tie it to sales, it doesn't have as much meaning to them, right? They're not negotiating with a customer, they're not selling anything.

Chris: They're just moving it along.

Gary: Yeah, they're moving, which is important, right? Taking a part from the shelf and handing it to a technician is a sale, it's happening, right? We're selling the part.

Chris: The quicker the better.

Gary: The quicker the better. I would incentivize things that would incentivize that. We had a poker chip game that we used to play a lot. What I would do is if I found you doing something right, I would give you a poker chip and so right things that would lend itself to sales is like perpetual inventory, which is not very sexy or fun, but it needs to be done. What is does is it-

Chris: Most don't do it.

Gary: Nobody does it. But what happens is if you do it three or four times a year, your inventory becomes very clean. What happens then is when the technician needs that part, that guy can go find it and have it out there in a couple of minutes. That means I can move more parts across the counter and we can increase shop efficiency.

Chris: And fill rate.

Gary: Yeah and fill rate goes up. I figured out pretty fast that if the most profitable sale I could make is when the technician asks for the part, the guy turns around and hands the technician the part and he hangs it on the car. That's the most profitable sale you can ever make. I wanted to make that happen as many times that I possibly could. The only way you do that is if you have clean inventory. They're not excited. I mean, counting a bin is probably one of the most boring things you could ever do. Anyways, if they did their bin counts and they'd bring me a sheet, I'd give them a poker chip. If I saw them cleaning a bin or straightening a bin, I'd give them a chip. If I saw them really being friendly and nice and helping a tech, I'd give them a poker chip. It was pretty much anything I could see that they were doing right. At the end of the week, we'd play roulette. I'd get a stack of cash and I had a roulette wheel and I had a big felt canvas or blanket, or whatever you want to call it that I would lay out. I'd put the roulette wheel on there and they'd bet their chips and I'd spin and I had cash on there. It was fun, I mean they had a great time. They wanted to do bin counts. They caught the fever and they understood that what we were doing was important and it made a difference for that dealership and it got them engaged.

Chris: That's good. I've done it with runners, when we've tracked runners before. When the pick ticket prints, there's a timestamp. When they deliver the part to the tech, the tech will initial in the time. You can play a game on that with the runners. You know, because you're new taking over parts that you probably should do a perpetual inventory yourself.

Donnie: No, that's one thing we don't do. I don't even think we've done a yearly inventory very often.

Chris: Yeah, you're going to want to take a couple months off and just go through the inventory.

Donnie: No.

Chris: Right?

Gary: Yeah.

Donnie: I'll delegate that.

Chris: No, you need touch every bin! How can you manage your department if you haven't touched every bin?

Donnie: Well I know where the parts are.

Chris: Well you need to touch them though and count them.

Donnie: No, that's a delegation.

Chris: And go through a big sheet.

Donnie: That's a $10 an hour job.

Chris: Well yeah, but sometimes you got to do that in the beginning to understand it. You cannot teach somebody how to do a perpetual if you haven't done the perpetual.

Donnie: I have worked in parts before.

Chris: But have you done a perpetual?

Donnie: Not in about 10 years.

Chris:	Don't you agree he needs to do a full inventory?
Donnie:	I actually had them teach me how.
Chris:	What's your parts inventory? How much?
Donnie:	You know, I couldn't even tell you that.
Chris:	Oh boy.
Gary:	We're in trouble.
Donnie:	We're in trouble.
Gary:	We're starting out blind.
Chris:	Okay, let's talk about the book.
Gary:	Moving on!
Donnie:	Moving on!
Chris:	You ordered this, right Donnie?
Donnie:	I did.
Chris:	"You're a Badass." So this was suggested by Steve and Gary from Galpin Motors and the Elite Group.
Gary:	I was actually intrigued by the button.
Chris:	Yeah, the button is dope. I didn't want to drive everybody crazy about it. At one point it says "You're a badass," but then it says a bunch of other stuff, let's see. **Button:** You create your reality.
Chris:	"You create your reality."

Button: Feed fear a suck it sandwich.

Chris: "Feed fear a suck it sandwich," that's the worst one of all of them.

Button: You are a badass.

Chris: There you go, Donnie, "You are a badass." My favorite chapter in here is "Your brain is your bitch."

Gary: What's with the little book?

Chris: I don't know. The little book came with the button. When we were in the Elite meeting earlier this week, they were talking about this book, so I go on Amazon. There's this crazy thing here in LA and in some markets. It's one in the afternoon, you order it on Amazon and you can have it delivered same day. I thought for the two guys that suggested the book, I would buy them the buttons and then I got myself a button because they didn't have the buttons. I bought the book for everybody else in the Elite group. The button, you ordered the button right?

Donnie: I did.

Chris: Yeah .**Button:** You can do it!

Chris: "You can do it!" Basically this book is really about kind of what we were talking about today, that you choose kind of to look at things in positive light and you own your result. The Magic Johnson we were watching today at the very end he says "The one thing that I always had - you know I was poor," whatever - but the one thing I had was I controlled my work ethics and my results." This is is kind of about that. It's about owning your results and then meditating. They talk about meditating. They talk about having a mantra that you tell yourself. Basically to boil it all down is have a good attitude, see the positive and go after it, but it's fun. It's a fun name and it's a fun book. If you gave it to your advisers that they got to own their stuff basically.

Donnie: It's got a badass title.

Chris: Do you want to touch it? You're looking at it like you want to touch it.

Button: Do what you love!

Chris: Do what you love Donnie!

Donnie: And touch it.

Gary: Did you guys talk about meditation in the meeting today?

Chris: Yeah, JD brought that up, but that's always weird.

Gary: JD likes TM.

Donnie: Yeah, is he doing it?

Chris: But Donnie's never done it!

Gary: No?

Donnie: No, but it's got me interested.

Chris: Actually I was talking to a client, a dealer last night and she paid for a bunch of her managers to go to TM and their lives are messed up. She's like "I paid for them to go TM and they don't do it." It's one of those things if you needed TM, you'd probably find it on your own.

Donnie: Yeah.

Gary: Yeah.

Chris: To tell people about it, they just think it's weird.

Donnie: Well I always think-

Chris: They're like "You're from California!"

Donnie: When you were going through the morning routine, that's kind of one of the things I always try to do is tell myself a positive, while I'm shaving in the mirror in the morning is tell myself a positive, try to give that vibe.

Chris: While I'm shaving in the mirror? What are you shaving bro?

Donnie: Well yeah, it's multitasking. The neck area.

Gary: I was going to say, he's got a beard!

Chris: It's a quick morning ritual!

Donnie: It is. It's a quick "I'm great!"

Gary: My head was going there too! I said, "The guy's got a beard, what's he shaving?"

Chris: "I'm very handsome."

Donnie: I have to shave the neck. The neck gets too burly, you can connect the hair sweater to the neck.

Chris: I know, but it is all joking aside, it's a real thing. If you start out everyday thinking positive and being grateful for what you have and kind of the rest of the day you got that going on, the negative bounces off.

Donnie: The thing I actually thought about even before I came here is I was talking to myself and I've actually had people tell me that you need to meditate more, find some personal time for yourself to reflect on the things that you've done. That's one thing I'm grateful that my owner gives me the time. She's like "You don't stop and celebrate the small victories," and you've got to do that more. A lot of us, I'm always looking at that next step, looking to be ahead. I always want to do better and I think I can do better and I'm always harder on myself. I have made a lot of accomplishments, I've just got to stop and look back and them.

Chris: Yeah. No, I think we're all terrible at that.

Gary: Yeah, for sure. Yeah, no doubt.

Chris: For sure. Yeah, we talked about meditation a little bit, JD brought it up. Mostly we talked about a morning ritual and some of the guys were talking about how it's hard as a service manager to stay up all the time and always be positive, it's a lonely deal. We talked about framing yourself in the morning and being grateful.

Gary: Working out.

Donnie: Right.

Chris: Working out.

Gary: I was talking with one of the guys earlier and we were talking about teams and one of the things that I learned really early on that became very important to me was having guys that worked for me that wanted to work for me. I learned pretty fast that I was going to build a team of people that wanted to be there. If they didn't want to be there and be on my team, they want to be the Terrell Owens and do their own thing, then they weren't there. I was remembering a story when I didn't have that, when I had a team of guys that were just terrible and I didn't want to work with them. I remember going to work every day just miserable, not wanting to go. In my car, just pissed at myself because I'm driving in and that's not a good place to be. You do that for a couple months and it's really a lonely and depressing spot. I couldn't see the way out, but what changed that for me was listening to Brian Tracy on the way in. Somebody had given me a couple of CDs and he's all about positive affirmations. He starts talking about it and it's hokey and it's corny. "Hey I like myself and I love myself," but I can tell you right now, listening to that on the way in that day, I felt better than I had in months. About halfway through the day I thought "Wow," I needed to wake up that morning and remember what the things that I'm happy about and the things that I'm good at. Have some celebrations and celebrate some small wins because otherwise, there are some tough spots in life. You got to get through them. There are some winter season and that's just how it's going to be. At that point, we were in a winter and I had to see my way through it, but I wasn't going to do it by getting depressed. It really helped me get to the other side. I'm a firm believer in it even though it is kind of corny, but I'm definitely a firm believer in it.

Chris: Yeah, it's always hard for me in those situations with the group and a bunch of dudes to talk about that stuff because, you know half of them are just like "When can this be over?" It feels almost like it's very touchy feely or something, but I just know it's worked for me.

Donnie: No, I think the morning-

Chris: I'm happier than most people.

Donnie: The morning ritual has got to be ... I mean, I go back to the thing of actually putting sayings and things on my mirror. I used to do that when I was a service advisor. One of the best things is I had a service manager tell me one thing is "What do you want out of life? What is it that you're shooting for?" At the time when I was an advisor starting out, it was like "I just want an Xbox Three," you know? "I just want an Xbox." He's like "Take a picture of that and put it by your computer."

Chris: Yeah.

Donnie: I was just starting, my spiffs, every time I sold tires or batteries, that's what I was shooting for. That spiff money was paying for that thing. I just started putting that everywhere. I put it in my truck. I had it by the speedometer. Every time I looked down to see how fast I'm going, that's what I'm seeing. It's kind of that visual thing you know? Visualize what you want and how you're going to get to it and it'll happen.

Chris: Yeah I think the thing that freaks most people out is they think it's some spiritual thing like there's some angel that's like "Oh okay, well he looked at his Xbox picture enough, we're going to give him an Xbox." Really what it's doing is it's making you try a little harder, work a little harder. It's constantly refocusing you on the goal, which makes you perform better, feed your subconscious. It's like following a map more than it is winning a lottery.

Donnie: I think it embeds it in your subconscious that you're focused on that then, you know?

Gary: Yep.

Chris: Yeah. Let me read you ... Oh, wait. No, I lost my page.

Gary: I think if you read the book, and we should talk about that book on the next podcast we that we do, but-

Chris: I refuse to talk about that book.

Gary: *10% Happier* - really?

Chris: Oh, I thought you were going to say another one.

Gary: No.

Chris: No, I like that one.

Gary: *10% Happier* will give you a whole new take on meditation.

Chris: Yeah, he tells it in a good way too.

Gary: Yeah, that to me changed my opinion of meditation.

Chris: Okay, Donnie.

Donnie: Hm-mm-hmm (affirmative).

Chris: "Your brain is your bitch, remember everything you desire already exists, you just have to shift your perception in order to see it made manifest. Your job isn't to know the how's, it's to know the what and to be open to discovering and receiving the how." Little book, comes with the button.

Donnie: That's deep, "Your brain is your bitch."

Button: You create your reality.

Chris: "You create your reality." We talked about parts.

Gary: I have another parts idea and I can share it with you.

Chris: Oh, okay.

Gary: We're done talking about cholesterol and marriages.

Donnie: Proposals.

Chris: We're never done with your cholesterol, no come on.

Donnie: That's the highest he's ever seen, remember.

Gary: Oh my God. We were talking about making the parts your ally, right?

Chris: Hm-mm-hmm (affirmative).

Gary: I know that service managers are very removed from what it takes to run a parts department, they have no clue what's going on back there and vice versa. You're a service manager. You're used to playing games and having fun and doing fun stuff and you got your parts manager back there that's not included in that, maybe he's not doing any of that. You can make a bet with him. Maybe it's CP hours, maybe it's parts sales, maybe you want to help him increase parts sales and by helping him, he's helping you, right? Because if his part sales go up, your techs are hanging more parts, which means they're turning more hours. By connecting the two together and having some sort of common ground or going after a common enemy will help build the bridge and get him on your side and get him thinking about something different because honestly, in the parts world you can get lost just thinking about inventory. It's all about the boxes and the numbers. When I became a parts manager, I had nightmares about numbers chasing me around. If you can help them, bring them out of it-

Chris: 11 digit numbers.

Donnie: Oh, God. Stacked.

Chris: And superseded to another 11 digit number. I always love that how parts managers are like "Oh no, it's not the SK5233777 that's been superseded to the SK-"

Donnie: Yeah, when they can rattle those off, it's scary.

Chris: Oh my God.

Donnie: Well I like the idea.

Chris: That takes a talent thought.

Donnie: I like the idea that we were talking about earlier too. Even taking the technicians out of the element and then asking them where they see the roadblocks at.

Gary: Yeah, for sure.

Chris: Oh yeah.

Donnie: I think that was a great idea. I always have to hear that. Techs walking out of parts and they're blaring obscenities "The stupid parts people, they don't know what the hell and they're stuck back there and meh!" Gary and I were talking about how when he took over parts department, he gathered all the techs and bought them pizza and then said "Give me all your problems," then sat back with one of those court typewriters. What do they call those?

Gary: A stenograph?

Donnie: Yeah, a stenograph and was trying to type fast enough to keep up. He wasn't ready for all of the information the techs were going to give him. He said it was really good, he got a lot of good information.

Gary: Yeah.

Donnie: You did that how often, about one a month?

Gary: Yeah I did it once a month for almost an entire year. You got to put on your Kevlar underwear because they're coming at you.

Donnie: Draymond Green's kicking you?

Gary: Yeah! I was telling Donnie it was like Normandy! Like missiles were just coming at me. I had 70 techs in the room, it was just full and they were just firing stuff at me.

Donnie: He's like "I wasn't trying to take it personal, but it was getting violent."

Gary: Oh, it gets hard and some of it gets personal.

Chris: Yeah.

Gary: It's good to let it out. After 12 months of doing that, I had my next meeting and they didn't have a single thing to say, not one. I was telling Donnie "If you address the things that you can address and then you talk about the things you know you cannot address, you just strike those off the list, they don't come back again."

Chris: Yeah, you're not hiding from it.

Gary: No.

Donnie: Yeah.

Gary: It is what it is.

Chris: Yeah.

Gary: As long as I was communicating with them, then they were like "Okay, we're good."

Donnie: Some of the things you take care of on the top of the list and handle the things on the bottom of the list, so you work your way to the middle.

Gary: Yeah. All the counter guys thought it was nuts. They're like "You're going to get crucified. They're going to kill you." They were just terrified of it, but once we got the information, some of the stuff was simple. We couldn't get a transmission through the hallway because the tool room was in there. Remember where the tool room was? You couldn't get a transmission through there and it was designed to deliver that part through there. They'd have to go all the way around through the parking lot. I don't know if any of you guys has dragged a pallet jack through the parking lot, it's not fun. The transmissions, nobody would want to pull them, first of all. Then, it would take forever to get to the shop, but it was a simple fix. We just cleaned up the tool room and told the guys "You keep the tool room clean, we can deliver parts through there." Guess what happened? The tool room was clean. It's funny that stuff like that, stupid things.

Chris: It's communication.

Donnie: That's part's fault.

Gary: It was our fault, yeah.

Donnie: Yeah, it's part's fault. Yeah.

Chris: Yeah, but I think when you don't have an open dialogue, perception is different than reality.

Donnie: You got to knock down the walls.

Chris: Yeah, you got to put that aside. It's about the result.

Gary: It's funny too how sometimes that didn't cost us a single nickel, to clean that room up and we improved productivity just by doing that. You don't know that that exists, this almost goes back to that theory of constraints. Try to figure out where the constraints are, where the bottlenecks are and then what can you do with them. You don't know what they are until you start talking about them.

Chris: Yeah, that's good.

Donnie: Keeping an open line of communication.

Gary: Hm-mm-hmm (affirmative), absolutely.

Chris: In closing Donnie, any other words of wisdom?

Donnie: Watch your cholesterol, trans meditation.

Chris: Transcendental meditation!

Donnie: Whatever...

Chris: "I'm going to try that trans meditation! It gives you herpes."

Donnie: The TM and your testosterone level, you take an injection.

Gary: If you've got low T, that's a problem. Low T and high E don't go together.

Donnie: You don't want no TM on that either.

Chris: Yeah, you're crying.

Gary: You cry a lot.

Chris: You cry a lot.

Donnie: No communication, I think that's it.

Chris: How is your estrogen?

Donnie: My estrogen is ... Well, since I work out a lot it's pretty low.

Chris: Oh, okay.

Donnie: I don't have that problem.

Gary: I'd be interested to see after what I dead lifted and squat over the last couple of weeks, where my estrogen is now.

Donnie: I do get kind of scared at your two videos. Working out together, that's kind of odd.

Chris: You know what's great? I had a trainer for years and then when Gary started working on the office I'm like "Let's work out." I told my trainer "Hey, the deal-"

Gary: "I found Gary."

Chris: "is Gary and I'll figure it out on our own or you're training both of us." He's been training both of us at the same time. It's been fun.

Donnie: Two for the price of one.

Chris: Yeah, I haven't paid anymore. It's pretty good. Gary's upped our game on some stuff because I was benching, squatting and dead lifted ... Well no, dead lifting was more, but still Gary upped our expectations on that. He's got us squatting a lot more than we were because we were kind of doing the same. It's been fun.

Donnie: I don't see how you did that on the bike this morning, I was dead today. My lung's are a mess.

Chris: I'll tell you what it is, bro. I have the heart of a bulldog.

Gary: It's the HGH. His HGH levels are strung like bull.

Chris: I beat you by like four miles.

Gary: He destroyed me, I don't know. I didn't fight. I didn't have it in me today.

Donnie: Poor Gary.

Chris: I know.

Gary: I had two lead weights strapped to my body.

Chris: Not me, I did it. I laid it all out.

Gary: Tuesday, though, Tuesday!

Chris: Lance Armstrong's got nothing on me. I played this trick on him. I was gone for two weeks. I didn't work out for two weeks. I'm on the road and I don't have a system for being on the road with working out that well because in the hotels they don't have good stuff ever. I told him on Tuesday, so we lifted on Monday and then Tuesday's cardio and we ride the bike. I told him, I said, "If there's a day Gary, if there's a day you could beat me, today would be the day." He probably did his best ever.

Gary: He was visualizing it.

Donnie: I was there.

Chris: He did his best.

Gary: He was in my head.

Donnie: He had his morning routine going, he was visualizing it.

Chris: I'm nervous about him catching me. Even when we're done, I'll do another sprint or two, just trying to stay there because I don't want him to catch me.

Gary: Yeah and cycling is my thing too, so it makes him extra proud that he dominates me on that.

Chris: Well cycling is his thing on a real cycle.

Donnie: You wear a onesie when you're real cycling?

Gary: Oh yeah.

Chris: That would be funny, but on the stationary bike it's a little different.

Gary: I'm all estrogen, of course I'm wearing a onesie!

Chris: All right, cool. Well thanks everybody for listening and I hope we fixed your parts department and look forward to Donnie doing a perpetual.

Gary: Yep.

Chris: Because the key to everything is perpetual.

Donnie: I'm all up for it.

Chris: Perpetual inventory.

Donnie: Perpetual inventory.

Gary: Four times a year, maybe five.

Chris: Constantly perpetual, keep that clean. It's all about your turn rate.

Donnie: Yeah, estrogen four times a year.

Chris: No, perpetual four times a year. Bye.

Gary: Bye.

Episode #4: Dave Anderson Perfects Our Mindset To Maximize Dealer Performance

Chris: Welcome everybody to Service Drive Revolution. We have an amazing guest today, uncle Dave Anderson. How you doing Dave?

Dave Anderson: I'm doing great Chris, how are you?

Chris: Good. Are you worried at all about Gary's cholesterol?

Dave Anderson: Yeah.

Chris: We start off every show asking Gary how his cholesterol is, because his cholesterol is a lot like a milkshake.

Gary: Jeez. It gets worse every show-

Chris: Do you have your cholesterol checked?

Gary: ... worse every show.

Dave Anderson: My cholesterol's fantastic.

Chris: See?

Gary: Oh, man.

Chris: Now Gary's going to say it's genetic.

Gary: Man.

Chris: He can't help it, right?

Gary: That's the theory right now, that's the theory

we're going with that it's genetic. I can't help it, so we'll see.

Dave Anderson: It's bad luck.

Chris: Besides fixing Gary's cholesterol, we have some fun stuff that we're going to talk about.

Gary: Fixing? There's no fixing. It's not fixed. It's getting worse.

Chris: I'm sure because Dave's is good, he could tell you. You probably put an effort into cholesterol, right? Eating the right stuff?

Dave Anderson: You've got to do stuff. It's not ...

Chris: What's the strategy?

Dave Anderson: The strategy is to live right, Gary. Give it a try.

Gary: Oh, okay.

Chris: I would guess Dave isn't leaving the office with a Crown Royal and a cigarette.

Gary: Oh, that sort of thing, yeah. Okay.

Chris: Cigars.

Dave Anderson: It's the cheap booze that kills you. Step up. Get the good stuff.

Chris: Yeah, Gary. Then french fries. Do you dip your french fries in mayonnaise, or how do you handle the french fries?

Dave Anderson: Don't do the fries. Don't do the fries.

Chris: Skip the fries.

Dave Anderson:	Got to skip the fries.
Chris:	Gary, you should be writing this down.
Dave Anderson:	This isn't rocket science Gary. It's not that tough.
Chris:	Write it down.
Dave Anderson:	You got to stop blaming bad luck. It's bad decisions, Gary. It's bad decisions.
Gary:	I'm taking mental notes. No french fries, no mayonnaise.
Dave Anderson:	Basics.
Gary:	I think I got it covered.
Chris:	You don't know how many burgers I've seen Gary eat, just full on cheeseburgers.
Dave Anderson:	It's genetic, though. It's genetic.
Chris:	This applies to all aspects, Gary. To business, to everything.
Gary:	Okay, all right.
Chris:	It's the market. The market's down.
Gary:	My market is different. My gene pool is different than you guys. That's what I'm sticking with.
Chris:	That's funny. We both, Dave, we're huge admirers of yours, and we both have stories about our ... I call you Uncle Dave, because when I was in my 20's coming up in this industry, you were my dad when it came to leadership. Your books and your training were my first real entry into any kind of leadership

training. Same for you, right?

Gary: Oh yeah. No, exactly the same for me. I was a young manager, and then of course we don't have any training, there's no manuals to tell you how to lead people, and you kind of feel lost. Then I just happened on to some of your stuff, and without being too dramatic, it definitely shined a beacon of light and helped like, okay, now there's a solution. There's someplace where I can go to learn this stuff.

Dave Anderson: That's awesome. You guys talk about when you were young and I was like your dad. I'm not 100 you know.

Chris: It really wasn't that long ago, it wasn't. It goes by fast.

Gary: It feels long but it wasn't that long ago.

Chris: How long has it been Gary, like 18 years? About that?

Gary: Yeah just about that.

Chris: My story is, when I took over the dealership I was running I bought your series of videos and I would do a video every week in my management class. It was a great entry to me to get them talking and thinking but I learned just as much as they did. It created a culture of getting better and learning and the exercises, I forget the name of that course. Maybe it was *Learn to Lead?*

Dave Anderson: I think it was *Growing Great Leaders*. I think you had the *Growing Great Leaders* course. Great way to use it.

Chris: The best, honestly.

Dave Anderson: Thank you.

Chris: I've watched that so many times and gone through that workbook so many times. It created a conversation and then I remember - and this is a funny story - and I don't know if I've ever told you this, maybe I have. We asked you to come out, we hired you to come out. You came out and did a day, I think it was on a Saturday, Sunday or something.

Dave Anderson: It was, right.

Chris: Then the next month I read in your newsletter they used to do. Do you still do the newsletter?

Dave Anderson: No I don't do the newsletter.

Chris: We subscribed to the newsletter.

Dave Anderson: You did. We did it a lot of years.

Chris: I got it and your very first thing in there was about how you were speaking at a dealership and then just something to the effect of, "How can people ever want to succeed when they have losers?" You were describing our conference room and the sales boards that we had up. How could you ever want to succeed when you've got 6 car guys on the board?

Dave Anderson: I didn't name you though, I didn't name you.

Chris: No, but I knew.

Dave Anderson: If you're going to have me come over you got to do something with the sales board. You've got to make stuff up or something but you can't have that up there.

Chris: Make a note of that Gary. If Dave comes to the office we've got to hide everything. It was very accurate and great stuff. All that did was motivate me more. It was great but it was funny because I'm reading that sitting in my office going, oh man what?

Dave Anderson: You paid a lot for that insult.

Chris: You can do that? You can write about me like that? It was pretty funny, but no, we're big fans. One question that I had for you; is it 12 books you've put out?

Dave Anderson: 13.

Chris: 13 books. What's your favorite book that you've done?

Dave Anderson: They always say the favorite book is either the last one or the one you're working on. My favorite one really was the last one, which was, *It's Not Rocket Science.*

Chris: Which is a great title. Says it all.

Dave Anderson: Thank you. Well, it built on all the others because it's about execution. All the others would lay out a lot of vision and strategy and here's what you need to do. What this book really did is really got into here's how you do it. You've got to execute. You can have all kind of goals, you can have plans that fill the walls, but if you can't execute it. I present an execution process. Most people don't have one. If you sit down a group, even with owners and you ask them, "List for me your execution process, write down the steps." You get that blank, deer-caught-in-the-headlights look. They end up saying dumb stuff like, "Well we hold meetings, we set objectives, we follow up," and still nothing's getting done so that's not much of a process. In the book I present a really concise workable process to help close that gap and it's done really well. That's why it's my favorite one because it ties together so much of the other things I brought up in the other books. It really is the bridge to getting more of that stuff done.

Chris: Yeah the wisdom and experience of time kind of all in one.

Dave Anderson: I couldn't have written that book 15, 16 years ago, I didn't know that stuff. You get better. You figure out what works. You work with people who figure things out and each book should reflect that and should be even more relevant than the last.

Chris: I love that. How long does it take you to write a book?

Dave Anderson: Four months.

Chris: Four months? Wow, so you've got a real system.

Dave Anderson: I have a system.

Chris: How long did it take you to write the first one?

Dave Anderson: The first one, you know going back, that was a long time ago, the first one took longer. The first one took about a year, you know why? I gave myself a year. If I'd have given myself two years, how long would it have taken? Two years. You know when I started to be able to write them in four months? When the publisher said, "You need it done in four months." So I started to figure out how to get them done in four months. Back when I had more time I

	took more time. Isn't that the way people are wired?
Chris:	By the way, my first book took me three years but I wrote three books basically. I started off with ghost writer, and then because in the car industry it's so specific it just doesn't work. It has to come from you.
Dave Anderson:	That's true.
Chris:	What I learned from that is it took longer with the ghost writer redoing everything than it did if I just did it. Then the second one was okay and then the third one I got it but it's hard. It's not easy. Now I have a system, the same and it's much easier but the first one is hard.
Dave Anderson:	I write most of them on airplanes and in hotel rooms, just taking that down time and making use out of it. If I'm flying from LA to Atlanta, I know that's about a four hour flight. I can get about 1,200 words done if I'm focused and I'm not watching the movie or talking to the guy next to me about how uncomfortable the seat is. If I'm actually doing something productive, I can pretty well budget how much I can get done in that flight. It's kind of a system.
Gary:	That made me think of one of my favorite Dave things. In his training he said, "You talk about reading and personal development and getting better and you say you don't have time. You're sitting on a toilet for 15 minutes a day. You can read for 15 minutes a day." Dave's really good at getting rid of excuses.
Dave Anderson:	The older you get the more books you should be able to read based on that. It's crazy. If it's important to you, you find a way. If it's not, you find an excuse.

Chris: You really do. Gary and I were in a situation yesterday, I brought up, "Well you got dressed today, because it was important to you. It was a priority. You don't come in naked." These things need to be a priority too. It's just focus is what it is.

Dave Anderson: It's amazing how little time people spend working on their mindset everyday. I was with a group - we had 1,000 people - I was giving a speech to a good high energy group. You ask the question, "How much time do you spend every morning, preferably in the morning before your head gets screwed up, working on your mindset, doing something to build your mindset? Whether it's reviewing goals, reviewing your why, listening to something inspirational based on whatever your spiritual beliefs are, maybe reading something, meditating, praying? What do you do early in the day to build your mindset? The answer is mostly nothing. People leave their mindset up for grabs. They may have talent, they may have knowledge, but if the mindset's not right, if you're not really dialed in and focused that stuff's not going to be leveraged. It's not going to be maximized. You've got to make time to work on the mindset. I don't care what your position is. That's part of what reading is about - staying fresh, staying relevant, staying energized. I like it early in the day because I like to burst into the day. I don't like to start the day in neutral. I don't watch a lot of news, don't read the paper. I'll scan the headlines on Twitter and see what's in the news. I don't dwell on it. I don't want to be ignorant of what's going on, but I don't want to be rehearsing that nonsense, that garbage, those murders or the fires or the earthquakes or whatever, the famine, in my mind over and over that day. That's not productive. You've got to work on mindset, most people don't and it's a great edge if you do.

Chris: You probably find it impossible then to watch the Cowboys the last couple seasons because you don't want that bad news.

Dave Anderson: It's excruciating. It's excruciating. Here's how you watch the Cowboys the last couple years - straight bourbon.

Gary: And not the cheap stuff Dave.

Dave Anderson: The good stuff, 24 years, yeah.

Gary: For everybody listening to this I'm surrounded by Cowboy fans. What's the coach for the Cowboys, what's his name?

Dave Anderson: Jason Garrett.

Gary: Who's a better coach Garrett or Pete Carol?

Dave Anderson: Oh Pete Carol's a much better coach. Jason Garrett's a clown, he shouldn't be there.

Gary: He can just put up with the owner though, that's his thing.

Chris: Yeah, I don't even know how he landed that job.

Dave Anderson: He's over his head. He's over his head.

Chris: It was pretty obvious the first year.

Dave Anderson: It was. Are you a Seattle fan?

Gary: Oh yeah, well I grew up up there. I was born a Seahawks fan. It's not a new thing.

Dave Anderson:	You had a better run than we have lately.
Chris:	He's a Seattle super fan.
Dave Anderson:	You sucked for a long time though.
Gary:	It was brutal. My Mariners too. We lost our basketball team so the Sonics now are the Oklahoma Thunder. It's a sad thing being traded. I think the Browns fans probably have it worse because the Seahawks did turn it around and we have a good owner who cares about winning.
Dave Anderson:	You do have a good owner. That's big.
Gary:	It was interesting, I was a fan of Pete Carol when he won but I wasn't a huge fan of Pete Carol until he went to the Seahawks. Just seeing him turn it around and the culture and how he relates with that younger player - He's adapted.
Dave Anderson:	He has, that's a great leadership lesson: if you're not going to bring the energy who is? If you're not going to shape the culture you're going to leave it up for grabs. It's not going to be what you want. He understands that. You've got to go in and set the pace. In my book, *It's Not Rocket Science*, I kind of messed with people and I put a little bit of rocket science in it anyway just to be ornery. I put in the second law of thermodynamics just to mess with people. It's so true. The second law of thermodynamics is what Pete Carol understands. What it says is things don't naturally wind up, they naturally wind down unless outside energy is applied. Most leaders don't get that. Things are not going to naturally wind up. They're going to naturally wind down unless outside energy is

applied. Guess who's supposed to bring that outside energy? It needs to start with the leadership, with the clear vision, with the enthusiasm, with the passion, with the making the tough decisions. That's what energizes a team. He gets that. He gets that really well.

Chris: We're all fans of Coach Wooden and his pyramid. Does he call it "Pyramid of Success?" Pete kind of copied that and at the top he has won forever. Wooden was a huge mentor to him when he was here in California. Yeah it's great stuff. You can write a book in four months. What is your system for writing a book? Do you start with an outline?

Dave Anderson: Yeah.

Chris: On your phone or in a notepad?

Dave Anderson: In a Word document. I used to hand write it out and now it's just easier. You've got to start with the big picture. I start with the big picture and I start to get ideas for chapters. Then as I come up with a quote, a story, an analogy, I'll file it under that particular heading and the book just starts to evolve. You start with the outline, you get an idea of the chapters and you start to fit stuff in each chapter. Then you decide how to arrange the chapters and tie it all together. I'll usually discipline myself to write X number of words per day. I want to stay in a rhythm. What I like about doing it in 4 months is you stay focused. If you drag it out too long you can lose that rhythm. I've found that when I have a tighter deadline I'm more focused, I'm sharper, I'm more precise. Whether I'm writing a magazine column or a book, it turns out better. I think if it takes too long, you're all over

	the place, it doesn't always flow as well. At least that's what I found out for me.
Chris:	Yeah I think it's like hit songs like McCartney and anybody will tell you, the ones that come easy are the hits. If it's a struggle ...
Gary:	Do you have a place you like to write? A specific place you go to that .
Dave Anderson:	A lot of it on airplanes, a lot of it in hotel rooms. Then I have a loft in my house with a library and that's my place where I write when I'm at home. It's quiet. I've got 1,200 books around me there and it just makes you feel surrounded by good stuff so it inspires you to do good stuff.
Gary:	That sounds like the closer, you go into that space and that gives you the creative freedom to just get it done?
Dave Anderson:	It does. That's where you tie it all together, in that comfort area there. It's good.
Chris:	What is your morning ritual? On a typical day when you're at home, you wake up and then pour the bourbon?
Dave Anderson:	No, not in the morning. That's with lunch - don't get ahead of yourself. No, that's for weekends. I have a pretty intense morning routine. I have about a two hour routine of reading, studying. I go through seven different devotionals. I do study, I do research and then I use what I learn and there are a number of people in my phone that I mentor. Then I'll send them encouraging texts, encouraging information. That helps me share it, helps me learn it, helps me live it. About two hours. I get up really early. My mind is very focused. By the

time I get to work there may be someone smarter than I am, but they're not going to outwork me, they're not going to out-focus me out-hustle me, out-tough me, out-last me. I'm mentally ready. I'm mentally dialed in. I spend a good two hours. I don't do the workouts in the morning. I'll sometimes go to karate in the morning before I go to the office, but usually I like that in the evening. Some people are better in the morning, I like it better in the evening. I like to get it done in the evening.

Chris: Yeah we're morning guys. We meet at the gym at 5:30 and then we get it out of the way. I find that if I don't do it in the morning I just don't get to it. I get busy. Often times we're in the office until six or seven and then it's dinner. That's good. During that two hours, do you visualize?

Dave Anderson: I do sometimes, I do if it's a day of a big speaking event. I like to visualize before a speaking event. I'll try to get into the room the night before, especially if it's a big speech, not always feasible, see the room, see the crowd, kind of put yourself there. I think that helps. I started doing that a long time ago. That's what I generally save the visualization for is just the event itself, not all sorts of other stuff.

Chris: What are your favorite crowds that you've spoken in front of, location and who was the group, ones that are memorable?

Dave Anderson: I have some amazingly fun clients. They're not all in the auto business. I have a lot of clients, because of the books I write, outside of the auto business. I will tell about dealership groups that I get energized with as well because they've been with me a long time. I've seen them make progress. I see them sticking with processes and not just sticking their toes in and then, Oh that was hard so I'm going to try something easier. I get fulfilled when I work with people who are committed to process. Overall, probably the most committed group I ever worked with was on mission trips. I volunteered for eight years to go overseas and teach leaders of the underground church in Iran on biblical leadership principles. These are people who frankly would come to the meetings at risk of being arrested. We couldn't have the meeting in Iran. We would hold them in a surrounding country. We'd bring them out 50 or 60 of them. It was the only meetings I've ever done where you actually have a security detail. You're just worried. These guys, four of them have prices of their heads but they come to learn. We teach them all day through an interpreter which is another challenge, to teach through an interpreter, but to see that commitment, to risk their safety, to risk imprisonment, to risk their lives to get better for something they believe in. You've got people over here that are so full of it. They say, "I want to get better." They won't walk across the street into a library and check out a book that's free to improve their state in life. That's the most committed group. Then the hungriest group, the Hoosiers. They won the Big 10 last year so I get a ring.

Gary: Oh really?

Dave Anderson: Yeah I get a ring. Part of the deal man. I haven't shot a hoop in years. I'm going to have a big championship ring.

Chris: What do you say to those kids about social media and what they're putting out there, because it's a different game now, everybody's a brand. Do you work with them on just, that accountability?

Dave Anderson: The coaches work with them on what to do and what not to do social media-wise and they are very disciplined in that regard. Through the season you'll see most of them don't send out much of anything. They'll retweet a good, safe quote, something like that. Won't get into rants and so forth. What I help them do is find their hunger. Until they have that 'why' figured out, until they start to develop that mental toughness - I share mental toughness principles with them. I send them videos. I make special videos for them that they watch before each game on a different mental toughness or persistence or bouncing back from adversity. I send them texts before the game and after the game, each individual player. We kind of have a program that we've developed to work on the mental aspect. I don't know anything about X's and O's. I know the mental game and that's what I work on them with.

Gary: Yeah and it's 99% mental.

Dave Anderson: It is. I see so many talented people. Talent's great but it's only potential. You can have talented service advisers, sales managers, but if they don't have the mindset... That's why I'm so big on working on mindset. If they don't have the mindset to really apply it and to have that hunger to use it, it's going to be largely wasted.

Chris: Yeah that's the thing I see all the time is you've got guys with talent and you just see them wasting it because they just don't have that mental toughness to go execute. It's just too

	hard. It takes too much. It's not for me. It's sad in a way to see that happen because it's really just being wasted.
Dave Anderson:	Well you do, and often-times talent can also make you lazy because things do come easy to you. You do take shortcuts. That's that old adage, Hard work beats talent. When talent doesn't work hard, that you see in play over and over again. I've seen a lot of people with marginal talent with ferocious drive run circles around people with superior talent that don't have the hunger to apply it. You see it everywhere.
Gary:	Yep, all the time.
Chris:	You see it in sports especially. The guy that put in the work and the hustle and that has the mindset. I think, just watching the NBA finals this year with Lebron, he's just on another level mentally. Even when things don't go right for him he just goes right back. Kobe had that. Michael had that times ten.
Dave Anderson:	He did, he did.
Gary:	You see those guys too, they turn it into chess. Lebron was not playing basketball the whole time. He was playing chess with these guys. Every move he made, everything he did he was angling towards the finish line. The refs, the coaches, getting into the heads of the other players; it was pretty amazing to watch him. He was not going to be denied.
Dave Anderson:	No, he wasn't. What a comeback right?
Gary:	Yeah crazy.

Dave Anderson:	That was amazing. Like him or not, you have to respect what he did.
Chris:	I'm a Golden State fan and I wanted Golden State to win but I was marveled at what he did, what he pulled off.
Gary:	Our trainer when we go to the gym, he was kind of making fun of me because I said that they were going to win, it was Lebron's year. When they were down he was like, "You still think they're going to win?" I'm like, "Yeah I kind of do." And he did. You could just see it in his eyes he wasn't going to be denied no matter what. It's mental more than anything. You can see the other team just didn't have it in their eyes.
Chris:	Game after game, you could just see it on their face. Steph Curry was just crumbling. He's a talent, extremely talented basketball player but his head got in his way. He couldn't wrap it up.
Gary:	Jordan had that. There's so many players that played against Jordan that would say how intimidating, or some would say he's intimidating, some would say he's your friend ,and then he would flip it on you. I don't think anybody could figure him out. He was always a step ahead of everybody mentally.
Dave Anderson:	He was, he was. He's not a guy that ever paced himself. Some of these guys, they have a couple big games, they let up a little bit. He never paced himself. He went in, one of the few guys in any sport that really went in and gave it all every single game with that relentless, relentless mindset and attitude that typifies Jordan.
Chris:	It's funny because you watch him and you think, okay he's just an amazingly talented guy.

I think on the face of it you assume that's all there is, that he just was born with this amazing talent. I read that book and it's incredible the amount of preparation and the amount of work that he put into making it look that easy. When he got onto the court he made it look that easy.

Dave Anderson: During the Olympics, when he was on the Dream Team, it bothered him that some of the players weren't taking it seriously enough. He's watching game film right out until he runs out onto the court. These other guys are just loafing around and, "Oh it's going to be low-hanging fruit." He respected himself so much and he was so disciplined in that regard. He's not capable of turning it off and dialing it down because he's wired a totally different way. He couldn't do it if he wanted to.

Chris: Yeah it's funny, Magic Johnson tells a story, his favorite Jordan story happened when there were no cameras in a practice. He said he decided he was going to talk trash to Michael. They were beating Michael's team in the Dream Team, in practice. Then Michael goes, "Oh okay," and he flipped a switch and nobody else scored but Michael. There's two players kind of like that, Michael and then Jerry Rice, where whenever you hear other players talk about, "Oh I went and practiced and did workouts with Jerry Rice or Michael." They all of the sudden realize the gap in practice, because they're like, "Wow." People are like, "Jerry Rice is running hills and doing things," it wasn't a mistake. He wasn't the fastest, the tallest. I don't even think he was drafted that high but he had the mental part and the work ethic. When nobody was watching he's running hills. When other people are out clubbing or whatever, he's working and taking it very serious.

Dave Anderson: This is what athletes understand. I think that sometimes people in our business don't understand. You don't get better on game day. You get revealed on game day. You get better with what you're doing in between game days. Its like our sales people, service advisors, you get revealed in front of the customer. It's what you do in between those customers. Are you thinking about the last one? Are you running the game film through your mind? Are you doing any training? Are you practicing anything? Most people in our business they just show up on game day and want to play and there's not a whole lot of practicing going on. If you compare, you look at an athlete, you compare the amount of time they spend running drills, studying game films, studying their play group, doing scrimmages, working out, and you compare it to the amount of time they personally are in the game, it's really lopsided. They practice all the time. They play very little by comparison because they understand that the level of their practice determines the level of their play. We're in an industry where people don't want to practice, especially if they've been at it awhile. They think practice is for the rookies, the new guys, the losers. They're not sharp. They may be successful but they're missing their potential by a mile because they're not paying the price in practice. Even practicing a script 10 minutes a day, practicing a presentation, a walk around, 10 minutes everyday, really is compounded. Those right decisions just compound success overtime. Most people don't do it. They'd rather go read the paper, put out a fire, eat a donut, than to do something that actually could change their life.

Gary: Yeah five minutes could make the difference between success and failure. They won't spend the five minutes.

Dave Anderson: No, they're going to complain they have bad luck.

Gary: Bad genes.

Chris: Like your cholesterol Gary.

Gary: Did you catch when Dave was saying that things naturally go down?

Chris: I did. You're propping that cholesterol back up with cheeseburgers because naturally it wants to regulate and then you're like, the french fries and the cheese. Maybe cut the cheese off the fries. It could work.

Gary: What about the chili? Do I leave the chili on the fries and then, because it's Fritos and then there's chili also on those.

Chris: No, none of it's good. Maybe just the chili, no fries. The other funny thing with that is in our industry they don't practice and learn most of the time, but they also aren't aware of what's coming. One of the things in your leadership training, they always said "A leader's job is to be 50 feet out filling the potholes." - that's a quote of yours. When we're looking at the industry, I've done speaking engagements where they're like, "Don't talk about Tesla. Don't talk about the changes coming." In every industry in the last 10 years the consumers have voting. In our industry the consumers are going to have a vote on how they want to buy a car and how they want to service it. We're not going to be able to hold them captive. There was recently, was it last week, last Monday, or maybe two weeks ago? Wall Street journal did an article on Cadillac and how they're going to virtual dealerships or virtual sales departments, and that video is actually better. They're going to reduce their size. Basically what we've been saying for a long time is, the manufacturers don't have to, they're not going to need the dealers if we don't provide a value.

Dave Anderson: That's a great point.

Chris: Cadillac is just saying it. Lexus has 300 dealers and they sell more cars than us. We've got 1,000 dealers and so we're going to trim it down. Then Ford, GM, it'll happen where there will be a hybrid where they're going direct to consumer. The lid is off the jar but nobody wants to talk about it. We have to get better. We have to offer the customers a great experience. We can't just hit them over the head. We can't do the bait and switch. I don't know how many times in the last month we've had friends buy cars and the experience is terrible. They get into trouble, it's different than what the desk had told them. It's just crazy.

Dave Anderson: It is, and it is all about the experience. The great experience makes price less relevant. That's what people keep saying, everything's about price. It's not about price. It's about price because you don't create an experience, so for your customers it's about price because they think you're terrible. They think you're mundane. Why would I pay more for you because you're not driving value? If you create a better experience... We pay for better experiences or you wouldn't have first class on an airline, you wouldn't have a Ritz Carlton right next to a Budget Inn. You can get a night's sleep and a toilet and hot water in both places. Why is someone paying a grand when they can pay $50? They want a difference experience. Its up to the person to create the experience. If they don't have passion, their skills, their knowledge is not up to speed, then why not just buy it from a machine? I see no value in you.

Chris: Actually the machine would have higher grosses.

Dave Anderson: It would - the machine's more credible.

Chris: What did the guy say when you went to ...? Gary recently went to buy his daughter a car and they're there in the dealership. Salesmen was terrible. Sits down, you go to the bathroom and come back and what did the sales manager say?

Gary: The desk manager goes, "Hey I need to sell a car today. What are we doing?"

Chris: "I don't want to inconvenience you." That's where we're at, still today.

Dave Anderson: Unbelievable.

Chris: Then they're in a meeting talking about grosses are down, we can't compete with the public. Its like no, you just don't care about people.

Dave Anderson: They blame the incentives, they're not high enough, advertising's not working, we can't compete with the public. No, you're not doing your job. People have said to me before, "I bet when you buy a car you're really hard on people." Only if they're terrible. I'm a really easy sale and I will let you make money if you do a great job. I get that, I respect that. I'm not going to cut your throat over nickel and diming you on stuff. You create a great experience, you're going to make money from me and I think that's the way it should be. The last guy I bought a car from, amazing experience. Came out to the car, programmed all of our phones, programmed it into the garage door opener, sends me texts on Father's day. Who sends a text on Father's day? Happy Father's day. Sends me new ideas how to pimp out my car. We just had this one come in. We could do this for the wheels, we could do this for the seats. He didn't just make the sale and then move onto something else. We have a relationship. He creates a great experience. Who am I going to refer people to? Who am I going back to again? You think I'm going to cut his throat over a few bucks?

Chris: No, nobody would.

Gary: You want to spend money too. Somebody like that, you want to spend money with them. It makes you want to go buy whatever he's offering because he makes you feel good and that's the whole thing. He connects with you.

Dave Anderson: Where my wife gets her cars, the sales department is terrible. We go back because of the service department. We have that relationship with that service advisor. Has to be him, won't deal with anybody else but him. We'll take whatever recommendation he gives us because we trust him. He's earned that trust. He's been our service advisor for years. We literally hold our nose to do business with the

	sales department in order to be able to do business with the service department. That's the power of someone that creates that type of experience.
Chris:	Yeah it'll be interesting to see what happens in the next 10 years in our industry. Gary and I were talking a little bit about you. I know you were running a dealer group in the Bay Area. What made you, when the dealer group was sold, what made you decide to go into training instead of being a pastor?
Dave Anderson:	That's a good question.
Chris:	You're very much like a pastor in a way, in the way you teach. You could be on a pulpit in church, just the way that he delivers right?
Gary:	Yeah, the pattern.
Dave Anderson:	Some of the books I've written are business books based on biblical principles now that you've mentioned it. How to run your business by the book and how to lead by the book. I was responsible for the front-end operations of six dealerships but I also did all the leadership training and I created the programs and it was really the part of my job that I loved best. I've always liked speaking in public. Even in school it was the one thing I could do. Everybody was worried about having to write a speech or give a speech. I'm blessed, I've never been nervous in front of an audience in my life. I just never have been. People ask me how do I handle nervousness? I can't tell you because it's not an issue for me. It's the one thing I really, really do well. I love the car business so I wanted to stay and help people get better in that business. Public company bought the group. I left it and

started *Learn to Lead,* two decades ago. I decided to stay with what I knew best and that's what I knew best.

Chris: You still do a tremendous amount of missionary work right?

Dave Anderson: I do. We have a foundation. We have a nonprofit foundation that we run out of our offices here where we help take care of over 400 orphans every day, that live in camps. We work with skid row down here in LA, where, as you know, there's a 50 square block area where 17,000 people live in boxes and tents. We actually work through the police departments to get them the help and the aid they need. We're involved in a lot of that. I've not done the overseas mission trips with the Iranian Christians in three years now just because of a couple of things. The increased danger, even the places we used to have, they're more dangerous. Pretty much everyone that came to those classes is now either dead or in prison.

Gary: Really?

Dave Anderson: Yeah, yeah.

Gary: You're looking for new audience.

Dave Anderson: We're looking for a new audience, that's right. We're looking for some new up and comers.

Gary: That's rough.

Chris: It's tough to sell tickets to that event. It's funny how good we have it.

Gary: It puts it in perspective right?

Chris:	Yeah.
Dave Anderson:	I was in Ukraine at the Gypsy camps where we help the orphans and just to see the filth that they live in and to hear people over here complain. The whiners, we've just become a nation of whiners and cry-babies.
Chris:	We're a little soft.
Dave Anderson:	Absolutely, soft-bellied bunch, spineless bunch, this pampered age we live in. There are people over there who pray everyday for what we throw in the garbage. They're praying for what we're throwing in the garbage and we don't have that perspective. You've got a guy over here demanding $15 an hour, he thinks he's entitled to it, for flipping a burger. He's that spoiled, he's that entitled. He's 38, he's still living in mama's basement and he doesn't understand what the real world is all about.
Chris:	Same experience when I was growing up. My parents were missionaries and we lived in Mexico. One of the things my step dad would do, and at a very early age I made this connection, the youth groups that would come down were so entitled and were so miserable, these kids. Me, I always dreamed of being, it'll sound weird, but if you put yourself in my shoes as a kid, I always dreamed about being an American because I was a missionary's kid in Mexico. I was the only white kid. It was kind of a reverse thing where I never felt like I fit in, but I couldn't relate to those kids either because they were so miserable. The kids in Mexico that literally were living in a cardboard house, like if it rained their house washed away, were happier than the kids that came from upper-middle

class. They graduate high school and they get an M3, a BMW, and somehow they're miserable. It's all perspective and it's all mental.

Dave Anderson: People, if you're not happy with what you have, what you want isn't going to make you happy either because it's the wrong mindset. Gratitude's an attitude. Entitlement is an attitude. You get to pick either way. A lot of people today, they're pampered, they're picking entitlement and they're miserable. It's their choice. No one can make you that way. You chose it.

Chris: I think where we live here, I think a lot of the younger generation of these kids would be good just to drive south of Mexico and live there for a year and see what it's really like because we're so lucky here, the opportunity.

Gary: I did that with my kids in a smaller way.

Chris: You took them camping?

Gary: I took them to the neighborhood where I grew up. It's a rundown poverty-stricken neighborhood and not the most fun place to grow up as a kid. I drove them through there and I was like, "This is the alternative. This is what's out there. If you work hard and you put your mind to it and you don't complain about the great things you have and you appreciate them, then you get to have more and you get to go further. If you're constantly feeling like you're not getting what you're supposed to be getting or you got this entitlement attitude, then really what you're in danger of is slipping right down. You've got to earn it. You've got to go out there and go get it."

Dave Anderson:	You know what? Let your kids struggle a bit. Quit making it easy on them. Let them struggle. Struggles make you-
Chris:	Gary listen to this, listen to this-
Dave Anderson:	The struggles make you stronger, the struggles make you stronger. Everybody pampers these kids and they're not ready for life. They're not ready for life. I was talking to a dealer group and they were horrified. My daughter just got married, they weren't horrified for that. They were happy-
Chris:	Do you like the kid?
Dave Anderson:	I do, I do.
Chris:	He's a good kid?
Dave Anderson:	He's a good kid. He does really well. He's a good, hard worker. I really like him. They dated for three and a half years so we had a good chance to vet him and to look into all the nuances and we really like him. He's a good guy. They got married in April. Everybody says, "Are you going on a honeymoon?" She says, "I don't have the days." She works for me. She's my general manager. She doesn't have the days. "Oh your dad and mom are the boss." "I don't have the days coming. I have to wait until I accumulate the days before I can go on a honeymoon." That's the way it is. Do you think that earns respect from the people she works with? I know dealer kids who get to take off whenever they want. They get to go play golf whenever they want. They get to go party whenever they want. They have no set schedule and they wonder why people think they're a

freaking joke, why they don't respect them, why they can't take them seriously where they're just a ceremonial leader in their eyes or just a pretender with a title? Because they haven't earned that respect. Let your kids struggle a bit. It toughens them up. They live in this participation ribbon culture where they suck at every sport possible but they've got eight 12th place ribbons that give them this false sense of self esteem, laziest most disrespectful kid has a shelf of trophies not worth anything. That's the mindset they come into the workplace with. Look how special I am, look how unique I am, you should make me happy. Let them struggle. It toughens them up. Character is forged in a pit, it's not forged in a hammock laying around all day.

Chris: Yeah you've got to have some pain.

Gary: My kids were on the swim team when they were little kids and they came back from a swim meet that I wasn't able to attend because I worked in the car business, you know you're there every Saturday. Anyway I came back and she had a ribbon and it was 10th place. I told my wife, "What? 10th?" She goes, "Oh yeah they get ribbons all the way down to 10th place." I go, "How many kids were in her division?" She goes, "Oh 10." What does that mean?

Dave Anderson: That's crazy. My daughter had a 7th place ribbon and she was proud, when she was a kid, she was eight or nine, that there were 8th places so she felt pretty good about herself. Had to put things in perspective. That's the culture. The problem is then they come into the workplace and we have to influence their mindset from you owe me, to I have to earn it. You have to build that earn and deserve culture. We entitle people with bad decisions every day. We give them free lunches on Saturday. We give them spiffs they don't have to qualify for. We give them promotions because they've been here the longest and we think we owe it to them, rather than the fact that they're actually the best person for the job. We give the house deal to five-car Fred because we feel bad for him instead of using it as a reward for good performance and celebrating excellence. We use it as a welfare check for someone that shouldn't be on the team in the first place. We create this entitlement, people that know better. We create these conditions where people don't have to earn it, they don't have to deserve it. They get rewarded just for showing up, not stepping up, and then we curse them when we've created the conditions for it to happen.

Chris: Yeah I'm going right back to 15 years ago when I first saw you speak at NEDA. It was actually a sales class I was in. I was looking for some way to learn how to hire and motivate people. I think the class was how to retain and hire the best people. It's funny you were saying the very same things. We're incentivizing bad behavior and the people that are at the top of the food chain, we're just leaving them alone because they're doing such a great job but we never talk to them.

Gary: But it's getting worse.

Chris: It's very straight forward and it's very simple. It seems like that. Yet we still see it everyday, 20 years later and we're still doing the same things.

Dave Anderson: Think about how stupid it is to ignore a top performer because you're spending all your time with these people. You've got to wind them up everyday, everyday you've got to hug them and burp them and nurse them and give them a pep talk and wind them up. You have limited time. That means you're going to ignore the top people. Here's basically what you're saying. You're saying, "Gary when you get great, what you can expect in return from me is less time and attention because I'm going to be down here on another rescue mission hugging and burping and nursing five-car Fred trying to talk him into six so he can have a record month, do his victory lap around the dealership and ask to be promoted. You're kind of on your own. Terrible message. Then we wonder, 'Why can't we get other great people to work here?' Because you're ignoring the ones you have.

Chris: Yeah the chihuahuas attract chihuahuas.

Gary: Yeah and the low performers get the joke, they're getting all the attention. They're getting exactly what they want.

Dave Anderson: It disgusts me to see them handed spiff money that they don't have to qualify for. Come up with a 90-day qualifier. If you don't average X over a 90 day period, you have to sit the spiff program out. You're not going to get the $5 for a demo, $10 for a writeup. It should sicken us to be handing this welfare, $10 for this, $5 for that, to people who are still going to underperform and we're trying to trick them into competence. I've had people say, "Well if we give them the spiffs they'll produce more." It doesn't work that way. You can't trick someone into competence.

102

Chris:	No and they're just getting entitled.
Gary:	You can't buy it. You just can't buy it.
Dave Anderson:	A spiff should be to reward the right people for doing the right thing so they continue to build healthy habits, become financially enriched and hang around.
Gary:	Right, and another strategy that we learned from you is the minimum requirements. That just gets the rid of the bottom. Don't focus on them. Let them do it to themselves because you spend so much time trying to fix somebody who doesn't care. It's funny when you put minimum requirements in, how people end up working an extra week and they figure it out.
Dave Anderson:	It's a negative guarantee because just because you hit the standard, doesn't mean you still retain your employment here. We're going to still look at 'Do you live the values, character, integrity, CSI?' But if you don't hit it, you're not going to work here anymore. There's really nothing more fair than that because you're telling people what they have to do. People are so afraid to come up with a minimum standard but what they do is it causes the wrong people to fire themselves, it takes the emotion out. Then the mistake I see is they'll set the minimum standard, somebody won't hit it, and they make an exception.
Gary:	Then its over. It was a big waste of time.
Dave Anderson:	Standard's worth nothing and neither is your credibility.
Chris:	Yeah you lost all credibility. The top performers are going, "See? I knew it. I knew

they didn't really care about performance."

Dave Anderson: That's right, it's all talk.

Chris: Dumbs everything down.

Dave Anderson: It does, it does.

Chris: Yeah it's funny. Dave has another saying that applies to your cholesterol, that "Sacred cows make the best hamburgers."

Gary: Well, you know I love burgers so you're singing my tune.

Chris: You could help your cholesterol with sacred cows, eating sacred cows. I love that saying. That wasn't a book right? That was just a saying?

Dave Anderson: No - it was a little bullet point in a book, "Sacred cows make the best burgers."

Chris: I love that.

Gary: My favorite, most favorite thing I took from that thing that I went to, I think it was 15, 16 years ago, whatever it was, is the interview question that you ask. You say, you tell them, "I don't think this interview is going very well." Then the answer back is, the funniest thing you said, you said sometimes they blame you. "You're not asking me the right questions."

Dave Anderson: I don't believe you should make it easy on someone during an interview, and they will blame you. Here's the deal: the stakes are too high to have a lousy interview process because if you make a mistake everybody's going to pay for it over and over again. The objective of an interview is not to include the candidate. The objective of the interview is to eliminate the candidate. You've got to go in looking for a way to eliminate them. If you can't, that's a good thing, get excited because you're onto something special. But if you go in looking for a way to include them you're already making exceptions, making compromises and dropping the bar. One of the things I like to do that brought up that question, I like to see how someone handles pressure before they're cashing my paychecks. By the way, it'd kind of be nice to know how can you handle pressure? I like to ask a question that puts them on the spot, creates a little pressure, see how they handle it. That's one of the ones I like to do. It's funny you remember that. I'll put the pen down about halfway through the interview and just ask them, "How would you feel if I told you the interview's not going very well at this point?" You'll really see what's there. I've had people get all defensive and blame me. "You're not asking me the right questions," one guy told me. "You're not doing this right." What does that tell me about, how coachable is that guy going to be?

Gary: Not very.

Dave Anderson: Not very coachable. He's defensive. On the other hand I've had people say, "Wow really? Where do you think I could get better because I really need to get a job and I really want to get better." Does that tell you something? Now you got something. Then I'll tell them, I'll say, "Actually I thought the interview was going well. I just wanted to see how you'd feel if I told you it wasn't." Then you'll see if they have a sense of humor, which is kind of important in the workplace as well. I don't say it disrespectfully or to be a jerk. I want to see how you can handle pressure because in every job there's going to be some and I need to know how you handle it. I'm going to be interviewing somebody tonight by phone. I'm on the board of directors for a foundation and they have limited resources so they can't make a mistake. I'm going to be doing a phone interview with this person. It's going to be very intense. My objective during this phone interview is to find a way to eliminate this guy. Deep down, I hope he makes the cut because we really need somebody but we're not going to make a mistake. I'm going in with the right mindset. Pre-structured questions. It's not going to be a casual conversation. It's not going to be a good old boy get acquainted session. People start asking these stupid questions like, "What do you like to do in your spare time?" Which has nothing to do with performance and can actually lead you into illegal areas when people say, "I like to go to the mosque or the temple or the church and I volunteer for the Republican party," and now they don't get hired and they can say, "Things were going pretty well until they found out I was a Jewish Democrat." Now you've got liability on your hands so we shouldn't even ask some of those ridiculous, trivial, work list questions. We should focus on performance because that's what matters. Do they live the values? Do they have the performance? Anyway, I'm looking forward to the interview tonight but there's too much at stake to make a mistake for any of us.

Chris: Yeah and people think that's mean but really, what it is is, you're being steward of the opportunity and protecting everybody else, because when you let in somebody that doesn't have the same values and mindset and performance and doesn't want to improve, you're poisoning the well.

Dave Anderson: That's right you are.

Chris: You have to.

Dave Anderson: It doesn't take six does it Chris? It just takes one. How many poisons does it take to destroy the chemistry in a locker room? You see it in sports, you see it in business.

Gary: One.

Dave Anderson: Then we keep them too. We want to give them house deals. We want to fix them.

Chris: Yeah we were talking about this the other day. I've never fixed anybody.

Gary: Me either.

Dave Anderson: No, no. You guys figure it out tell me I'll write a book and we'll split the money.

Chris: No, there's no book there.

Gary: I hired a guy Chris absolutely told me not to hire when I was at the dealer. I just felt like I could fix him and yeah it was a disaster. In the end I really felt like it was unfair for him. I knew it wasn't going to go well and I took a chance on him anyway. As much as I felt like I was doing him a favor when it was over, really it's just more pain for him.

Dave Anderson: What you did is common. We want to think we can do it. We want to think we're the one that can bring it out and that can help them really

	make it. They've got to give you something to work with. If they don't have the character, the attitude, the drive, the energy, the talent, if they don't have it, you can't teach them those things, they've kind of got to bring it to the table. You can't put in them what was left out. You can only draw out what they have.
Chris:	Most great leaders; the key is they've surrounded themselves with people that are better than them. We're not going to fix people. What we want is people that are pulling us.
Dave Anderson:	Absolutely.
Chris:	That's the key. Did you ever try Dave's question in an interview?
Gary:	Oh yeah, a bunch of times.
Chris:	You set the pen down and you're like, "So what if I told you this isn't going very good?"
Gary:	Yeah.
Chris:	Did anybody blame it on you?
Gary:	I never had that scenario where people blamed it on me but I did get the people that just didn't know what to say. They were just like, oh well, okay. They were just like, "I'm leaving now." That would happen a lot. I remember I was training my BDC manager and she had a whole group of people that she was interviewing and she's like, "Oh I got this person. I really like him." I'm like, "Okay well did you try the question?" I used to tell all my people to use it. "No, no, I can not say that. I just can't do it." I go, "Okay well let's go in there." I go in there and I use it on her and I turn to my BDC

manager, her eyes were like saucer plates. She got so uncomfortable she turned beet red and it was funny. The girl was good, she was like, "Well, you tell me what you need to see from me and what would you like me to say, what things can I do?" She just kind of went right back to the table. Turned out to be a great employee, ended up being a service advisor in the end. Went from BDC, really, really solid employee. That was definitely the difference-maker for me. It helped me to decide, between all six of them she had the best answer.

Chris: I like that.

Dave Anderson: I've had people say, "Well if somebody asked that to me I'd get up and leave, well, then I'd go." You flunked the interview, go. That's the whole idea. If you're that type of person we would want you to go. Who's going to lose here? I'm not losing, you're losing. You were here because you wanted something.

Chris: Gary will tell you, I have a move for that. I just stand up. Where'd he go? I'm gone.

Gary: I will say we're letting the cat out of the bag during this conversation though, by letting people listen to this.

Chris: You can prep for an interview, I wish you would practice.

Gary: We've got to come up with a new one.

Chris: That's funny. Do you see Dave, what a great impact you've made on us?

Dave Anderson: Well, except his health, I'm concerned about his health.

Chris:	We just started on that today. You're not responsible for that until today. Going forward he'll check in with you.
Dave Anderson:	I am very encouraged to hear how much you guys have learned and retained and still talk about. That's what it's about. That's awesome.
Chris:	No, it's great. We're really excited to have you again this year at our Top Dog event. The theme this year is performance, so just what we're talking about.
Dave Anderson:	Love it. We're going to talk about mastering the art of execution. We're going to talk about getting it done which is what performance is all about and the people that come are going to learn a really nice five step process to master the art of execution. They'll be able to go back immediately and get better results.
Chris:	I'll tell you, because you did the Top Dog event for us last year, people still talk about Dave at the Top Dog event, it was so fun. Same thing: this year we're giving away, I kind of mentioned it to you, but we're giving away a $50,000 award to the top service manager. Performance, so numbers. Half of its performance and half of it is their story that they tell. It's our first year for that.
Dave Anderson:	That's awesome. So not everyone's going to get something for just showing up right?
Chris:	There's no 10th place.
Dave Anderson:	I like that, I like that. That's terrific.
Chris:	We're not wasting that ribbon. That'd be hard for somebody to convince me to even do a third place really. I'm like the Ricky Bobby with

that.

Dave Anderson: Yeah I mean third place is the second loser.

Chris: Yeah it's a long way down already.

Dave Anderson: It is.

Chris: I've been third place before but I was never happy about it and I didn't want an award.

Gary: Yeah you just want to try harder to be first place, just drives you to do more, I don't want a ribbon for that.

Chris: I remember, even in track and field in high school, I would get third place in something at the state thing and I won gold in a couple, but they did it like the Olympics. They were trying to find me to go on the podium. I'm like, "I don't want to go on the podium." I didn't win.

Dave Anderson: How many bronze medal winners do you remember? Who was bronze behind Mark Spitzer, Michael Phelps or any of those guys? Nobody remembers.

Chris: I was playing through in my head what I could have done different or... I didn't want the ribbon.

Dave Anderson: That's the way to use it. Use it.

Chris: Yeah it's a lesson.

Dave Anderson: Sure it is.

Chris: There's always a lesson there. Well, we thank you, you're an amazing host and this is an amazing facility here, this training center.

Dave Anderson: Glad you guys came out.

Chris: Dave's always so great with candy, drinks, he's an amazing host.

Gary: Yeah I've heard a lot about this place and wandering around it's really, really cool. I love the situation room, which is what we're in right now and the war room is my favorite I think. The Lombardi room is cool but the war room is-

Dave Anderson: We have some neat themed rooms here. Again, you've got to create an experience. People come here for training. We don't want it to be like a Marriott or a Sheraton, typical sterile room. Want them to have a great experience and take great care of them while they're here. It works.

Chris: When they're doing the training you use these themed rooms as breakouts right? They break out into little groups and then come back together?

Dave Anderson: I will. I'll do teaching for a while out in the main room that you guys were in. The classes here are intimate. They're intimate, they're interactive, they're very intense. I'll teach for a while, then they come with the groups they came with, usually they'll come from the same team, and they'll debate, they'll work on action plans, they'll prioritize things. Then they'll come back into the main session and we'll talk about what they came up with. They get so much done while they're here. So often in a training session people take a lot of notes, shake their heads and they have to go back to start figuring things out. We want them to make as many decisions as they can here, so when they get back they can hit the ground running. Yeah. We tried to come up with themes that lend themselves well to debate and discussion and planning. We have the situation room, we have the war room which is planning for D-day. Then we have the Lombardi room. I'm not a Green Bay fan, I am a Lombardi fan. He came up with some pretty solid plans. People loved it and it gets them in the mood. It gets them in the feel. There's a lot of original memorabilia in each of these rooms. There's stuff from the Kennedy era here. There's stuff from his Secretary's of State in this room. There's stuff from actual the World War II era. There's stuff from ... It just creates an experience and they get into it.

Gary: Isn't there an ashtray or something from Kennedy?

Dave Anderson: Yeah over there. There's a bust that Abraham Lincoln had, his secretary, that was her personal bust. Her pin, the White House matches from him are actually there. We have pictures on the wall here of actual photographs from the Cuban Missile Crisis. They were taken on the ships that were leaving with the missiles to verify them. Those were actual photographs from that. There's a letter behind me which was signed by Abraham Lincoln sending to someone. There's a letter up there signed by President Kennedy. There are magazines from that era. There's a lot of original stuff just in this room.

Chris: It creates a great vibe and a great mindset.

Gary: Yeah you feel it right away when you walk in.

Dave Anderson:	Well, people don't expect it. They expect the same old room. We have three dozen different types of coffees, three dozen different types of soft drinks. Create an experience, you'll get more out of people. The people that work here love it too. It's a great, great culture for them.
Chris:	Good well thank you Dave and we're looking forward to the Top Dog event. It'll be fun.
Dave Anderson:	Going to be a blast, going to be a blast. Thank you for having me on the show.

Episode #5: Tim Kintz Talks Customer Retention. Is It A Sales Function Or A Service Function?

Chris: Welcome to Service Drive Revolution, how you doing G-man?

Gary: Doing good! Really good.

Chris: We have a very special guest today. Flew in all the way from Texas, Tim Kintz.

Gary: Wow, my favorite state.

Tim: That's right.

Chris: I don't want to endorse a lot of people at all, but I get really tired of the sales guys out there that are all talk, but never give any good content. But the thing I love about Mr. Tim Kintz is he gives great content and he's a great guy. He's not as full of it as everybody else. I think that's why we connected.

Gary: He's from the great state of Texas.

Tim: At least I live there.

Gary: America's team, my friend, America's team.

Chris: Would you marry a Texan?

Tim: No, I'm not from Texas, I just got there as quick as I could.

Chris: That's funny. We love Tim. He's great, although he has terrible issues with math. Where did you go to college?

Tim: Arizona and California.

Chris: Really?

Tim: Yeah. But I grew up in the state of Missouri.

Chris: On your shirt ... he's wearing this shirt, you guys, I don't think everybody can really see this, but I'm going to describe it to you. It's a t-shirt, and it says, "6+4+3 =2," but clearly it does not equal two.

Tim: It does, you just don't understand it.

Chris: Explain it to me.

Tim: It's like Missouri math, right? Home of the best baseball teams in the country, Saint Louis Cardinals, Kansas City Royals. It's a double play, man. Anybody knows anything about anything knows that six, four, three double plays are a pitcher's best friend. That's common sense, the only thing about common sense though is what?

Chris: It's not that common.

Tim: Apparently so, at least in California. It is the San Francisco Giant's turn, but that was my whole background, baseball. It's all I ever did was play baseball. It's how I kind of ended up in the car business, went to Alaska to play baseball and they got me a job washing cars at the Honda Acura store. I figured what the heck, let me try the car business out and thought it was a great opportunity. It's like Denny's, right? You never make reservations, you just kind of end up there at two in the morning, well that's car business. Most of us didn't plan on getting into it, we just kind of ended up there. You'll always hear me use sports analogies, baseball, football, doesn't matter what it is. I always said, we were talking about this earlier, "Selling is a sport, are you in the game?" That's really what it comes down to. Are you in the game or are you watching the game? Are you in the bleachers, or are you on the field?

Chris: Yeah, I agree with that.

Gary: For the lame people out there, can we talk about what those numbers are?

Tim: Oh, yeah.

Gary: 6, 4, 3, double plays ...

Tim: It's the shortstop is six, second base is four, first base is two ... is three, and two is two outs. So it's six, four, three, double play, shortstop, to second base, to first base for two outs.

Gary: Oh okay.

Tim: There we go.

Chris: I like it. On today's podcast, what we're going to talk about is sales, some sales tips, and you're going to give us some sales tips. We're going to talk about the difference between selling in the front end and selling in the back end service. We have a book today that Gary loves that he read, called *Pitch Anything*. He's going to give you a book report, a little book review on it?

Gary: Yup.

Chris: Then we're going to talk about Gary's cholesterol again? Do you get your cholesterol checked?

Tim: No.

Chris: See that's what you should do, bro, don't check it.

Gary: That's the answer, just don't ... that's right.

Chris: Denial.

Tim: It's like my seatbelt.

Gary: Ignorance is bliss. I think we covered this last time. Ignorance is bliss.

Chris: He basically has a milkshake for his blood, like it's a chocolate milkshake.

Gary: I'm trying your method now, I'm doing chocolate milkshakes in the morning, burger and fries in the afternoon, I'm going to see if that works versus my vegetable juice and salads.

Tim: You got to die of something, right?

Chris: Right, exactly.

Tim: I mean, what the heck.

Chris: You want to prevent that as long as you can.

Tim: I want to die like my grandpa, in his sleep, not kicking and screaming like his passengers.

Chris: Bet you they were having sex.

Tim: No, his passengers were kicking and screaming.

Chris: Hey, one thing that you said in NDA that really got my attention that I agree with is when you walked in, and I kind of had a feeling but I didn't describe it as good as you did, but when you walked in and you were like, "Wow. Everybody is doing too good."

Tim: It was unbelievable, it felt like 2007. I walked in and Cock's automotive and all them booths, millions and millions of dollars. They had liquor in every one of the booths, and hookers, and dancing girls were everywhere. It was-

Chris: I was not at that convention.

Tim: It was Vegas. It was unbelievable. You had a CRM come, You had a million dollar TV screen, for crying out loud. My

first thought was, "Dang, we're going to have a recession next year."

Chris: Yeah, I felt that too. Everybody's high on the hog, but nobody's focused on fundamentals.

Tim: It goes right back to good habits are formed during bad times, bad habits are formed during good times. Right now there's a whole lot of bad habits going on.

Gary: It's a spending spree.

Tim: It is. We forgot about 07. Quite frankly, so have the banks. So have the manufacturers. So have the used car managers. We've all forgotten about it. That's why retention is so important moving forward. We put these product experts out there, paying 1,500 bucks a month. That's great when people are buying cars. What happens when people have to be sold on cars? Becomes a different world, huh?

Gary: Yeah.

Chris: No, it does seem like everything's running very loose, and very ... Everybody's very happy, and we have this thing in America we do, is we like to live in denial.

Tim: Yeah, "Those who forget history are doomed to repeat it." a Yogi Berra-ism, Since we're in LA. Yogi Berra played for ... Oh, he played for the Yankees.

Chris: For the Yankees. Go ahead.

Tim: Same thing, same thing. It's de-ja-vu all over again. That's exactly how it feels, man. 07, nine years later. Pow. Kapowie.

Chris: Yeah, it feels like that for sure.

Gary: I like the way-

Tim: But that's all right though. Look, that's not a bad thing. Look, first of all, that's not a bad thing. That means right now, if you get prepared, then you can gain market share. In the down time is when some of the most successful dealers, and dealerships, and sales people succeed. We were just out in West Texas. They're dealing with a recession right now, based on oil prices. Well, the dealership I was in, you were in a different group, but the dealership I was in, they had sales people in there that recession-proofed their business, because they focused on the retail automotive customer. They did their follow up. They took their onetime customer, and turned them to a lifetime customer. Brandon is the guy's name. He's got a baseline now of 23 cars a month. It doesn't matter if the oil prices are thirty bucks a barrel, or if they're $130 a barrel. He knows the worst month he'll ever have, because of his customer retention, is 20 to 23, 25 cars a month range. Right now is the best time to guarantee market share dominance if we do have a recession. Nothing wrong with that.

Chris: Just for everybody listening, to kind of clarify, in Odessa, Texas is where we were, right?

Tim: Yeah, Odessa.

Chris: Midland Odessa. The oil companies, because of oil prices, have all their big rigs that basically drill, stacked up.

Tim: That's right, over 1,000.

Chris: Oh, I got in Tim's pickup. We were going to lunch? I got in his pickup, he was driving to lunch. The first thing I had to ask him is, "Where's your gun?"

Tim: Which one?

Gary: Under the seat, in the glove box.

Chris: He said, "My little Chevy pickup." I'm like, "They make a smaller pickup than this. This isn't little." He has a compartment in the center console for guns, which is kind of crazy.

Tim: Shy built that in.

Chris: So we're driving and he says, you know, "See that over there?" You just see these towers of Pisa. One after another, stacked up. They're out of commission. They were talking about, today on the news, the feds said that Halliburton and the other company they're trying to merge with cannot do it. They're all hurting. This part of Texas is desolate. The dealers there - I actually think the dealership you were working for used to be the number 1 Super Duty dealer in the country.

Tim: Absolutely.

Chris: I mean guys would come in and buy a hundred trucks at a time.

Tim: That's right.

Chris: Like a hundred. Now, it's dead. There's no pulse. Each one of those towers is worth how many jobs?

Tim: Anywhere, depending on who you talk to, forty to a hundred jobs per tower. Per platforms. Per oil platform.

Chris: Those are what they drill in ... They're looking for oil, and they're drilling, right?

Tim: Of all the jobs, based on - depending on who I asked - it was somewhere between forty to a hundred jobs.

Chris: When you're counting on fleet sales, in that environment, and all of the sudden the economy's dead. People are moving out of there, right? They're going somewhere else.

Tim: Yeah.

Chris: You've got to really have retention, and really have a connection with customers, in order to still be selling cars.

Tim: Well, and a couple things. You know, we talked about that a long time ago. About, you know, "You're doing a great job with your fleet, in-fleet tail customers, right? You're getting them in, you're taking care of them. But our retail customers are disappearing. We're not retaining any of them." That's all, you know, it's all unicorns and cotton candy when oil is $120 a barrel. What's going on? I brought up Brandon selling 20 to 25 a month right now, because he continued to focus on the retail automotive customer. There's another guy, I don't want to say his name. He was selling 50 a month, but his 50 were all fleet tail, and fleet accounts. He was killing it, but now, last month, when I was there he had nine and a half out. It was the 29th of the month when I was there. You can just see the difference between preparing, you know, if something's going to happen, right? If something's going to happen, whether you're a leader or a sales person, it doesn't matter. You fail to prepare for it, then that's just a failure of leadership, whether its self leadership or leading a team. If you know that potential is there, and the probability is there, but you do nothing to prepare, then shame on you, because right now is when we need to be preparing. It's the time to train, but we're too busy. That's when you need to train. "Yeah, but we're selling too much service. We don't have time to train." Yeah, well you better make the time. If you don't make the time to do it right, when are you going to find the time to do it over? That's the reality of it.

Gary: Tim, let me ask you a question. When you're talking to these dealerships about retention, how are they responding to that, and what actions are they taking?

Tim: Depends where I'm at. If I'm in West Texas, they're "amen" - they're all over it. They know they need to do it, because they have to.

Chris: Because they have to, not because they're ahead of the curve, right?

Tim: Right. It's the pain of discipline or the pain of regret, right? The pain of discipline's doing the right thing, because it's the right thing to do, not because you want to do any of it. Does it take effort to do it? Yeah, but the best thing about the pain of discipline is the pain only lasts until you do it. Your follow up, your retention. Problem is there's the pain of regret, and there's a whole lot of people dealing with that. "If only I would have, could have, should have, but I didn't." That lasts forever. I think the good dealers, the Fred Beans of the world we go into, they understand that, and they're making the guys do their follow up. They understand that retention isn't a sales job. It's not a services job. It's everybody's job. It's a total dealership, we all have to be in this thing.

Gary: I think, especially for me, when I think about the cost of acquiring that customer, and what they spend on marketing to get that guy in the door and buy a car. Then that's it? We don't care about him anymore? At what point do we decide that putting money into retention, keeping the guy around is worth more than trying to acquire a new customer?

Tim: Think about this right now. Think about how great our times are. Take West Texas out. Take some of the Dakotas out, from the oil being down. Think of the majority of our country right now. We're in the best of times for the car business. Think of last year, what we sold. 17,500,000. This year we're projected to beat that. What else is great about the car business right now? Cars are better than they've ever been. What else?

Chris: Quality's up.

Tim: Quality's up. Banks are buying - you've got tier one banks buying like they're subprime lenders. Interest rates are all time low.

Chris: Yeah. Leases are low.

Tim: Leases are phenomenal.

Chris: Options are through the roof. You got Hyundai's that have the same options as BMW.

Tim: Absolutely. Consumer confidence has never been better. Traffic, you know, the internet, it's unbelievable to generate traffic. Think about advertising now. In the past, we'd advertise with radio, TV, newspaper, right? Our advertising was pretty much target shooting with a shotgun. Every now and then you might hit that bullseye. Now, with SEO, digital marketing, reputation management, social media, you're target shooting with a rifle. You can hit your exact demographic you want when it comes to marketing now that we never had in the past. All the internet is unbelievable. Leads that we're getting is amazing. The tools, the technology. Think about CRMs. It's unbelievable. That's when we need to really buckle down, because it is unbelievable, because it's so good. I think our competition sucks, if you want to get good. If you want to be a top producer. If you want to gain market share. If you want to dominate your market, your competition sucks. If you're serious, this is the best time in my 26 years in the car business, it's the best time to become great.

Gary: That's what I always felt, too. The gap between the top performers and the guys that do nothing, it's just so wide.

Tim: Right.

Gary: There really are no levels in between. If you're going to do it, and you do it right, you just rocket past everybody else.

Tim: How many times you hear a guy say, "Well, let's get kiosks, and sales. That'll sell cars." Or, "In service, "Let's just put a kiosk in service, it'll sell service."

Chris: In service they say ... They get, you know, the pads or whatever, and the drive-

Tim: Yeah, tablets, that'll sell.

Chris: Yeah, the tablets.

Tim: Just all that crap. It's all crap. People sell, not product, right? Programs don't sell. People sell.

Chris: Yeah.

Tim: I think sometimes we forget about the people part of it, until we have a pull back. Then we just say, "Wow." Then your--

Gary: That's like the nature of this industry right now. Everything's about the technology. They're not investing in the people. They want to go buy tablets, and different kinds of CRMs and systems--

Tim: If I get a cool program, we'll sell cars.

Chris: Let me ask you a question about that, because I don't know if we talked about this or not. The tablet thing, right? We were talking about tablets. This comes up all the time. People ask me, "Hey. Should we try tablets?" To me, there's something seriously wrong with the tablets, and the idea of it. Lets say if you had them, the technology usually is wrong, but let's say the technology really, really worked. The steps to the sale and services, you know, you run out and attack the car. You attack the car and the driver. Your time at the car is to build rapport. It's nothing about the car. The car is a commodity, because anybody can service the car, right? Your time at the car is about building rapport. The idea of a tablet, and doing it all at the car, and that the customer is in a hurry, and that's the way to do it. I've seen that sales usually drop when you're trying to do it at the car, because there's something about ... I'm curious what you think it is. There's something about taking the customer inside and sitting them down, then presenting the maintenance and the things that are due for, that increases your closing ratio. Instead of doing it at the car. The car is about building rapport, but when you try to do it all at one time without that change in scenery, for some reason the closing ratios aren't the same.

Tim: I guess the answer is it really depends, right? Some guys want technology to sell everything for them. They want to show them a little video on what a front end alignment does. That's crap.

Chris: That never sells anything.

Tim: It doesn't sell anything. Videos don't sell nothing. They tried it in FNI for years, doesn't sell anything. What I think the benefit is is that, you know, you've heard in sales, "Speed kills." Right? It's not how fast you get through the sales process, its how effective you get through the sales process. Well, I believe it's also right in service, except at the beginning of that sale. Whether its a sales or service doesn't matter. Slow kills. It's 100 degree, it's mirror image.

Chris: Yeah.

Tim: Slow kills early on, so I think if you do have a tablet, similar to sales people. We just implemented this with a dealer group that I go into. They got 18 stores, they have an unbelievable CRM, but it's garbage in, garbage out, because nobody's actually doing anything with it. They all have an amazing app for it. They come back from a demo, and it was dragging the sale out. They've got to go in and manually input, you know, Bob Jones. He lives at Main street. It takes forever. Slow kills, because of the ether, right? The excitement, the customer ... It's a little opposite from service, but its the same principle. It's speed kills when I'm selling the car. Slow kills when I'm negotiating it. I believe when a customer pulls in the service lane ... I can be wrong, because I'm sales guy, but we do no more than you guys back in service do.

Gary: What? What?

Tim: I think when the customer first comes in--

Chris: Wow, wow, wow. Slow down.

Gary: Hold. Wow.

Chris: Can't we all just get along?

Tim: I am in LA. Yes, we'll all get along. I think when they come in, I think the slow kills. I'll tell you why. I brought my wife's Lexus into a dealership by my house. Unbelievable dealership. I remember standing there for 15 minutes, being pissed off that I'm standing there for 15 minutes waiting for an advisor to come over. Then when they come over, are they speeding up the process? If you have technology that's great, as long as it helps you be more efficient. You have a - I'm looking over your shoulder - you have a John Wooden book behind you. You got Wood, and you got like 100 John Wooden books there. John Wooden always said be quick, but don't hurry. It's was all about be quick and efficient, but don't rush or hurry.

Chris: That's good advice.

Tim: He said don't rush or hurry because you made mistakes. Be quick and efficient, and you can be effective. Can a tablet be effective? Absolutely. But it's the execution of it, right? It's the people part of it, not the technology part of it. Does that make any sense, or am I just losing my mind?

Chris: It makes perfect sense. I mean, how many times have you had a customer come in and say they're in a hurry, then spend two hours.

Gary: Right.

Tim: Everybody's in a hurry.

Chris: Yeah. They're in a hurry because they don't like you.

Tim: Just give me fifteen minutes. It's easier.

Gary: Yeah. They don't want to talk to you, that's why they're in a hurry.

Chris: Until they like you, they're in a hurry.

Tim: Yeah. They don't like you. You have to earn that, right?

Chris: Because once they start to like you, they slow down.

Tim: I always talk about this in sales, I call it your buyers quadrant. When a customer comes on the lot, they're guarded. Then they become open minded, if I do my job. Build some rapport, get to know them. They're open minded then, during my high impact presentation demonstration. Then, they become confident in me when I come back and I say, "Hey. You guys are going to love your new car." Because I've earned that. Then, when I get to negotiation, they trust me. You think about service, and that same, subconscious process that customer goes through. When they pull in the service lane, they're guarded. Why they're guarded in sales, and why they're guarded in service, could be two different things. I mean, you tell me. Why is a customer guarded? What is the fear factor they have, when they pull in the service drive?

Chris: I think the first part, because we've done such a bad job historically, is the fear factor of just getting helped. One fun thing that I like to do in our coaching group meetings is I take everybody's cell phones away, then we start calling their dealerships, trying to make an appointment. It's a joke.

Tim: Oh, it's--

Chris: You know. They have a hard time making an appointment, most of the time. Right now, the people--

Tim: Hard time?

Chris: Yeah. Right now, the people listening to this will say, "Oh, that's not my store." But it's their store. Then they come in, like your Lexus experience. They sit there for 15 minutes. The trust barometer just is like--

Tim: Oh yeah.

Chris: Dropping. Then some guy walks up and says, "Do you have an appointment?" And most--

Tim: Yeah. In wrinkled dockers and a wrinkled polo.

Chris: Yeah.

Tim: His hair looks like it was combed with a live chicken, and he used a five iron to iron his shirt.

Chris: Yeah.

Tim: That's bad.

Chris: Then what? It's all uphill from there?

Tim: Oh yeah, then it's ... That's why they end up getting their stuff done at other places. My wife's a perfect example. She went to this place up the street to get an oil change this last time on her car. She didn't want to drive all the way over to Plano Celebrity Carwash or whatever. They do the whole thing up there. She goes up there to get the oil change and the car wash. She comes back and says, "Hey. I just want to let you know I also got the tires rotated." Like really, you got the tires rotated too? Okay. She says, "I know. I know. I could have went to Firestone. That's where we got them. I know I could have went there. It was just easier. It was just ... It was only $29, but it was just easier." I've never seen any of those third party guys have one line RO's It just doesn't happen.

Chris: Right.

Tim: The craziest thing is Celebrity Carwash and Firestone could have a rock fight. You don't even need to have a rock fight with them. They're in the same freaking parking lot. It's convenience man, is all it was. How often does that happen though?

Chris: No, that's everything.

Gary: Happens all the time.

Chris: Imagine if your wife pulls into that Lexus dealership, and somebody greets them right on the curb. It's like, "Oh. We're so excited to see you. Just do me a favor. Pull into lane one and stay with your car." Then an advisor comes running out, and is like, "Good morning. How are you? I love your car. What are you planning on doing today?" You know, built a little rapport. Just a little rapport. Complimented your wife on her eyes, maybe her shoes. What would we compliment your wife on?

Tim: Everything.

Chris: Everything.

Tim: Yeah. That's the right thing to say.

Chris: Compliment her on everything? That'd take a while.

Tim: On her husband.

Chris: Think. No, that wouldn't happen.

Tim: Oh, okay.

Chris: Built a little rapport, then made it convenient, because you got to make it convenient.

Tim: Big tip.

Chris: What wouldn't she buy?

Tim: Absolutely. If you--

Chris: That's why I say it's not about product knowledge and service. The service advisor that knows the viscosity of whatever, I never knew any of that stuff, I just knew how to make friends. Because you lose trust when the customer doesn't know where to go. You lose trust when they wait. You lose trust when you come up, you're not friendly, and it's a transaction. Right here in LA, there's all these new restaurants, all these fancy chefs from all over the country are coming in. There's too many restaurants for the people. You go into them, and they're empty. You walk up, they're like, "Do you have a reservation?" Then they make you sit there for half an hour, staring at an empty restaurant. That's what we do in service, it's a joke.

Tim: It is. Especially when you charge sales, but that's a whole different story. It's-

Gary: It's justifiable.

Tim: It is. It's justifiable

Chris: I know you don't understand this, but the dealership makes a little more money.

Gary: Yeah.

Tim: Yeah, right.

Chris: On the internal--

Gary: There's a little door at the back of the dealership. You walk through that door, there's some people that work back there, so check it out.

Tim: It's justifiable homicide that prints money. That's right. It's like when I lived in Alaska, it was always the saying, "You get more trouble for shooting a moose out of season than shooting your wife." Well, it's kind of the same thing. You guys can charge us whatever you want. It doesn't matter. You guys will just freaking crush ... But-

Chris: No, but what we shouldn't do is take 14 days to do it.

Tim: That's for sure. But why does every one of my cars have to have a front end alignment, and windshield wipers, and take 14 days?

Chris: Well, you'll pay for it, so--

Gary: Well that's when--

Tim: We're not even ... We don't have a 10% penetration on front end alignments. But that nice machine over there, we're paying for it.

Chris: Yeah, that's a legitimate point. A lot of guys are living on internal, and hence what we were talking about in West Texas too, right?

Tim: That's right.

Chris: From living on internal, then when that goes away, the fun starts. Now all of the sudden they--

Tim: New inventory's piling up like chord wood. There's no more PDIs to do, and they're wholesaling out used cars. Huh, what do we do?

Chris: Now what?

Tim: It's like the dog that caught the car.

Chris: Yeah. Talking about sales, and the difference between service in the front end. There's guys in our industry that will teach service advisors to ask five times. But anybody that's ever written service knows that you cannot ask five times in service, you'll scare a customer away. I know from owning and running a dealership that we'd peel customers off the curb in the front end all the time, and it worked. But in service, you just don't do that. So it's trust based more than anything. What do you think about, or what tips do you have for building trust?

Tim: You have to earn it. Its not given, right? First time that customer comes in for their first service, is going to be the toughest sale. It's going to be the toughest time. Second time that customer comes back in, if they go to you, now you become their friend in the service department. Third time they come back in, now when you tell them they need that front end alignment, and they need a tire rotation, its just what they need to do, because you've earned it. The nice thing when they buy a new car, or even a used one, for the most part its pretty easy the first time to get them back in, if we do a good job. I'm a huge believer that just like in the front end, the most successful sales people have a high repeat and referral business. I don't understand why we don't do the same thing in the back end. Why does that customer not see the same service sales person, or service advisor, every single time when they come in? Because now when I come in, you're a friendly, right? You're a happy face. If me as a service advisor is doing a good job, putting notes in the CRM, or the DMS. Putting notes about, I don't know, whatever I found out. If they have kids. If they're a Cowboy fan. Whatever it is, if I do a good job of taking notes, I open up that customer screen. You open up your new RO, whether it's pulling it from the CRM ... Now all of the sudden I have something in common to talk about with that customer, right? We always say build rapport. What is rapport? What the hell does that even mean? It's ... No, you're finding common ground, so you can have an ongoing conversation. Right? Rapport is this big word everybody uses. Okay, you mastered opening a question so you can build rapport. Rapport is all about finding common ground. Once you have common ground with that person, now it's just a conversation. When you can have a conversation with somebody, you're not selling them. I think sometimes we're so ... We begin with the end in mind, and we stay at the end. We just try to sell them something, because we're getting hammered that we're not selling front end alignments, we're not selling enough tire rotations, we're not doing enough of our core product in service, to raise our effective labor rate.

Our effective labor rate is too low. We start beating people over the head, but we never earn the right to sell them every single time when they come in. The other thing is I think its your job - it's everybody's job - but I think it's the service job to make your dealership sticky, right? We sell the car, how do we make the dealership sticky? You know, the manufacturer is making it harder. How do we keep that customer stuck to our store? How do we keep them coming back every three months, or six months, or once a year, depending on your manufacturer? What are you doing to make your dealership sticky? I'm a huge believer in doing re-deliveries with people. I sell you a car, you come back in two weeks so I can go through the technology. You probably didn't retain more than 10%. Then, within 30, 60, 90 days, we do a new car clinic. Service needs to champion them and be part of it. We do female car care clinics. We do traditional car care clinics. We keep our store sticky. Let's keep these people coming back. Once we can figure out how to make our store sticky ... That comes down to us being loyal to them, and then they'll be loyal to us. Then, moving forward, you'll dominate the market, because most of us don't retain customers. Most of us replace customers. We write the same amount of RO's this month, this year, as we did last year, this month.

Gary: If you look at businesses like Starbucks and Apple, in my home town back up in San Francisco area, the Bay area, there was a Fixture Max store that was on the corner. I'd go by there constantly, it was near the dealership I worked. It was empty all the time. There was nobody ever in it. I don't know how they paid the rent. There was nobody in there. You go to the Apple store, you got to stand in line to get somebody to help you, but you'll do it because you're going to get good help. They're friendly. You want to be there. You want to be part of that. You go into Starbucks and the Barista knows your name. I get friendlier service there than I would pulling into a service department in some cases. That's where we're missing it.

Tim: Oh yeah.

Chris: For a $5 cup of coffee.

Gary: I'll pay $5 because I'm going to get good service. I don't know...

Tim: Convenience, because there's one on every corner.

Gary: I don't think its that hard. For me, its not that hard. I look at that scenario and think, "You treat people right. You offer them, you do more than what they're paying for. You treat them well. They're going to come back.

Tim: But that's a bigger challenge, right? That goes back to vision for the dealership. What's our long term? Is everybody tied into it? That's a whole leadership conversation that we need to have. I'm not going above and beyond, I'm going to do what I need to do if I don't buy into it. There are tasks that I have to do every day. We've talked about that versus a career, right? Too many guys have jobs and not careers.

Gary: Yeah, that's--

Tim: Therefore you don't want to take care of customers.

Gary: That's the leader's responsibility.

Tim: And Chris, what's job stand for?

Chris: I forget.

Tim: Just over broke.

Chris: I like that. So Gary reads a lot.

Tim: Yeah.

Chris: That's a good thing.

Tim: Yeah.

Chris: You don't seem excited about it.

Tim: I am. I'm very excited.

Chris: He read a book called *Pitch Anything* by Oren Klaff?

Gary: Oren Klaff.

Chris: Are we sure we're saying that right?

Gary: Yeah, I believe so, Oren Klaff.

Chris: *An Innovative Method for Presenting, Persuading, and Winning the Deal.* He loves that book. Can you give us a little synopsis on what the big takeaways were?

Gary: Yeah. His thing is he pitches deals to venture capitalists. He has a start up company, lets say it's a software company. He's looking to get $10,000,000, $100,000,000. So he's pitching to billionaires, trying to get them to invest in something that's not proven. He'd go in against these other companies that do a similar thing; they're trying to raise money. He was a small fish in a big pond. He realized one day that he needed a different approach. So he just did the analytical thing. He went through and decided, "I need to create a system." So that's what he did, so he could go in and pitch a deal in less time, capture the customer's imagination, and be able to get them to buy or invest in this product. He sold and closed more deals than just about anybody in that field. He had a method that he calls the Strong Method, let me just read it real quick. He says, "S is set the frame. T is tell the story. Then R; reveal the intrigue. O, offer the prize. N is nail the hook point. Then G is get the deal." For me, the biggest takeaway in the beginning is the "set the frame." I thought a lot about this when I was reading it. I read it probably five, six times, because I was so captivated by what he did. He talks about frame collisions. In every social, you know, interaction, business interaction, there are frames that are coming together. Very simply, he put it like, "You're getting pulled over by a police officer. The police officer has a frame. He's going to give you a ticket. You have a frame, I'm late for work, I'm trying to catch my flight. You know, whatever it is. So, you're going to have a frame collision. Its coming. You have the frame collision, well the moral authority takes over, because you're breaking the law. So, he doesn't have to give in. His frame takes over for yours, and that's it. That dictates the rest of the interaction. His frame now owns it." In a service drive, I thought about that. I was like, "Wow. That's genius." Because a customer comes in. What's their frame, right? Their frame is, "I'm going to wait too long. I'm going to get mistreated. My car's going to take longer than it should. They're going to try to upsell me things I don't know that I need." Then, here's an advisor coming along, going, "I'm behind on my alignment sales. I got my manager breathing down my neck. I need to sell this customer something." Immediately when that customer pulls in, there's a frame collision. The customer used the - he talks about this in it - they use the time frame as their ability to overcome the service advisor's frame. The time frame is, "I don't have time to talk to you. I'm in a hurry." So the advisor then gives in. Guess which frame takes dominance. Now the customer's frame is dominant. The advisor gives in. No sale happens. The worst part about the whole exchange is the customer leaves with service and maintenance due on their car that would help them. They don't get it, because we cannot even have the conversation. I just thought to myself, "It's so genius." He talks about ways to kind of overcome the time frame. That customer comes in and says, "Well, I only have five minutes." He goes, "Great, I only got two, so lets get moving. I'm here to help you." You know, he'll just go right back with the time frame. Then he'll create a joke out of it. "I only really have one, so maybe we should get moving a little faster." You were talking earlier about creating rapport, it's a way to create rapport. He's joking back and forth with the customer, and building rapport with them. It's friendly. I thought, to me, that number one takeaway was that if anybody could do one thing to try to improve what they do in their sales and their closing ratio, especially on the service side, is just consider that. That the frames are coming at you. The fact that you know its there, you cannot go head on at it, because they're going to break yours, then you're done. Then the customer owns you. You know, we talk a lot about control. That's one thing, they overcome control by using that frame.

Chris: There was another great story that you told me about in that book about him walking into a meeting--

Gary: Oh the Apple story?

Chris: Was that what it was? Tell me that story.

Gary: The other part of it ... I'm going to skip ahead to offer the prize. One thing he always says is that, "At some point, you have to consider that you're the prize." Again, if I can put it in terms that we understand is, if a customer is coming in, they're coming in to get their car fixed. Guess what we know how to do? We know how to fix cars. Whose the prize in this scenario? We're the prize, You have to think that way. We're not chasing them to get their money. We're offering something that they need, and are required to get done. He wants to be the prize. When he loses somebody's attention, he needs to do something to get that attention back to him. He goes into this meeting, and he starts pitching a deal. The guy on the other side of the desk puts his feet up on the desk, grabs an apple, and starts eating this apple. He's cutting pieces out, and he starts eating this apple. Oren quickly realizes, "This guy's not paying attention to me. I've lost him." In his mind he's swirling. He's telling the story in the book. He's like, "I've got to do

138

something. I've got to figure something out." He walks over to the guys apple. He grabs the knife, he slices the apple in half, and he says, "Let me tell you how deals are done when you do business with me. Everybody gets a piece." He grabs a piece of the apple and just starts eating it. Then, the crazy thing--

Chris: Which is a huge pattern interruption.

Gary: A huge pattern interruption.

Chris: Nobody would have the balls to do that.

Gary: Right, exactly. That's exactly how it ends. He ends up finishing his presentation. The billionaire on the other side of the table doesn't break character. He stays, you know, stone faced. He just turns around to walk out. The guy goes, "Wow, wow, where are you going? Come back over here. Nobody does that. Why?" They all start laughing, then they start joking about it. Then he closes the deal with the guy. That's the other thing he talks about in the end, when he says, "Get the deal." He says, "At some point you kind of got to be willing to walk away." I think in the service department, that's another thing we're talking about. The five closes of an alignment. Begging, pulling, and "Come on customer, buy from me." It becomes disingenuine.

Chris: Yeah, even with CSI, when the advisors are begging at the end. It's the same thing. You frame upfront.

Gary: Yeah.

Chris: When you commit to CSI upfront, you're like, "Hey, I'm going to do this."

Gary: Right.

Chris: "But you're going to do this. I'm promising you I'm going to give you great service, but you're going to answer the survey." That's control, and that's framing too, right?

Gary: You got to earn it. If you're going to say you're going to do it, then you got to do it.

Chris: Because if you're waiting until the end, the customer's frame is, "I want to get out of here, and do the least amount possible."

Gary: Right, exactly.

Chris: This jerk is begging me for something he didn't even earn.

Gary: They're like, "Can I put my fingerprint here, then run out the door with my car."

Chris: It's probably scratched.

Gary: Yeah, right, exactly.

Tim: That's funny.

Gary: Yeah. I loved the book. I read it, and I also listened to it a couple times in my car, driving back and forth. I love the way he tells the story in it. Very captivating. His method of connecting and bonding with customers, trying to sell. It's just completely different than what we do here. Or what we do, what most people do. For me, it was fantastic. He focuses a lot on stories as well. The tell the story side of it. He says, "When customers come in to the drive, they're in a part of their brain that's primitive, right? They're in the fight or flight section of their brain. Is this going to be a threat to me? Am I in danger? Are you going to push something on me that I don't want?" That's where they're thinking. That's where they're at. Tim, you were talking about it earlier. You said that customers come in guarded, right? That at some point, we're building rapport, we're connecting with them, and trying to get them to be open minded. You're trying to open them up. That's exactly what he's talking about. They're in this portion of their brain where they have to be guarded. It's what we've been ... it's what evolution has taught us. We don't want to get eaten. What normally we try to do is we try to crash that with analytics. We try to talk about the molecules and the nitrogen we're going to put in your tires. Or the—

Tim: Show you a video.

Gary: Yeah, or the viscosity of the oil, like you were saying earlier. We try to break through that with facts and figures, but they cannot accept that information, because they're not in that mindset. What he says is you got to start telling stories.

Tim: Sure.

Gary: It's the stories that get through. You hook their emotions. You speak to them, then they start to open up. Then they become, like you said, open minded. Now you can have a conversation. You've built rapport with them. Now we're open. Now they're like, "Okay, this is no longer a threat. I trust this individual. I'm going to listen to what he has to say." That portion, they shift out of that mindset, and into their neocortex as he puts it. Into the section of their brain where they can reason, and has logic. Now you can talk to them about what's going on with their car. Understanding that just changes that dynamic between you and the customer. Between that and the frame collisions, it's pretty powerful stuff.

Chris: I remember when I wrote service for Volkswagen. You know, is it a timing chain or a timing belt on a Volkswagen? It needs to be replaced.

Gary: That's a belt.

Chris: Yeah. So the thing ... Different from the Subaru's, by the way, because you worked on Subarus, right?

Gary: Briefly.

Chris: When the timing belt breaks, no big deal.

Gary: Yeah.

Chris: No big deal. But when it breaks on a Volkswagen, it's a big deal.

Gary: Oh yeah, it's a scatter.

Chris: So the valves, they turn in. We call it ... The techs would say, "It turns into spaghetti." Right? I remember I would use the story thing in the commonality of other customers. It was an easy thing to do, but I would tell customers, "You're due for your timing belt on your GTI 16 valve or whatever." They're like, "Oh, I don't want to do that." I'd say, "I understand. If it's budgetary, I understand also. I just want to tell you, I've had customers that I told them that they were due for their timing belt. They didn't do it, they neglected it, and the thing that's different about Volkswagens is" ... I don't remember now, because it's been so long. What do you call the valves that will collide?

Gary: They have interference.

Chris: Yeah.

Gary: They create interference.

Chris: When the belt goes, it's, you know, then I would quote them whatever the price of the engine was. Just be really careful. It worked, telling them that story.

Gary: I had a similar time, because BMW was the same way. I had a timing belt story. I bought a used car from somebody really cheap. I knew it was behind on the maintenance. I drove it off the lot, I think I made it eight miles or something like that. The timing belt broke. It scattered the valves. It cost me thousands of dollars. I would tell clients that story when they would come in and talk to me, and they didn't want to do their timing belt. I get it, it's not something you want to pay for.

Chris: It's no joke.

Gary: The story tells itself. You don't want to be that person, sitting on the side of the road, thinking, "Man, I should have spent the $300 to get the timing belt done.

Chris: It's funny, when you're an advisor too, you're not telling them that story because you want to sell it to them. You're telling it because you've seen so many times people that don't do it. They come in, and the car is basically over. It doesn't make any sense to spend the money. Then they're in a weird position, and they owe $4,000 on a car that's worth nothing. That's why you're telling them the story. It has nothing to do with selling. You're really trying to do them a service.

Tim: Doesn't it go back to you have to earn the right to tell them that story? Otherwise their mind's not open to listen to you. How'd you do when they came in?

Gary: Yeah, it sounds like a pitch, right?

Tim: I think so often though, if you think about it, and whether its on the service floor or service, I think we sell out of fear, instead of selling them inspiration. We're so afraid that we may lose a deal, that we never make a deal. It's that emotion that we got to create, right? In sales, I'm creating a positive emotion. Selling is getting a customer to think, act, and feel in a positive way. In service, its almost that pain. That, "If you don't do this, this is potentially what's going to happen. Let me tell you why." You're creating almost the opposite emotion. But it's all about emotion. Selling is emotion. How do you get a customer to think, act, and feel in a positive way. Whether they're positive they want to fix it or not, they hold off. All of the sudden it's your fault that they didn't do it. Then you get a bad survey. By the way, CSI. Is that a score, or a process?

Chris: Its the grade of a process.

Tim: Right. We just look at it as a score, or a number. VOC or whatever it is. We look at the number, but we forget about the-

Chris: Man, CSI is the easiest thing to get.

Gary: I know.

Tim: Yeah.

Chris: Easiest. I think this was pretty fun. I have one question for you in closing. How fast of a fastball could you throw?

Tim: Not fast enough to make it to the big leagues. I could throw over 90 miles an hour back then.

Chris: That's pretty fast.

Tim: It was.

Chris: I couldn't hit 90.

Tim: Just the same old story about the old guy.

Chris: I'd be sitting there staring at it.

Gary: Yeah.

Chris: Right? I couldn't wind up like that.

Tim: I'd just hit you with it.

Chris: In fact, I've gotten in the 90 batting cage before.

Tim: Oh no.

Chris: If you even make contact it hurts your hands.

Tim: I couldn't either.

Chris: Ouch.

Tim: I never understood how guys could hit.

Chris: That's awesome.

Gary: What's the little league distance? You know, the mound to the plate? It's like 46 feet?

Tim: Give or take. It's 60 feet, six inches in the big leagues.

Gary: In the big leagues, yeah.

Tim: But that's what's so great about baseball, though. It's all uniform, right? Every field you go to, every field's different. The distance down left field, center field, right field, left center. It's weird. So unique. You've got a hill in Houston's field. I think they took it out. But everything in baseball ... It's the coolest sport, because of that. Every other sport has uniform ... Football fields. You've got 100 yards. It's 120 with the end zones. It's this wide. Baseball's just unique. You got 60 feet six inches pitching mound. You got 90 feet base pass. It's kind of weird because the foul pole is actually fair.

Chris: You hear that bro?

Gary: What's that?

Chris: That football sucks, and baseball rules.

Tim: No, no, it's just we're creative in baseball, right? Because in baseball, the foul pole is actually fair. If the ball hits it, it's fair. In all the other sports, if you step out of bounds, except tennis, it's not fair. Name me another sport where the guys play out of bounds the entire game. The catcher-

Chris: Cricket.

Tim: I don't know. That doesn't count.

Gary: Soccer.

Chris: One thing that we do agree on, because none of this I agree with.

Tim: That's all right.

Chris: The one thing we do agree on is that Safeco Field is pretty bitching in Seattle.

Tim: It's one of the best.

Chris: Every seat in that. It was built for baseball.

Tim: Yes.

Chris: That's all they do there.

Tim: It's a great town.

Chris: They're not having a football game, they're not having a soccer game. I don't even think they have a concert there.

Tim: Not the best field.

Chris: It is baseball.

Tim: Not a bad seat in the house.

Gary: It's nice.

Chris: It's magical.

Tim: It's not Saint Louis, as far as quality. But it's more fun.

Chris: I saw a game in Saint Louis.

Tim: It's good. State of Missouri.

Chris: Like 18 innings. Do you know when they stop serving beer?

Tim: In the seventh inning. When I left.

Chris: No joke. I was in Saint Louis. I was like, "Hey, lets go catch a game." We go. I forget who they were playing, but anyways, it ends up being like the longest game in Cardinals history or whatever. Yeah, no beer for a long time.

Tim: I'd went to the bar across the road. Jack Bucks.

Chris: They don't let you back in.

Tim: Joe Bucks. It was 18 innings, brother, you wouldn't have missed anything. There was a whole bunch of zero to zero innings. Three up, three down.

Chris: As is usually the case. Well thank you, this was fun.

Tim: Yes. It was awesome. I loved it. Thanks.

Chris: We learned some stuff. I love how you can come up with the stuff you come up with. It's great.

Tim: Yeah. Thanks.

Chris: Fun.

Tim: It was fun. I might read that book, check it out.

Gary: Yeah, no, I recommend it. Its good.

Chris: Watch your cholesterol.

Gary: Yeah, and watch your cholesterol.

Chris: Get your cholesterol measured, Tim.

Tim: How do you watch it?

Chris: Next time you come back, I want to talk about your cholesterol. We should compare blood tests.

Tim: I don't want to know.

Chris: You watch it by eating the right things, and doing the right things. Doctor Lau gives you a list of stuff, then Gary just ignores it.

Gary: He gives it to my wife, then she forces me to eat whatever is on the list.

Tim: I live in Texas. Is red meat and french fries on there?

Gary: No. That's not Doctor Lau Approved.

Tim: Fried chicken?

Gary: No. No.

Tim: Baby back ribs?

Gary: Nope. No.

Tim: Well I just don't want to know.

Gary: Kale. I think kale, sprouts, mung beans are on the list.

Tim: Yeah. Super foods.

Gary: Sprouted mung beans.

Tim: Cool.

Chris: Thanks. Cheers.

Tim: Cheers.

Gary: Cheers.

Tim: Awesome, guys.

Episode #6: Battlefield Leadership And Business Fundamentals With Navy Seal Jocko Willink

Chris: Welcome to Service Drive Revolution and my co-host Gary, better known as "G-Man." Now recently Gary and I went to San Diego and interviewed Jocko Willink, who's going to be a speaker at our upcoming Top Dog event here in Los Angeles where the top service managers and advisers from all over the country get together and workshop for a couple days. If you don't know about Jocko he was a Navy SEAL for two decades. He fought in Iraq where he was highly decorated and his unit there was Task Unit Bruiser which was instrumental in retaking and stabilizing the city of Ramadai and on top of that just a cool name, Task Unit Bruiser. After Iraq Jocko became an officer-in-charge of the Navy Special Warfare Detachment for three years where he oversaw all the west coast Navy SEALs and from his work in Iraq he was awarded numerous medals including the bronze and silver stars. How we came to know Jocko is by reading his book, which is a New York Times best seller, the name of it is *Extreme Ownership: How U.S. Navy SEALs Lead and Win*. It's an amazing book; best book on leadership I think I've read in the last five years and if you haven't read it, it's a must read. Jocko currently has a company called Echelon Front where they do leadership and consulting for businesses. He makes parallels in the book and in his leadership training from the battlefield to business. The stories and analogies are amazing. It's hard to not appreciate on top of the great leadership training and everything that we learned from Jocko. It's also hard not to really appreciate the fact that guys like Jocko are out there representing our country and sacrificing, what they do. It's very selfless and love-of-country when they serve in the military at the level that they do. So we owe them a huge amount of gratitude for that also and everybody else who serves. It's awe-inspiring that these guys are out there protecting us. So you're gonna enjoy this podcast. Jocko is very generous. We learned a lot from him and it was a lot of fun. So enjoy. Hey welcome everybody to the podcast, with the world-famous Jocko Willink and G-man.

Jocko: Hello

Chris: Jocko, you're kind of like Madonna in that it's one name, really. Jocko.

Jocko: I guess, there's not that many Jocko's in the world.

Chris: No.

Gary: It's a brand now, Jocko.

Chris: G-Man, I recently got my cholesterol back. Do you have your cholesterol checked regularly?

Jocko: I haven't had it checked in a while but I eat and live pretty clean so it's not a huge factor for me that I'm thinking about all the time.

Chris: So we consider tequila a food group, so we're getting checked quite frequently.

Gary: You need to have it with every meal, it's gotta be there.

Chris: We have tequila right over there, actually.

Gary: I started with Chris in the office and he's got this doctor, Doctor Lau. Doctor Lau's whole goal, and he's only for men, is to make every day the best day possible. He doesn't want you to have bad days. So he runs this blood panel on you and then he'll go through and figure out ways that you can improve your chemistry. So he runs a panel on me when I first got there, it was pretty bad. So he gives me this regimen, I start working out with Chris everyday. Every morning we go to the gym. I'm working out, I'm eating right, I'm losing weight. I was on the road for two years so I'd put on like 25 pounds. I was eating french fries and hamburgers with every meal.

Jocko: I can't even laugh at that.

Gary: It's bad, it's bad.

Jocko: I can't even laugh at that, I don't like that at all.

Chris: I can laugh at it.

Gary: So I've got the best wife on the planet, she gets up at 4:00 o'clock in the morning and presses fresh vegetable juice for me and puts it in these mason jars, packs it, protein shake, packs my lunch-

Chris: It's ginger, beets, it smells like it's good for you.

Gary: So I've been feeling good. I'm getting in better shape, I feel better, I started riding my bike again, things are going well. I get my next blood test, which I think is going to go well. This time I'm on the phone with Dr. Lau and Dr. Lau's like "I can't believe it, we've gotta do something. Change your diet today, you've gotta stop eating Carl's Jr, you've gotta get on the treadmill." He starts telling me all this stuff, I said "Woah Dr. Lau, I'm drinking vegetable juice three times a day. I'm eating clean, I don't understand." He goes "Well, when I look at your blood what I see on the other side of the phone is a guy that's 300 pounds and eats Carl's Jr for lunch every single day." I'm like "Oh my god." So I don't know.

Chris: So my theory is he should probably go the other way and his blood type probably answers to milkshakes and cheeseburgers better and the healthy stuff is what's killing him. Maybe, I don't know.

Gary: I don't know, I cut all that stuff out, my cholesterol didn't move.

Jocko: When you say you cut all that stuff out, what did you cut out?

Gary: Really stopped eating out, stopped eating french fries and burgers everyday. Start eating more chicken, vegetables, brown rice, pasta.

Jocko: Just FYI, you might want to check out cutting out all those carbohydrates. When you say brown rice and pasta, that stuff is not good for you.

Gary: Yeah.

Chris: He eats a lot of carbs.

Gary: I do. I probably still eat too many carbs.

Chris: And you drink too much.

Gary: Yeah, and the alcohol thing too.

Chris: That's not good. You need to go on a fast, I think. So we're super-excited Jocko that we have you at our Top Dog event this year and I was telling you we give your book away. We have a stack of them in our office when people come in we give them away. Best leadership book I've read in five plus years. The thing that got me when I started reading the book is the way that you wrote it is like you give an analogy from war and then you relate it to a business lesson. The thing that I got right away in it was we're such pussies in business because the first story you tell is life and death and then it's like "Oh yeah, and in the boardroom." It's crazy how terrible leadership is nowadays and how it's life-and-death really when you're talking about it in your book.

Jocko: Yeah, I usually have to explain that to people when we start working with customers. For me, customers are businesses that want help with their leadership and management. So when we start talking a lot of times they'll throw something at me along those lines such as "Well, you know, when you were overseas you were dealing with life-and-death and we're just dealing with paychecks." I always throw back at them that we were dealing with lives but you're dealing with livelihoods. If I take away your mortgage payment and I take away your ability to feed your kid, that's your life. That's what you do. Even though it might not be as extreme as life and death it is a person's livelihood. It's how they make their money, it's how they pay their mortgage, it's how they feed their kids, it's how they take care of their family. When you take that away from them because you failed as a business leader that has a huge impact and that's what causes stress in business. That's what causes stress in combat from a leadership perspective in combat what worried me was something happening to my guys. That's what worried me, it wasn't about me like "Oh, I hope I don't get wounded. I hope I don't get killed." I didn't care about that. What worries you is "Can you take care of your guys? Are they gonna be okay?" As a business leader when you're in charge of a business, maybe you're concerned a little bit about your own financial good but your real concern should be "Am I taking care of the people that are trusting me and counting on me to lead them?" That's a lot of pressure regardless of what the business is.

Chris: I think on the flip side of that is the companies or leaders living up to their full potential because the things that you lay out, there's a roadmap and some of the recipes that you give. A lot of it is mindset, but the mindset is the companies living up to their full potential and not just being average. There's the part of losing, but really most leaders don't understand that their full potential is probably four times what they're doing, at least.

Jocko: Absolutely. Every human can do better than they're doing right now. Everybody in the world can do better than they're doing right now. It's a big step and it takes work, hard work, to improve. Especially the better you get the harder it is to improve more so the better you get the more you have to work to get better. It's a challenge and that's why you do find people that are okay with being average.

They're okay with being okay. To me that's not a good way to go through life.

Gary: That top 20% is always the hardest. Getting them to move into that 80% range is usually you can pull a big lever and they'll move really fast but that top part's really hard to get there. Gotta have a lot of discipline.

Chris: We're very much conditioned in our country that average is okay. A lot of things that are taught and that are said are in the tone of keeping us average. We do it to ourselves more than anything else.

Jocko: That's very disturbing.

Gary: When you come into a company like you were talking about and you want to get those guys to move and to do things, how much push back do you get when you come in? Are there egos involved? How do you get past that?

Jocko: You can definitely get egos, there's always egos involved in every situation but most of the time when we're talking to people there might be a small percentage of people that will give some pushback but most of the people are saying "Yeah, yup, that's right. Yes, I wish we would do that. Yes, I could do that better." The things that we're talking about aren't revelations. They're not revelations and they're usually not radically different from what people already know. I didn't invent anything new but through the application of those simple things, simple not easy, it's another thing that we wrote in the book, it's simply not easy. These things are simple to understand, they're not easy to execute.

Gary: We were talking about that the other day. It's funny, we were talking about the nutrition part of it and there's this billion dollar weight loss industry and all these books written and a million different diets on how to do it and really the thing is simple-

Jocko: And there's a new discovery of how to lose weight. It's new from NASA on how you lose weight and get in shape.

Gary: Yeah, work out and eat less. Eat the right foods, exercise more.

Jocko: It's hard to find somebody who doesn't know how to lose weight. It's doing it that is the problem. Everybody knows how to do it.

Gary: So the strength is having a coach like yourself. Is that what you guys bring in to those organizations? Being able to carve out the path for them, clear the forest, get 'em through?

Jocko: Sometimes I think it's an analogy I use, or a story I talk about a lot is the movie Terminator and in the movie Terminator the beginning, opening narration says, "In August 27, 2023 the machines became aware" and a lot of this is about awareness. People are going through the motions and they're just not aware of the mistakes that they're making. When we point out "Hey, this is the situation that you have going on and here's what's causing it." They go "Oh, I kinda knew that." Yeah, they kinda knew that but when we explain it to them and show it to them and hold up the mirror so they can see it for themselves it becomes very obvious and the first part in winning any battle is recognizing the enemy and identifying them and knowing where they are. When you become aware of your own faults and your own mistakes that you're making that's when you can finally begin to take the steps towards improvement.

Chris: You have a voice for movies, you could be doing those intros... "From Star Wars." So what characteristics do you see between the businesses that you work with that perform at a high level and the ones that struggle? What are the different characteristics between the two?

Jocko: It's the same bulk of problems that people have, and there's a variety. The number one thing, people ask me all the time is "What's the most important characteristic of a leader?" They say "About a business?" just the same question that you just asked me. I get asked that question a lot. The key component that I always talk about is humility. When you lack humility what that does to your personality and thereby does your to your team's personality is immensely impactful. When you're not humble that means you think you're the best. That means you think I can't do anything better, I'm doing the best that anyone can do. That means you're not listening to anybody else. That means you're not taking any suggestions from anybody else. You're not even doing a critical honest self-assessment and saying "Hey, what can I do-." No, you're thinking you're doing everything great. And what do you think about your competitor, or the enemy? From the battlefield it's the enemy. What do you think of the enemy? "We're smarter than them, we're better than them, we don't have to worry about them." In business world what do you think about your competitor? "Oh, we're the best. We're the industry leaders, therefore we don't have to work hard. Then we can start cutting corners, we can start taking shortcuts. We can start to relax and rest on our laurels." That's the difference between people that excel and people that don't. The people that excel are constantly saying "What can I do better, how can I improve? I better watch out behind me because the enemy's trying to sneak up on me, the competitors are trying to sneak up on me." I'm going to work today harder than they're working. That's the huge difference between people that excel and people that don't.

Chris: They're willing to take feedback and process it. They don't take it personally.

Gary: I've heard you say that before too. That you like people that are hungry and humble.

Chris: Yeah, hungry and humble.

Gary: Want to climb that mountain? Then humble, have humility. Without that you don't see the mountain, you think that you're at the top of it already.

Jocko: Indeed.

Chris: What would you say, Jocko, is the one thing when you walk into a business scenario, what is the one thing that you see that everybody else doesn't see?

Jocko: Well immediately you have an outside perspective, which is very helpful. As an individual I call this being able to detach yourself. In other words when you're on the battlefield you're out there and there's all kinds of mayhem happening, there's craziness happening. There's people wounded, there's people dying, there's things blowing up, there's bullets flying around. If you get emotional and all of your head goes into that scenario, you can no longer make good clean decisions because you're emotional. Your mind is trapped in the chaos. You're not perceiving what's really happening around you because the things that are going on are so overwhelming. So what you have to do as an individual is you have to be able to detach from all that. You have to be able to step back and say "Okay, here's what's happening, I'm not gonna be emotional right now. I'm gonna look at the things as they are and I'm gonna make decisions based on what's really happening, not on emotions and chaos." When we walk into a company that's the first advantage that we have that most of the companies don't have. They're in it, they're in the firefight, they've got the chaos going on. They don't see those egos. I walk into those companies and I can see these egos. They're very clear, whose got them, who they're rubbing up against, who they're offending. Because I'm walking in I'm already very detached, I'm de facto detached. We're able to come in and look and assess very easily to see where the friction points are and what we have to do to fix them.

Chris: I think we have a painting in our office that says you can't read the label of the jar you're in. It's always a fresh set of eyes and I'll tell people we're really not that smart. What it is, is we're a fresh set of eyes and we get to go to all these other companies and see what they're doing and what isn't working and then we're sharing that with you. We have some basic fundamental skills but we're observant. We're students more than anything.

Gary: Right. That is the danger. I traveled for a couple years, consulting, and you're out there on your own. When you first get there you get the freshest perspective, you get to see it, but when you've been at that company for a year and you're showing up there month after month you do get to that point where you almost kind of get sucked in to their reality.

Chris: You become a part of the team and then you're not as fresh.

Gary: You can't be objective anymore. We talk about that with our group.

Chris: We flip our guys.

Gary: Yeah, it's like "You gotta pull back." And I love that chapter in your book where you talk about that and you bust through a door and there's a bunch of a guys, there's a lot of chaos going on and you literally almost physically took a step back and had to assess the situation. I just think that is such a clear example of what you have to do. You literally have to get out from a 30,000 foot view and look down on the battlefield and see what's going on.

Chris: I think you tell that story on a podcast, I don't think it's in the book but you talk about taking somebody up on a hill? And you were watching the battlefield from up there and you're like "This is where you really see it."

Jocko: Right, right. That was just one of the guys that had worked for me and now he had stepped up and he had taken my position. To make a long story short yeah, we were out there watching this. It was training - we were watching this training event happen and we had all kinds of chaos going on in the training and it's so obvious when you step back. We weren't even on top of a hill, we stepped back 20

158

meters. That's all it took, was just 20 meters out of the chaos and the answer is so obvious when you're out there. He looked at me and said "Wow, it's so easy to see from here." When we went through training together and he was a guy with me and we were in the jar, so to speak, we were in the chaos. I still stepped back mentally, a little bit physically. Maybe you can't get 20 meters but you can get three meters and you can change your perspective and you can open your mind, open your ears, open your eyes. You can dislodge your emotion and you can make a much better assessment and the answer becomes very clear when you aren't caught up in all that.

Chris: You can train your mind to go there quicker when you're aware of it. I love that analogy when you talked about going up on the hill, that you have to mentally do that even if you're in it, it's funny. The one question you wanted to ask you was about your kids and them serving in the military. What advice would you give them?

Jocko: The same advice I give everybody. Be humble, work hard. I've got three daughters and one son. I don't think my daughters are gonna go in the military, they might, I don't know. My son I think is more encouraged by, or he likes the idea of going to the military. He's seen my life and said "That looks like it was pretty fun." He's a kid that likes being outside, likes to surf, likes to shoot guns. When I was a kid didn't I think about "Hey, it'd be really fun to go to an office somewhere and sit in a cubicle and look at a computer screen." I never thought that. I never had that idea. I thought to myself "You know what would be cool? Jumping out of airplanes and hucking grenades at people. That would be cool. That's what I want to do." So it's no shocker to me that my son has the same type of feeling. I think a lot of boys have that feeling but at the same time I'm trying not to pressure him to go in. I'd want him to make the decision on his own. If he makes that decision, that's cool. If he doesn't make that decision, he wants to go do something else, that's cool too. I try not to put massive expectations on the kids. Try not to do that. It's hard not to, cause you want your kids to be the President of the United States of America and everything else but if you try and put that on them they're probably gonna end up with not good situations.

Gary: Yeah. My wife and I were talking about that. I have two kids, a boy and a girl and they're 19 and 20 now. So we were saying we pushed them to do better in school and to try to excel and keep talking to them about trying to get into college and doing the thing that all parents tell their kids to do. So then they get accepted and my wife's like "Well, this is gonna cost a lot of money. I don't know if we can do this." I'm like "Well we told them for the past 12 years that they gotta do this. It's time to pony up. So they're both in college now.

Jocko: That's good. Good for you. That's one of the mistakes I think parents make is that, just like business or military leaders, they don't explain why something's important to their kids. They say you need to go to college. Kids never connect that. They say to themselves "Well that sounds like four more years of high school to me. That doesn't sound like a good deal. I want to go out and make money and get a job." We don't explain to the kids why this is important, what it'll do in the long-run, how much money you'll be able to make in the future if you do go to college. That's not necessarily the right path for everybody. I think in this day and age there's a generation of kids that are coming up - if they make this move and they go become an electrician or a metal worker or a plumber they're gonna end up more in demand than a lawyer or a software developer because guess what? Everyone's trying to become a lawyer, a software developer, a finance guy. Who's gonna fix your toilet is my question? Who's gonna rewire your house, who's gonna fix your car? I think there's gonna be a generation possible in the coming years that decide to go more in the trade route and I think they're going to be very successful.

Gary: I was a mechanic for 15 years, that's how I started my career. It was good, it did very well for me. It took care of me and my family, it was a good business. That's what we talk about now. When I came into the business I was the only apprentice in a shop full of master techs and now it's just so hard to find people that want to do that job and I agree with you. I think think that's the coming trend, it's got to be those jobs are gonna get more in demand. The income potential is going to get higher and people are going to start going into that. It's a good field, it's just a dirty business. It's not glamorous and not everybody wants to do that. Everybody wants to sit behind a computer screen and create apps and games and they just don't want to get their knuckles dirty.

Chris: What kind of cars do you have?

Jocko: My pride and joy is a 1974 Ford Econoline Quadravan. Which is a factory four-wheel drive van that was made in the 70's. That's my--

Chris: Like Starsky and Hutch kind of van? Scooby-Doo?

Jocko: The Ford Econolines at that time had the snub-nose, so it's like a really flat nose and the engine is right in between the seats. It's a pretty awesome vehicle.

Gary: Is it lifted? The big tires like that-

Jocko: Yeah, it's lifted with big tires. It's turning into a project so I've got a ton of work to get done on it.

Chris: Do you work on it yourself?

Jocko: I did work on it myself but right now I don't have the time. You know you either have time or money? Right now I have more money than time so that's why I'm holding off. It's something I wanted to do myself but now I'm thinking "Okay, do I do it myself? Do I wait? Do I pay somebody to do it now?" Then I told my son "Hey, this could be your chariot of glory in years to come if you want to break out the wrenches and make it happen."

Chris: This is what you get son. This is what I'm handing down.

Gary: Does your son want to do it? Does he like the wrenches?

Jocko: He's been fired up but I would say he's not got the craftsman gene so I don't know, we'll see. This day and age there's not a lot of... at least when I went to school you could take auto shop, you could take wood shop, you could take metal shop, all those things are gone.

Chris: They're writing code.

Jocko: Yeah, they're writing code now.

Gary: Yeah, shop class is gone.

Jocko: Unfortunately, he can't bring it into school and work on it as a project in his freshman and sophomore year and his junior year when he gets his license he's the man, right? The man with the van. Instead maybe he can program apps, I don't know.

Chris: That's funny. One commonality that I see in top performers and I call it. I felt like sometimes I'm sadistic, but you were talking about this. And something else I heard about how when you were going through SEAL training, like the harder it is the more you like it? Am I saying that right? You were saying "When everybody else is struggling," you were like "that's the fun part for me."

Jocko: Yeah, I think that, and again I always say this, when you're in the SEAL team, SEAL training is no big deal. No one cares about SEAL training, and in the civilian word people think SEAL training's a big deal but you compare SEAL training, which is "Hey, I had to carry a log around and put a boat on my head and I had to run and swim a bunch and it was hard and it was cold and I didn't get to sleep a lot."

Okay, that sounds real rough but then you compare that to combat where I got guys rolling out for their sixth night in a row into downtown Ramadi on a foot patrol where they got in three firefights over the last three nights and they're gonna get in another one tonight. There's IEDs all over the place, they could get killed. They know it, I know it, we all know it. So the SEAL training thing is sort of like "Whatever." Some people make a big deal out of it, it's just not that big of a deal. Back to your question, yes, I want things to be hard. I'm looking for a challenge. I want to push myself, I want to push my team and get after it. When you're going through SEAL training and people are quitting - I was watching people that are quitting because they don't want to be cold, they don't want to be wet, they don't want to be tired. Hey, okay, you can quit, I'm actually gonna take possession of your soul and use it to build my own strength up and become more of a destroyer. That's what I'm gonna do.

Chris: That's so funny Jocko, cause you're like "It's SEAL training, it's not that hard." What's the percentage of guys that make it through?

Jocko: There's like an 80% attrition rate.

Chris: So there's 80% of people that if I was sitting here they'd be like "Oh my god it was the worst thing ever."

Jocko: That's one way of looking at it, but 100% of my friends made it through. So the guys that I knew that were good dudes, 100% make it through. It's 80% of-

Chris: So the other guys look like Gary and I? I think if I committed to it I'd make it through. It would just have to be something I wanted to do. We were talking about this yesterday, is that I have this flaw that I won't do something unless I know I'm gonna win. I've been that since I was a kid and we were debating whether that's good or bad, it's probably a little bit of both, but I think if I decided to do it I would do it. There would be no quitting but I'd think about it really hard before I committed.

163

Jocko: Yeah, it's really difficult to tell who's gonna make it through and who's not. It goes beyond "Are you gonna quit or not?" There's actual physical limitations that human bodies have and they're weird. For instance, we had a guy in my SEAL training class that was a NCAA water polo team captain and champion so the guy was a physical stud but for whatever reason he didn't have strong forearm grips so he couldn't climb ropes and hang on to ladders and they just broke him down on the obstacle course which is very grip intensive and he just quit. So here's a guy that's a way better athlete than I am but he just had this one weakness that made him quit. The other thing that happens is people get injured. People get pneumonia. People get hypothermia. People get stress fractures. There's a whole litany of things that can catch you that have nothing to do with your will to make it through. Now your will to make it and not quit definitely goes a decent distance but even if I knew you were a completely committed person that never quits or anything, I still wouldn't put any money on it. I can't put money on anybody going through SEAL training, just like I can't put any money on people going into combat and what they're gonna be like.

Gary: That's a liability ...

Chris: It's a 100% chance that I would decide that I didn't want to do it anyway. You know when you grow up as a kid there's just certain things, you wanted to do. My passion was something else. That's an interesting thing you're saying, how much of it is mental and how much of it is just physical and luck of not getting hypothermia?

Jocko: It's both because if you can't climb a rope, physically, it doesn't matter how much mentally you want to climb the rope, if you can't do it physically you're not gonna make it.

Chris: But you don't know that before you get there?

Jocko: You don't. So you could put that back on the mental side and say "Well if you know and you're mentally tough then you're gonna train yourself to a certain point." But there's people that break down that don't make it through and they physically break. They physically break and they can't make it. Also some people that are really gifted athletes, they're making it through more based on their physical attributes than their mental attributes. Get a kid that's a horrible athlete, that's slow and weak, but he's good enough. He's gonna make it through on his mental toughness and his grit so it varies for different people what's gonna get them through.

Chris: What was your favorite part of that? Of the training?

Jocko: I loved it all. I thought it was all fun. There's a week in there called Hell-Week which is where they keep you awake for five days and you do physical evolutions the whole time and you're not allowed to sleep. Everyone's scared of that and that's where a vast majority of the people that quit. They quit during that week and to me that week was a joke because it was very easy for me because all you had to was keep going and you make it. You run, but there's no time limit on the run. You swim, but there's no time limit on the swim. You paddle the boats all over the place, but there's no time limit on getting there so you just have to keep going and they're trying to break you mentally and I wasn't breaking mentally. It was a fun time for me, I was laughing.

Chris: That's awesome. When you're training to be a Navy SEAL how much of it is physical and how much of it is mental? I would call it like "schoolbook part" where you're reading and learning the mental side of it, not diving and jumping?

Jocko: Well the first part, when you go through the basic SEAL training is 95% physical. That's what it is. You learn a little bit of stuff along the way but it's nothing important and they're basically making sure you have a functioning brain. That's all they're doing. Can you figure out dive physics? Can you figure out the weapon systems and know the nomenclature of the weapon systems? So you do that but that's just basic memorization almost. None of that really matters. You get to the SEAL teams which is where you actually become a SEAL. Where you actually learn the tactics, techniques, procedures that make you into a SEAL that learns how to close with and destroy the enemy. Learn small unit tactics. Learn fire maneuver. That's the stuff and that stuff is all mental. There's a little bit of physical stuff on it but it's almost all mental. "Okay, here's where the enemy is, here's where I am, here's where my team is, here's where my supporting elements are. Here's how I'm going to move these pieces on the chessboard to win this situation." That is all mental. Part of the reason it feels like it's all mental is because your physical baseline has to be good enough, that just because you're carrying a heavy load and sweating and getting dehydrated and moving at a high rate of speed through long distances, you're not gonna pay attention to any of that and you're gonna be mentally aware and paying attention and learning how to move those chess pieces on the battlefield. So there is a physical component that's a baseline, that's just always present, but the mental training is then the primary part of it. Especially for the guys in the leadership positions which everybody in the SEAL teams, as they come up through the SEAL teams, they grow and advance into more and more leadership positions.

Chris: Pardon my ignorance cause I don't understand at all but the one thing, when you're dropped in somewhere on a mission and there's a small group of you, like six or eight on a special mission, in your experience was there ever a time where it was hard getting out?

Jocko: Sometimes it is.

Chris: So how do you get out when it's...

Jocko: It just depends on the situation and where you've been placed. One thing that we do well is we plan contingencies so that we'd look at a situation and say "Oh, we're going to this location, this seems like a place where bad things could happen. It seems like a place we might not be able to get helicopters into this spot so let's figure out a way, let's have a secondary location that we can get to. Let's have a way to bring in close air support that can come from the sky and drop bombs and provide cover while we bring helicopters in or we can have a secondary place we get picked up by vehicles. We will plan accordingly to prevent as much as possible, getting into a situation where we're feeling like we can't get out of here. We're gonna plan accordingly.

Chris: Was there a situation in reference to getting out where you were on like the third contingency?

Jocko: Well I think a great story in the book that Leif (and Leif is the guy that wrote the book with me.) Leif Babin - he was one of the platoon commanders that worked for me in our deployment to Ramadi, Iraq and he's my business partner. He wrote a great story in there and they were in an overwatch position which meant they had snipers. They were watching an area of Ramadi looking for bad guys, killing bad guys and the enemy. This was in a building, so they're in a big building and while they're in the building an enemy came and planted an IED outside the front door. The guys, our EOD guys, they're explosive ordinance disposal, guys that look out for bombs and try and keep us safe from stepping on IEDS, those guys spotted it before the platoon broke out and left the building. So luckily they saw it and they said "Okay, now what are we gonna do? How are we gonna get out of here?" Well, for whatever reason, this building had one door. That was the only door and the bomb was right outside the door and so Leif and his guys sat there and thought about, "What can we do? If we walk out the front door they're probably gonna have an ambush, they've got the bomb, it's gonna be bad so what else can we do? How can we get out of here? Can we rappel out of one of the windows?"What they ended up doing was getting out their sledgehammers and sledgehammering through a concrete wall to get out of the building from another egress route. So there's a good example of "Hey,

167

we're in a really bad situation, how are we gonna get out of here? I know how we're gonna get out here, we're gonna get out sledgehammers and pound through this concrete wall until we make a man-sized hole then we're gonna crawl out."

Gary: Literally smash through a wall to get to the objective.

Chris: Breaking down walls.

Gary: That's good. If I can shift gears for just a minute, in the book you talk about mentors and people that you had with you when you were in the military and then I was listening to your podcast with Steve Austin and you were talking about when you came out and you started to get recognized. Somebody asked you to speak to a group of managers or leaders and share some of the principles that you learned and then it grew and started to escalate from there and you grew a business out of it. Did you have a mentor? When you said "Hey man, I've got something here, this could be a business." Did you have somebody that helped you, that walked you through it, a mentor that kind of showed you the path?

Jocko: No.

Gary: Not on the business end of it? Nobody that-

Jocko: Nope. What I did have was good relationships with people that were in the business world and as I talked to them and uncovered things. Plus it all just makes sense - it's leadership. The fundamental principles of leadership, they don't change. Do they nuance? Yes. Are there little variations? Yes, but the fundamental principles of leadership, they don't change, whether you're on the battlefield or you're in business, or you're running an eight-year-old-and-under girl's soccer team, the leadership principles stay the same. I don't care what situation, you are leading humans, there's a science to it. There's also an art to it. There's an absolute art to it, so you have to understand the science and you have to know the fundamentals and you have to understand the disciplines of the science in order to become an artist and start to work those nuances. It's like you were showing me earlier a guy that's a woodworker. The fundamental principles of woodworking are the same but every piece of wood is different. It's got a different grain to it, it's got knots in it, it's got all these different types of wood. I've got wood at my house, Brazilian type that's four times harder than teak. The principles are the same but you have to use certain techniques and it's the same thing with being a leader. The principles are going to stay to same but the techniques that you use and the tools that you use to lead people are going to vary and change but they won't violate the basic principles of leadership.

Chris: We always say you're painting a Picasso. It's the timing, it's all of it at one time, especially when we're trying to turn something around really fast, the timing is a big part of it because you have to do everything. There's just certain stages that if you don't do it, it doesn't get momentum and once you have momentum it's hard to stop, but yeah, I always say painting a Picasso, it is art. That's the fun part, great leaders, it is like art. Steve Jobs was art in a way.

Jocko: I think a good example is Jimmy Page from Led Zeppelin. Are you familiar with him?

Chris: Oh yeah.

Jocko: He was a studio musician for many many years. Meaning they told him "Play this piece of paper right here. You follow this music." He did it, he did it perfectly for all those years and he was highly disciplined and he understood the fundamentals of music, but then in Led Zeppelin he was able to just take that and now create. That's why he's considered to be one of the greatest guitarists of all time because he knew those fundamentals so well that when he broke out and set his mind free he was able to just express in a way that many people haven't been able to do.

169

Chris: Yeah, in a lot of ways he kind of reinvented some of it, with his approach to it. What kind of music do you listen to?

Jocko: I listen to primarily heavy metal and old school.

Chris: Specifically which bands?

Jocko: Well, I mean we're talking about Led Zeppelin but Black Sabbath would be my all time favorite.

Chris: I thought you were gonna go heavier than that.

Jocko: Makes sense.

Chris: Journey. Foreigner. What else?

Jocko: I'm sorry, I didn't hear that.

Gary: He's just making fun of me.

Chris: It can't be all Journey, bro.

Gary: Come on, Journey comes on in a bar, everybody goes nuts, everyone's singing.

Chris: What do you think about Kanye?

Jocko: Who's that?

Chris: I don't know. He's just a rap guy. He's married to Kim Kardashian? He's actually pretty good, I like him, but he's pushing some boundaries for sure.

Jocko: Cool.

Chris: Anything else, G-Man?

Gary: So when I went to high school I was in the weightlifting class. I lifted a lot when I was in high school. Everybody always wanted to know what your bench was. So I am curious, so Chris and I lift at the gym, we do a lot of power cleans and deadlifts and all that stuff, so I'm curious, bench and squat, do you have a number?

Jocko: I don't bench a lot anymore. I just don't find it to be good for my shoulders. If you ever trained any Jiu Jitsu there's certain moves in Jiu Jitsu that are actual submission holds that make you tap and submit because they're hurting your shoulder and some of them are very similar to the bench press. I think the most I've ever benched is 350, I'm not a very strong bencher. I can deadlift around 500 and squat. You know I do a lot of higher-rep squats and I also am very particular about full range of motion all the way down for my squats but I squat some higher reps with a decent weight.

Gary: Is that your routine? You do mostly power lifting exercises like that like squats?

Jocko: I do calisthenics. I have rings at my house so I do all kind of gymnastics-type, well, that's a stretch because you gymnasts are actually incredible. They do a lot more than what I play around with, but I have rings at my house, I have bumper plates so I squat, clean, deadlift, clean-and-jerk, snatch, I have kettlebells, I have a rowing machine, I live by the beach, I spring, I run, I do Jiu Jitsu every day just about, I surf, I definitely stay active as much as I can.

Gary: What about the surfing? I lived up in San Francisco most of my life and I moved down to L.A. to work with Chris and I live by the beach, I live out by Venice beach so I took up surfing. I had a guy teach me how and I'm still struggling with it but I'm trying to get the hang of it. When did you pick up surfing?

Jocko: I grew up in New England and so I started. I had an old lifeguard guy that was older than me that just, for whatever reason, said "Hey I'm gonna teach you how to surf." And that was when I was 10 years old. so that it was a real help to me because that familiarity with the water and comfort in the water is something that really tricks up a lot of people going through SEAL training. Because a lot of it is in the water and they come pretty close to drowning you in a lot of situations and if you're not comfortable in the water you're not gonna make it through. I was super comfortable in the water from growing up surfing in the wintertime, cold water, hurricane swells up in New England so it was a real benefit that the guy reached out and said "Hey, I'll teach you how to surf."

Gary: That's funny that you mention that because when I talk to people about surfing that's the one thing they say is that they're afraid of the ocean. They're afraid of drowning, they're afraid of the waves tumbling. Sometimes you get under a wave and you've just gotta wait for it to stop before you're gonna come up.

Jocko: Yeah, if you're not comfortable in the water surfing its not gonna be fun for you. I would tend to agree with that.

Gary: Yeah, absolutely. I'm out of questions. I probably have 100 more but we don't want to hold him up all day.

Chris: It was fun, thank you for doing this.

Jocko: Thanks for having me.

Chris: It was great.

Gary: We appreciate it.

Chris: Sweet of you and we'll see you at the event.

Jocko: Awesome. Looking forward to it.

Chris: Thanks Jocko.

Gary: Thanks.

Jocko: Thank you.

Episode #7: Dealership Leadership Techniques To Create Top Performers With Tim Kintz

Chris: Welcome everybody. How you doing G-Man?

Gary: Doing good.

Chris: And we have our famous friend here, Tim Kintz. How you doing Timmy?

Tim: Excellent, good to be back.

Chris: Tim's mad at Gary for taking him to the gym this morning.

Tim: Yes, and you too.

Chris: Why me?

Tim: Oh, I hurt. Well it's Gary's fault, cause it was actually his free pass that got me in. We did deadlifts.

Chris: Yeah, that's right. That's a good point.

Tim: I'm too old to be doing that. My tendons will snap like piano cords if I keep doing that.

Chris: I'm outta free passes.

Gary: I was actually afraid of the weight at some point. I looked at it in fear.

Chris: We're gonna talk about that today because we're gonna talk about leadership and the law of the lid and then we're all gonna talk about our favorite leadership books. I have a story about you and the law of the lid at the gym, right? I think you probably know what that is?

Gary: I do know what that is.

Chris: We're gonna talk about that.

Gary: I have a story about you, my favorite law of the lid story.

Chris: But it doesn't involve the gym.

Gary: It does not involve the gym.

Chris: Does it involve cholesterol?

Gary: It's fifteen years old. No it doesn't involve cholesterol. I'm really curious if Tim had an opportunity to get his cholesterol checked since we last spoke.

Tim: No, but I'm working on keeping the levels high. I want to be in first place when the test comes, when the score comes out.

Gary: It's a competition? You're winning?

Tim: Yes, I just want to have the hightest number.

Chris: Gary's hard to beat, I think. Didn't Doctor Lau say you were the highest or something like that?

Gary: No, not the highest, but he's unhappy with my score, let's just put it that way.

Tim: Not like golf? Right, you're suppose to have the highest score to win?

Chris: Well, no in golf you want to have the lowest score to win. You don't play a lot of golf, huh?

Tim: My dollar cost per an average stroke is much better then everybody else though. When you break down what I pay versus what I pay per a stroke is way better.

Chris: That's a good point.

Gary: Explain that?

Tim: I spend forty bucks to go golfing and I see the buck twenty. I paid a lot less, per a stroke then you for shooting an eighty.

Chris: Oh, you got your money's worth.

Tim: Former "F" and "I" guy. Reduce it to the ridiculous clothes.

Chris: I'm way too young to play golf.

Tim: Yeah? 34?

Chris: 54, whatever. I'm way too young to do it. Okay, so we all believe or will have experienced that part of the fun of achieving stuff is that a lot of people don't believe that you can achieve stuff and really it starts with setting yourself a little goal that sometimes scares you a little bit. Have you ever set a goal, Tim, that scares you?

Tim: Regularly.

Chris: Like what? Give me an example.

Tim: My income level that I want to be at right now scares the hell out of me. I'm not going to bring that number up, but it scares the hell out of me.

Chris: You want to make $50,000 a year?

Tim: Yes, $4,000 a month.

Gary: In Texas that's big money.

Tim: It is, we don't have any taxes. I get to keep most of what I make.

Chris: You've been here in California for a couple of days. What do you think about the taxes here? Do you think it's worth it?

Tim: Well, that's why I moved from San Clemente, California to Dallas, Texas because I had an 11% raise the day I moved there.

Chris: Yeah, that makes sense.

Tim: It was nice.

Gary: I'd miss the beach though, I don't know. I can't do it.

Tim: It's a great place to visit.

Chris: Gary lives right on the beach.

Gary: Yeah.

Tim: That's cool. That's where we lived in San Clemente.

Gary: Sand, sunsets, surfing. I can't give it up.

Tim: Birkenstocks.

Gary: Live in Texas, love my Cowboys, but I've got to visit.

Chris: Back to the point of the law of the lid is there's people out there that would never even dream about having a goal. Let's say your goal, and I don't know what it is, but let's just use a hypothetical number of you want to make $100 million a year.

Tim: That'd be nice.

Chris: There's a ton of people out there that couldn't even think about making $50,000 a year, right? And really the difference between you and them is they have less opportunity, less hours in the day, less days in the week.

Tim: It's all there. Some people get a week's worth of use out of a day, other people get a days worth of use out of a week. It comes down to your dreaming.

Chris: I love that. "Timism." Start calling them out.

Gary: That's the book that's coming out, "The Timisms".

Chris: I told him he should make a book of "Timisms." They're great.

Gary: It's like a dictionary.

Chris: He doesn't even know he's doing them, honestly.

Gary: Yeah, they just flow.

Chris: When I tell him, I'm like, "I'm going to write that down," he's always surprised. But no, they're great.

Tim: It's true. There's no such thing as time management, it's activity management. What are you doing with your time? Don't we all get fooled by the clock? We think we have all this time in the day because you looked at the clock and you looked up and you're like, "Holy smokes. What happened to today?"

Chris: We got more done today than most people get done in a week.

Tim: Yeah, or noon.

Chris: It's crazy. Okay, so my story ... You know, you met out trainer this morning, right? I've been going to him for a while and then when Gary started working in the office and out in the field he started going with me and I'm not a ... I can bench as much as I can squat which is a problem, right? You being a former pro athlete, you should be able to squat twice as much as you bench?

Tim: At least.

Chris: Early on I hurt my knee and so I never really put my heart into it and then same thing with deadlifts. I would deadlift - what was the weight? Like two something?

Gary: 250.

Chris: 250, so I would bench 250, I would deadlift 250, and I would squat 250. Gary goes and he's like, "No, come on." I was really comfortable with that.

Tim: The law of 750.

Chris: I was comfortable with that. Last week he comes in all fired up and he says on our walk to the gym, we meet here like we did this morning. Then we walked to the gym and he's like, "We're going to deadlift 300." Right?

Gary: Yeah, 315 was the number.

Chris: 315.

Gary: Three plates.

Chris: He was just fired up, didn't matter, there was no stopping him, there was no convincing him otherwise, and we did. I didn't have on special shoes. Nothing but Gary saying, "We're going to do it."

Tim: My sleeves were an inch too short for me afterwards.

Chris: He did good. He worked it out. You're going to hurt tomorrow, but you did good. That's the law of the lid. The only difference between me going for a year doing 250 and all of a sudden doing 315 was he said, "We're going to do it."

Tim: Kicked you in the ass. Who's that leader to push you?

Chris: It was Gary.

Tim: Yeah.

Chris: He's a leader.

Tim: Locker room leadership.

Gary: I'll take that.

Chris: In a lot of situations, it's really just saying, "Why not?"

Gary: Yeah. I think it's a pattern, too. When I see things like that, I think that's a pattern, that's not reality. When you see, 250, 250, 250, no. It's got to be some heartbeat in there somewhere. We see patterns like that all the time and it's never-

Chris: You just want to break them. As soon as you see it, I can see it in your face.

Gary: I just want to break it. Because it's never reality, it's all mentality. That's a "Timism."

Chris: "Timism." Would you use that?

Tim: I might.

Chris: It's never reality, it's mentality.

Gary: It's never reality, it's all mentality.

Tim: I like it.

Chris: Oh my goodness.

Tim: It's your beliefs.

Gary: Is that a word? Lucas, look that up. Is that a word?

Tim: It is now. Put a Wikipedia, make it a word.

Chris: That's funny.

Tim: We're not rubber bands, we're not going to bounce right back. We stretch and keep stretching. I always say that's it's not that most people dream too big and miss it, it's most people dream too little and hit it. Right? People are afraid to dream and think big and be pushed and be challenged. You've got to be challenged. I always talk about locker room leadership, or as John Maxwell calls it, lateral leadership. What is that? Lateral leadership? Leaders keeping leaders accountable. Leaders pushing leaders. If somebody's not pushing you to become a better leader than you're never going be a better leader, therefore your people will never get better and if your people don't get better because you're staying the same that's pretty much becomes the law of the lid. Then, you have high turnover because people get frustrated, they get tired of working for you. Because they're not growing.

Chris: It's amazing what people do. They get in this comfort zone and then they don't see it, but from the outside ... I think an advantage we always have coming in as a fresh set of eyes, right? We have a painting here in the office that says, "You can't read the label of the jar you're in." Right? A lot of times if we talked about the results that we get going in, most people wouldn't even believe it. They never believe that.

Gary: They don't believe it.

Chris: They're like, "Well, how are you going to do that?" They can't even put their head around it. The only difference is we're going to.

Gary: Yeah.

Chris: It's like hiring techs. The guy's like, "You can't hire techs." You're like, "Well, the first problem. You want to know how to hire techs? Stop saying I can't hire techs."

Gary: Right, you've got to believe.

Chris: There's this football coach, I don't know if you're heard of him because you only like baseball, but his name is Pete Carroll and he coaches a little team called the Seattle Seahawks.

Gary: Yeah.

Chris: He tells a story about when his son was looking to go to colleges, he was the coach of the Jets at the time, so this was way before he coached USC. His son wanted to tour USC and so he came out with his son and he toured USC and the head coach of the football team at the time, and I don't remember the name of the coach, heard that Pete Carroll, an NFL coach, was there. He requested could he meet Pete. He gets Pete up in his office and Pete's sitting there and the coach says, "You want to see the 21 reasons why USC can never win a championship?" He pulls out a laminated sheet and shows Pete the 21 reasons why USC can never win a championship. Pete goes, "Well, the reason why you can't win a championship is this sheet."

Gary: You're carrying around your losing manifesto.

Chris: Funny story, Pete won a couple of championships at that same school not that long after that. It's all mental.

Gary: I never heard of the guy. I'll Google it when we get out of here.

Chris: You never heard of Pete Carroll?

Gary: Never heard of the guy. No, sorry.

Chris: Well, Jerry Jones has. I can guarantee that. You Dallas Cowboys fans are all the same.

Tim: Didn't USC go on probation forever after he left? Just saying.

Chris: Yeah, they did and I think USC could've beat most pro teams that year, too.

Tim: Yeah.

Chris: Right?

Gary: All right, I'll bite.

Tim: They had like 12 NFL players on their team. NFL team has like 49 NFL players on their team.

Gary: If Pete's flaw is too much hype, I guess that's his flaw, but it worked.

Tim: One thing he did that he was phenomenal at, is he had fun. He understood rule number one: have fun and his guys had fun. They threw mannequins off the roof and freaked people out, and he would just do crazy stuff. When you're a leader that has fun with their people ... Joe Maddon, the coach for the Chicago Cubs, he has fun when he was at Tampa Bay. They have dress-up days. They get on airplanes and they're all dressed in 1960 clothes and its dress up as your favorite superhero and they all get on the plane and fly to their next place as superheroes. It's just is having fun enough? If you're having fun, are you working?

Chris: No, I feel that a lot of times.

Tim: Don't you feel when you got into some stores ... The one thing that the recession did is it took away the fun in the stores. I always go in, little things I do on the sales side, is I have golden bat that I'll get. I'll go to a sport goods store and get a golden Louisville Slugger. I'll Krylon it shiny gold and for every deal they get, depending on their grosses, like any deal over $10,000 you get to autograph the bat and we keep it at the sales office. The sales people love it. You start doing the math, you start filling in all those signatures, it's a quarterof a million-dollar bat. But I've got one store, they guy's always sending me a picture of it when they autograph it. One of the guys at the store, he makes his customers autograph it because he's that low volume, high gross guy. He sells like six cars, but he averages $14,000 a deal and he makes his customers autograph it. They don't know why, but I guess my point is they're having fun. If you've got a guy with the best closing ratio gets a dumbbell and the guy with the worst closing ratio gets a fire extinguisher because they're burning. Whatever it is, that's what leaders do and that's what Pete Carroll did. That's why Pete was so successful there.

Chris: He created a different environment and then the kids wanted to come because the whole thing, the college is recruiting more than anything so he got-

Tim: He did the same thing in Seattle.

Chris: It's funny. Two years ago, the year after they won that first Super Bowl, I went to opening day on a Thursday. My cousins and I, we all went. They were playing the Green Bay Packers. You've got the Green Bay Packers warming up on one side of the field and you've got the Seahawks warming up on the other side. Do you know who the first person on the field is for the Seahawks?

Tim: Sherman?

Chris: Their DJ.

Tim: Oh, really?

Chris: He's playing the most hard-core rap and these guys come out and they're bouncing around and they're having a blast doing all these drills and lobbing and then you look over at the Green Bay Packers side and it looks a lot like Tyler dancing. The whitest, stiffest, thing you've ever seen.

Tim: That bad?

Chris: That bad. They have swagger, too.

Tim: Yeah, they do. Attitude, fun, swagger.

Chris: I don't think you know this story, but I had a bet with one of my coaching group guys. I think he was in the elite group. When the Cowboys played the Seahawks and I bet that I would wear a Dez Bryant jersey and $100 if the Cowboys could beat the Seahawks. Oddly, they beat them. Which is the worst.

Tim: Last year?

Chris: Yeah.

Tim: I love it. That's one of four victories, huh?

Chris: I wore a Dez Bryant jersey for a day.

Tim: Could be worse though.

Chris: Then, I gave it to him.

Tim: Could've made you wear, like Romo.

Chris: It was bad.

Tim: Randall, the guy that keeps getting arrested that used to be with them, he could make you wear that one.

Chris: Yeah, they kind of attract that, but people in Texas are like that. They don't care.

Tim: Yeah, don't mess with us.

Chris: Everybody's carrying a gun. It's very fun.

Gary: This is stereotype radio. Welcome.

Tim: Yeah, everyone's scaring him.

Chris: Everyone's packing heat in Texas and they eat barbecue. Was that bad to say?

Gary: No, we're just going down that road so I'm just following along. I'm not leading anymore now, I'm just following in.

Chris: That's the law of the lid? It's all mental?

Tim: Yes.

Chris: It's mental more than anything else.

Gary: I want to tell my lid story.

Chris: You can't read the lid of the jar you're in?

Gary: No, I have so many lid stories it's ridiculous, but I have my favorite, which is when I first realized the law of the lid.

Chris: How old were you? 17?

Gary: No. How old was I? 30-31, something like that.

Chris: Really?

Gary: Yeah, it was pretty old.

Chris: 30?

Gary: I always knew that you are what you believe. I've always felt that. You've got to believe big if you want to achieve things and you've got to think differently. But the actual law that there's this perceived lid that will hold you back, I never really thought about it in those terms until I was working at the service department up in the dealership I worked at in

California. Along comes this guy Chris and walks into our store and we just built this brand-new building. They spent $12 million. It had 25 bays, it was beautiful.

Chris: With the big round front which was unique, but it looked amazing.

Gary: It looked like a museum.

Chris: Yeah, and a customer backed their car through the ... They had this front, it looked like the White House kind of, but it was all glass. I don't think it was open a week and a customer accidentally put it in reverse and went right through the glass.

Tim: That's cool.

Gary: That's not my lid story.

Chris: No, but it was funny.

Gary: I was working in the shop and we were only half full because we moved from literally a cracker box into this huge building.

Chris: It used to be in a barn, right? A dairy barn.

Gary: Literally, in a barn. We're working in this huge shop. I've got two or three bays, we've got space. My kids used to come and scream around the shop in my creeper while half the shop was working. It was empty and then Chris comes along and says, "It's a nice shop, but you guys built it too small." I thought, "This guy's crazy. He has no idea what he's talking about."

Chris: Oh yeah, it was too small.

Gary: It was too small. What was it? A year, maybe year and a half later? Maybe less.

Chris: Not that long.

Gary: No, it wasn't that long.

Chris: We were in four 10s right away, right?

Gary: Yep. We maxed the shop out almost immediately. We went to four 10s, we maxed that out and then it wasn't shortly after that we were building a new building on the other side of the lot. Put in 17 bays, and I remember shortly after that I was listening to a book in my car and they were talking about the law the lid and I was like, "Holy cow. The guy's got no lid. He's literally got no lid. He just sees further down the racetrack than anybody else." I just realized that whenever I come up to that point where I see my lid I just need to tear it off and look as far out as I can possibly see. That's the only way to get there.

Chris: I remember that. You guys were booked out like two weeks. It was crazy.

Gary: We couldn't catch up. We kept growing and growing and we just couldn't catch up.

Chris: The better we took care of customers, in that market, I remember, the better we took care of customers ... We made loan cars easy. We were eating up everybody.

Gary: Yep.

Chris: We did for a long time, right?

Gary: Yeah, we went two and a half times the gross where we started. Two and a half times.

Chris: Yeah.

Gary: It was big.

Tim: You helped them see a vision. Big, long, further out. Most people live month to month in this business.

Chris: What's funny is years later, Gary's going out and fixing service departments, right?

Gary: Right.

Chris: Same thing. They look at you like you're crazy.

Gary: Yeah.

Chris: Just recently, the boys hired over 30 techs in a month and a half.

Gary: Mm-hmm (affirmative).

Chris: The stores doubled their sales.

Tim: I thought there weren't any techs to hire.

Gary: That always makes me laugh.

Chris: The first thing you need to do if you want to hire techs is stop saying you can't hire techs. Gary kind of pioneered it, but he got really good at hiring techs. I remember, we had a guy working for us that needed to hire techs in a northern, snowy city, very close to Canada on the east that has a football team that lost four Super Bowls in a row?

Gary: Yeah, four.

Chris: We can leave it at that. The guy that worked for us didn't believe that he could hire techs which was the oddest thing. I made a bet with Gary. Gary was working in other stores and I said, "Gary, can you make a bet?" What was it, for $2,500?

Gary: $2,500, yeah.

Chris: I said, "Gary, if you can ..." He had a week or something free time. I said, "Gary, if you can hire ..." Eight techs in 30 days?

Gary: Yeah, eight techs in 30 days.

Chris: "I'll give you $2,500," I think was the bet. The guy that was in the store that worked for us, like did everything he could to sabotage you. Remember?

Gary: Yep.

Chris: He kept telling him we don't need any more. It was the oddest, crazy thing, but he got seven. He would've had more if it wouldn't have been for the sabotage.

Gary: Yeah, I had nine and I got a couple sabotaged. One guy showed up with his giant toolbox and the service manager actually threw him out. He hired this A tech, this factory trained, the whole thing. The unicorn and the guy shows up on deck and his toolbox is 27-odd feet long and the service manager throws him out of the shop. That was the one guy, he cost me $2,500. I wanted to fly out there and choke him.

Tim: You didn't pay up anyway? You didn't say to retain eight, you just said he had to hire eight.

Chris: I was mad, too, because of another leadership thing for another podcast. But the thing with my team is these guys, like even Gary, was they were too nice to this guy. Nobody would stand up to the guy at workforce. Nobody would stand up to him and tell him that his thinking was stinking except for me.

Gary: His thinking was stinking.

Chris: Everybody was nice. It was like Lucas' Yelp review of the organic corner bakery. It's like the nicest bad review you've ever read. That's how everybody was. I was screaming, I was so mad. I don't know if i handled that right, but to the bigger point was while everybody was saying they can't hire techs here comes Gary, and in our company, he's got all these things that nobody thought of with ads and keywords. He would run blind ads when we'd go into a market and he'd have techs already lined up before he knew if he needed techs. Right?

Gary: Well, I always needed techs, but yeah.

Chris: Before it was time - everybody would wait the 30 days - you were already dialing in your keywords. He created a system, so everybody's sitting around saying you can't. He was like, testing. It was all testing because you made a lot of mistakes, but you never gave up.

Gary: Oh, yeah. I struggled there for a little bit. I remember showing up at that dealer. He gives me the bet. I was in Colorado, so I've got to find out how to get to the other side of the country and the only seat I could get was middle seat, redeye, and so I was dying. I show up there, I'm in shorts, in the middle of winter in Buffalo and I had to change in their locker room. Then, I sit down in the manager's office and he goes, "Well, I don't know what you're going to do. I don't know why you're here." I looked at him and I go, "I don't either yet, but we're going to figure it out because I've got a bet and I'm going to win it so let's go to work."

Tim: You're not going up there for nothing.

Gary: I was looking for the path and trying to find a way and I didn't know what I was going to do yet.

Chris: How much more fun is it to be the guy on the other side of the desk saying, "I don't know, but we're going to figure it out." It's way more fun than just sitting there going, "You can't."

Tim: Misery loves company, though. They attract each other. It's the law of attraction that kind of goes right in there.

Chris: You're just going to get the same thing. You're never going to discover-

Tim: Let me defend those guys. Let me defend all the service managers, sales managers, everybody. Most of them guys are the least trained people in the dealership. Most of them get a lot of training on how to manage the dock, how to manage the inventory, how to manage stuff, but they don't get anything on how to manage people, how to lead people, how to have big vision, and how to dream big. You see it all the time. You guys go in the stores and you go in there and they have nothing but a team of top producers. Then, they hire a new guy and bring him in, he's a top producer within a short time. Right off the bat, because that's the culture that great leaders create. They don't have that low lid. That lid is always getting pushed up. But then you go into other dealerships whether it's sales or service and it's just a team of average people. Why can you take one guy and put him in a dealership and he sells six cars or he's an average or below average advisor, but then you could take that same guy and put him in another dealership right across town. Same environment, same structure and they're top producers. What is the difference? Well, it's leadership. That's all it is. You see it in sports, right? You ever see a sports team where you had a great coach and they go to a team that's average players and that team overachieves. How often does that happen?

Chris: All the time.

Tim: The Patriots do it. You can go on and on about that. You see what Jim Harbaugh did at Michigan. He took a team that was, I don't even know what the record was, four and eight or two and ten.

Chris: He didn't even recruit them.

Tim: Not at all.

Chris: He headed a team that was four and ten. Ten and four.

Tim: Ten and two or whatever it was after that. You see it the other way around, too. You see an average coach go to a talented team and that team underachieves. I live in Dallas, it happens here all the time.

Chris: Yeah, all the time.

Tim: In reality, it comes down to the coaches. Here's the funniest part, the scariest part: In sports, when things go bad and the team fails, who do they get rid of?

Chris: The coach.

Tim: Yeah. Who do we blame and get rid of when things go bad?

Chris: The player.

Tim: They were not sports, huh?

Chris: You know a really good "Timism: that he says is: "You've got to stop coaching the department and start coaching the people." Is that how you say it or do you say it differently?

Tim: Yeah. Stop trying to manage your department and start managing the individuals within the department. We spend so much time trying to win the game, but we forget it's about the process stupid. Follow the process. Focus on the process. Clear out all the white noise. Do the right things all day, every day. Care about your people. spend time with your people and the victory is going to take of itself. What other industry worries about the end result in the middle of the game? That's all we ever do. All we ever care about is the results. We never ask, "How many ups came on a lot? How many incoming calls? How many appointments? How many did we confirm on the sales side?" It's always about, "How much did we make? How many did we sell?" It's always just the result and most industries are always looking at the activities. The leading indicators.

Chris: It's a game of inches, right? You're always looking to get down the field a little bit further and not necessarily shooting for the end zone on every play.

Tim: Right here, what John Wooden said, "It's about the details." Everything he talked about was it's all about the details. It's about the fundamentals, it's about the details. But it's funny, you look at guys like we're out here in LA doing this and you've got Phil Jackson. You've got that book right in front of you on Phil Jackson. He was the ultimate guy that could take high achievers. Kobe Bryant, Shaq, any of them that other leaders have a hard time, coaches have a hard time controlling and leading and inspiring and look what he does with them. He just stands there with Michael Jordan and Scottie Pippen and all those guys when he was with Chicago. Joe Torre did that with the Yankees and they can get the most. There is no lid with those guys. They're always pushing, they're always driving and they figure out what motivates each guy. Whether it's a kick in the butt, a pat on the back, or a combination. Maybe you need wall-to-wall counseling, four wall counseling. They know what makes their guys tick, what motivates them, and they use it against them in a good way.

Chris: There's a great story that Phil inherited the Chicago Bulls from another coach.

Tim: Collins.

Chris: Yeah, Collins. He worked for Collins as an assistant coach and so the owners really wanted them to try the triangle and so that's why they hired Phil. Collins said, "I don't think it'll work, but go ahead. You tell Jordan to do the triangle." They did the triangle for two weeks and then Jordan nixed it and the coach stood up to him and that was it. Phil thought Jordan hated him and guess what? Same thing happens in the playoffs. They meet Detroit, Detroit double teams Jordan and they knock them out because there was no answer. Phil knew that they had to have some sort of system where if they double team Jordan, there was another way. They had Pippin, they had everybody on that team with Collins and he couldn't win and then Phil comes in and he puts in the triangle. He sticks to it, he makes Jordan do it, and they end up being one of the best ever. Jordan was convinced that Phil just cared about him not getting a scoring title, but he ended up learning that he could still have a scoring title, but there was an alternative. They could still win in the playoffs.

Tim: Well, he helped him also. Big thing back then is he really helped them have that lateral leadership. Jordan was the best leader they had on that team. He'd kick your ass if you weren't practicing hard, if you weren't trying.

Chris: The locker room coach.

Tim: That locker room leadership, that lateral leadership.

Chris: Kobe, too.

Tim: Oh, yeah. Kobe was that way-

Chris: He empowered him.

Tim: Shaq a little bit, but then you have other teams. You look at Cleveland right now and their superstar keeps running their coaches off one after another after another.

Chris: They call the plates. It's like everybody to the right and he goes down the left.

Tim: They don't have that leader.

Chris: There's no system.

Tim: Didn't happen when he was in Miami with Pat Riley.

Chris: Yeah, he's got a system.

Tim: He was a strong leader. Ultimately, everything we do is about leadership. Leadership, I always say, leadership is overrated. Not really, but he word is overused. What is leadership in the store? Isn't it being out front and leading? Taking that first arrow, saying, "Guys, you know what? This is new stuff and we're going to figure it out and we're going to mess up, but we're going to learn this thing together." Being the first guy there. Managing, focusing on the detail, having your stats, your probabilities, training your guys so they gain more knowledge and coaching them so they're developing skills. That's what leadership is. Giving them big vision and goals and something to shoot at.

Chris: Giving them big vision, taking off the lid, giving them big vision, getting their buy-in and their involvement and then going after it together and understanding it's not going to be perfect. You're going to hit some obstacles.

Tim: What you just said, "Getting their buy-in." What's one of the most important things great leaders do? They get buy-in. You have to be sold and not told on what the vision is. I need to sell it to you, not tell it to you. I can tell you what the vision is, but if I don't sell you on what that vision is you're never going to buy-in and if you don't buy-in you'll never do anything to change. If you don't do anything to change then that's the definition of insanity. Keep doing what you're doing and keep getting what you're getting. I don't believe that definition of insanity applies as fast as the world changes now. If you keep doing what you're doing, you're going to get your ass blown away because somebody else is going to steal your market share now.

Gary: You're a sitting duck. You're just sitting on a fence.

Tim: There's no such thing, if you keep doing what you're doing you're going to keep getting what you're getting. No, you're going to get less and then less and then less and before you know it you're going to be working at Denny's.

Chris: Really?

Tim: Yeah.

Chris: I'd better get busy.

Tim: It's where all the car guys end up.

Gary: I thought that was McDonald's.

Tim: You sent me that sign from McDonald's that was hiring all former car salesmen.

Chris: Gary, favorite leadership book of all time? Can you pick one? It's hard to pick one.

Gary: It is hard. I just actually was thinking about I really like Maxwell's book *The 21 Irrefutable Laws*. It was one of my first leadership books that I read and I really enjoyed it and it meant a lot to me. But we're just discussing this and I was thinking about Jack Welsh and his book.

Chris: *Winning?*

Gary: Yeah, *Winning*. He was talking about the stretch strategy and I remember using that when I read that book and I used that when I went into a department. It worked like a charm.

Chris: What is it?

Gary: It's funny because it doesn't mean anything other than we are going to do more with the same amount of people. We're not going to hire, we're just going to produce more and we're going to stretch. Every single person within the department is going to help each other and stretched to do just a little bit more than we did last year. I was stuck in that scenario where I couldn't hire anymore heads and we had to stretch to get there. I thought, "What am I going to do?" when I read that. He just was such a great leader and had great vision and a great mind and I used his principles and they were great.

Chris: Yeah that's a great book. What about you? Favorite leadership book of all time.

Tim: Different, personal leadership, that kind of paradigm shifted me. I was going to listen to and read Robert Kiyosaki's *Cashflow Quadrant* stuff back in the early '90s when I was in Alaska. It was kind of a get serious on setting goals, having long-term vision because that's everything he talks about. You know *Rich Dad Poor Dad* guy.

Chris: That was his second book, right? *The Cashflow Quadrant?*

Tim: *Rich Dad Poor Dad* was his first one, but within there he talked about the *The Cashflow Quadrant.*

Chris: Yeah, but that was its own book.

Tim: Yeah, and then I think probably the thing that was, once I got in the business was *Good to Great*, Jim Collins. I loved it and it's not so much leadership, it's a combination of leadership and management. He really talked about the flywheel effect in there. How you have 100 foot flywheel made out of cast-iron, you've got a little crank, and you need to get that thing started. It takes all your energy and all the effort you have to get one revolution out of that flywheel, but if you put the same amount of energy in the second crank as you did the first, you're going to get more. It's a law of multiplication. Then, the 10th crank, if you put the same amount of energy in the 10th one, you're even going to get more results on that 10th crank than you did on the first one. We do that the dealership so often, but then we say, "You know, let's try something different." Now, we always try to stop that flywheel so it takes all your energy to stop that momentum you just created, so you can then start over to get that first revolution going just so we can keep changing direction on that flywheel and it just hit me. We always have these damn start and stop programs that we always do and with all this technology and we got this cool program and this and this and tablets for service. All that stuff out there is going to help us sell cars and we forget programs don't sell cars, people sell cars. We're always changing direction and we wonder why we never get that positive momentum. We wonder why we never create that culture of growth and development. We don't give them a chance because it's like a schizophrenic thing. *Good to Great* is phenomenal and then I would recommend what he just said was *21 Irrefutable Laws of Leadership* is-

Chris: It's a staple.

Tim: Yeah, it's a staple. It's a great starter if you haven't read a lot in the past, it's a great one. If you really want to make it simple he's got one similar, *21 Indispensable Qualities of a Leader*, which is kind of the Reader's Digest, the playbook version of *21 Irrefutable Laws of Leadership*. Just go, get you going. If you haven't read a lot, crawl before you walk, walk before you can run. Maxwell's always easy to read - embeds some stories, analogies, sports, everything along with it.

Chris: I have bunch. What's the Navy SEAL one?

Gary: *Extreme Ownership*

Chris: *Extreme Ownership*, I gave you that one, right? Did you start reading it?

Tim: No, I got it last night at like 11 o'clock.

Chris: It's amazing, every chapter. What he does is he tells some sort of story or analogy about being at war over in the Middle East and then he ties it back to leadership, but it's riveting because the thing that you walk away with is they'll die. They'll die if they don't backstop a deal to put somebody in a CRM. We let that stuff slide. Just the level of intensity, they have no choice. In those extreme situations real problems are solved very quickly. Attention to detail, it's the real thing.

Tim: That's awesome.

Chris: Pete Carroll. Have you read it, *Win Forever*?

Gary: No.

Chris: I've got a bunch of copies of that. You could take one.

Gary: I've got to Google that guy's name.

Chris: Who inspired Pete Carroll was Wooden and I think this Wooden - It's just called *Wooden: A Lifetime of Observations and Reflections On and Off the Court*. Wooden, Coach John Wooden. He inspired Pete Carroll and a lot of guys, but one take away from that book is when he would get new players, he would measure their feet. Most coaches would take for granted that the players coming in knew what their shoe size was and he said they never knew what their shoe size was.

Tim: Interesting.

Chris: Having the proper fitting tennis shoes kept them from getting blisters and they could play longer, they were more effective. Those little tiny things and that attention to the individual. Really getting to know them. Then, *Eleven Rings* is pretty good, by Phil Jackson. Let me read you a quote and you need to tell me what this means, this quote here: "Life is a journey, time is a river, the door is ajar."

Tim: Is this like riddle me this Batman?

Chris: Yeah. What's that mean?

Tim: I give up.

Chris: "Life is a journey, time is a river, the door is ajar."

Tim: We need to do some bong hits.

Gary: Phil wrote it.

Chris: Phil smokes weed?

Tim: No.

Gary: No, he vapes.

Chris: He does?

Gary: I don't know.

Tim: Just kidding. We don't know that.

Chris: This chapter is the first chapter in the book. It's called *The Circle of Love*. "Life is a journey, time is a river, the door is ajar".

Tim: If I read the chapter I could tell you.

Chris: Have you read this?

Tim: No.

Chris: Oh, you'd like it. It's good. Lots of good stuff. Those are the best leadership books for me. Just to recap, *Win Forever* by Pete Carroll.

Gary: *Win Forever*, that's number one?

Chris: *Wooden*. I don't know if there's a number one honestly. They're all really good.

Tim: Depends on where you're at.

Chris: I love Dave Anderson, too. I love his stuff.

Tim: *No Nonsense Leadership* is probably the best book, in my opinion that Dave ever wrote. It's very good.

Chris: It might have been one of the first leadership books I read.

Tim: It applies especially for the variable ops managers. It's a perfect book for them.

Chris: To me, really, it's useless to try to pick a favorite because if you really want to be a good leader you should be reading a bunch.

Tim: It depends.

Chris: You're going to take something out of everything.

Gary: I think my favorite is the last one I read. You always get something good and you're like, "Wow, that was great!"

Tim: *The Seven Irrefutable Laws of Leadership.* I mean *Seven habits of Highly Effective People,* isn't that kind of a staple that everybody needs to read to become a great leader, too?

Chris: Who's that by?

Tim: Covey.

Chris: Oh.

Tim: Stephen.

Chris: I just can't keep track of everything all day like that.

Tim: Story telling?

Chris: Have you ever tried that?"

Tim: I picked up a lot of good ideas that I could, like, "Begin with the end in mind." When you sit down to figure out, "Okay, what's the end result of something that we're trying to accomplish?" Whatever it is - then, back up to first things first. Second habit of highly effective people is they begin with the end in mind. Whenever I sit down to do goals, projects, doesn't matter what it is, I'll always sit down - kind of like we did. We were talking about the conference coming up. It's, "Okay. What's the end result look like?" When we talked about 360 or anything, it's, "What's the end result look like?" Figure that out and then first things first, but too often we try to start with now and work our way to the end and they have nothing to do with each other. There's a lot of great lessons in there. Most all of those really smart guys are kind of boring on some stuff. They're really good book writers, but really boring to listen to. Not like you.

Chris: I'm really interesting.

Tim: Yes.

Chris: I don't have "Timisms" though.

Tim: You do now. "Chrisisms."

Chris: I'm trying to write them all down as you say them. Seriously, you need to think about ... Oh, one thing that Tim told me, because we were telling him he should write a book of "Timisms," he writes in his underwear.

Gary: That's a thing. Like, you have write in-

Tim: It just happens that way, I think.

Chris: Is it a Texas thing?

Tim: I put my cowboy hat on and a guitar. I think that'd be a New York Time Square thing.

Chris: What is your "Timism" about Texans. I wasn't born there-

Tim: I'm not from Texas, I just got there as quick as I could. I grew up in the state Missouri.

Chris: Anybody who every buys one of Tim's books, understand that he writes in his underwear.

Tim: Yes. You just have to wonder what kind of underwear I've got.

Chris: What room in the house are you in when you do that?

Tim: My office, third floor. Looking out over the lake.

Chris: Kids allowed to come up?

Tim: No.

Chris: "Dad's writing. Leave me alone."

Tim: Yeah.

Chris: How many hours a day do you write when you're home and you can write?

Tim: I just power through it. Drop them off at the bus stop, come home, and just sit up there and go. If I don't go then I don't get going again. I've got to get my motor running. It could be 12 hours, it could be two if I'm done. It's all about the creative juices flowing. It just seems to work when I'm free.

Chris: You know, it's funny. You were saying the other day that you're not creative or you're not an artist or whatever, but really you are. You're very creative.

Tim: Only when I am.

Chris: You come up with great stuff.

Tim: It's fun. Thank you.

Chris: That's creativity. It comes from somewhere, right?

Tim: Somewhere.

Chris: I don't think that's any different from writing a song. When you come up with your training and stuff.

Tim: I'm sure. Yeah, and so much of what we do is from experience. You go into a store - we're just a unique business.

Chris: Well, yeah, but it's how you package it is like writing a song, right?

Tim: Yeah, it is.

Chris: I know a lot of your stuff and some of my stuff is the thing is taking it and then putting it in a way that people can use it.

Tim: Right, or how can I simplify it.

Chris: Yeah.

Tim: My whole thing is to try to simplify things nowadays. A lot of trainers have spent years trying to make three steps in the 33 steps for validation and stuff. Less is more, man. Keep it simple.

Chris: It cracks me up when people are like, "How many hours of training is your VT?" I'm like, "Really? That's the question? I don't know. A million. Are you going to get through it? Do you want quantity or quality?"

Tim: It's not a race. It's not how fast you get through it, it's how effective you get through it.

Chris: I hate some of these books you read from other guys in the industry that are just like - Gary has this funny saying, "Ask Madden how to win footballs." He'll say, "You've got to score points." It's like, "Yeah, but how do I score the points?"

Tim: How to make a long story short.

Chris: Give it to me quick.

Tim: Mr. how-to-make-a-long-story-short.

Gary: Yeah, if you want to win football games, you've got to score more touchdowns than the other guy. If you do that, if you score more than him, and he ends up scoring less than you, then at the end of the game you win and he loses.

Chris: Yeah, but these guys are like, "How do you sell more cars?" They're like, "Well, you've got to up more customers." Like, "What? No, give me a system. Give me one thing I can do tomorrow." That's what I love about your stuff. You've got goods, it's just not fluff.

Tim: **K**eep **I**t **S**imple **S**tupid, or **K**eep **I**t **S**imple **S**alesperson if you want to stay positive.

Chris: Why are you calling me stupid? I don't get it.

Tim: Shoe fits.

Chris: Okay.

Gary: On that note...

Tim: He's got a gun. He's going to burn me with that cigar.

Chris: We don't have guns in California. That's a Texas thing. One more time, "Life is a journey, time is a river, the door is ajar." Thank you for listening.

Episode #8: Top 5 Traits Of Leading Service Managers

Chris: Hey, everybody. Welcome to Service Drive Revolution. Today, we have a special guest: Mario.

Mario: Hello.

Chris: And G-Man. How you doing, G-Man?

Gary: Doing good.

Chris: Mario's with us. Mario works with us in the field, so most of the time he's in stores.

Mario: In the trenches.

Chris: This week he was at the home base, the home office. We asked him to join us here because he has a lot of wisdom. He's a little closer to the front line than Gary and I sitting here in our office, right?

Gary: Right.

Chris: He's actually out there fighting.

Gary: Shielded from that.

Mario: Not that pansy-ass stuff Gary's doing up in his office with his feet up.

Gary: Yeah, we're hiding behind all the shrapnel that's coming.

Chris: We have an exciting podcast for you today. Today, we're going to talk about what the top service managers have in common. We have some of the top service managers in the country in our coaching group. What brought this up is we're a week away from our Top Dog event that we do every year, where all the top service managers from all over the country come and convene on us. We're giving away for the first time a $50,000 service manager prize. Or, actually, even $50,000 to the manager that showed the biggest increase in CSI, net to gross, and their effective labor rate, and then wrote an essay about their journey and their leap of faith. This topic's very relevant because Mario's out in the field all the time, the things that the top-performing managers have in common. Before we get to talking about those managers and the commonalities, Gary got his cholesterol, and I know ... Nobody talks about the ...

Gary: Bum, bum, bum

Chris: On the podcast when ... nobody talks about: "Well, that was great information about my service drive and how to increase CSI or profits." "Is Gary going to die?" That's what everybody says.

Gary: We had that great Magic Johnson conversation and that awesome video that he did-

Chris: Not one comment. Is Gary going to die?

Gary: "How's the cholesterol? I'm worried about you?"

Chris: The way Uncle Dave handled it was pretty funny. Gotta stop buying the cheap booze Gary. He went right at me. Gary and I both recently had our cholesterol. I would like to announce to everybody, not that anybody's worried about my cholesterol, it was the second best it's ever been.

Gary: Wow.

Chris: Second best. I owe that to not drinking the cheap stuff and niacin and--

Gary: Niacin

Chris: Gin and not the french fries and chill and all the stuff that you're doing. So where on here...?

Gary: The carne asada fries or the trailer trash hot dog.

Mario: That niacin's no joke either man. If you have never tried it, that opens up your pores and it cleanses.

Chris: Oh yeah. That's good stuff. Have you ever had your cholesterol checked Mario?

Mario: Perhaps. A long time ago. I don't recall.

Chris: When you get as old as Gary you've got to do this all the time.

Gary: Your still a little young for that.

Mario: I've got about 50 years.

Chris: You've got a while.

Mario: Just playing Gary.

Gary: Nice.

Chris: Where is this on here? See, now I'm lost.

Gary: I can find it.

Chris: These things are terrible.

Gary: There's too much information.

Chris: Is it the triglycerides that we're worried about? Bro, that's an all time high!

Gary: I know. I know.

Chris: So look at this Mario. So this is this months, right? Gary we really need-

Gary: I love that Chris you get such a kick out of this. You love it so much.

Chris: Everybody listening to this. I forgot it was an all time high. Listen guys, Gary might not make it to the Top Dog event. You might want to call him.

Gary: If you're watching this. It's not like I'm not floating over my chair. I'm not 300 pounds.

Chris: Dr. Lau said, "It feels like by looking at your chart I'm talking to a 300 pound man. What did he say? 300 pound man that can't -

Gary: Eats Carl's Jr every day for lunch. That's what he said. Yeah.

Chris: So look at this. See this chart?

Gary: I wish.

Chris: All time high. Your cholesterol went up 80 points bro. 264

Mario: Supposed to be getting better Gary.

Chris: The range you want is 150 or lower.

Gary: I'm tying to win.

Chris: He's a ways away. He's twice what they want you to be at right?

Gary: I'm going for high score.

Chris: It's Pac Man? That's so funny. So now in Gary's defense I think this was done a couple days after you got back from vacation right?

Gary: Yeah. Yep. It was two days after. That was a rough one because we were here until midnight the night before working, remember, and Ben was here. I didn't get to bed until two in the morning. That was not a good day.

Chris: It's a normal week at Chris. What you're saying is, basically, you didn't have a chance to fudge it for a couple days. It was real.

Gary: I was going to dilute it down but ... I had one of those blood scrubbers at my house I was going to run it through a filter.

Chris: That's so funny, that's hilarious. So say a prayer for Gary.

Gary: I'm going to be all right.

Chris: You're going to have to start taking it seriously bro.

Gary: There's some good things on here. It's not all bad.

Chris: So Gary, just bought your daughter a car?

Gary: Yep.

Chris: How did that go?

Gary: We talked about it a little bit on the previous podcast a couple of times about the experience and what happened to her when she went in to buy the car. And all the different dealerships she went to and just how bad it was from a customer experience standpoint and it really had my daughter turned off. At some point she just didn't want the car anymore. She's just over it. What we decided to do, because she goes to school up in the wine country, up in Sonoma, and we have a client that's got a dealership up there that sells Honda's. We were going to just drive up there and buy it up there. I figured I'd call somebody and have them set me up and just take care of it all through phone, email, and then just pick up the car, but she couldn't decide on the package that she wanted, the color interior, and she was still going back and forth. So I said, "Why don't we go to Santa Monica because they have a dealership there and we'll just pop in. We'll just pop in. You can look at the car. We're not going to buy it here but we'll figure it out." So we go in. First of all they have valet parking there and so the guy he comes up super nice, "Can I help you?" and I have the top down on my car and I don't want to park my car outside. "No, no, no," I'll put it over here inside. We'll take care of it. Everything's good;" 'm like, "Great" We walk inside we get greeted right away.

Chris: So they de-horsed you?

Gary: They de-horsed me.

Mario: Well that's in Santa Monica, you got to remember--

Chris: Did they throw the keys on the roof? He's about to tell us this great customer experience he had; they threw his keys on the roof. They called it valet.

Mario: He had a red vest on.

Chris: So let's recap. You pull in. They take your keys and your car. Were you trading your car in?

Gary: This is the Chris way of doing it.

Chris: Did you trade the car in?

Gary: No, no, I wasn't trading anything in.

Chris: Oh okay. So that's why they didn't throw your keys on the roof. Okay. Keep going.

Gary: They took care, it was nice. The salesman greeted us promptly, smiled, very nice. It was a Sunday and they were crazy busy and so he said, "I'm in between clients right now. One person's looking at a car, another in finance, but I have some time. I'm going to help you guys. What can I do for you?" I told him what we were there for, just to look at a car and she just wants to see it. He said, "No problem, I'm going to take you and show you inventory." So he takes us upstairs and shows us the car and he spent all this time with my daughter. I walked away. I didn't care to hear it all. I was just wandering around looking at cars, but he just went over options.

Mario: So you left your daughter with another man?

Gary: I left her.

Chris: She can handle herself.

Gary: Technically, she's 20.

Chris: She takes after her Mom. She's fine.

Gary: She's got Brazilian blood. She's fine. He's answering questions and my daughter really liked him and really started to fall in love with the car again and the experience. The deal was my wife was really committed to this idea of buying the car up north because it fit the schedule.

Mario: It's our customer. We're keeping it in the family.

Gary: We got home and I thought about it and I thought, "You know, he really just went out of his way and didn't try to close us and didn't try to hold us hostage there and didn't give me a credit app like the other guy did."

Chris: What do we gotta do to make a deal?

Gary: He didn't ask me, "What do we gotta do to close the deal?" He just said, "Hey look, I'll give you all the information you want. If you guys want to buy a car great." If not he's okay with it. So we thought about it. We talked about it. I thought man, I appreciated that. I wanted to buy a car from him. It took us about a week or so because we were kicking it around. We figured out the logistics and drove down there and bought a car from him and he set us all up. The second experience was better than the first, literally. He topped it. The car was clean. It was perfect. It was beautiful. He had it parked underneath. The process was relatively fast and he put a big red bow on the car and had my daughter pose for pictures. We were the last deal of the night. It was 9:00 at night because I left here and met him out in Santa Monica so we got there really late. I think I got there at 8:30 or something like that. It was 9:00 at night and they were wrapping up. They were closed. Everybody's out going home and so I told him, "Look bro I get it you did a great job, you don't have to stay. We'll figure this out." He's all, "No, no, no, no, no." So he got in the car and started going over the whole car with her again and did this amazing delivery with her and was just a great guy. I asked him at the end. I said, "How many cars did you sell this month?" He said he sold 37 cars that month.

Chris: Wow.

Gary: I know.

Chris: Why didn't we hire him?

Mario: Does he want to come downtown?

Gary: He may want to come downtown.

Mario: It's more fun downtown. Who wants that beach? That's terrible, homeless people in Santa Monica.

Chris: Yeah.

Mario: That's awesome - of course he sells 37 cars. He makes friends.

Gary: That's the thing, it was so simple, so nice, easy to deal with. Just gave us what we wanted, what we were asking for. I guess the other thing I thought, I thought about this a lot, he was just a really good listener. The one thing I remembered about almost everybody I dealt with is they did not listen to us and he stopped and listened to what we needed and delivered what we needed and it made me feel good. Made me want to buy from him and we went back and bought a car.

Chris: That's funny, we were talking about that last night because we were referencing - have you ever read *How to Win Friends and Influence People?*

Mario: Yeah, yeah.

Chris: In there he talks about how if you listen to people they'll end up actually telling you what a great conversationalist you were even though they talked and blabbed for two hours and you never said anything.

Mario: Oh yeah, absolutely.

Chris: A big part of connecting is listening.

Gary: It's being interested. Genuinely interested. That was the thing. He was really interested in my daughter and her first car and this experience that she's having and he just got-.

Chris: School and probably the whole thing. What did she say after?

Gary: She was just ecstatic after it. After the first time that we met him she came to me and said, "I think we should buy it from him. He did a really good job." She was connected and she was excited. That's the other thing, hen we first started this experience, we talked about this the last time, she was terrified to go to the dealership and then they proved her right when she got there. Now she's even more scared. She never wants to buy a car again. In this experience she's excited. She was excited to go back, excited to meet the guy again and it just completely changed her perception of things and it's amazing. Amazing how simple it was. They didn't have the best facility, it's not like their show room was a luxurious Taj Mahal. It was just a typical store. It's in Santa Monica. It's in a small place. It's an older building, an older facility, but that didn't matter. What mattered most was just how they treated us.

Chris: What's his first name?

Gary: Enrique.

Chris: Good job, Enrique.

Gary: The other guys. I probably talked to ten guys. Maybe more...

Chris: So much work.

Gary: I couldn't tell you their names. I couldn't tell you. His name I remember.

Mario: The difference, I think he went above and beyond where most of us, whether in sales and service advisor, we drop the ball once, we collect the money once we got you to sign at the dotted line. We just say, "Okay. We're done." And we finish and we wrap up and we go on to the next. I think the reason he's selling 37 a month is because he goes above and beyond. It's not over until the customer is 100% satisfied and I can almost guarantee your daughter's going to go back when she thinks of a new car, regardless of the brand she bought, she'll go back towards him because of the experience she gained.

Gary: I think so. I almost think for sure on that one Mario, because of the fact that she was afraid in the beginning, she's going to want a go-to person. She's going to want someone she feels comfortable with. She doesn't want to go through that again. So if she wants to go back you hit the nail right on the head it becomes a repeat customer. She's going to want to go back to him. She might drive down here from Northern California to Southern California if she had to buy another car.

Chris: He'll be the manager by then.

Gary: Right. He'll be a dealer.

Chris: Gary, I was on vacation last week so I went up to, In Washington my grandfather always had property by this lake up there called Mesa Lake. It's a huge lake a little past Bremerton, Washington, kind of the area that I grew up and my family goes out there in the summer. In the *Farmers Almanac* the last couple weeks are the best times in Washington to not get rained on, historically. There wasn't any rain it, was perfect weather. We got a house on AirBNB there on the lake. Basically, Mario, I think my cousins and I, the whole time, I don't think we talked about anything else but the Seahawks and how they can kill the 49ers. I don't think anything else came up. I think we prayed to beat Carol.

Mario: You need some praying. You guy's definitely ...

Chris: The only time. It's the greatest thing. My cousin Jeremy - I'm sitting there and during the week, he came out on the evenings. One time, He comes out the very first thing he said to me, "Did you see Carol's press conference?" I mean, it hadn't been up an hour. I'd seen that it was up, but I hadn't watched it. I was like, "No" But no one ever says that in my world.

Gary: I want to add a little context to this. I don't know if you know, but everybody that's listening, Chris is a Seahawks fan. You've probably figured that part out, but I'm looking at Mario right now and I can just see out his shirt sleeve his San Francisco 49ers tattoo.

Chris: Grounds for termination right there.

Gary: He has it written in blood on his arm.

Chris: Chip Kelly's the answer. I was just reading a thing this morning that Chip Kelly's top five to get fired. They're predicting in Vegas.

Mario: I have wishful thinking at this moment. I don't know how he's going to come out and make a difference. I was happy with our previous coach, but I guess we all have to take a chance and try something different because whatever we had before wasn't working so ...

Chris: Harbaugh was working.

Mario: I get it but ...

Chris: Harbaugh was working.

Mario: Once he was gone what happened?

Chris: You went to the Super Bowl with Harbaugh.

Mario: Once he was gone ...

Chris: I would have got out of that guys way. Just get out of that guy's way.

Gary: When teams do stuff like that it's hard to be loyal. They've got a great coach. All they've got to do is pay the guy and he'll stay there and you'll win.

Mario: What the problem is-

Chris: Did you see the Sunday conversation with Harbaugh the other day?

Mario: Uh uh.

Chris: Oh man, it's so funny. The guy's asking him stupid questions like, "People say about you that you're obsessed or whatever". He's just looking at the guy like, "Yeah I'm obsessed. It's what I do - football." He's like, "The only three things in life I care about basically: my wife, my kids, football. That's what I do."

Mario: Simple as that. Right?

Chris: He bleeds football.

Gary: Yep. Yep.

Chris: I'm not a 49ers fan, but when he was there you couldn't argue with the fact that he was a leader of men.

Mario: One of the things that I was going to say to answer that question is, just like in a football organization, is when there's not a clear path to what we're trying to accomplish, everything falls apart and you can relate that to any service department, any sales department. Everybody has a head, they all have their own agenda, what they want to do, but unless it's all geared towards the same goal things going to fall apart. It doesn't matter how good one rock star is and how bad a manager is if they're not geared and it's not tailored to the same goal, things ain't going to work out.

Chris: Success is attracted to clarity.

Mario: Yes. Clarity is one of the keys of success.

Chris: So our Top Dog event this year we're giving away the $50,000 service manager challenge.

Gary: Exciting.

Chris: We're doing that on the last day and Mario's the MC of the event. He's got funny jokes. It's going to be great. You have funny jokes right?

Gary: No pressure.

Mario: No pressure.

Gary: Mario's hilarious, by the way.

Mario: We're paying out some jokesters right now.

Gary: Bring your tissues.

Chris: The speakers we have ... We have Uncle Dave Anderson and he did it last year and he's amazing. So he's going to do a thing on performance, and then we have Tim Kintz, sales trainer master friend of ours.

Mario: Slow down I'm getting excited Chris. I'm getting excited!

Chris: Listen to this: I was telling my cousins, who we had at our event, and I was telling them about Jocko, did I tell you this? They go, "Oh. He's consulting for the Seahawks." Remember when we did our podcast he said they are working with the Seahawks.

Gary: Yep. Yep.

Chris: I didn't know that. It's not Jocko. It's his partner, I guess, but Pete Carol's hired him to come in and do leadership training with the locker room.

Gary: The Eschalon.

Chris: I don't see Chip Kelly doing that. What's the coach for the Cowboys? I always forget his name. He's forgettable. What's his name?

Gary: I can't even remember. You put me on the spot. He's the back-up quarterback.

Chris: Some of our coaching clients are Dallas Cowboys fans.

Mario: I'll be there Saturday watching the Rams and the Cowboys go at it for the pre-season. That'll be fun.

Chris: Big deal.

Mario: I'm just trying to see a game in LA, that's it Chris. Don't beat me up over that. I'm just trying to go catch a game. Have a good time.

Chris: Do you think people around here are going to catch on to the Rams?

Mario: You know, it's give and take. This community out here has been ... We didn't really have a team so people kind of branched out. We had San Diego way far out there. A lot of people didn't go. We had the Rams back in the days and the Raiders. For some odd reason a lot of people took on the Cowboys out here in this area so those are generically-

Chris: A lot of people? Only Gary.

Gary: America's team, my friend.

Mario: Let's not forget San Francisco right?

Chris: There's more Raiders fans out here right?

Mario: It's been growing. It's kind of hard to tell now.

Chris: They were saying on the news, the Rams are very disappointed with the turn out for practices.

Gary: For practice?

Chris: Yeah, but they're practicing in Orange County.

Mario: Right.

Chris: That's a thing that ... We need to sit these guys down, like the guy from the Angels and the guy who owns the Rams, "Listen. Orange County's another country."

Gary: Yeah.

Chris: You keep trying to tie them together. They're not the same.

Gary: They're not.

Chris: Nobody from LA's going to Orange County to watch the team practice.

Mario: Well I think when Anaheim changed their name to the Anaheim Angels, went to LA Angels, they thought they were going to bring on a whole new crowd and everything and they just flopped.

Gary: It's too far.

Mario: It's the Dodgers

Gary: I'm telling you almost West LA is almost too far. It's almost not LA anymore. It's 15 miles.

Chris: Who's going to sit in traffic for three hours to go watch them practice?

Mario: That's the funny part. 15 miles. 3 hours.

Gary: Yeah right.

Mario: I was across the state, I forgot I was having a conversation with someone and in conversation we brought up when you ask someone how far something is they tell you in distance, where when we talk in LA we talk time. That's the difference.

Chris: The first thing you would say if you said, "I'm going to Orange County to Irvine to watch the Rams practice." The first thing I would say is, "What time of day."

Gary: Right.

Chris: Then you would say, "How long?"

Gary: That's true.

Chris: Because it's only 7 miles

Gary: We start talking about the freeways you're going to take: "Oh, you're going? Well, what route are you going? "Oh I wouldn't go that way."

Chris: Yeah, what you want to do--

Mario: We got to the point where there's no right way to take it - you just take it. Deal with it.

Chris: Mostly now it's all side streets I think.

Mario: Because of Waze.

Gary: Yeah Waze. Even that now everybody's got Waze so it's just clogged there too.

Chris: It's funny. So part of, for everybody listening to this podcast, part of the $50,000 service manager challenge is they had to write an essay in their entry so they gave their before and after numbers for CSI net to gross and ELR. And that average increase was astronomical for all three of those because we charted all that and I should have printed that so we could say their numbers, but in those essays, man, some of them really got me.

Gary: It was tough.

Chris: They got me. It's just crazy how real service managers get supported in. It is crazy. How little support and how little training they get and what a big bat they swing. It's the next car sale. It's retention. It's their view of the manufacturer. It's everything and they get nothing.

Gary: They're touching so many customers and there are so many moving pieces. Whereas the sales department, there's a lot going on, but they're not managing nearly as much. There's not many customers coming in. There's not many employees that you need. You got techs. You got BBC personnel. You got advisors. You've got porters.

Mario: Inventory. You're selling time.

Gary: It's crazy.

Mario: That's irreplaceable. It's gone when it's gone. Hiring techs. It's crazy.

Gary: It's really sad that that's how the industry has been over time right? From advisor you got, "Here's your pen. Here's your clipboard. Get out there." Right? As a manager, "Oh you're the top advisor. Get out there and be a manager." And it sucks when you had a really poor manager or leader in front of you, you're going to lead just as bad or even worse than they did, right? That definitely does not help.

Chris: In reading some of those essays. Some of these guys that we have in our coaching group are salt of the Earth. The greatest guys ever, and when you read the essay about, just when they were given the tools and we just showed them how it works, they took it and they ran with it and they made it their own and they got unbelievable results just because they were taught how to read a financial. They were. It's crazy how one of them, I think he said 14 or 15 years he's been a service manager. Nobody taught him anything. We see that over and over again and it just infuriates me that as an industry we think we're going to get ahead treating them that way.

Gary: How he could go that long? 14 years, and have no training or support and you're just floating along and then all of the sudden somebody comes along and says, "Hey do it this way, and he's like "Why didn't anybody tell me that?"

Chris: Yeah. If you would have told me, I would have done it. It's funny what happens with managers. We see this a lot too, and I don't know if you've noticed this Mario, but I definitely do, is if they've been a manager more than five years they're scared to ask.

Mario: Yeah, because they should know all the answers.

Chris: They should know, but they were never trained.

Mario: Absolutely

Chris: They get a dealer that reads a 20 group composite, comes in and says, "You've got too many people. Fire 5 people." Their ELR's $50. If you have an ELR today that's less than $100 you don't understand how to run your business.

Gary: At all.

Chris: It's crazy. What the top service managers have in common, and we made this list: The first one is, we have five here that we think are the commonalities, but the first one is they've got to understand the financials. If you don't ... What happens in our industry to the same conversation we're having is the dealer always has a financial statement on his desk. Anybody who runs an independent shop or anything, what they're looking at is their financial statement. It's never shared with the manager, but he's graded on it and it's his trick bag that they get him. Unless we're sharing the financials with them. Unless we have an open book and we're teaching them how effective labor, how expenses, how everything is affecting the overall outcome. There's only two measurables that matter. It's customer satisfaction, and you could say customer satisfaction and retention, but it's the same thing, and profit. Unless we're teaching them, its all for naught. They're in a trick bag.

Gary: You're just flying blind. You've got no idea where you're going or what you're doing and you're just showing up every day and trying to keep the wheels on the bus and what difference would that make and why would you change prices if you didn't know that that was going to have an impact?

Mario: Right.

Gary: Then it makes it easy to make price on emotion and not on what makes sense for profitability. This feels like the right price, verses I need to do this to be profitable. They just don't know.

Chris: If you're a service manager listening to this I just want to tell you that half of the time the guys that show up for the boot camp, it's the first time they've seen a financial; don't feel bad.

Get in our coaching group and get here and we'll teach you. We'll give you the tools. We'll help you, because we care and we will mentor you and guide you through it. Don't feel bad about it. It's not your fault, but don't feel bad coming because we'll teach you. We'll teach you how to read the financials and you'll be better than anybody in your dealership at doing it.

Gary: The one thing I thought was interesting too... I worked at my dealer for 20 years, some od, and had my little pocket of people that you kind of had in your little circle and once you get outside of that it's amazing the amount of information that's out there in the field that people are doing right now. And one of the things I thought was probably the best part of having that group of people, that you could be with, is sharing those ideas and learning from guys that have tried something else on the other side of the country. And when I see that take place - it's the magic of bringing that group together and that coaching group, it's just.. it pushes them to the next level. Gives them the new ideas.

Chris: For a long time bro. That's what makes us look smarter than we are because we're in all these stores and we see what's working and then we share it and then it makes us look smart but really we're just observant. We're collectors.

Gary: We get to test. Which is awesome. Being out in the field and working with stores and being able to test stuff and stuff works an you're like, "Great" and you just want to share that with everybody. Especially being in this environment where you have access to them all. It's like gold. You just want to hand it out.

Chris: It's totally true. The next one that I have on here: So what the top service managers have in common, is a passion for customers. I think about you, because we've talked about this before Mario, you worked at Longo Toyota and Longo's number one in the world. I ran the number one BMW store when I was there at the time, and there were a lot of commonalities between Fletcher Jones and all the number one stores in the country and the commonality was the customer was always right. We never wanted to win an argument with a customer. It didn't matter. They got over on us. The got over on us. It was okay.

Mario: Absolutely, and I know where I'm working on a couple new modules out there, and part of the modules... I was explaining this story of how as a porter I really got impacted on what Longo brought to the table and as a porter, as a supervisor, as you get into advisory and management, every paycheck has the same description on that paycheck. Didn't matter what position you were at, but it simply said, "This paycheck has been brought to you by our customer" and that registered so deep to me as an employee. Knowing that if we don't provide great customer service for our customers, eventually we won't have anyone to serve and eventually they won't have a service for me. Knowing that as a porter, I really owned that, and I had a different mentality of going out there and making sure I took care of every single customer to the best of my ability. Even at times I would take care of other people's customers because I knew if they're not doing the right job eventually these customers leave too, so it was very impactful and to this day I remember that like the back of my hand.

Chris: How many times could you get a bad survey before they launched you?

Mario: I think right after you go under your national you go on prescription, which is probation, and you have three months to pick it up. If you don't pick it up, the average, over those three months you're done. That quick. That easy. Doesn't matter how great your numbers are. If you've been a rockstar for the last three years. Doesn't matter. They'll replace you because CSI was their number one. They'll find people to sell.

Chris: You were never right with a customer?

Mario: No. No and I think years later I ended up finding out this phrase, "Would you rather be right or would you rather be rich?" And I realized I wanted to be rich.

Chris: It's true though. I remember my managers at Crew View would be mad because there'd be some policy thing or something for 1000 bucks and it would go from the advisor to the service manager to the guy to the guy, and then it would get to me and I'd give it away. I'm not going to argue. They're like, "Ah! We make good money. We'll be okay" but that customer-

Mario: We'll never gain them again.

Chris: They're locked in. To let the customer come that far down the path. At that point it isn't about the $1000. It's about they need to win. We've made it about winning or losing, not about the fact that we wrote down the damage on the war ground. We positioned it all wrong. You just got to fade. You can't be right.

Gary: The goal is to keep them long term too, so if you start out ... It's funny, we used to say it at my store, "If you're going to give it away then why argue about it?" Why get in a fight with them before you give it to them? Why don't we just make friends and admit that something bad happened and just move on and, like you said, if they get over on us, they get over on us. It just is. You're not going to win anything by starting an argument then paying for it. Let's just take care of them. They're going to come back and get their car serviced for many years hopefully. They're going to know that we take care of them, stand behind it so we're going to have that customer for a long time, and then they're going to buy another car. Isn't that what we want? Then we've got them for another five years. That's the goal. It just doesn't pay. It doesn't pay to do that.

Chris: No. The next one: So, what the top service managers have in common, the first one was understanding their financial, second was passion for the customer, the third one is hit the sales button. They got to know how to sell.

Gary: Retail.

Chris: Effective, elaborate and sell.

Mario: Yep.

Chris: One of the essays mentioned you going out to the store and playing games and training the advisors and hitting the sales button. It's an easy thing to understand. It's like a super power that the managers get when they understand how to hit the sales button. It really is.

Gary: Yeah.

Mario: The very first thing you've got to know is what they're saying, how they're selling, right? So you, as the manager, got to go out there in the forefront and listen to your advisors. Listen to them present because only then will you know how to guide them and give them tips because not every advisor is at the same level, right? You have to go out there and find out what levels are my advisors in? Where I can guide them and give them the proper tips? The excuse every manager gives is I don't have the time or I haven't been out there and we tell them time and time again you have to spend time out there to realize what's going on. That's the heartbeat of the dealership and if you're not constantly checking that heartbeat than you're not knowing where we're going or where we're headed.

Chris: Part of hitting the sales button too, and this happens sometimes in the bootcamp, when guys come is, say for example they're all excited because they have a 100 alignment machine and they're selling 100 alignments, half what they should be.

Gary: And 100 come on it.

Chris: Yeah. We had one the other day. It was, like, $70 I think. They're paying the tech 1.8 hours and they're charging $70, $69.95. So they're losing money on every alignment they sell.

Gary: Right.

Chris: But they're hitting a sales button. They're spiffing the advisors to do it. They've got half of it right, but you have to know how to price things.

Gary: I think too that's the common misconception. We're talking about hitting the sales button and the thing people go to first is, "I need more traffic", right? "I'm going to run a loss-leader and I'm going to get more people in and all those alignments, they're going to become something. Well, they don't become something unless you plan for it, but the bottom line is you really don't need to do that. There's no reason to. You've got customers. You're not offering them what they need and when you learn how to pull that lever and you learn how to get your advisors focused, like you were saying Mario, focused on the presentation and what the car needs and how they sell. I mean, that's the thing, and then playing the games and putting that behind it and getting it fun, that's where it really just takes off.

Mario: Yeah you've got to start out with your current customer before expanding to new traffic because all we're going to do is the exact same poor job we're doing with our current customers.

Gary: It's just more of less is really what it is. You know, it's funny Chris , you did a math problem a long time ago where you kind of penciled it out and you're like, the last thing you need is more cars. You're just going to loose more money. When I looked at it I was like, "Oh, my God, you're right!" It was so clear in that moment we just had to change what we were doing. We had to stop thinking about "more, more, more" because it's just going to hurt your CSI because you're just overwhelming your staff and it just doesn't work.

Chris: You've got to build the foundation first and then grow. The next one I have on here is they're people collectors. They're collectors of advisors, techs. You get the good advisors, good techs follow them. They collect people.

Mario: They basically just need to connect with each other because good breeds more good. You want to hang out with people who are out there performing. That's typically why when we hire an advisor onto a store they have a couple technicians that are willing to follow them because they know they have the secret of success, and how to sell, and how to turn their hours. And in return we've hired some technicians that say, "Hey I've got a great advisor" and it's because they want to continue up a path where they know they almost have a guarantee, per se, the little cushion, the little window, that they're going to this new department or new dealer and they know that someone has their back and it's what it comes down to.

Chris: And then the last one I have here is that they transcend their department and what we mean by transcend their department is that the sales department doesn't hate going there. They're affecting all department's internals, the used cars don't take 15 days to get through the shop. They have a system for that and that's another thing nobody teaches service managers how to do that, and so there's clear systems on how to do that. But you have to understand that. You have to transcend just your department because inside of a dealership if you're running it like only your department matters, you're negatively affecting four or five other departments. You've got to be able to get PDI's done. Customer's that come in with WIOs. A customer that just bought a car and the check engine light turned on after. Used cars have to turn quick. There's so many things that you affect, and just attitude. Your advisors have to radiate customer services so the sales people want to turn people over to them. I don't know how many times we go into a dealership and the sales staff are like, "I wouldn't send my Mom back there."

Gary: Right and that's all the time.

Chris: It's two weeks to get our customer in...they'll have used cars that are 30 days.

Mario: That's why the saying goes, "Sales sells the first car, service department sells every one after." A lot of it comes down through the service department like you said. The WIO's, all the additional parts, any warranty issues, they come through

231

us. That experience that we provide for those customers is going to be the difference on whether they're going to continue to stick with the brand. Stick with that dealership, right? We continue to look at them as, "Well it's not my customer - sales should have taken care of it, then we're being pretty negative and we're not being a serving mentality by proving great customer service to our customers.

Gary: I always felt that same way. You've got to create a bridge. There's very few businesses in this country that have a system like ours where we have a front end that's manufacturing customers for us. They're just constantly feeding us with new customers to service and that's an amazing thing, and you have to fall in love with that a little bit and create bridges so that they want to send customers back to you. And they're going to tell you everything that's wrong and sometimes your ego gets involved and you get offended by it, but I just say, forget it. Let them say what they're going to say. I just tell them I'm going to fix it. I'll straighten it out. I'm going to help you, because I just want to keep those customers coming, right? Every customer they send me is a customer I don't have to go out and buy and go get. It just comes to me automatically. There's a lot of methods for doing that, but communication, I think, is the main thing. I think if you're a manager and you're listening to this, my best advice is, you've got this place that is feeding you customers, go out and sit with those guys for a little while. Sit with them, hear what they have to say, create a bridge like we were talking about earlier. Listen a little bit, talk a little less than you listen, take it in. And then do your best to try to modify to meet their needs, but you'll be a lot happier.

Chris: Don't stay in the dark. Don't ignore it.

Gary: Don't ignore it.

Chris: Transcend.

Gary: Exactly.

Chris: Transcend.

Mario: Like they said, "God gave you two ears and one mouth" right? So we can listen more and talk less.

Gary: That's right.

Chris: If you're a dealer service manager out there, and you don't have the training, and you're not surrounded by other winners in our industry, get in our coaching group and so we can help you. We've got some amazing talent and our training's pretty good.

Gary: And fun.

Chris: Gary says the best out there? Our training?

Gary: Yeah.

Chris: It's really kind of the only of it's kind, really. Nobody cares about service like we do.

Gary: No.

Chris: We bleed service.

Gary: It's unique. There's a lot of other people that do it but it's not the same. Ours is different.

Chris: They don't love it like we love it. Also the Top Dog event. Don't forget if you're not coming to that you can buy tickets to it, and come as a guest, and check it out and dip your toe in the water of our little-

Gary: I've been in this industry 30 years now, maybe more than 30 years, and I could tell you, honestly, it's the only event like it that I've ever seen. There's no place where advisors and managers come together like that and get to work together and workshop together and see some of the same things. It's just such a powerful event.

Chris: The goal in the beginning was sales gets all kinds of cool stuff and service doesn't, but I think we've transcended sales. Nobody in sales has what we have. The speakers and ... People leave there with real tools and we're sharing-

Mario: The networking. I mean, I've been surprised going all across to the East coast and the advisor he's telling me about an advisor that he just finished texting that's out in California. And I'm like, "What are you guys texting about?" "Oh, that I'm going to beat him in the Comp and that he might be beating me in CSI but I'm coming with Customer Pay."

Chris: About his Momma.

Mario: I'm like, "Where did you get his number?" "At the event." Networking goes around. People get each other's numbers and they're either poking or motivating each other to be better and to get to the event next year. Because, only because, you made it to the event that one year doesn't mean you're guaranteed the next year. It's all about performance and continued performance.

Chris: That's it. Totally. We'll work on Gary's cholesterol. I hope you feel better because you're a little sick, right?

Mario: I'm getting over it. I'm getting over it. This helped out. It was exciting.

Chris: Work on some jokes for the event?

Mario: I need that. Please send your jokes in. If you guys got any jokes that I can use I would really appreciate that.

Chris: They would all be inappropriate probably.

Gary: mario@chriscollinsinc.com, by the way, I want to see what comes in.

Chris: No. Don't do that. It's got to be clean. PG.

Mario: Just keep it PG guys. 13 maybe.

Gary: I'd like to make a commitment here.

Chris: On your cholesterol? Okay. Let's hear this.

Gary: I'm going to go out on a ledge here and I'm going to say by my next test I will have it under 200.

Chris: Or you'll get a Seahawks tattoo?

Mario: I like that bet!

Gary: My low's 185. I'll go under 200 by the next test.

Chris: I was here at the office and the lady showed up to do his blood and he wasn't here, he was running late. And I told her, "Do you got the big needle because his blood's like a milkshake" and she looked at me like, "Oh, I don't."

Gary: "Should I get it?"

Chris: So you'll get a Seahawks tattoo if you're not under 180, is that what you said?

Gary: If I'm not under 180 I'll get a Seahawks tattoo.

Mario: Wow!

Chris: Bro you don't want to do that.

Mario: That's pretty big! Just to clarify, you're a Cowboys fan. You're willing to get a Seahawks tattoo if what? What are the stakes?

Chris: You've never been under 180.

Gary: I'm sorry. Under 200. What am I saying.

Chris: I tricked you.

Gary: You did. Under 200. That's that little "p" thing. You just got in my head.

Chris: You're funny.

Gary: 264 right now, by the way. 264, so I've got to get it down 65.

Chris: Testosterone, HDL ...

Mario: That's compared to a 300 pound man?

Chris: 300 pound man might be better. You really do though. For me being Irish it's very hereditary. You just gotta eat good you can't - I can't have french fries and all that. Your testosterone's good bro.

Mario: I think the last time we had a conversation about, we were talking with Ben, and it has a lot to do with your blood type.

Gary: Yeah.

Mario: On what you eat, right?

Chris: If it's hereditary, you've got to dial it in.

Gary: Yeah. There's a way, there's a way.

Chris: You're not taking your vitamin D.

Mario: You need vitamin D?

Gary: I take my vitamin D every day. I just ran out. So you're right. I'm not taking my vitamin D.

Chris: So was he or was he not taking his vitamin D Mario?

Mario: Was not.

Gary: I'm standing behind the--

Mario: After all the fluff and smoke and mirrors he was not-

Gary: This was not a fair test man. This one was not. I was not in the right spot.

Mario: Did you know it was coming up?

Gary: I forgot. I totally forgot it was coming.

Chris: The other one that worries me is his cortisol.

Gary: Yeah, yeah. so ...

Chris: It's funny how good you get at reading these after a while, right?

Gary: It's like reading a financial statement. The first time I looked at it, it was like a magic eye poster. I had no idea what I was looking at and then you kind of tune in and now I can look at it and I can tell what anybody's doing. It's the same thing with this; you start to get good at these blood tests, look at them and see what's going on.

Chris: It looks like you have Herpes.

Gary: Yeah. Love it. A big case.

Mario: That didn't stay in Vegas, huh?

Chris: He doesn't have them. He's a good boy.

Gary: All in all, relatively healthy. Little high on the estrogen still so he's up in the blocker but still okay.

Chris: You're setting an Olympic world record for cholesterol. What is it? 260?

Gary: 264

Chris: "I'm okay." In denial.

Gary: Over 200 they start to get really worried about you.

Chris: I wish I would have printed mine out because there was a time mine got bad and I just went into boot camp.

Mario: Eat a lot of shrimp? I heard that kind of affects that? Gets that ...

Gary: High?

Chris: I don't eat shrimp. I can't eat shrimp.

Gary: I do eat a lot of shrimp.

Chris: No but it's steak. It's all that. I eat way too much steak.

Gary: I eat chicken. Lot's of fish. I almost never eat red meat.

Chris: Well thanks everybody for listening. We will see you again next time and make sure you still have time to make it to the Top Dog event. Sign up.

Mario: Make sure you guys get your barking voice ready! Still thinking about his cholesterol.

Chris: That was a 260 cholesterol bark.

Gary: Little hesitation on it...

Chris: Stop drinking the cheap stuff Gary. So funny. Thanks everybody. Bye.

Episode #9: The Do's And Dont's To Building Customer Relationships

Chris: Welcome everybody to Service Drive Revolution, where we're changing drives and changing lives. Probably the worlds only podcast for service drives I would think.

Gary: So far.

Chris: Do you think so? How's your cholesterol G-Man?

Gary: High and getting higher.

Chris: I've got my blood test next week.

Gary: Oh man. I need to cut back on the steak.

Chris: Yeah, my diet this weekend was not great so I-

Gary: Let's check it today.

Chris: I know. I cut my finger and blood didn't even come out, it just bubbled.

Gary: Chocolate milkshake from In-and-out.

Chris: It's not good.

Gary: That's funny.

Chris: Today on this podcast we have an exciting agenda for you. We're going to talk about snackification, not gamification.

Gary: Snackification?

Chris: We're going to talk about "Service advisors, lost me at hello." Pretty fun story about that. So "Service advisors, lost me at hello." We're going to talk about the $50,000 service manager challenge, our upcoming Top Dog event, which is going to be really cool.

Gary: Super excited.

Chris: And we have a book, it's called *The Obstacle Is The Way*. We're going to talk about that. We should talk about the $50K challenge up front. We decided, I don't know, eight months ago, to make it really exciting for our coaching group members, that we were going to do a challenge, and we're going to give away $50,000 to the service manager that takes our systems, and its kind of four things right? They increase their CSI, their effective labor and their net to gross, and then they kind of write a summary of their process or their journey more than anything.

Gary: Right.

Chris: 50% of it is on the story, the other 50% is on the numbers. I mean we have guys increasing effective labor rate by $60 and it's great. But the idea is, you know the sales department is sexy, and service isn't that sexy, so we want to throw out a prize that would really profile the guys in the back, really on the front lines of this war we have.

Gary: Right.

Chris: I don't know who we're at war with, we're actually more of a hospitality, serving people. Why do I think war? I know why I think war; because of one of our speakers at the Top Dog event. So we're going to announce the $50,000 service manager challenge winner at our Top Dog event in August. We have a Top Dog event every year where we invite the top service managers and top advisors from around the country that are in our family. I think this year you're thinking about opening it up to maybe some other guests that aren't in our coaching group or in our family?

Gary: Yup.

Chris: But we're going to announce the $50,000 winner then. Then we also are going to have some speakers, so the theme this year is about performance. We're going to have Tim Kintz right?

Gary: Right, yeah, Tim will be there.

Chris: He's going to talk about performance. We're going to have old mean Uncle Dave Anderson there doing a thing on performance. I say that with the most love, we love Dave.

Gary: Oh yeah, Dave's awesome.

Chris: But Dave tells you how it is and that's it.

Gary: It's the brutal truth from Dave, that's for sure.

Chris: Yeah, but we will all get better because of it.

Gary: Yeah.

Chris: And then we're going to have Jocko who wrote the book *Extreme Ownership* and it's probably the best leadership book I've read in a long time.

Gary: Yeah.

Chris: So he's going to be a speaker, so some big names. It's going to be fun.

Gary: Yeah.

Chris: Then we'll talk and we'll do stuff and then we'll have the finalists for the $50,000 challenge.

Gary: Should they read the book before they come out? I almost think maybe they should read the book.

Chris: Yeah, no, that's a book, too, when you start it you can't put it down.

Gary: Yeah.

Chris: Cuz of the way that, well we'll do a book report on it at some point, but it's a great book.

Gary: Yeah, no, recommended read for sure. Should be on our book list, and Jocko podcasts.

Chris: Yeah, and his podcasts are pretty good. Sometimes. Sometimes they're a little crazy, he's weird.

Gary: Yeah, they're long, they can be dry.

Chris: Yeah, all about war all the time, maybe, I don't know. We love Jocko though and we're excited to meet him and have him there. Really good.

Gary: Yeah, no, his stuff is good. I mean--

Chris: That was a get, you worked really hard to get him.

Gary: Yeah.

Chris: It's not easy.

Gary: No.

Chris: It's not easy to get somebody to come on a Sunday.

Gary: Yeah, yeah, Jocko's a talent man. He's in demand so, I had to--

Chris: Some sweet talking.

Gary: I had to wrangle him. He's flying in and doing his thing and flying out.

Chris: It's funny, we have the event on a Saturday and a Sunday so the advisors and managers are, you know, aren't out of the store during the week, so it's hard to get a guy to come speak on a Sunday.

Gary: Yeah.

Chris: Dave. No way.

Gary: Yeah, he's no way. I don't blame him.

Chris: Church.

Gary: He deserves to take Sunday's off.

Chris: Yeah.

Gary: I'd probably, for the money we're paying Jocko, I'd go on a Sunday.

Chris: Yeah, I think so too.

Gary: I think so. And he's coming up from San Diego before he goes to Boston so it's a 'tweener.

Chris: He's going to Boston on the way?

Gary: Yeah, Sunday after the event he's flying to Boston.

Chris: That...

Gary: Yeah.

Chris: We just got back from Boston.

Gary: He's a busy cat right now.

Chris: Yeah, that's fun.

Gary: Boston in, I don't know, in June.

Chris: Anything else about the Top Dog event? Except it's going to be a blast?

Gary: No, I think. I'm excited, I think it will be the best event that we've-In fact I know it's going to be the best event that we've thrown-fantastic.

Chris: It's going to be big.

Gary: It'll be big. We've got some great speakers. I think we're going to have a really cool venue, There's just going to be a lot of fun stuff.

Chris: We always learn a lot from the advisors.

Gary: Oh yeah.

Chris: It's always good.

Gary: Tons of good content. I just think it's going to be fun and educational, motivational, the whole thing. It's going to be the whole package.

Chris: Yeah, good networking. It'll be good. So Missy came in here, we were shooting a video before, we were recording this with the dogs. And Missy came in here and she took them back and she goes "Oh I got a new thing." She goes "it's snackification, forget about gameification." So she's using snackification with the dog. I thought that was pretty funny.

Gary: Snackification. All right for all you guys out there get some Reese's peanut butter cups and--

Chris: Oh no you can't give that to a dog.

Gary: Well for the advisors, they could sell more alignments, they get a stack of Reese's peanut butter cups.

Chris: You've got to be real careful with bulldogs about snacks because they get gas really bad.

Gary: Yeah, that's no bueno.

Chris: Their snacks are the Red Regional that they get. We've got to be careful. But our dogs are, they fall in this classification, we have this dog trainer come out especially 'cause we're working Tequila to be a movie dog. And she said "He falls in the classification of food motivated." Which is very true. He's food motivated, so snackification works really well with that chubby boy. We have a story, and we experienced this story together, right?

Gary: Yeah.

Chris: So we go to the gym in the morning. We were there this morning, Gary was lifting, I don't know, 400 pounds. How much do you lift?

Gary: No, not 400, I was having a rough day today. My body was feeling hurt and punished today.

Chris: Well let's pretend you lifted 400 pounds. I was the only one there as a witness.

Gary: I'm in.

Chris: It looked like 400 pounds, but everyday we walk by this office furniture store when we go to the gym, so we've got to walk by it to get to our gym. We moved into new offices and the one thing that we don't have going for us is good office chairs. Like this chair I'm sitting in kills my back.

Gary: Yeah.

Chris: So we needed office chairs, right? So I'm like "Hey at lunch we should cruise down to that place by the gym." It's always closed cuz we go at 5:30, or whatever, in the morning.

Gary: Yeah right.

Chris: So they're always closed, so we're like, we made a plan. We went down there right, and we were going to get us some office chairs.

Gary: Right.

Chris: There's some parallels to service advisors and the service director.

Gary: We thought it was that easy. We grabbed our wallets, we walked down to the store, we're going to buy chairs.

Chris: How many customers think "Oh I'm just going to go in and I'm just going to get an oil change and I'm..." you know, right?

Gary: Yeah, right. Same thing.

Chris: So we wander into this place that obviously has huge overhead. It's in downtown. It's in a nice spot, and huge. There's is office furniture everywhere. I mean that place has got to be 10,000 square feet.

Gary: Yeah, it's big.

Chris: It's big.

Gary: Their server room was massive. I couldn't believe it. Like I wonder what they're doing?

Chris: Yeah. So we walk in and there's nobody there, nobody at the front, right? There's like a little desk there at the front but nobody. And we're walking around and then this girl from the back says "Oh can we help you?" and we said "Yeah, we want to get some office chairs." She said "Okay, I'll get somebody." Then she comes back and she says "What was your budget for office chairs?" I said, "I don't know. It's more important that we find the chair than the budget, right?" But she instantly went to price, which advisors do so often. So how did you feel when she said "What's your budget?" and then I said "I don't know." And then she followed up with something to the effect of "Well, I just want you to know that these chairs can be $500 to $800."

Gary: Right.

Chris: Then, my response to her was like "What? Do I look like I can't buy a chair?"

Gary: I think in that moment, I think what I said to you was, "Chris, I think we need to upgrade our wardrobe, because apparently we look like we can't afford it." I felt like I was being profiled like the minute we walked in. They're like "Oh you guys, what are you guys doing here?"

Chris: Yeah, it was crazy. And it wasn't even those, what are those really fancy chairs like you guys used to have at Concord, whatever they're called?

Gary: Herman Miller.

Chris: Yeah, they're not even Herman Miller. Herman Miller's are like a grand?

Gary: Yeah. I was looking at Herman Miller chairs a couple of weeks ago and the one I sat in was a couple of thousand dollars actually.

Chris: A couple thousand?

Gary: Yeah, they're expensive, expensive chairs.

Chris: Okay, we're probably not in the game for those, but I mean we want a good chair.

Gary: Honestly, it wasn't that comfortable either.

Chris: So that's the starting of the relationship is, "Are you sure you can afford this?"

Gary: Right.

Chris: So how many times has that happened that the service advisors will say, and we hear it all the time, we'll go through and we're like, "Hey why didn't you present this to the customer?" "Oh, they didn't want it, they can't afford it." I remember when I was an advisor I would sell so much work that was there just because I got the customer. We had an open drive so there was no loyalty, so if I got the customer and the advisor before hadn't recommended the work or hadn't sold it, I could sell it almost every time, just because I'd ask and they didn't.

Gary: Yeah.

Chris: You know we, half of the cars, 'cause we were Volkswagen, were girls from the University of Washington that had no money and they were there going to school from Idaho or wherever, you know, and guess who would call with the credit card?

Gary: Dad.

Chris: Dad. I just had to ask. I remember one time a girl cried. She had like a, what was that thing called, a Jetta GLI, like the 16 valve one and the thing was leaking oil. You could pour the oil in the top and it would leak out the bottom. She's crying "I can't afford it," and then I get this call, you know, "Hi this is dad, what's it need? Can I give you a credit card?" I mean it was that easy and all because I would ask. That's it. I didn't prejudge. You never know. Especially here in California, guys walking around in flip-flops and a tank top are billionaires.

Gary: Right, yeah, exactly.

Chris: But they just don't care.

Gary: It's not like it used to be 50 years ago where the guys, you know, everybody's wearing $5,000 Armani suits. Now it's jeans and flip-flops, the dot comers with millions of dollars look like they're homeless half the time, so it's...Yeah to profile people like that doesn't make any sense at all.

Chris: Yeah, well we got profiled, bro, for sure.

Gary: Yeah,

Chris: And we do not look like we can afford an office chair.

Gary: It was not the profile we wanted to portray.

Chris: She's like, "Listen Jesus, listen hipster Jesus, you can't afford this. So, like stop wasting my time."

Gary: You and your thin bearded friend should leave.

Chris: Yeah, it's funny. I was pretty put off by that. That was not fun. But I see it all the time, so advisors walk up to customers in the drive and they're like what brings you in today? They're qualifying, right? That's what everybody wants to do, even on the front end with sales people. I remember we'd do hidden cameras, literally sales people within five minutes of the customer walking on the lot, it was like, "Do you know your credit score?"

Gary: Right.

Chris: Credit score is not the problem. The problem is getting them to fall in love with the car. It's the same thing in service. It's like they're going to have to fix the car, I mean the car's coming in on a tow truck or you're doing it cuz they like you, but they're doing the work somewhere. Nobody's driving around with a car leaking a ton of coolant or oil very long.

Gary: Yeah.

Chris: Especially if it's a repair. You can prejudge all you want, the work's getting done. But what is it...70% of the time customers are going to an independent or a private mechanic because we're pre-judging? We're asking them, "Did you have an appointment?" We're making them jump through all these hoops in order to earn our service. When they're really the ones voting, they're the ones in control.

Gary: Yeah, and I think like Eric was talking about that, who came out and did the, you know--

Chris: Tequila Eric?

Gary: Tequila Eric, yeah. He talked about his liquor store and he said something pretty profound to me. We were just kind of chatting about it beforehand and he was talking about when customers come in. He said that they're afraid, and he was telling me that he had a conversation with a client who was looking for wine. I know for me, I'm not a big wine connoisseur, I don't know wine from wine, but I like to drink wine and I'll buy wine if I'm hosting a dinner or something like that. So it is uncomfortable, 'cause you don't know what you're getting and wine's a very complicated and expensive thing and you don't want to sound stupid. So you don't want to say "Well I don't know, I want a red one that tastes sweet please, you know doesn't taste like an oak barrel." So you need somebody that's sensitive to that and's not a snob that goes "Oh, well you don't know what you want? Then I just can't help you." He was saying he has to have a conversation, "Well tell me what you're serving, what's the occasion, what do you like, what don't you like?" And it makes them feel a little bit comfortable and he learns a little bit about them and then sells them wine. I think in the service drive we have a lot of that going on. Where people come in, they're afraid, they don't know what to ask for, they don't know what they've got going on. They're in this big dealership, there's all this stuff happening and we don't stop and take that time to make them feel comfortable. Then they just want to leave. It's no surprise to me that they're going and they're flocking to these independents where it's smaller. It's smaller, they're going to get a little bit more personal attention. They're going to get to meet and see the people and become friends with them and they get a more intimate relationship. We know that it's occurring and I just think as an industry, we've got to figure that out. At some point somebody's got to stop and say "Enough's enough."

Chris: He brings up a good point too, is that customers come in and they're afraid.

Gary: Yeah.

Chris: They're put back, they're scared. They know what's going to happen. They don't know if they should trust. So a customer comes in and he's like "I'm going on a date, I need some Cabernet Sauvignon," or whatever, (I think that's how I said it.) He's like "Yeah, okay, what's the occasion?" He really figures them out and then makes them look like a hero. It's the same thing. Do you know how many times I've had a female customer and you know that in that situation sometimes there can be a weird thing with their husband, right. They okayed the work and the husband's like "Why'd you do that?" Right? So a lot of times just really showing them, taking them out and showing them what the car needs so they visually saw it so there isn't any weirdness or anything. Or the same thing with husbands, showing them. So like with the instant inspection: they see it, they know exactly what it is, they really understand it, so they can speak to their spouse either way in a way where they know. "No I saw it. I mean it's really there. I mean this is really what they're doing." and taking the time to understand the client and what they're up against. I don't know how many times a spouse has called and said "Oh cancel the work." You're like "Okay, well you still need the work. Why?" So really doing it up front, it's the same with him. Really caring and showing empathy really is the difference maker in that situation.

Gary: Yeah, and that's just a lack-t's just poor communication- that's a lack of explanation. That's just, you know, it's just, "Okay well you need this this and this," and then she says "Well okay I need it, let me get it" and then the... Or the other way, but the spouse says "Hey what is it that we're buying?" and they don't know. Then of course you call and say "Wait a minute"

Chris: They're like "I don't know but it's $800." They're like "no."

Gary: You don't know what you're buying for $800? You've got to know and you've got to know what you're paying for. To me that makes a lot of sense. Taking the time and making sure they understand, a little hand holding, the Cabernet Sauvignon, whatever it is, you know. But explaining that to them so that they understand it. It's not that hard, we just have to do it.

Chris: Yeah.

Gary: I don't know if you want me to share this, if we have enough time today to talk about my sale experience with my daughter?

Chris: Oh and the Honda?

Gary: Uh-hum (affirmative).

Chris: Oh yeah, that's fun.

Gary: So, not to make a long story...

Chris: Not fun in like "fun." Fun in how disappointing our industry is.

Gary: Yeah, I mean it was disappointing but it goes, what made me think of it was talking about that fear. And so, my daughter wants to buy a new car. She's--

Chris: Your daughter wants you to buy her a new car.

Gary: My daughter wants me to buy her a new car. Let's get straight. She's got an old car and it's about done, and she driving—

Chris: Most of the time she's driving your car.

Gary: Yeah, she's been in my car too much, but she's driving from northern California to southern California a lot so she needs a new car. So we went out looking for cars. I want her to kind of live the experience of finding a car and driving a car and dealing with the staff there and understanding the whole experience. I'm kind of playing back a little bit and letting her take the lead role on it, but she's terrified. Like terrified. Like "I don't know what to say. I don't know what to do. Do I drive the car? Does the guy get in it?" She was just terrified of the whole experience and it was a real eye opener for me because that's how people start. Where are they going to buy a car? This will be my daughter's car, she'll buy another car maybe in 10 years, so she's going to have this one experience and if we don't do it right then what's her feeling? Like what's the frame, what's her perception going forward? Anyway, so we end up at this Honda store. There's a whole bunch of sales guys standing outside. It's real intimidating 'cause they're huddled up as a group so we don't want to approach them. It just doesn't feel right. Fortunately a guy walks up to us and finally says "What can I do for you today?" We say "Well, we're here to look at some Civics" and he says okay and walks us down the line. He goes "Here's our Civics" and just stood there and looked at us. I'm like well, "Options? Can you tell me the packages, like point me in the right direction?" We get into a few cars, look at a few cars, and she says "Okay I like this one." I say "Great, let's take it for a test drive."

Chris: Which color was it?

Gary: It was white.

Chris: Heated seats?

Gary: Yup, heated seats.

Chris: The full thing, right?

Gary: Back up camera.

Chris: You've raised a princess.

Gary: Side view camera, yeah.

Chris: You've raised a princess.

Gary: I raised a princess.

Chris: It's going to be expensive for you.

Gary: Uh-hum (affirmative), yeah. The wedding is what I'm really worried about. The car thing is probably inexpensive in comparison to what the wedding's going to be.

Chris: Oh wow.

Gary: I'm more worried about the wedding. But, anyway we get a car, we drive it, she likes it, and we sit down at the desk with the desk manager and he looks at us and he says "Hey, you know I need to sell a car today, so what are we doing?" "Hey, I need to sell a car today, so what are we doing?" And my daughter was like "What are we doing? I don't know. I just want to look at cars." She just was freaking out.

Chris: You lost me at hello.

Gary: We went to another store and drove another car. It was a Hyundai, I think, and she was just kind of comparing the cars, and in that store they gave her a credit app. They're like "Here, fill this out, sign here, who do you want the car registered to?" They did the hard--

Chris: They just presume the close.

Gary: The hard punch you in the face close. "What's there to think about? Let's do this." She just doesn't want anything to do with the whole thing and it's just, for me, it's sad because I grew up in this business and it's given a lot back to me and...

Chris: It's so douche.

Gary: It's... yeah, I just expect more. I wish for more. I want my daughter to want to go and patronize those establishments, you know?

Chris: Yeah, meanwhile you go to a Tesla dealership, and everyone wants to hide from the idea of it, and they don't want to talk about it. But we're not going to be able to be douche for that much longer. People aren't going to stand for it. It's the same thing with my girlfriend's car. She's buried in this Nissan. Buried. What's even funnier is her cousin was the finance manager, and she's buried in this thing. She's been paying on it, I think, for four years and she's still owes $13,000 on a $12,000 car. It's crazy. And what about Lucas' experience buying the Jeep down here?

Gary: Yeah.

Chris: Downtown. Oh man I wish we could put Lucas on the microphone. He learned a new term he didn't know. Lucas, for everybody listening, is from England, and so there's still, (he's lived here for awhile), but there's still things that are new to him and so he learned a new term during his car buying experience. Bait and switch. His experience might as well have been, they threw the keys on the roof.

Gary: Right.

Chris: That basically was his experience, and he's so sweet and nice. I was like, the whole time, "Why didn't you leave?" He was like "Well the car was there and they had it all cleaned and detailed and I wanted it." I'm like "Yeah but it's $3,500." He drove away in the car, but he didn't feel good about it.

Gary: My daughter said "Dad I really want the car, but we're not buying it there." That's what she said. "We'll drive somewhere." I was kind of proud of her at that moment. Like "Yeah you got to demand more for yourself." For sure.

Chris: Yeah, we really have to as an industry, we have to connect with people. We have to have more empathy and we have to care. We have to play the long game. We can't play the short game of just shredding everybody. Just taking their skin right off.

Gary: Yeah, it just doesn't work anymore.

Chris: You're killing the lamb. You've gotta shear them, right. Is it lamb or sheep that you shear?

Gary: Sheep.

Chris: Sheep. You're killing the sheep. Gotta get my animals right, you're killing the donkey.

Gary: You can shear the sheep many times but...

Chris: You can shear the donkey--

Gary: You can only skin it once.

Chris: So funny. I think a lot of advisors lose the customer at hello. With their greeting.

Gary: Yeah.

Chris: It's such a turn-off.

Gary: Yeah.

Chris: It's a turn-off when customers have to go in and find an advisor. You want to walk out, you want to put them at ease, you want to talk about everything except for the car.

Gary: Right.

Chris: The things that are important to people which for us it's family, Tequila, cigars, Seahawks, Cowboys. Talk about any of that, right?

Gary: Right.

Chris: I mean it's funny our trainer, if you talked about ... I've told you this story or maybe you've seen the video of it. You can't hear Jimmy but he says to me, "Oh, I hate it when they pet the dog." I go "What do you mean?" He goes "Your pet the dog thing. I got in an Uber the other day and the guy's trying to talk to me and "How are you?" and I'm just "Drive me to wherever he's going or whatever." I said "Well that's not really petting the dog." I said "What if the guy got in and said, "Oh, you know you like soccer. Best player of all time, Messi or Ronaldo?" He's like "Oh you know," 'cause that's the conversation, 'cause he says "Messi" and I think "Ronaldo." Lucas is shaking his head no, but Ronaldo, by far and away, has the stats and he's way better looking.

Lucas: "Way better looking? Messi looks like me. I mean, don't looks count for anything in soccer?"

Chris: Well at least he's acknowledging soccer 'cause he usually calls it football.

Gary: Throw a name out, Lucas.

Lucas: What's that?

Gary: Throw a name out, who's the best one?

Lucas: Messi.

Gary: Messi, oh okay.

Chris: Ronaldo. But the point is he'd talk about that all day. That's petting the dog. The things that people want to talk about, right? You talk about the Cowboys, or maybe--

Gary: Yeah, plus or minus. It's been a rough couple of years.

Chris: We can talk about the Seahawks.

Gary: Yeah, Seahawks.

Chris: We can talk about them for a long time. So, it's really, you lose customers at hello, that first impression. I was pissed when that girl said "You know, what's your budget?" And she's just like, she was the police, like she was trying to price us before we even got to value. It wasn't about how great the chairs were, how comfortable, or how they never break, or they'll fix your back or--

Gary: Right.

Chris: You know, they have a button you hit and a cocktail pops out and it comes with dancing girls, and ... No it was, "Can you afford it?"

Gary: Yeah.

Chris: "We want to prequalify you."

Gary: "Hey, you guys are in the right place 'cause we have the best chairs. So have a seat."

Chris: "Have you heard about how great our chairs are?"

Gary: Yeah.

Chris: "That's probably why you're here."

Gary: Right, exactly.

Chris: Because...

Gary: "Oh you walk by everyday, you see them, you know. That's why you're here."

Chris: "Come on, come sit."

Gary: Right.

Chris: But, "Let me get your blood." You know if they would have tested your cholesterol they wouldn't have sold us the right chair.

Gary: Right, "You can't sit in this chair."

Chris: Yeah, they're just playing god, and it's so easy for people to play god, but it's so boring for customers to have somebody do that to them.

Gary: I don't know. I want to enjoy the experience. If you're going to spend money, I want to have fun. I want it to be light. I don't know I just ... everybody takes it too seriously and they're all upset and this lady's profiling, it's just too much.

Chris: It's nuts.

Gary: I don't know. Life's too short and we interact with each other so often nowadays, especially. It's like we got to make it light, make it fun.

Chris: Or we got to start dressing up more when we go places.

Gary: Yeah.

Chris: Maybe we just look like hobos.

Gary: Yeah, I don't know.

Chris: I don't think so. Okay, so in everyone of these we try to do a book report.

Gary: Yes.

Chris: And your idea for this one, which I think is great, was to do *The Obstacle Is The Way*. I'll kind of tell you that my understanding of this book and then we'll talk about your favorite story in there.

Gary: Okay.

Chris: There's something called Stoicism. People who follow that religion are Stoics. Marcus Aurelius and Seneca were two of the main ones. So Seneca's written a lot of stuff that you can get on it, and some of it is really good and some of it is impossible to understand.

Gary: Yeah.

Chris: But the idea of Stoicism is that you don't overreact to things and that the obstacle in most situations becomes the way. I'll kind of read you the quote the he devised this, and actually I think in his he doesn't say it is the way, he says it is the path." The obstacle is the path" is what he says. But here's his quote, and this is just a great way to understand how to turn obstacles into opportunity more than anything else. It's *The Obstacle is the Way, The Timeless Art of Turning Trials into Triumph* by Ryan Holiday. Mr. Holiday. So the quote here is: "Our actions may be impeded but there can be no impeding our intention or dispositions because we can accommodate and adapt. The mind adapts and converts to its own purposes the obstacle to our acting." So basically the way that I read that is that there can be obstacles, but what the obstacles can account for, is that we can adapt and change.

Gary: Right.

Chris: So we can go through it, we can go around it, we can figure out a way, but there's usually in every situation, five to ten ways to overcome it if you don't get emotionally involved. That's the biggest thing, is not to get emotionally involved to the point that you shut down or give up.

Gary: Right, yeah.

Chris: That's usually the difference between the really successful leaders or managers compared to the ones that give up and just kind of get by, right?

Gary: Yeah. They hit that first wall, and it may even be small and breakable, but they just stop. Just because their perception is they can't get past it. Can't do it. Can't be done.

Chris: Yeah, and then that quote concludes with: "The impediment to action advances action. What stands in the way becomes the way." So "The impediment to action advances action, what stands in the way becomes the way." And I know this from just about every obstacle in my life looking back, and it's easy to look back, that I was way too concerned in the moment. Because you're not going to die, that everything's going to be okay.

Gary: Right, yeah.

Chris: And a lot of times if you think, "Will I remember this in a year?" you won't. But it's such a big deal, we get wound so tight sometimes. I'm a big fan of Stoicism and Stoics and just managing to the middle and not overreacting. What was, there was a story in here about the rock that you really liked?

Gary: Yeah, my favorite passage in there, the one that really stuck with me the most, was the - you know I'm going to paraphrase and butcher it a little bit - but it was about a king who put a large boulder in front of his castle and saying block the main entrance. Underneath that boulder he put a pot of gold and put the boulder on top of it. So he would watch from the tower and just watch people over and over and over come up and maybe give the rock a push or maybe just see it and turn and go the other way. This went on and on and on, until finally a farmer came up and came against the rock and looked at it for a minute, kind of scratched his head and then walked away. Then came back with a giant tree branch and put a lever underneath it and popped the rock up and lo and behold there was this pot of gold underneath. There's a really favorite quote and everybody uses it. It's "When opportunity knocks, it's usually wearing overalls and looks like hard work."

Chris: Yeah, I love that quote.

Gary: It's one of my favorites. I use it on my kids all the time. They hate it, but it really makes sense. I think this book and that story really lends itself to that statement because it's true. You walk up to something, "Ah it's going to be too much work, I don't know how I'm going to move this thing." And if you really stopped and reframed and really changed your perception of looking at it and saying, "I probably could move this but I need a bigger lever." Right? Like "I need help. I need something to help me." And then in that you find opportunity there. You find the gold or the whatever it is you're trying to achieve or accomplish. It seems like a pretty simple metaphor.

Chris: Yeah, and it's 100% mindset. It's what you want it to be. 'Cause you can make it into a problem or you can make into a solution. It's completely up to you.

Gary: Yeah, I mean how many things in this world did we determine were impossible, right? You couldn't sail around the world, it was flat. You know it's round, and you can't go to the moon. I mean, it's just, you can't have a computer in every household. There are just so many things that we perceive.-you can't run a five minute mile- that we perceive is impossible that are possible now. For me, like at some point let's wake up and say "Man we've just gotta just change our perceptions and just go after it."

Chris: Yeah. You run a four minute mile don't you? Ten minute mile?

Gary: It was ten, yeah, ten minute mile. Which is actually really slow. Which is plodding along.

Chris: Which, oddly, was faster than me.

Gary: I think my brother-in-law runs like a six or something like that, six or six and a half.

Chris: Man, four would be fast. It's good. So, big fan of Ryan Holiday. His other book *Trust Me I'm Lying* was really good too. But that's about his time in American Apparel and marketing and how it's all fake. Marketing is fake.

Gary: Right.

Chris: But I mean he goes into details, it's really good. But I love this Stoicism, *Obstacle is the Way*. It's a little book. Easy.

Gary: Yeah.

Chris: Easy to read.

Gary: Yeah, that's the great thing too.

Chris: It's like a snack.

Gary: And you can pick it up and just read one of the passages, the chapters are short, and you usually pick something up.

Chris: Yeah, it's all relevant.

Gary: So if you're looking for a little motivation for the day or maybe you need to reframe yourself or rethink something, it's good to start by doing that, they'll help you.

Chris: And listen to this quote: "When a man knows he is to be hanged in the fortnight, it concentrates his mind wonderfully." So I guess I'd quote: "if a guys going to get hung, it's over."

Gary: Right, you know the freight train's coming, so...

Chris: Yeah, it's great. Good book. So what we've learned today is how to raise a princess and buy her a new car, right?

Gary: Yeah, yeah.

Chris: How not to sell office furniture?

Gary: Or anything for that matter.

Chris: Prequalify.

Gary: How not to sell anything.

Chris: How service advisors lost customers at hello. We learned about snackification.

Gary: Snackification?

Chris: Food motivated bulldogs. And we're changing drives and lives. That's going to be our new thing. We should have tee-shirts. Changing drives and lives.

Gary: Everyday.

Chris: And the book *The Obstacle Is The Way*, and getting everybody excited about the Top Dog event and the $50,000 challenge.

Gary: Yeah, so look out, watch your inboxes. We're going to start sending some emails out. Talking about what's going to happen and teasing it a little bit. So yeah, super excited.

Chris: Thanks everybody. Thanks for listening. We'll see you real soon.

Gary: See you.

Episode #10: Top Dog Service Manager Challenge Finalists, Awards And Winner

Chris: Welcome to Service Drive Revolution Podcast with your host Chris "the Bulldog" Collins and Gary, "the G-man". Hey everybody. Welcome to Service Drive Revolution. Today, we have a great podcast for you with the finalist for the $50,000 service manager challenge and I'm glad to announce that Gary made it.

Gary: I survived, is that what you're saying?

Chris: You lived.

Gary: I made it. One more week of life I have left in me.

Chris: Did you guys hear when we read his cholesterol last week? Yeah, it's not good.

Gary: 300 or...?

Chris: He's on 400 at a time.

Gary: 264. Is anybody over 264 in this room?

Chris: No.

Gary: I wouldn't...

Chris: Of course not.

Gary: I knew it, I knew I'd win that one.

Chris: That's a bad thing to win bro.

Gary: I'm in first place.

Chris:	He's so proud. But he did bench what, 200 this morning, or what was it?
Gary:	205 baby.
Chris:	205. 205; he's strong.
Gary:	Yeah, feel good. I don't know, I feel great.
Chris:	Wow
Gary:	So Dr. Lau...
Chris:	Don't look at your blood.
Gary:	We did see Dr. Lau recently at a party, walked in and he didn't even recognize me. He walked right past me, he walked up--
Chris:	Yeah.
Gary:	He walked up to you, Chris, and then started hugging him and that was it. He didn't...And then I said, "Hey, Dr. Lau." And he goes, "Gary?" And I go, "Yeah." And then he goes, "Oh my god you look good." And I must. "That's what I've been telling you, I look good." I don't know what my blood test says...
Chris:	He's looking at your blood test.
Gary:	I'm not.
Chris:	He thinks you're a 300 pound...
Gary:	I'm not 300--
Chris:	So...

Gary: Pounds man, that's my promise.

Chris: It was funny you guys. We're at this big party, at this big house, and I don't know, there's like a thousand people there and all of the sudden the power goes out. And like it's a hundred degrees and it starts getting hotter and hotter in the house and people don't know what to do. And people are coming in like "We're looking, we're trying" and they would come back and they would come in. And then Gary disappeared for ten minutes, power comes on and he comes back. Then you see we're all just staring at the panel?

Gary: Yeah they were at the circuit panel that was in the garage with all the breakers and they didn't check the main. And I asked them, "Check the main?" "Oh no we looked at it, we looked at it." I'm all "No, its the main, check the main." They didn't. They didn't.

Chris: So I squeeze him...

Gary: I walked outside and went ...

Chris: The conclusion is that Millennial's don't work on stuff. So we're asking them like, "Do you know how to replace a fan belt? Or...?" Nothing.

Gary: No.

Chris: Like they don't work on--

Gary: No.

Chris: That younger generation isn't getting their hands dirty.

Gary: No.

Chris: Right?

Gary:	Yeah and I mean they had no, they literally had no idea. They were calling an electrician!
Chris:	Yeah.
Gary:	To flip a breaker.
Chris:	It would've taken hours.
Gary:	Yeah.
Chris:	It was so funny.
Gary:	Yeah there's this, you know, a half a million-dollar party going on and they don't have any power, the music's gone, and they're gonna call an electrician 'cause nobody knows where the main breaker is on the side of the house. It was hilarious.
Chris:	Gary's like "I'll replace a wire harness, lets go." "What's it pay?"
Gary:	"Car need breaks? Let's do that too while we're here."
Chris:	22 hours. So, I'm really proud of you guys in reading your...couple of them honestly I got choked up with your summaries that you submitted, your essays. And I want to give you guys some numbers, some stats really quick to spark this conversation. So everybody that entered the $50,000 challenge: on average they were up 9.2 points in CSI, their net to gross was up 13.7%, and their ELR was up $23.30. The six that are the finalists, your CSI was up an average of 19.24%, your net to gross was up an average of 17.1% and your effective labor rate was up 22.54. Its pretty impressive!
Gary:	Nice job!
Chris:	There's a groove...

Gary: Good job.

Chris: And I mean, in that average, some guys were up you know, huge numbers in each one of those categories, but kind of the key is to be up on you know on everything. But it's amazing, amazing results. So, lets start kind of with you, Adam, and talk a little bit about your journey as, I know in here you talk in your essay you talk about you're a technician and then...

Adam   Correct.

Chris: How did it happen? You were on our list of people to be a potential manager?

Adam   Yeah, right.

Chris: There was a change, right?

Adam   Mm-hmm (affirmative)

Chris: We moved somebody to parts.

Adam   Ken, yeah.

Chris: We moved him to the parts.

Adam   Ken moved to parts and then I think that the idea was for Eric to be able to just handle it by himself. That was four, five months and you know, just I guess it wasn't working, right?

Chris: And that's when--

Adam   Went back workin' on cars and you come up--

Chris: And you're--

Adam   To be a manager--

Chris:	Studying to be. The whole thing was everybody that you had asked about Adam, like we would say like "Well Adam would be great, you know, he'd be a great manager." And he's also, there's that BMW mini, he was a mini technician but the best. He'd just gone on a trip to like the Philippines for being-
Adam	Thailand, yeah
Chris:	For...How do you win that trip?
Adam	I was one of the top eight tech's in the country.
Chris:	But how do they determine that you're-I always hear that how you-
Adam	There's a bunch of tests and then...
Chris:	Like they put a car with a bunch of tricks and then you gotta fix it?
Adam	Well they start out doing that. I mean I was in that competition for ten years so I did the beginning two years of it was that. You would do dumped cars and you would fix 'em and then you'd win. So...
Chris:	And you were studying to be an actuary?
Adam	Correct, yeah.
Chris:	And so everybody would say- the President of the company would say: "Well, he won't do it because he's gonna be an actuary." And I'm like, "What's that?" First, so I think the first thing I asked you when I called you in is "Why do you want to do that?" And then you got all excited and you were explaining it to me and then I was like, "Oh man, he does want to be an actuary. I don't know..."
Gary:	Hey when I heard that I thought, "That does not fit, there's no way." I can't imagine you just sitting like

staring at a screen for--

Adam   You had met me before you found that out.

Gary: Oh yeah, I had known you for a little while before somebody said that.

Adam   Well that's what I thought would be the winning combination, where I got a guy that's good with numbers and then I, you know, some personality at the same time and then...

Gary: They don't need personality in that field.

Chris: I told you.

Gary: They don't want it.

Adam   They do.

Chris: I told you that was in-

Gary: -I knew you were gonna lead the actuaries.

Chris: I was in Nashville.

Gary: That's what I thought.

Chris: And there was an actuary convention right?

Gary: Right, yeah you told me that.

Chris: I told you that? And they don't have personalities.

Gary: Well the guys that lead a bunch of people always have personality so I figured I could get in there and--

Chris: Its very rain-man like.

Gary: Yeah I don't know that the lead accountants got the...that's the same.

Adam   But if he did wouldn't he revolutionize this world? That's what I thought.

Chris: But yeah, I'm glad you didn't. Long story short, you didn't.

Adam   Right.

Chris: You're not studying?

Adam   Correct. Yeah I did not do that.

Chris: For actuary anymore right?

Adam   No, no I...

Chris: We were--

Adam   Put that aside.

Chris: Going to ruin somebody else's life with the car business.

Adam   You've ruined several people's businesses.

Chris: Yeah.

Adam   By stealing me away.

Chris: So the part of your story that for the podcast, that I think is really interesting, and really is a tribute to how much this is mental, is that you were a tech.

Adam   Right.

Chris: You went from a tech to a manager?

Adam   Right.

Chris: Nothing in between?

Adam   Correct, yeah, no services.

Chris: And there was...

Adam   Advisors.

Chris: And the advisors...?

Adam   Right.

Chris: Tried to tell you that you didn't know what you were doing.

Adam   Right.

Chris: Because you've never written service?

Adam   Right, right.

Chris: All that right?

Adam   Yeah. They tried to game me a little bit.

Chris: But it's all the same, it's taking care of customers, following a system.

Adam   Yeah, I mean there was a big learning curve initially. I, you know, didn't know anything but at all, so but, anytime I undertake something I'm gonna push to figure out whatever it is I don't know and I'll go figure that out. So, if I didn't know something and somebody was telling me something, I'd say, "Okay, well tell me about that." And I get a chance to learn whatever it is and then I know, okay. And how much time do you have to spend in the drive looking at what's going on and hearing people talk to customers and then talkin' to them yourself after you know they got blown up, you know, after they blow up the advisor and you gotta handle 'em? I mean at some point you figure it all out. You know? So, for me that part of the journey was...it was the dedication I had to put into trying to figure out the new position and then determining who I wanted to be as far as a manager, you know? And if I'm going to lead people, I have to gain their respect, and you can't gain their respect through expert authority if you weren't an advisor before. No advisor's gonna respect you as an expert, as an advisor. So there's gotta be other ways. But if you know your stuff, if you're serious about what you do, you have a passion for what it is that you want to accomplish, you dream big and have a big vision and people buy into that. Then you're leading people even though you haven't done what they've done. You know, so for me that was kind of the push. That and-

Chris: -dream big?

Gary: Like long division in your head if I helped out?

Adam   No.

Chris: Or he tried to game...? I'm not trying to game - or have you heard that story with the missed opportunities report?

Gary: No.

Chris: Do you guys all know we have the missed opportunities report right? And like they were struggling in their numbers and I'm there and I'm like "Bro, its all about the missed opportunities." And he's like, "Well, I've been thinking about..." and I'm like "Oh shit, here we go, I've been thinking about it." So he was trying to build into the missed opportunities report some sort of element of chance or error.

Adam   No there's...

Chris: I don't know what.

Adam   A component for measuring the mechanical work that's also sold on the vehicle. Okay so you've got measurement of the missed opportunities when you look at maintenance and then also you look at what's been sold mechanically on the car. So because, and invariably I would get stuck in a conversation with the advisor who sold three-thousand dollars to a customer and decided to not say anything about all the maintenance, and he missed 100% of the maintenance which is maybe another $2,000 and he's like "What are you talking about? I sold three thousand dollars of stuff to this guy." And so on one hand you have to say, "Okay, yeah, good job, but you forgot all this other stuff." So what I wanted to do, and your thinking I'm gaming the system, but really it was a tool for me. I put that into the report to show a measurement of how much actual mechanical work they sold so I could take that off the table for 'em. Like, "Hey Lip, look-great job-but look at all this other stuff you missed." You know so, I'd beat them to the punch of using that as an excuse. And that's the best missed opportunities report we've got by the way. Bro that's a great spreadsheet.

Chris: I don't think I've ever seen it.

Adam   I tried to use it, it made my head hurt. I couldn't and I'm an excel guy.

Chris: Bro I noticed- I noticed- lets get it out of the way.

Adam   Okay.

Chris: I'm not as smart as you.

Adam	Its not about that.
Chris:	They came in, they bought it, they didn't.
Adam	Yeah, right.
Chris:	That's it, I don't know.
Adam	Well I still got you just doing hatch-marks. I'm like all right.
Chris:	Yeah, like if we could do with a rock on a string still, well that would work. Its just I'm very visual.
Adam	I just think in spreadsheets so I had to--
Chris:	Well yeah, you're smarter.
Adam	Pretend a way that made sense to me and I could use it as a tool to leverage performance. All right, that's basically what I did with that. So, its a good time.
Chris:	Before we, so before closing, Adam, can you hear me? Before we move on, real quick, can you just say where you're from?
Adam	I'm from Chicago. Right.
Chris:	I don't think we should say the stores.
Adam	The stores?
Chris:	No.
Adam	What about how long?
Chris:	Call him.
Adam	How long have you been with...?

Gary:	Chris?
Chris:	How long have you been with this management?
Adam	So, we are, (our whole store), we've got three stores, and the three stores have been with Chris for four years. So I was a tech for the first like nine months of that basically.
Chris:	Okay.
Adam	So and then I moved over to management spot.
Chris:	There you go.
Adam	Maybe less than that actually.
Chris:	Yeah, and Adam definitely has embraced the instant inspection moral too. You're a ninja with that.
Adam	Yeah.
Chris:	Watch out.
Adam	The poster child...
Chris:	Yeah. Okay.
Adam	All right. Jeff.
Chris:	Jeff Spencer?
Jeff:	Hello.
Chris:	I'm looking at a picture right now of your--
Adam	Keep him posted.

Chris:	Holdin' up the...?
Adam	Posted.
Chris:	Right. One of your advisors with nerf guns.
Adam	I know. I sent them a text after that, I love that.
Chris:	Yeah.
Gary:	Yeah
Adam	I give high respect for the giant.
Jeff:	Every time I come out here there's a new Nerf gun and then I go home and buy it.
Chris:	Jeff Spencer what do you say we close today and go huntin'? Kill some Deer.
Adam	I'm always looking for new Nerf guns.
Chris:	So tell us just a little about your initial reaction to the Chris thing and then kind of the-
Jeff:	Well, for me it made sense immediately. You know you always hear the other service training that's out there, you know, been through some of it and its just, I just couldn't buy into it. And I saw a couple youtube videos and I'm like "That is what's up." You know, its the customer experience and--
Chris:	Making friends.
Jeff:	Exactly, making friends, the whole deal. After that, you know, it was probably about a year before I could finally convince the GM to get any, some training. Because I'd been service manager probably about, oh six years, and I got to go to a service management one in 2010 so that's it, that's all I had.

Chris: Was that like any DA or...?

Jeff: It was NCM.

Chris: NCM?

Jeff: Yup - and everybody else, you know, in my group got to go to even the second part of it, but I just got to go to one so and that was it. So, but yeah, I really liked the program and you know, its so easy.

Chris: Any obstacles? Like when you went back were your advisors like, "you're crazy."?

Jeff: You know what? You know its... you don't eat the elephant all at once, you know? One bite at a time; so you just kind of get the maintenance menu's set up. You know, get your... everything in place and then you just slowly introduce new things, and like he says its about 90 days and then you're good. And they start seeing the results, they love the games, you know, you make it fun. You know, and then the accountability always sneaks up and gets 'em and they don't even know it. So...

Chris: That's the trick.

Jeff: Its pretty awesome.

Chris: What's a favorite game there?

Jeff: Well, we do a little pie in the face.

Chris: Oh yeah.

Jeff: Yeah, yeah and-

Chris: -like the real-...like Mario did?

Adam	God, no!
Jeff:	No, the you know... the little hand that throws whipped cream in your face?
Chris:	Yeah.
Jeff:	And if they sell three things on one ticket, I'll take the pie. Oh they love it, its awesome. So, good times.
Chris:	Yeah whenever you're having a slow day, if you throw yourself in front of a Nerf gun or something. Though usually-
Jeff:	Yeah.
Chris:	They want to shoot you mad. They want to.
Gary:	And Jeff, you've been in the program, I was looking at your accounts, five months, is that right? Does that sound right?
Jeff:	We signed up in April, maybe?
Gary:	Yeah it was March or April, something like that, yeah.
Jeff:	Well March, right, and then April boot camp.
Gary:	That, mm-hmm (affirmative).
Jeff:	So again we got rock and rolling right away, just embraced the whole deal.
Gary:	Mm-hmm (affirmative).
Jeff:	And it's awesome-three record months.
Gary:	Wow.

Jeff: Immediately.

Gary: Yeah I was looking at those months, like you made a massive turn around fast. It was good.

Jeff: Yeah it was awesome, yeah. It's unbelievable.

Gary: Yeah, you're helping with sales now, right?

Jeff: Right, yeah. So, the sales department is the weak link and I was always kind of, you know, profitable. But now that we're just killing it, I've actually helped the sales managers interview sales associates and trying to get the sales department turn around and big picture guy. You know, I know the more they sell, you know the more opportunity I have in back.

Gary: Yeah, they're building you new customers right?

Jeff: Right.

Gary: All the time, yeah. The more cars they sell the better off we are.

Jeff: Yup.

Gary: For sure, cool. Thanks, nice job Jeff.

Chris: Now Jeff, JD, and I hit it off right away cause of our beards. So we had that in common and then didn't I send you beard oil?

Jeff: You did.

Chris: And then he went and got he got a trim from Homer actually yesterday.

Jeff: Yeah I was happy to use him.

Chris:	So, whenever he comes in for a meeting or something, he goes to Homer.
Gary:	You get him today?
Jeff:	Yesterday.
Gary:	Yesterday? Okay.
Jeff:	He squeezed me when I landed-so I had to represent-so.
Chris:	Yeah, when we met Homer he was just making beard oil in his kitchen and now he's got like an empire.
Jeff:	Yeah, now he's got beard box's, and beard combs, and-
Chris:	-just the whole thing. We should've started the beard thing.
Gary:	Yeah.
Chris:	Right?
Jeff:	Always behind the eight ball sometimes.
Chris:	Yeah. No but so tell us a little bit JD..., I mean we clicked right away.
Jeff:	Right.
Chris:	And we were speaking the same language right away and a lot of the stuff that-
Jeff:	-yeah it was...
Chris:	'cause...
Jeff:	I mean, I met you last year. You know, I've known Chris and the organization since probably when...?

September of last year? And it was that "ah-ha" moment finally that somebody that looked outside the box or you know the law of the...that had no lid. You know, I was always the outsider with most of my organizations cause I had this very gung-ho approach to taking care of things, and I was sitting there in the meeting listening to Chris. I'm like, I look at his petty plans and look at this, I said: "Oh my God!" Kind of like the you-fell-in-love type of moment. It's like you know, there's somebody else that spoke your language and so I mean, it wasn't even before I left Portland that we were gonna try changing alignment prices. And you know I had always had a good, better, best, program about alignments and I've always wanted to implement and finally at the meeting we got it taken care of. And its just...it was like wildfire down there.

Chris: You were doing lifetime alignments right?

Jeff: I'm doing, yeah, one year, three year, and lifetime alignments.

Chris: Tell us how that works.

Jeff: The standard, you know, alignment was $139-is $139, and it's good for 12 months, 12 -15,000 miles.

Chris: So you warranteed an alignment?

Jeff: Mm-hmm (affirmative)

Chris: **Awesome.**

Jeff: Then there's: if its the alignment your car is potholed or damaged within that 12 months, they can come back and get a reduced price for $89.95. And then we offer a three year alignment which will take care of all the leased (primarily most of the leased) vehicles and that runs $169.95, same type of parameters. And then we have a lifetime alignment which is good for as long as you own the vehicle for $199.95. Its just a gross monster.

Chris: And you're selling them like crazy, right?

Jeff: Yeah, well the best month we had was just shy of 200.

Chris: Wow, nice.

Jeff: It was good.

Chris: Any obstacles?

Jeff: You know, the biggest thing that I had I learned, you know, and being with the coaching group and working with you guys, is that I've actually had to start to read. Listening to books has come a long way but what I've learned is that I had to become, you know, the leader that I want to be to be able to lead my team. And, there's that natural growth, that painful growth that comes along with wanting to be a better leader and fail, and make those mistakes. And you know I'm not sure if the greatest obstacle was getting out of my own way and me growing or having to almost love the team enough to treat 'em like your kids, and listen to 'em and deflect coming back and just growing with them. But I mean, I'll sit here and say it, the team that's down there in Corpus Christi right now, they're the results and I couldn't have been happier to lead that team down there.

Chris: Yeah and I think most of the time you're, you know, same thing always right?

Jeff: Mm-hmm (affirmative)

Chris: It's us.

Jeff: Mm-hmm (affirmative)

Chris: What are some good books that you read?

Jeff: Actually I see the book right over there on the windowsill, I just got done listening to that: *Ego is the Enemy,* the new Ryan Holiday book.

Chris: Good?

Jeff: Oh its phenomenal.

Chris: Still a cysim again?

Jeff: Yeah, but he actually goes a little deeper into it. He still has a little bit of a Stoic base to it but he actually goes into how, you know, good leadership. There has to be a humility that goes along with leadership. But I was talking to Gary on Monday about *Pitch Anything*, the Oren Klaff book.

Chris: Oh yeah.

Jeff: About frames. That to me was... the webcast you guys had a month or so ago but listening to that book really made it, you know, a good impact. But the first one of course with Jocko, *Extreme Ownership,* was one that you're really tugging in. You know, the really instrumental chapter for me was when he swapped both captains-

Chris: Oh yeah-

Jeff: Different buds-

Chris: Yeah that's a great chapter.

Jeff: And it really showed that it's not the team but it's the leader on the team.

Chris: Yeah.

Jeff: That can motivate the people, and when I heard that it really kind of just ignited that fire that's like:" No, you have to be the best you can be." Not just for yourself, but for your team, because you have people and then, you know, just do a lot of podcasts. You know, not to keep going on but when Rogan had Jocko on last year in December and he was talking about how can you really compare business to *The Ballad of Grimaldi* - and Jocko looked at him and says, "Have you ever had a firing, buddy?" He says, "You just terminated that person's career, you just ended that guys way of earning a life for himself and his family." And of course, you know, Rogan jokes back and says, "Well that's why I'm not a leader." But you know that's what we have to look at as leaders and as managers, that's the level of accountability that we have. We're in the trenches everyday.

Chris: You mention the-

Jeff: Good intent.

Chris: -Law of the Lid. Did you read Maxwell's book *The 21 Irrefutable Laws of Leadership*?

Jeff: I did.

Gary: So where did you find yourself bumping up against your lid? Do you know where that's at?

Jeff: For me, I can dream big, I can see it. But it's the actual implementation and actually buying in that can be done. And a lot of it's just, you know, my own excuses and that's where my lid was. Chris, you know, like I said in my story, I mean he asked me what I wanted after just meeting me and he had that look. You know I said, "That's bullshit, whatever you want you can get, you don't stop." And in a lot of ways my lid was me. You know, I could think it, I could see it, I could dream it, I could want it, but its the actual... it's the rationalization that gets into the day to day of life that you know, "Oh well this is gonna happen, or this is gonna happen..." instead of just saying "Just go after and go get it".

Adam   Yeah.

Jeff: It happens to all of us.

Gary: Yeah. No, that's my favorite thing in being close to Chris for all these years is that's the one thing I saw 20 years ago, you know, when we got together and I said "The guy's got no lid." Like that was one of the first books I bought when I became a manager was *The 21 Irrefutable Laws.*

Jeff: Right.

Gary: To this day it's one of my favorites and then Chris comes along with no lid and I'm like, "Oh my god, what am I thinking?" Like, I have to do something about it and, you know, everyday we get challenged but it's interesting too when you become aware of it, to see where you bump up against it. You know? Or you say "Wow that's not possible, that's really hard and I can't do that." Its interesting to be aware of that.

Chris: What's the most recent thing that I've challenged you with? With the lid, that drove you crazy?

Gary: The 200,000 was a tough lid to get through.

Chris: You busted right through that.

Gary: Yeah, but that would mean, you know it was tough, that one.

Chris: You didn't even do 200, wasn't it like two...what was the number?

Gary: First one was 209, and then it was like 275.

Chris:	Yeah.
Gary:	So we just... three was easy. He taunted me with the little thing that I wanted, put it up on a shelf and "Yeah, there's the watch." Yeah, so it took me a minute to get there but in the end it helps you grow, helps you move, its good to have somebody challenge you like that.
Jeff:	Oh it does and I think you know, almost into a new Gary Vaynerchuck book, *Ask Gary Vee* and there's a big chapter about fear.
Gary:	Mm-hmm (affirmative)
Jeff:	And I think a lot of times that our lid is fear. It's the unknown on the other side of that we actually get it, but I will say that you know you hear a lot of these people, that have these goals that want to obtain a certain, you know, and get an IPO or they want to get this. You know they want to sell their company and you want to obtain a certain goal and you know, "Oh we had a big goal for March of this year and we hit it." And it was the most exciting but also the most defeated time because you got to the goal and you know that it was just the first step on the path to keep going. There's really never that pinnacle, never that top, you just gotta keep going with it.
Gary:	Yeah its a journey not a destination. Right and what-
Chris:	I like what Jocko says: "I'm gonna just roll a rock back down that hill."
Gary:	Yeah, he says he like to-it was in one of his podcasts right? He likes to...somebody asked him like, what happens? He looks to push the rocks is what he says, "I want to push the rock."-
Chris:	I want to push the rock.

Gary:	And he says "well what happens when you get the rock to the top of the hill?" And he goes, "well I don't know, I'll just roll it back down and start over." 'cause for him it's not the top that's the goal, it's the journey that he went beyond. Thanks Jenny. Rocky?
Rocky Barnes:	Hello.
Gary:	Are you a Dallas Cowboys fan?
Rocky:	Yup.
Chris:	Yeah.
Jeff:	You and everyone.
Chris:	My Seahawks lost last night.
Jeff:	Did they?
Chris:	I mean, I know its a pretty season but still, come on. There's a lot of Dallas in this room.
Gary:	Yeah they sold out the coliseums. Dallas Cowboys came out here to play their new something... I don't know, maybe a new football team in L.A. I don't know who they are, they mean nothing, but yeah, they sold out.
Chris:	They sold it out.
Gary:	They sold it out, yeah.
Chris:	So I know-
Gary:	'Cause the boys came to town.
Chris:	I know Rocky, you've done an amazing job and had a huge turn around in numbers but you really haven't...

there hasn't been much. It was too rough, right? You were just game like "I'll try it."

Rocky Barnes: Oh yeah. It was just smooth sailing all the way...

Chris: No.

Rocky Barnes: Not really.

Chris: I was like "You worked really hard."

Rocky Barnes: Yeah, so it's like a lot of hard work.

Chris: You didn't.

Rocky Barnes: A lot of preparation.

Chris: It doesn't seem like you sabotaged yourself, you just went to work.

Rocky Barnes: That's what it took, yeah, just a lot of work. We launched in April but it took too much to get ready to launch and that was probably the hardest two months. Not only just physical work but the psychological part of it, all the kickbacks felt different, the big change that you had to hold everybody together for as far as anybody from the advisors, the technicians... Everybody said "Oh well all that's too good to be true." And that's kind of what had to go around and finally you know, we launched and then it even got harder, or more hectic.

Chris: Yeah the speed and the momentum picks up right?

Rocky Barnes: Yes.

Chris: So what are a couple things for any manager listening

	to this that you could give 'em tips that, you know, would inspire them or help 'em to increasing their CSI and increasing your sales?
Rocky Barnes:	Well it's just this process is, there's some basic stuff but then there's new stuff as far as getting that stuff going. It's your processes and accountability. The accountability is the main thing. We have the tools now to hold them accountable and it holds us accountable too.
Chris:	Yeah, its funny that in some scenarios we have the new stuff but in most scenarios it's paper.
Rocky Barnes:	Right.
Chris:	Like it's not digital, it's not sexy, it's just paper.
Rocky Barnes:	Well...
Chris:	If you're gonna do it.
Rocky Barnes:	The new stuff, the gameification, the getting the advisors excited, that's where it pushes you up. And the process shows it's word the focus to get the results that we're looking for.
Chris:	Yeah, exactly.
Gary:	How long did it take you to get to buy in and like to believe? Did you start out like "Yeah we can do this." Or were you like "Eh I don't know."?
Rocky Barnes:	Well, I was in a 20 group meeting for the first time when Chris was doing the meeting. A lot of good stuff there. I automatically started picking up on some of it and took it back to the store and started talking about bringing the CCI crew pin into the store. And the GM and I sat down, we have a good working relationship,

and he said, "You really want to do this?" I said, "I always want to know where my store could go." November, I'll be there nine years and we've grown every year pretty solid, just you know, a little bit at a time, but we know there's a lot more that we were not capturing. And we don't know what the lid is as you would call it. So, we talked about it and said "You know what? We'll meet and be totally exposed to everybody at our company" 'cause you know - wind comes in. So but from the start I was anxious, but once we signed up for it I says, "What have we done?" But then actually, kind of started looking at everything and went "Okay I agree with you, this is when we'll struggle." The different areas 'cause that's- I know that's my weakness- but I'm gonna do it. I said, "Don't think I'm not balling in but you gonna' have to push me on this." So... but that was a whole the thing about having a consultant, seemed to help us get it all launched and that's what's-

Gary: I know I hate the word consultant 'cause in our industry its like, I experienced things when I worked at a dealership, that the guy comes in and he makes everybody feel stupid and leaves. You know, like he didn't really teach me anything, he just made me feel stupid.

Rocky Barnes: Well that's no - that's what I said before. That all the consultants that I've dealt with before actually couldn't do it in-

Gary: Yeah.

Rocky Barnes: Get the job done.

Gary: Yeah that's the joke that you know what a consultant is? Its a guy in between jobs.

Rocky Barnes: Yeah, yeah but not the case here. Not in any shape, form, or fashion.

Chris:	Yeah, I wish we could think of another word for 'em but I mean it's--
Gary:	Just because of the stigmatism in our industry.
Rocky Barnes:	Yeah it's just like a four letter word now. It's just been beat up too many times.
Gary:	Yeah.
Rocky Barnes:	Well, that was like, for the kickback too, 'cause everybody comes in promising you'll... then promising you'll... Everybody's, well made more money, we're gonna take better care of our customers, all this and says the consultants gone, it all goes back to normal. But not with this process. So yeah.
Chris:	No and its a collaboration too. Like you're contributing to the overall success of everybody else because what we're doing is taking what's working and spreading it to everybody in the group.
Rocky Barnes:	Absolutely.
Chris:	Which makes us look smarter than we are. Really, the industry needs somebody to be a conduit to how can we get better.
Rocky Barnes:	Absolutely.
Chris:	You know, and make it fun too, it doesn't have to be so oppressed.
Rocky Barnes:	Right, for sure.
Chris:	Oh, I meant to give you guys these hats that we still have. We're pulling out all the stops you guys. Free gifts.
Rocky Barnes:	Oh that's Doug's.

Chris:	Good. Thank you Rocky, great job. Matt Eschliman; so your essay got to me a little bit 'cause you definitely were conflicted.
Matt Eschliman:	Yeah, totally.
Chris:	You were having a hard time.
Matt Eschliman:	Well, its like we just talked, I'm pretty stubborn for one thing so that's a roadblock. That's one of my lids is that I'm very stubborn and hardheaded sometimes. But you know, I've been in this game of the auto industry for 17 years and in one form or fashion from you know, in different positions and so forth, but I thought that I was pretty smart you know. I thought that I had my stuff together and saw you at a NADA, you were doing one of your sessions at NADA a couple years ago, and talking about Service Drive Judo and I went "Well that's kinda an interest", you know, it intrigued me. And then my GM constantly brought your name up over the next several months and it really fought spending a bunch of money to get a "consultant". All the reasons I just said, I mean I've been around enough, have dealt with plenty. In fact, the organization you know that I'm with now had brought in a whole other group at another time to consult and not one thing stuck you know. And so I really fought it for a long time. And then finally I decided to kind of give it a shot and the first thing that I learned is: I gotta change all my pricing. And then mentally I just shut down again because all I'm hearing is, I just gotta charge more, and then things would be great. You know that's not...shame on me for not learning about it more but my stubbornness kicked in and I said, "No way in the world am I gonna price an alignment at $129.95, its crazy." You know, we got a guy down the street from us that has sign up "Home of the 59.95 alignment". You know I said, "There's no way that I'm gonna do

that, I'm gonna drive people away." And it took a lot of pondering and thought and prayer and different things that I believe in and I just decided you know what- we're losing money, you know. I need to do something different so I just decided to jump in with both feet and once I took another look at everything. And I learned more about the customer experience piece and I learned more about the financial statement, how that all works and I realized that every time we sell a service we're essentially losing money, you know? I decided it's kind of amazing what you can do when you price something so you don't lose money every time you sell it, you know? Amazing how that works.

Chris: First you have to know that you are losing money on it right?

Matt Eschliman: Yeah absolutely...

Chris: They're kept in the dark about that.

Matt Eschliman: My whole career, it's maintenance is cheap.

Chris: Yeah.

Matt Eschliman: My whole career, that's all I've been taught and that was a really hard roadblock for me to get past. But I'm so glad that I did. You know, I'm so glad that I learned what really needs to be competitive and what the difference is between competitive and maintenance. You know there's a difference. There's certain things that we do need to price really inexpensively you know? Oil changes, tire rotations, and breaks, and batteries you know what I mean? That's essentially it. You know the quantity there is very few and we re-priced everything. We put in a labor grid, we trained on maintenance, we put in the games. You know having Mario go out was really great, it kind of really helped me understand the whole process. But I probably took two to four months of analyzing all the data and doing the training and pricing and playing with numbers and you know I was kind of slow to really launch everything, even from when we signed up way back in September.

Chris: Oh yeah I remember when we would talk originally when you were here for a coaching meetings.

Matt Eschliman: Yeah.

Chris: You'd be like, "So I'm gonna ask you some questions because...", and you'd preface everything with "I'm not buying into this yet, but explain this again four months in."

Matt Eschliman: Yeah that's the way I am you know.

Chris: You were always very sweet about it and be like, "Okay I don't know about this but it's...what does this mean again?"

Matt Eschliman: Yeah.

Chris: It was pretty funny.

Matt Eschliman: And you know then finally Mario coming out just made it all click and we launched it. Over the next few months, we saw tremendous growth. We saw, you know, our whole service advisor team is all green. I mean the reality is myself, my two service managers that I currently have, have quite a bit of experience but you can take all the advisors and add up their combined experience and it's not as much as any one of us alone. And so we saw some of them really rise up and you know, we brought one with us on this trip. Jason is doing a phenomenal job. I mean, I'm so excited about his future. And you know our net gross went up 40 points. I mean that's like - what? That just means we really sucked before okay? So that's...

Chris: Either way that's a big, that swing doesn't happen by accident, you worked really hard.

Matt Eschliman: CSI's always been something I've been really frustrated with on with one of our manufacturers and just feeling totally out of control. Last meeting that was my prime focus of really understanding it and the two of you helped me there. We've made a huge turn around there. We've gotten more responses in the last three months alone than we did at any quarter prior, you know, so there's a lot of things going in the right direction. I feel like we're just barely scratching the surface. I mean, I really feel like we're only like ten percent of the way into this thing. You know, I mean, that's the reality of it and I just feel like you know we can just accomplish some great things. Because of all this stuff we just got a twenty dollar an hour rate increase for warranty at one of our stores. I mean-unbelievable! I mean, my owner like did back-flips and everything else, so very excited about everything. I cannot say enough about the training that you offer and I think in my essay I call you my mentor.

Chris: After you've seen the beard and the crazy bulldog.

Matt Eschliman: Yeah I did. I may have said something like that but, you know. I think I mean that's the term to use instead of consultant is coach or mentor because I feel that like when we come to training. You know I've learned more about the financial statement this past year than I have the prior sixteen.

Chris: But doesn't it blow you away that our industry, we have all these great managers out there like working in stores and they've been service managers forever. And our industry never trains them on what they're judged on. And they're in this trick bag where, 'cause like once you understand it, its not a big mystery. Once you understand it then you make the right decisions, you're a good steward. But you know, why do we keep everybody in the dark? It's the craziest thing, that you have all this talent and all these great managers out there and we don't give 'em the tools.

Matt Eschliman: For years-

Chris: That's what I'm saying...

Matt Eschliman: For years I got one page of the financial statement and all I would do is scan down to this number that I got paid off of and I had no clue what the rest of it really meant. You know? I mean I had some idea in certain areas but there's never any training, there's never any learning to dissect it and really understand what's going on. So I feel very comfortable with that piece now and understanding what all these numbers are and how I can, for the first time in my entire career, I feel like I can truly effect change in those numbers. You know, I've been frustrated for so many years that no matter what I did none of this stuff changed, you know?

Gary: That's the most powerful thing is, I think when you get the statement, you get to look at it and you go to work and try to diagnose it and then you're like "Okay, well I can put some energy here and make something happen." And then it does and your like "All right I'm on the right track." It's like having a map, you know? You're able to start to follow it and you feel yourself getting to your destination, and you know. But if you don't have that map, there's no way, you're not going anywhere. I don't even know how you start.

Matt Eschliman: Yeah.

Gary: I mean at that point you're just running around circles.

Chris:	Yeah and to be excited to see the financial too; like you want you know your waiting for-
Gary:	Yeah it's growing and it's moving forward, it's you know, you're gaining grounds.
Chris:	Its a fun thing.
Gary:	It is a fun thing.
Matt Eschliman:	Well you know Shane, one of my service managers said he'll wear me out till he gets the numbers. But if I don't send him out the doc he's like "dude where's the doc?"
Chris:	No, I never understand why they take so long. Can I see it? No; and so then Doug isn't here but I just want to say, like the idea behind the fifty-thousand dollar challenge. And you guys know that our passion in here is to help managers just understand the things that they need to, in order do their job great. And your essays here from you guys coming in is going to help them jumpstart some of the leap of faith that you had to take. Hopefully this helps. That's the idea. That they read this and go, "Yeah. its not easy, and yeah, I'm taking a leap of faith." But you know, the other side is much better because it's a hard leap of faith. You know you all took it but it isn't easy. And you can't diminish the amount of work, and you know in the beginning it's a lot to understand and learn and then it's a lot to implement and do everything. So, huge tribute, and you know this will inspire other managers and you guys should feel really good about that 'cause you did the work and you took the leap of faith. It's a big deal.
Gary:	It's inspirational for us too. I mean like Chris was saying, like reading the essays. And you know the six finalists for sure, but just all of them in general, you know for us it was like it was a true inspiration to see people coming to these revelations. And they're having these breakthroughs and they're blowing their lid off and they're doing all these amazing things and the

emotional journey that they go through, just it was touching to read them. I've been using that and pulling quotes out and reading them to some of the staff here and this is just what we do, like these are the people that we're helping. That's what you see out in the field 'cause in a lot of cases you know they don't know what happens after they've spoken to somebody and you know we've gone to work and they're in the coaching group and now we're moving forward. And so I wanted them to know this is what happens in the backside and it's been inspiring them as well. You know it's- I just can't say enough about it. I commend all of you guys here in the room and everybody that submitted their packet. We appreciate it. It's been a great journey for me as well.

Chris: And so by the time this plays one of you guys will have won.

Gary: There will be a winner. Yeah.

Chris: There will be a winner.

Gary: So right after this...

Chris: They get really quiet?

Gary: Right after this...

Chris: They look like you when Jocko is talking to you about your cholesterol.

Gary: Oh my god.

Chris: I eat really clean.

Gary: Yeah, I got no grace. I thought the story was funny but he's like, "I can't laugh at that." I mean he looked me right dead in the bullets. He's like, "I can't laugh at that."-

Chris: I eat chicken and oats.

Gary: I was like, "I'm gonna leave now, I'm good."

Chris: Get a cheeseburger.

Gary: Yeah, right? Five days without a carb by the way, five days.

Chris: See I don't...I call bullshit on that.

Gary: What?

Chris: Well, that's a carb.

Gary: Where's the carb in there? There's no carb in there. Its diet Red Bull and vodka. There's no carb!

Chris: Vodka is a carb.

Gary: Is vodka a carb?

Chris: This is how you get a cholesterol of 300. It's a carb.

Gary: I'm lying? Are you saying I'm lying?

Chris: You cut back on the white starches and all that and that's great.

Gary: I would say I'm that guy. Yesterday, I was that guy at the meeting. Chris bought Togo sandwiches and so a big box of sandwiches come up and Dr. Lau's testing me so he wants me to go a couple of weeks without any bread, starch, anything. So I'm trying to be good and there's a box of sandwiches there for lunch. So now I'm that guy who peels the inside out of his sandwich and eats it and leaves the bread behind. I'm like...

Chris: It's really good.

Gary: "I hate myself." I'm looking at myself in the mirror, "I hate myself."

Chris: Nothing better than eating dry lunch meat.

Gary: Yeah exactly. Its good for you.

Chris: That's good I bet. You should take knives in too. I'll help you.

Gary: Yeah I'm on it.

Chris: Good well thanks you guys. Now we're gonna go party right?

Everyone: Yeah!

Chris: Have some fun.

Gary: Yeah.

Chris: Good. Thank you everybody. 'Bye guys, thanks.

Everyone: Thank you.

Episode #11: Proven Strategies For Profitability In Service

Chris: Welcome, everybody, to Service Drive Revolution, the favorite service drive training of the Westminster Dog Show, NASA, and the CIA.

Gary: NASA?

Chris: NASA.

Gary: NASA. All right.

Chris: On this podcast we share with you the latest strategies and techniques for collecting customers and running a healthy service department. Basically, everything that will help you get to the next level of performance from beginners to advanced. How are you doing, G-Man?

Gary: I'm doing very well today.

Chris: We have a guest here, Mario.

Mario: Hi, everyone.

Chris: Handsome Mario.

Mario: Glad to be here.

Chris: We brought Mario back. We're on this podcast. We're going to talk about a couple things, Mario. We're going to pick your brain. We're going to talk about smart goals, service advisor training or the lack thereof, your system when you were a top advisor, controlling chaos, high customer satisfaction, and KPIs.

Mario: I'm excited. Let's get it going.

Chris: So Mario... We'll get to your cholesterol in a second.

Gary: I'm waiting for the shoe to drop.

Mario: We're back to that?

Chris: We'll get to that in a second, but Mario--

Mario: Thought you were safe, huh?

Gary: I thought so.

Chris: Mario's podcast that we have has like a ton of views.

Gary: I know. We were just talking about that. Almost 3,000.

Chris: He didn't even know.

Gary: I know.

Chris: You don't know you're famous, Mario.

Mario: Nice, I love it.

Chris: You're going to walk in somewhere and somebody's going to go, "Can I get your autograph?"

Mario: Or looking through me right at you, right?

Chris: No.

Gary: Did you see the thumbnail for the video?

Mario: It's just a picture.

Gary: It's just a big picture of Mario.

Mario: Yeah, I saw that. That was funny.

Chris: Before we get into all the stuff about the service drive and all of that, we were talking about Kaepernick. Your quarterback, right? Do you call him your quarterback?

Mario: We were. We were. You know, I don't know how I feel right now about that.

Chris: Well, let me tell you how you should feel. That's what I'm going to do. I'm going to tell you how you should feel. Do you need a pen? I want you to take notes. Because I don't care where you fall on the point he's trying to make. That's irrelevant. It's irrelevant to the fact that he is the leader of an offense on a team, and during the National Anthem is your time to not distract the rest of the team and be checking out the other team on the other side of the field and talking about what's going to happen and how you're going to win. He's not talking about winning. He's drawing all the attention to himself, right?

Mario: You're absolutely right.

Chris: His point might be 100% legit, which I agree with it. Yeah, things aren't right and we need to fix them, but he seemed to be a backup quarterback in the Canadian Football League.

Mario: I mean honestly--

Chris: The 49ers are not going to win this year--

Gary: Mario, go ahead.

Mario: It's like we were talking earlier, you ended up saying, "It tells you where he's focused." You're absolutely right. I agree with what he's standing for or sitting there, lack of, right? But he's not focused on what we're paying him to do, just go out there and win.

Chris: Yeah. They're separate things.

Mario: Definitely.

Chris: You're the leader too. It's not like he's the backup tight end. He's the quarterback. You set the tone. You set the mindset. You got to be standing there with your guys, like, "We're going to kill those guys in a minute."

Mario: Absolutely. You can imagine the morale--

Chris: We want the ball first.

Mario: In that locker room, right? Just probably nothing going on, everybody's just ready to change, go home, and go kiss their wife and kids goodnight.

Gary: I mean, that's just poor leadership.

Chris: I'm not getting a San Francisco 49ers tattoo, bro. I'm just telling you right now. Not this season.

Gary: You just can't be. You want to lead a team. You cannot put yourself first. I get it, he's got principles and he wants to make a stand or a sit, as you put it, Mario. But I mean, come on, please.

Chris: Oh yeah. No, I agree.

Gary: He is the leader of that football team.

Mario: Act like a leader.

Gary: He needs to act like a leader and set his personal feelings aside and go out there and march that team down the field to victory. That's what he needs to do.

Chris: If Jason Garrett was the coach of the 49ers, he wouldn't allow that for a second.

Mario: No, and he shouldn't.

Chris: He's surprised I remembered the name of the coach.

Gary: You ask me every podcast.

Chris: The quarterback.

Gary: I can't even remember it.

Mario: Let's get back to Gary's health.

Chris: How many Super Bowls did Jason Garrett win as a quarterback? None.

Gary: No, he's got a couple rings because he sat on the bench--

Chris: The water boy.

Gary: When Aikman won.

Mario: Gatorade. H20.

Chris: I'd love to make jokes about your cholesterol, but ... You got your blood tests today. You were an angel, like you've been popping niacin. It was funny when you left the room today. Lucas and everybody was like, 'What's wrong with Gary? He looks like a mess. Because he's taking niacin. He's flushed red. He's spotty.

Mario: Oh, I have a story about that. I was out in New York and I was with Ben and he was trying some niacin. I was telling him, "I feel a little off," whatever, and he goes, "You got to try this." "What is it?" He goes, "Niacin." It absorbs ..." I forgot the detail, what he told me, it opens up your pores. You know, you flush out your system. I'm like, "Sure." Never knew nothing about it, and I'm taking it right before bedtime. Biggest mistake of my life. I sweated the whole night, I couldn't sleep, I'm tossing and turning, my pores are open, and I'm just sweating, thinking, why am I thinking about Ben right now? Because I hate him right now. He gave me this thing. Once you take it and you get used to it, you can see the improvement. You can actually feel your body feel better.

Chris: Well, it makes a huge difference in your cholesterol, because it eats the bad ones. It fixes depression and a lot of things, not that we're depressed, but it'll make you happier. But what's funny is ... Ben and I used to go to a different doctor, and when we started going to Dr. Lau, he doesn't prescribe niacin because he said, "The other client go to the ER."

Gary: Oh, because he turned red?

Chris: He took it and he went to the ER. So he's scared of it, but no.

Mario: I felt like the heart pumping.

Chris: The benefits of niacin are great. By the way, everybody listening, we're not doctors. Please consult your doctor.

Gary: I took a niacin and we were in the room on a call with a client. I popped it right before I got on the phone with him, and it closed up my sinuses. I couldn't breathe. So through the call, I'm getting more and more nasally. He's like, "Are you okay?" "I don't know!"

Chris: I thought you were going to say you're on video.

Gary: No.

Chris: So here's the thing. I have a theory, Mario, about his cholesterol, and we're going to see. Because I'm not joking. He wouldn't drink with me. He wouldn't drink, he wouldn't smoke cigars, he was eating chicken breast and lettuce basically for the last week and popping niacin. Everything that you need to do to have great cholesterol. But I bet, I bet there's a great chance that he comes back with bad cholesterol. Because he's the reverse.

Mario: He would.

Chris: I've been saying it's milkshakes and cheeseburgers. I think that NASA or somebody should study you. You're the anomaly that they could cure cancer with whatever's going on in his system because it's the opposite of everybody else.

Gary: I will say when I came off the road and I was at my worst, probably, health that I had been in almost my entire life, I would say. I was the heaviest. I was eating cheeseburgers and French fries every meal.

Chris: You got like Thousand Island dripping down your arm.

Gary: Oh my god. I come off the road and they get my blood tested and it was 220. No, it might have been 210.

Chris: But it wasn't terrible.

Gary: No, it wasn't terrible. Now that I've been working out every day for months and eating better, it's 226.

Chris: Bro, you're going t be 300. You're going to be 300 with all the good stuff you're doing.

Gary: I'm telling you. I would think.

Chris: You're exactly the opposite. It's going to be hilarious.

Gary: It's a fun experiment, though. I don't know, it's just...

Chris: I still love it that on this podcast nobody says, hey, that tip you gave about CSI, that really ... They're like, is Gary going to die?

Mario: How's Gary's cholesterol?

Gary: We had a phone call with a group of shop owners and they got on the call. We were just introducing ourselves. We did a round of introductions. They told us where they were from and what they had done. I was telling them my background and what I had done and who I was, and then the guy goes, "Hold on, hold on. Wait 1 minute, I got 1 question." I go, "Sure, what is it?" He goes, "How's the cholesterol?" Just out of the blue.

Chris: Terrible, that's how. Did you say terrible?

Gary: That's what I said, it's bad.

Chris: I'm going to die. Hurry up, we need to hurry up this call. I might die.

Mario: At least we know there's people out there caring about your health, Gary. Because we know you ain't caring about it.

Chris: Well, or entertained by it. One of the two. Oh yeah. We won't even go into Romo. He's out for 10 weeks. I feel bad about that, actually.

Mario: It's good for the Cowboys.

Chris: No. I wanted Romo to have a good season. I don't like the Cowboys, but ...

Gary: He just can't stay healthy. He just can't do it. It just seems like everybody thinks, 'This is going to be his year' and just he's too fragile.

Mario: Yep.

Chris: Okay, go ahead, G-Man. Take over. Quiz our boy here, Mario.

Mario: I'm on it.

Gary: I just wanted to mention a couple things about Mario. Number one is, Mario, when you and I were talking earlier about this, is that you worked for Longo Toyota. How long did you work there?

Mario: About seven and a half or eight years.

Gary: So eight years, and so...

Chris: Did you start in it as an advisor?

Mario: No, I started as a porter.

Chris: Nice.

Mario: Pulling cars, taking people home.

Chris: Worked his way up.

Gary: Yeah, so like most of us in the car business, started out in a relatively low position, worked your way up into a position of prominence. Those of you who are listening outside of the state of California, Longo Toyota has the distinction for being the largest Toyota store in the world. You were telling me a stat earlier, and I forget it. How many cars were they selling a month?

Mario: Gary, back in the days, about ten years ago when I was there, our goal in May was 2,500 new cars, new units. That's ten years ago. I can only assume now they're probably at 3,500, 4,000 units a month.

Chris: That's not the most interesting thing about Longo. They have their own jail.

Gary: They have a jail? They have a jail?

Mario: I don't know. They have a gym now. They've expanded, but they do have a subway, a Starbucks, they have a Verizon, the whole cellular-

Chris: No, a jail.

Mario: A jail. They got the El Monte PD.

Chris: That's what Nina used to say, that they have a jail.

Mario: No, they didn't really have a jail. We called it Penske College. We would go down there for training and some people would call it the jail.

Gary: Oh, they had a jail.

Mario: But I loved it. I mean, if you were out there trying to learn and get the edge, that's where to be at, and they had it down.

Chris: It's the big leagues. They know how to take care of customers.

Mario: Oh yeah, they did. CSI was number one for them, and that's what we worked on. That's something we'll talk about today.

Chris: That's why they sell so many cars, is because they know how to take care of customers.

Mario: Absolutely.

Chris: The customer's never wrong.

Mario: Never.

Chris: You do not win by whining with a customer.

Gary: We've talked about this several times on the podcast. It just doesn't pay to try to be right, and I think Mario, you said it on the last one--

Mario: You want to be right or you want to be rich?

Gary: Exactly right, and I think having customers and a rich uncle, like Chris talks about in the book, is, you've got to treat them right, and you got to take care of them. They've got to trust and count on the fact that they can come back and you're going to do the right thing, regardless of how much it hurts, regardless of how much pain it is. Which is what I put our internet guys through today, was lots of pain because-

Chris: Oh, those jackasses. Gary advised, have you heard this story, Mario?

Mario: No, I haven't.

Chris: Okay, so when we have a problem here with the Wi-Fi at this place. It doesn't work. It worked okay. It was okay, it wasn't great. I think we talked about getting a T1?

Gary: Yeah.

Chris: Because we do when we do the webcasts. We don't want any interruption. I forget what happened. Anyways, we spent $6,000 on equipment and it doesn't work. Like, for months the internet just goes out. They say it's our fault. Then they come out and then it's like this whole ordeal. Last time, they said we were crazy. I don't know, there was a computer that sat in here for like a day that you could see it like ... You could see every once in a while it would say that it shut down. Then they came back and they're like, 'Oh yeah, the head. The head is wrong. I'm looking at this thing and I'm like, "You know what? I'm going to Google this." Because Google's amazing in these scenarios. So I Googled the equipment. All these reviews come up that are like, it's garbage.

Mario: It's the system that ...

Chris: No, the equipment is garbage. It says it can't outperform the Apple one we had before. Today these guys are here, right? I mean, we're kind of at the end with these guys.

Gary: Yeah, we're getting there.

Chris: No, we're there.

Mario: Dun dun dun!

Chris: We're at the end. Trust me, we're at the end. I walked up to them. I'm funny with this kind of stuff, but I walked up to them and I said, "Have you guys read the reviews on this equipment?" They go into this whole thing, "Well, we got clients, and they have over 100 users on it, and blah, blah, blah." They go through their whole thing. "But have you read the reviews on this equipment?" They're like, "Yeah." We're not going to get a refund, either. We own that.

Gary: No, we're getting a refund.

Chris: But we're going to get somebody who knows what to do.

Gary: We're getting a refund.

Mario: Sounds like extended warranty, man. They make people jump through loops and holes.

Chris: See, and that's the thing with Longo. It's not the equipment. The equipment could be figured out. It's their mindset of, it's always our fault. They always come in here and it's our fault. That's the same thing. Advisors do that all day long with customers. It's like, prove it to me. You're like, "I don't know anything about cars. I just know that this happens."

Gary: Yeah, and that's a thing that made me think about that and them and why I mentioned it, is because I had techs like that a lot when I was working at the store, and they just want to be right, and they want to blame the customer. It just doesn't pay. They ask all these crazy questions, like, "Oh well, you know, do you know what gear the car was in when it was making that noise?" Or, "Do you know whether it was in a shift point?" They don't know. They're like, "I don't know. I was driving on 680, I have no idea what happened." That's what these guys were doing to me. I said, "Look, guys." I go, "I'm not an internet expert. I don't know how to fix the internet. I don't know how to do network a building." I go, "That's what you guys do. So I'll tell you as much as I know, but at the end of the day, I paid you to fix it, fix it."

Chris: You've been out here seven times. Right? This was seven today. It's the same guy. He had backup today, but that didn't look like that was promising.

Mario: There is actually two ways to fix that. Back, when you're dealing with certain things like that, right? As an advisor, one of the ways you would do it is you frame the customer. You explain to them, "I'm going to ask you a serious amount of questions to get the better understanding of what's going on with your car." So you tell them you're going to ask them a bunch of questions, and then they'll know why. Because if you just start asking, not knowing why, you're going to get the same answer you gave them. The other way I would do it is either I call my team leader, my foreman, up, and I said, "I'm going to put you on a test drive with them so you can try to duplicate the same sound, and we're on the same page together." That way I don't just write it up for nothing. The technician's chasing a sound that we don't really know where it's coming from. Those are two ways that I would handle that back when I was writing at Longo.

Chris: Yeah, what I used to tell customers, and this is good: What I would tell them was, 'You know, there's this weird thing that anywhere within two miles of this dealership, problems don't happen. It's a mysterious thing. Nobody's figured it out. They're working on it, but nobody's figured it out. So within two miles it just doesn't happen here. So I'm going to need you to go for a ride with the technician and get two miles out. Because, the technician gets it. Even if you had a couple hours of diagnosis, there's something about the customer being in the car. A lot of times the customer would come back and go, "It didn't happen." Even then I would tell them, "Hey, well, it's happening, so let's figure it out. Pay attention to if it's cold going over a bridge. Let's narrow it down." But I would tell the customer, "You've got to be an investigator." It's CSI Seattle. You've got to figure

315

it out. Then they're on your cause, and you're on their cause with them. You're not making them feel dumb. I would see the other advisors next to me, and they would be like, "Yeah, sure, you know." It's like, people don't make this stuff up. The last thing they want to do is come in here and waste their time.

Mario: Absolutely.

Gary: But you were talking about that earlier, and you were like, "We don't want to torture these guys. That's not the goal."

Chris: Now I want to torture them.

Gary: Yeah, we do now, obviously, but that's not the goal starting out. We just want to have internet that works.

Chris: $6,000 worth of torture.

Gary: That's the thing with customers when they come in. We're not here to torture them. We need to believe them first, I think.

Mario: We're here to help them. We're just here to service their car.

Gary: They're not making it up. They didn't get in their car and drive all the way over there because they made something up and they want to lie to you.

Mario: Maybe at Longo. They used to have hot dogs and balloons and everything on Saturdays. It was like a circus there.

Gary: They're there to check out the prison? All right, all right. I digress. Let's go back to you, Mario. We got sidetracked by the internet. I hit a sore spot for Chris with the internet thing. I see he's a little upset about that. We're talking about Longo, biggest Toyota store in the world. How many advisors were you working with? How many worked there?

Mario: We're about 24, 25 advisors with about 3 for an express loop.

Gary: With all those guys there in any given day, there was 25 guys on the floor?

Mario: We were open from seven to nine. That was back in the days. I believe now their new hours are seven to seven. But back then it was seven to nine, and so we had to cover all the hours. So we needed all men on deck.

Gary: Wow. So how do you compete in a field like that? What was your process? One thing I know about great service advisors, and we've seen this every time we've gone into a dealership to help a service department, is they always have a system. Sometimes they don't even know they have a system, but there's a system in place. They seem to be doing the same things methodically. Those are the guys that are the survivors, the ones that are doing the best. Then the other guys are just letting the wave come in and crash over them and destroy them. Tell me about you and managing that field of advisors, 25 advisors?

Mario: Well, just to give you a little rundown. I started as an express writer. I was one of three people that got put in that position when we just opened an express lane. I was there for about a year before I actually moved over. I took a lot of that opportunity as I was just writing oil changes to really get to know the other advisors and to really get to know how they're doing the job and what's hard about the job. One of the things that I remember asking one of the writers, I go, "Man, every time someone gets on an extended warranty call, they just see their demeanor just ... and slouch and just look over." I go, "Why?" He goes, "You know, it's just a headache getting through it, but you have to do it." I go, "It seems very difficult. I'll tell you what. What if you teach me how to do this, and that opens you up for an opportunity to get a car? How's that?" I would wait on the phone for 30, 40 minutes while they just have you on a wait call, and then this guy would say, "Hey, they're on the phone." He'd dismiss himself or be around me and kind of coach me on how to get that extra diagnostic hour, and additional time for the technician. Naturally I realized, man, people do want to help you out here. You have to go out there and kind of find it. One of the trades that I found that worked for me is, I would go ask an advisor how he sold a certain item, and then I would go around the whole group and ask them the same question. Surprisingly, there was a lot of them that would have a similar system, but they did it through their own way. But the biggest one that we were talking about earlier, Gary, was the confidence. I remember this one guy, he says, Matt was his name. He goes, "Man, I got to tell you something. You've got to be confident in everything you do. Even if you're wrong, you have a better chance of selling." That's what he told me, so I naturally knew. When I'm talking, I got to feel confident. I was never coming back from the technical side of the industry, so I always asked the technicians, "Hey, what happens if this breaks? How long can I go without it?" That's what I learned when I talked to my customers, when I did the walk-around, I got to know how tech-savvy they were and how important things were to them. I would gauge my questions to the technician as I was the customer asking him. When I got on the phone, naturally I hit all of them out of the ballpark because I knew and I was prepped and I was confident in presenting the information I found.

Chris: It's funny that you sell more when you know less.

Mario: Yeah, right?

Gary: Yeah, I had a salesman tell me that. "It doesn't pay to be smart."

Chris: No, it's hard for technicians. You did it, but it's hard for a technician to go from the shop to writing service. Because you want to fix everything.

Gary Daniel: You want to diagnose it right there.

Chris: You're god. You know

Gary: And you're guessing.

Chris: You can just look at it and go, "Oh, it's this," and you just cut out the whole thing.

Gary: Yeah, that was really difficult for me, but I got burned really bad the first time I did it, so I learned my lesson the hard way. Because I guessed wrong and it came back and burnt me. I realized, man. I talked to a sales guy that worked for us. The guy I used to sit with quite a bit and gave me advice and he said, "It just doesn't pay to be smart." You've got to let things unfold naturally, and if you jump to the end, and you're wrong, then you violate trust and then you lose the relationship with the customer.

Chris: It's hard because your intentions are to do the right thing.

Mario: Not to mention your technicians, right, too? You're jumping to their authority and their knowledge and their skill.

Gary: Yeah, they're like, "What are we here for, if you're going to fix the car, smart guy?" You were talking about confidence. One thing I know about you, Mario, and we've worked together quite a bit, is that you're always ... I mean, I was a client. You used to come out to my store, and we loved having you there, because we'd just get all this rush of energy and you're always upbeat and fun. Working in a drive like that, with 25 advisors, I mean, how many cars a day? Like, 300 cars a day?

Mario: At minimum, yeah. I mean, we had 25 writes. Everybody was doing anywhere between 30 to 40 to 50 cars a day.

Gary: Hold on, hold on, hold on. Stop right there. Hold on.

Mario: Well, 25 advisors. Not all of them are doing that.

Gary: You would write up 30 cars a day?

Mario: Well, if I wrote 30, they would make the joke, and the joke was, "Oh Mario, part-timing today?" when I was at 30. Naturally you got to get over the 40 hump.

Chris: Man, that's a long, long day.

Gary: Oh, yeah.

Chris: Oh, god.

Mario: But it was fun. It kept it going, you never knew what to expect. From one customer to another, it was a whole different story, and it was exciting just to help them and fix their car and their needs.

Chris: We do not have one story where we let that happen.

Gary: No.

Chris: There's no way.

Gary: Oh yeah now we know. I've learned a lot with joining the Chris team and whatnot, and yeah, we're doing things way different now than how I did it back then. And it makes sense.

Chris: We can help Longo.

Mario: Oh yeah, we can.

Gary: Yeah, for sure. They need 50 advisors.

Chris: Confidence.

Gary: So, confidence. Sorry. We got derailed. So confidence, and then ... How do you stay up in that environment? Those customers coming at you, writing that many tickets. How do you maintain that? What's your mindset?

Mario: Well naturally, I've always been a positive thinker. I don't allow too much negativity because there's no room to allow that type of mindset. I've always been a half-full type of guy, cup half-full. I was naturally always hyper because I love life. Then you're helping people and you're just constantly working. I loved what I did, and I naturally was always excited to meet the next customer, and I didn't let one customer say no, and say, "Oh, that's it. No one's buying off of me." I'd stay positive. I said, "Okay, great, no problem. We'll get it through the shop. "I'll give you a health report, and I'll let you know what the technician's findings are." Then I'd move on to the next one. There was always a next car going there, so we always had something to do, so I think naturally it just helped me just go to the next one. Just like a quarterback, right? You don't get caught up in that one play, you move on to the next.

Gary: Yeah, you got to have a short memory, right?

Mario: Exactly.

Chris: I felt bad for Mario at the event.

Gary: Why?

Mario: Because I was pouring sweat?

Chris: He has a reputation, l I felt that Saturday night when we were at the bar, it's hard being Mario. Because everybody expects him to be the life of the party. I'm so glad nobody expects that of me.

Mario: Do shots with me. Let's go.

Gary: Mario! All of a sudden Mario's in jail.

Mario: My trick is I talk to the bartender and I tell him, "Give me water and make it look like-

Chris: You do that?

Mario: You have to do it. You got to entertain the team.

Chris: I can't do that. I've heard of that, but I can't do that. I just would tell people I'm done. Like, I just left, right?

Mario: Right.

Chris: I mean, I got to speak the next day. I'm leaving, I'm sorry.

Mario: That's it.

Chris: Doesn't mean I don't care. But I'm human. But you're superhuman. With that I felt bad for you.

Gary: Yeah, for sure. The pressure's on.

Chris: You did a good job, though.

Mario: Thank you. It was fun.

Gary: The other thing we were talking about was goals, and we've been talking a lot about goals here in the office and I was thinking about advisors and the guys that we see out in the field when we go out to fix the store. We were mentioning, we were just discussing the system. They all have a system. But the other thing I noticed is that they all have goals. Even though, again, they might not think they do, and you and I were just talking through that a little bit ago ... Tell me what you were telling me earlier about your goals and how you guys in your team kind of defined what the minimum standard was and how you policed each other?

Mario: Well, naturally, we were broken up into 3 groups, and we had our group of technicians, and we would mandate them. We all had our own logbooks, and we had a master logbook. Naturally, you can see how many cars people are writing, and then we would have a tracking sheet in our lunchroom to see exactly where we're at. We would always go in there in the morning, we'll come out and we'll poke each other and saying, "Man, you're really slacking us. You're hurting us. I'm holding you." We'd make jokes back and forth. At the time I didn't think of it as goals, as we were discussing earlier today. I go, 'You know, I guess we did have a goal, but nothing was written down. I see the power in writing it down and constantly talking about it, and I can just look back and go, "I would've been three times better." But yeah, we naturally policed ourselves. We kind of pushed each other and made sure that no one was slacking off, and at the end of the day, Gary, the biggest thing that pushed me was I had to feed my techs. I knew they had a family, they had a house, they had car payments. I couldn't just sit down where there's cars here. I got to go write up another car, generate some work, and feed my techs, keep them happy. Because we know when you guys ain't having to work, you guys start talking and then just start kind of ... Bad type of feelings get around because you guys ain't working.

Gary: Oh, you got Mario's ARO?

Mario: Well, they love my AROs.

Gary: He can't sell anything. All right, man. That's it. That's all I got.

Chris: That's it. That's all you got?

Gary: Unless you want to share some pearls of wisdom?

Chris: KPIs. What's KPIs?

Gary: Oh, the KPIs. We were talking about that, too. I was asking you about what you guys were measuring and how you measured each other. Tell me a little bit about what you were telling me earlier, again, about how you guys measured each other, measured success. There was a number, remember we were saying?

Mario: Right, well naturally, we would never want to be under 30, and we would only measure labor. As a team, these other guys were a little stronger, so that's why they would put us together and kind of build each other up. Their guys were a little higher, but as a team, we were trying to push for 150, and that's what would create our paycheck. Actually, we didn't police each other. When people ain't looking at you, naturally you just start slacking off and getting comfortable and making your day-to-day as easy as possible. But not with my team. My team was constantly pushing and poking and just kept you on your toes to go out there and do better and just be the best way you can be. One of the things that I was telling you is, one of the biggest things that we do in our program is connecting with the customers, "petting that dog." That's one of the biggest fundamentals, where we impact the experience that we're providing for the customer. Like I was telling you, I naturally did that back in the days when I did a walk-around. I had the customer come around. Not so much follow me, and I didn't have that understanding of what I'm creating of control, but I would build rapport. I think that's what got me a lot of sales. People would love me and look at me as a, this guy's fun, and he's not really trying to sell me something, until we got to my computer. Then it was over, right? Then when I joined Chris, he explained to me the process of systems, and I was in love, because it was pretty much similar to what I did, but it was more of, this is why we're doing it, this is what you're creating by doing it this way, and it was the rapport-building, the control aspect, just the whole experience with the customer. I love it because I believe it.

Gary: Weren't you telling me, too, that you guys were… the biggest measurement for Longo was CSI?

Mario: Oh yeah, I mean, CSI is what they go by. CSI, I believe national was about 92. I was always about 2 or 3 marks up there. CSI will make or break you. The minute you're under minimum, they put you on a prescription, which is like a probation period, and you have three months to increase that back to over national, or you're done. That's it. It didn't matter how great your numbers were, you were done. No excuses.

Gary: I guess the point I was trying to make was that you had measurements, you had key performance indicators you went after. You guys had to be above 30,000 in customer paid labor, and you had to have your CSI at least 2 points above national. That's, again, goes back to what I was saying, when you see the best advisors in the country and you go and you visit them, they have those standards. They're not all the same. Not everybody's looking at hours per order or ELR, but there are key performance indicators that they measure themselves by, and instinctively they just do it. They hold each other accountable, and they go out and they get it done.

Mario: Yeah, top performers, you put a measuring stick in front of them, they're going to get to the highest point. Just naturally, right?

Gary: Right.

Mario: They want to perform, they see the stick, and I go, "I'm going to get past that."

Chris: Good job, Mario. Thank you.

Mario: Thank you guys.

Chris: Everybody listening, if you have a service drive, we're here to help you. We have the best training and coaching groups that is out there, and we're also good-looking. But we can help you increase your CSI, retention, and profitability.

Gary: We're in relatively poor health, but we'll help you.

Chris: Give us a call.

Mario: And have fun.

Chris: Hurry before Gary's gone.

Mario: Don't forget the fun, guys.

Chris: Get in while Gary's still around. Thanks, everybody.

Gary: Cheers.

Episode #12: Techniques To Convert Difficult Customers

Chris: Welcome everybody to Service Drive Revolution where we share the latest strategies and techniques for collecting customers and running a healthy service department. And basically everything that will help you get to the next level of performance of beginners to advanced. We also deal with health, football...

Gary: Football.

Chris: That's pretty much it. How are you doing Jair?

Jair: I'm doing great.

Chris: How are you doing G man?

Gary: Really good. Feeling great today.

Chris: Jair, you've recently joined our team. He's always been on our team, but he was working for somebody else. We get lucky sometimes, right?

Gary: It's weird how that happened.

Chris: It's funny, our team, we keep building our team with people that have been in the family so they get the culture and the whole thing. It works out really good.

Gary: Yeah, Jair worked for me when I worked at the dealer back in Concord for... How many years have we worked together bro?

Jair: About three, three and a half?

Chris: More than that bro.

Jair: More than that?

Gary: Yeah, it might have been more than that because you were at Mini for more than a year.

Jair: Yeah.

Gary: It was two years. It's been like five.

Jair: Yeah, like five years.

Gary: Anyways, we worked together for quite a while, and when I left there, I came down here. I moved to LA from San Francisco bay area, and came north for Chris, and I was in Santa Monica, just sitting on the street corner. He came out from dinner, we had dinner with some friends there right by the pier, I'm just standing there, and I'm calling an Uber, I got my phone out, and also I hear somebody yell my name. The first thing I thought was, "How does the Uber guy know my name? I haven't even requested him yet." I put my head up and I look around and it's Jair just walking by, just randomly walking by. How was that, six months ago, eight months ago?

Jair: Yeah, it was eight months ago. That's crazy.

Gary: Now you're here.

Jair: Now I'm here.

Gary: Now you're, out of the blue, now you're here. Anyway, it's just funny how the universe works, you know?

Chris: How do you feel being on this side?

Jair: I feel great, it's fantastic.

Chris: We get to help people right? It's fun.

Jair: I love it.

Chris: There's a lot of people that need help.

Jair: Yeah.

Chris: It's a different kind of reward, right?

Jair: It totally is. It's completely different.

Chris: It's great, because you've been through the process so you get it. You've seen it from both sides now.

Jair: Like a total believer, it's like, it's awesome.

Chris: I know the first week I was ... Jair was like, "This is amazing. I can't believe how much more fun this is."

Jair: Yeah. It was crazy. You're on this side, and I see it all happening. I was just the one in the middle of it back in the day.

Gary: Yeah. It is a lot more fun to be above the battlefield, planning the battle than being in trenches.

Chris: We're going to talk about, I want to talk about difficult customers which are here, then we'll talk about goals, smart goals, and system, right?

Gary: Yeah. KPIs.

Chris: Does that match your notes?

Gary: KPI is on there too.

Chris: KPIs, I don't know what that stands for.

Gary: Key performance indicators.

Chris: Oh. Can we make it dirty?

Gary: It is the things that we measure ourselves by. Let's just put it that way.

Chris: We could...

Gary: Maybe. I'll come up with something better for the next one.

Chris: Okay, I remember, the Vickster. I love you if you're listening to this.

Gary: Shout out, hold on, shout out to Vicky.

Chris: Shout out to Vicky! Vicky and I, when Jair was an advisor before he was a manager, Vicky and I used to do this thing when I would go up there, where we take out 100 bucks in 20s. Then we listen to phone calls. We would pull up like the equivalent of who's calling in the day or whatever, but you guys had an internal system, because you're a crazy weird IT god. We would pull up phone calls. Now, he game between Vicky and I listening to phone calls, and if you're dealer, general manager, any manager in a dealership, and you've ever listened to phone calls, you know you need tequila like we're doing right now.

Gary: It's painful.

Chris: It's very painful. If the call was good, and mostly our focus was the BBC. If the BBC followed all the key points of the script, they got it back to the last advisor, they got their email, you know, there's probably seven things on our BBC script that they had to get. I would get the $20 to Vicky, and then Vicky would call in the BBC rep if they were there, and usually give it to them. If the call wasn't good, I would get the $20, which you guys know how competitive Vicky is, right?

Jair: Very.

Chris: My thing was, when you're looking at the software with the calls, you could tell how long the call was before he hit play.

To my advantage, because I'm always looking for that edge, you guys probably don't know that about me, but, I'm always looking for that edge. The edge was any call that was ten minutes had not gone right. Vicky never quite got that, but I was like, "What's this one? What's this one?" I wanted the ones that were longer, because they were transferred back and forth, and it would be somebody going, "I need a break it's so much." "Let's transfer you to parts.", then, transfer you back to service, this whole ... Usually I make money on those. I was always trying to pick the longer calls. There was this one call I remember it's twelve minutes. It was Jair, and this, the advisor who originally helped him was gone on vacation or something. The ball had been dropped about as much as you can drop the ball. Jair took this guy, and owned it, it was incredible. I wish we would've saved that call just for training purposes. How empathetic, I think empathy, and owning it. You never were blaming the advisor who dropped the ball or anything, you're like, "You're with me now, and I understand and I feel the same way." You just owned it. You definitely have a system for difficult customers. Walk me through; can you think of a really difficult scenario that our listeners could relate with and then you could tell them your approach to it? A crazy customer?

Jair: Yeah. There was.

Chris: There were a lot there.

Gary: We had our moments.

Chris: Talking about an entitled customer...

Jair: It was crazy. There was one one time I'll never forget where there was a lady who was just at her wits end with her car. "I'm tired of coming here, this is crazy, you guys haven't fixed it, you haven't fixed it. What's going on? I'm going to throw it off a cliff." and everything. I spent about 45 minute with her and come to find out she'd just had been divorced, and the whole thing just trickled down. I just wanted to sit down and go...

Chris: That's the thing. He gets to know people. He cares, he really gets to know them. It's not just about the car, right?

Jair: Yeah.

Chris: Are you curious about people?

Jair: All the time. All the time. I always want to know, I want to figure out who they are, how they are, what they think, what makes them twitch, because you find that connection. The most important thing whenever I interact with anybody, is finding that connection. I loved it. I used to sit down all the time and Vicky would be like, "You just spent 35 minutes with that guy." I go, "I know." He goes, "You were talking about the new bridge that was just built to go across the bay."

Chris: He designed it.

Jair: Yeah. I thought it was fascinating. He was there to drop off his daughter's car, because she was going to go to college.

Gary: It used to crack me up, sorry to step on you, you used to drive Vicky nuts. He would just be at the desk with-

Chris: It was like the barbershop.

Gary: He used to be like, "You got to take it. The drive's backing up with ..." She would just go bananas. Man, the customers loved him, and your numbers were the best in the drive.

Chris: Insane. He'd write eight customers and beat everybody. What is your system? You're obviously a good listener. Do you have an idea of how you naturally do that?

Jair: Yeah. You first got to see the tone of the client. When they come into the door, you got to feed that energy, what kind of energy are they in? You got to read their facial expressions, and see what their tone is. One of the things I really learned, and it took a lot of practice, is trying to find that connection with just tonality. Getting to that same tone with the client.

Chris: Mirroring?

Jair: Yeah. Total mirroring them. It was really interesting. If they were like "I'm having a hard ..." I'd be like, "Okay, I'm going to get you out of here, no problem, we're going to take care of you." And boom, they felt like they were totally satisfied. If somebody else was coming like, dum du dum, I'd be like, "Slow it down, how's it going? Do you want to share a cup of coffee? We can do this together. It's going to be all right."

Chris: Cowboy's fan, obviously. Slow.

Gary: We just lost Texas. The whole state of Texas just quit the program.

Chris: You're a 49-ers fan, right?

Jair: I am a 49-ers fan. Me and Mario were both on the same team.

Chris: Go 49-ers.

Gary: We left that off your resume by the way, stuff like that.

Chris: You know Mario hid that he had a 49-ers tattoo from me for a long time. Somebody else told me.

Jair: No way.

Chris: Yeah. He didn't tell me.

Jair: Are you serious?

Chris: Yeah.

Jair: That's the first thing he showed off when he showed up at our store.

Chris: You might have been the one to tell me.

Jair: I might have been.

Chris: Do you remember Vicky and I calling you, after that phone call?

Jair: Yeah, I do remember it. You were like, "Dude, you just took care of this guy."

Chris: You thought you were in trouble at first.

Jair: Yeah, I did.

Chris: He comes in, and he...

Jair: Totally.

Chris: Vicky and I closed the door. I think I gave Vicky the 20 bucks, I think. Maybe we didn't even exchange money, I don't know, we were so blown away.

Jair: What I do remember is that I didn't get any money.

Chris: I don't think we exchanged any. It was more about the BBC.

Gary: Nobody else participated.

Chris: We told you, I think we played a little bit of the call and said, "Man you owned this, it was amazing how well you handled this situation, because the customer was crazy." Mirroring on the front, and then, tell me about empathy, because you ooze empathy.

Jair: It's really funny. I remember being a little boy, and my mom was a single mom. It was me and my sister, and I would never forget, one of the people that I looked up to that was one of my favorites, was the service advisor at the Toyota dealership in Atlanta. We had a 1992 Toyota Corolla. When I was a freshmen in high school, on a Saturday, we would wake up and we'd go in, "We got to go get an oil change." We go get an oil change. I'll never forget how the service advisor was so kind and generous and thoughtful to my mom. How in this business sometimes we're perceived like the female comes in, or whatever... but he empathized so much with understanding my mom's position. "You're a single mom, we're going to take care of you, no problem." Always was willing to look out for her best interest only to find out that in the future he was the number one service advisor. I found out this out years later. He did that with everybody by trying to find that connection and understand people's position to try to be able to assist them. I use that now. I always try to help my clients, and the way that I did things was, "You know what? Let's put a game plan together. Your needs are this, and you may not have the ability to do it all, but let's work with your budget." I remember that was the word that he used to say when my mom was, when I was younger. "Maria, what's your budget? What we can do? Let's work together with this." I try to take those, sort of the same practices, to have people understand that I understand, that we're all just humans, and I play a role. And I'm here to help you, and I'm just connecting with them. We fix your car, that's the no brainer, but at the end of the day, we're in the business of people.

Chris: What was that advisor's name?

Jair: His name was Frank.

Chris: Frank. Sweet Frank. What do you think about advisors handling female customers? Most of the time it's a male dominated service department.

Jair: Yeah. It is.

Chris: What do you think?

Jair: One thing, I mean, realistically nowadays, it's interesting. There was a report that got released the other day that 84% of all sales decisions are now made by a female.

Chris: Yeah.

Jair: 84%. You got to take that into consideration.

Chris: Gary? Yeah, 100% over here, 101?

Gary: It's a beautiful climb, 9.9

Chris: 101. What a beautiful... The rest of the world it's 84?

Jair: Yeah. It's 84%. It's interesting how powerful the female is, but you got to understand that there's respect there. There's always got to be respect. As the consumer, as the buyer, as to all those things, there's got to be respect.

Chris: I don't know, I never ... that's good and all. Maybe that will convince a douchy guy to be nice to females, but I'm in the same scenario where I grew up with a single mom. I don't know, nobody's any different. I think actually when I was an advisor with females, I think I would try harder to protect them in a weird way. I didn't want them to feel like it was a douchy world, I don't know.

Jair: I know I did the exact same thing.

Gary: What's funny about Jair though. If we had some heat, and it was a female customer and half of our service drive was females at the time. Half the service advisors were female. We'd had some heat, and Vicky and I would be talking about it, and she would get it to Jair. I think the big thing was that-

Chris: It's empathy.

Gary: That empathy that you had.

Chris: It just comes up and he has this way of like, "Okay, tell me." He doesn't have an agenda, he doesn't want to be right. He's not trying to impress his feelings on you even before he opens his mouth. You can tell, just even body language, when a guy walks up it's like, "Okay, what's the problem?" You come off and you're like, "Oh, man. What's going on?" And he listened.

Jair: One of those things that takes practice, another example, was one time a lady called in and the BDC grabbed me. "Would you please take this call? This lady's going crazy, she's going crazy, oh my god. She's stranded on the side of the road." I pick up the phone and I said, her name was Lisa, I said, "Lisa, how are you doing?" She goes, "Oh my god, I have a flat tire, I'm on the side of the road, I've been waiting three and a half hours for a tow," and all this stuff." I said, "Are you okay? Are you safe?" All of a sudden she just like ... dead silence. I said, "Hello?" She goes, "Oh my god, I've called in like 45 times and nobody's ever asked me if I was okay." I'm like ...

Gary: You're like, "Ma'am, we don't control roadside. We're not the phone company."

Chris: You need to call 1-800...

Jair: It's true. We get into these things like that happening like, "What?"

Chris: It's funny too because that question, oddly, brings you back to reality. It's like earlier with one of our sales people I was having a conversation, you were not here, they're talking about how rough their childhood is. And I'm like, "Did you ever go two days worrying about eating? No?" I'm like, "Then you're a middle class. Was there always food?" You're bringing them back to, you have the basics, you're safe. I know the tire's an inconvenience, but nobody's dead.

Jair: Are you okay? Is everything okay?

Gary: That's smart. They got to do an inventory check and say, "Okay, yeah. I am safe. I got that going for me. I just need to get off the highway." Then you can work their problem to a solution.

Jair: Right. We wanted to make sure that everything was okay all the time. Make sure that they're okay first. Anything else is going to be taken care of. That was what's most important.

Chris: That's good.

Jair: There were some times where I just couldn't handle some people. Gary and I went through one with a young lady, middle ages lady who had a five series, it was a green one--

Gary: She's not listening.

Jair: Oh my god. We tried.

Gary: I worked very hard at that. Very hard at that.

Chris: You guys failed?

Gary: Yeah.

Jair: Yeah, but we tried.

Gary: She had a file folder that thick of everything that she felt was dumb with her car.

Gary: She just ... Yeah. I don't know, that was a unique circumstance I got to say.

Jair: It was very much so.

Chris: How did it end?

Gary: She parked the car up in front of the dealer, and then walked away and left it there.

Chris: For how long?

Gary: It was there for a month?

Jair: Yeah, I think it was a month.

Gary: We had to have it towed away.

Jair: We towed it to your house.

Gary: Yeah.

Chris: What year was it?

Gary: It was a 90's car. We were, this was back in 2010. Yeah, it was used. It was, I mean it was a decent car, and she just had high expectations, and it was a car that was more than ten years old, and had a lot of miles on it. There was nothing wrong with it, it was very safe, but she was very hypersensitive, and we bent over backwards. I did everything possible. You and I together.

Chris: You did everything possible?

Gary: Everything possible.

Chris: Everything? I guarantee you I can come up with something you didn't do. Back rubs?

Gary: I didn't do back rubs.

Chris: On my first one I got you.

Gary: You got me. I'm the fixed operations director, I'm working on the car. I pulled out all the stuff. When was the last time you see me hold a wrench? It's been a while.

Chris: Around here, Gary's looking for stuff to fix all the time. He's like, "I can build that." What was I doing the other day? You got jealous? I was painting, you were like, "What are you doing? You can't have tools." It's great, Gary's here, we've got tools. We have tools next door. We have a toolbox.

Gary: Chris wants me to cut something off, he's like, "I'm going to cut this thing off, I was thinking about a hacksaw." I'm like, "You can't do that with a hacksaw." I said, "No, no. I got a angle grinder in the storage. I'll go get the angle grinder." He goes, "Is that like a ...?" I go, "It's like, on steroids." It's here, it's here at the loft. I'm just--

Chris: You can cut yourself with that thing. So funny! My drums, I want to cut the arms on a couple of my drums, so they can go lower. He goes, "Oh yeah, let me get the thing."

Gary: Zipped through that thing like knife through butter.

Chris: Let's bring your toolbox down here. How big was your toolbox?

Gary: It's big.

Chris: Like the condo?

Gary: No, no.

Chris: Is it snap on?

Gary: It's snap on. It's the big snap on 5000 or whatever. It's big and it--

Chris: Yeah, we're running out of room here, but in our next office maybe.

Gary: Yeah. Weighs a metric ton, but man, I love my tools. I can't get rid of them.

Chris: That's awesome.

Gary: They got six inches of dust on them but ...

Chris: People feel safer when you're around for sure. Gary can fix it. You should see this disaster over here in the corner he's working on. It was so sweet of you to do that, but it's not your fault the internet coming in is broken. You can't put a band aid. Look at that pile of wires over there. It's crazy right?

Gary: Yeah, I know, I'm still trying to. You were here when I started that?

Jair: Yeah, totally. You were totally like, "What if we pipe it. We could pipe it across and maybe ..."

Chris: Yeah, he'd love that. If you could dig a hole, you would love that more.

Jair: We would drill it, and then, Chris is like, "That's pure concrete man. There's concrete." "Yeah, yeah, yeah. We can make it happen."

Gary: There's a way.

Chris: No. Five series. What was wrong with it? Do you remember?

Gary: There was nothing wrong.

Jair: For her it was--

Gary: Everything yeah, she would say. The diagnostic system would spit out these reports, and on there they would say there was some sort of transmission failure, but it was really a communication failure between the software, and we knew that. As technicians we knew that was there because it was inherent in the system. She couldn't get her head past it. She thought there was something wrong. Meanwhile the car functioned normally, but this report said... Somebody had handed this piece of paper to her-

Chris: That makes sense though.

Gary: Said there's something wrong on it.

Chris: They didn't make a fix for that?

Gary: No, because they've moved on. The model was gone, and they just didn't care. BMW moved on, and there was no way to convince her otherwise.

Chris: You couldn't smooth her over? With your beautiful eyes, and warm voice?

Jair: Couldn't do it. I tried very hard.

Gary: We gave it to him. We gave her to him, he gave it right back to me. It was the monkey.

Chris: Wrapping up, I'm curious because you've been around the world, and now working with us, and being a part of the team. What are the just specifically two advisors? What are a couple of characteristics that you see in the top performing advisors that the bottom chiwawas, chi chis don't have?

Jair: Passion. Passion and joy in what they do. Being able to have a good purpose of doing something. Not just selling but connecting.

Chris: Serving?

Jair: Yeah, serving people. Having that gratitude behind it, and just connecting with those people to know that's their guy. It was always my goal, I always said to myself, "I want to be the person on my client's phone as important as if they were going to put the speed dial on their doctor, speed dial on their attorney." I wanted to be their car guy. I wanted to still be, "Hey, you know there's something wrong with the car? I'm going to call Jair. He's going to know how to take care of me."

Chris: I always felt that way too. It was very rewarding when it did. You felt like you had everything. They trusted you, and you had to be a good steward.

Gary: Extreme ownership.

Chris: Or leadership depending on who's updating our You Tube channel. We got a bunch of comments on the last one because whoever does our social media, they put the titles wrong in the thing. Maybe I say it wrong, I don't know, but guys were pissed. Calling it extreme ownership, not leadership.

Gary: He's got a loyal fan base.

Chris: He should, he's good.

Gary: Yeah.

Jair: He's really good. Yeah.

Chris: Sorry.

Gary: Can we talk about his goals before we wrap?

Chris: Smart goals.

Gary: Talk about goals and smart goals, yeah.

Chris: Are your goals smart, or are your goals stupid?

Jair: Both?

Chris: That's a good hit. Good job Jair. That's the purpose of ... that's funny.

Gary: My theory is that if you're a high achiever, pretty much anything that you do, even myself as a tech, I always came into the shop knowing how many hours I wanted to do that week in order to pay my bills and take my family on vacation and do things I wanted to do. I had goals. Not that I wrote them down in any kind of formal way, but they were always there. And I think with high achievers it's just instinctive that you set targets, and you're constantly going out to get them. Tell me about you, and coming into a month, you're starting from zero, you're getting ready to write out the juice, set goals. What was your system around that?

Jair: My system was always to beat my best ever, all the time. To be able to motivate my team to always be better than everybody else in the shop all the time. That we were going to become as efficient and as motivated, everything it took. To include them was the way that made me successful. That's what I loved being at the Concord is that I walked in there and they're like, "Okay, you have these four technicians, or three technicians, and you're going to have to feed them. You're just going to have to collaborate with them." One of the things I wanted to do is I told them, I said, "Guys, we're going to take care of people. I'm just going to be the communicator, but you guys are going to be the surgeons." I'll take care of them and try to give them things, and take it easy for them, but you're going to have to do your surgery. I got that right there from them because of something that happened to me years ago. I'm going to share something personal. Back in 2001 I was diagnosed with a brain tumor. I had horrible headaches and all sorts of stuff, and I'll never forget that. I went into the doctor, and I saw the surgeon. And it was this guy who looked like a genius, this older gentleman who'd done this, and he comes in, no personality, super dry. "Yeah, we're going to cut you open, I'm going to do this, we're going to remove that, and we'll put you back together, and that's it." I'm like, I was terrified. Then he had this P.A. (Physician's assistant) who was his personal assistant comes in and her name was Karen. I'll never forget, she sat down, she goes, "I'm really sorry, he's a surgeon, and he's one of the most masterful people in this planet that knows what he's doing; but I'm the one who's going to tell you what's going to happen in normal terms and relax you, and make it feel easy." Ever since then I said, "Wow, that's an amazing tool. Just to be the guy who just translates information to make people feel comfortable about what's happening." It's scary. Sometimes customers come in, and they have no idea what's going on with their car. It's their freedom. You're taking away their freedom, it breaks down, or whatever.

Chris: They don't pop the hood, they don't see under ... it's all-

Jair: They have no clue.

Chris: It's a different language.

Jair: It's a totally different language. I can go in there and tell them that their alternator, and this and that, whatever happens.

Chris: It's just intimidating.

Jair: It's just totally intimidating, and you're human. We're adults, and so we think that we're educated individuals and we should know, you should know, what that means, but you really don't. They really don't, so it's my job to walk them through the process and let them know that when you leave here you're going to be safe and sound because we took care of you.

Chris: That's great.

Gary: That was good.

Chris: What did she say? Somebody's going to come in, they give you a shot, you're going to go night night?

Gary: We got some really good drugs coming.

Jair: No. She was amazing. She's like, "I'm going to hold your hand, don't worry about it, we're going to walk in together," and she did. The day of the surgery she was there, my mom was there, she showed up, she was there, and she goes, "Are you ready?" I'm like, "Yeah, I'm ready to go." The surgeon was in O.R. ready to go, and she goes, "All right, just count back, and with the anesthesiologist, count back from ten." And I think it got to six and it was over.

Gary: Night night.

Chris: It's amazing. That's an amazing story, it's like the pet the dog story, but more real. That's real. A dog, even though I love my dog, it's different than that. It's the same thing.

Jair: It really is.

Gary: He was not a people person.

Jair: He wasn't. He was a genius at his trade.

Chris: The best techs, the best doctors, the best lawyers, they don't think that way.

Jair: They don't. They're just trying to fix something.

Chris: They take it very serious, and they're really good at their craft, but to them it's like, "It's a cut, it's a variable, it's a contingency." They're thinking about all that. They're playing god in a weird way. We're looking for like, "Hey, hold my hand." If I hold your hand, you'll die. You want me disinfected in there going to war for you.

Gary: We don't care so much about the technical process of what it takes to eliminate whatever it is that pains us. What we care about is that you show empathy, and sympathy, and you're there for us emotionally. We're more of a wreck. He's thinking about, "I've got to slice you open four inches, and get in there and take everything out."

Jair: To them it's easy.

Gary: To them it's just a thing. They might as well be putting on our break pad.

Jair: Exactly.

Chris: Thanks everybody for listening to our beautiful podcast. By the time you listen to this, 49-ers will probably be 0 and 1.

Jair: That's not right. That's not right.

Chris: It's true though.

Jair: That's dirty.

Chris: Don't look at Mario.

Jair: I keep forgetting I'm from Seattle.

Chris: Thanks everybody. We'll talk to you soon.

Episode #13: KPI'S To Increase Productivity With The GOAT

Chris: Welcome fellow car dogs to the Service Drive Revolution. You hear that music at the top? That's actually me, playing drums, laying down the beats for you.

Gary: The best bumper music in the podcast universe.

Chris: That's exactly it. On this Service Drive Revolution, we share the latest strategies and techniques for collecting customers and running a healthy service department and basically everything that you need help with to get to the next level of performance for beginners and experts. How you doing G Man?

Gary: Really well, feeling good.

Chris: We have a very special guest today.

Gary: Yes we do.

Chris: They call him the GOAT.

Gary: The GOAT?

Chris: GOAT stands for Good, Alternative, Aspiration... No, Greatest Of All Time.

Hassan: You missed a letter there.

Gary: I got to tell you a story. We were at NADA and some people came by the booth and I was talking to them and I was sharing Hassan's story and talking about your workforce and how we learn from you. I said, "We call him the GOAT" and the guy looked at me kind of puzzled, and I go, "You know, The Greatest Of All Time." He goes, "Yeah, I know what a goat is idiot." I go,

"I'm sorry."

Chris: Jeez. Fine.

Gary: I've never heard about it before.

Chris: Well, there's a book about Muhammad Ali called *The GOAT*. Muhammad Ali really, besides Hassan, is the only one that you can say that. We're going to pick Hassan's brain and we're going to pop him with questions and get a lot, but right out of the gate we need to get something clear:

Gary: Okay.

Chris: He has another level. People always think, "Oh he was lucky,"or "Oh this, or whatever…" No.

Gary: "Well, he was in the right market."

Chris: "He was a better advisor than the rest of us."

Gary: Yeah. Now "He worked for the right brand." "He was in the right market."

Chris: Yeah, "He's better looking" like, whatever...

Gary: "He was six foot four and sharp."

Hassan: That's for sure.

Chris: No. He has another gear, so get the excuses out and really pay attention because you could learn something.

Gary: Yeah.

Chris: He used to drive me crazy when I would say at the meetings and you remember when you were an advisor at the top dog events, I would say like "Hey, if you really want to get good and you want to take it seriously, take a vacation and go watch Hassan. He'll help you, he'll let you watch." Nobody ever did it, right?

Hassan: Nobody showed up.

Chris: No, everybody's a critic but nobody wants to learn.

Hassan: I even called people out to come in and check it out. Nobody showed up at all.

Chris: He was unbelievable, and we'll get into the things that I noticed about him and then we'll pick his brain, but he would write up three customers at a time. He just had the most amazing control and hustle too. I remember advisors in his drive would say like "Oh, there's no work." Meanwhile, he's out back with a tow truck. He just hustled like crazy.

Gary: We had the same brand and I would argue that our market was even better. It was up north.

Chris: By far, by far.

Gary: Yeah. Nobody even touched, even came close to those numbers. It's funny when people say that, "Oh, well, he worked it up."

Chris: There's a bunch of stores, even the one you're helping right now, that's in a better market than you're in, right?

Hassan: Everybody thinks their market is the worse. You know what I mean? Everybody is going to make that excuse. But it's not the market. It's you versus the region or the market that you work in and it's your process that helps you collect customers, not the actual customer himself. It's the way you lead them and the way you bring them in and the way you treat them. That's what keeps them coming back and wanting to spend money with you. It's out of trust.

Gary: Yeah.

Chris: It's funny too, like, now people at events are hunting him down and like they're honored to meet him and stuff. But it's funny, like, he's the quiet guy. He's not, like it's always the loudest guy that is the worst performer.

Gary: Right.

Chris: It's the quiet guys like him that you got to seek out and pick it out of him, because half of it comes natural, half of it he couldn't explain why he does what he does. To him it's like, "Well, you just hustle. You just get up earlier than everybody else. You just work later." Like you don't take a two hour lunch, or lunch at all.

Gary: Right. He'll just do it - yeah.

Chris: Yeah. To him, it's obvious, and so it's hard for him to explain. He's the quiet, humble one and the guys that are like yapping most of the time are the guys that'll never get there.

Gary: Yeah, exactly.

Chris: Does that always feel weird to you? Because you're not boastful at all.

Hassan: No. I mean, it's kind of tough to go out and share your experience with everybody else, especially when they know your numbers and what you've done and how you created or collected those clients. Some people just can't handle that and they can't understand it. You can be at a level one or level two or level three, but once you start reaching way beyond that. Most good advisors I meet, they average anywhere from 180 to about 230, $250,000. When you tell somebody like that that, "Hey, you can double that, especially if you work at a BMW or a Mercedes or a Lexus store." They have a hard time comprehending. You know what I mean? I mean we know that from our consulting side of things, when we tell people their ability to kind of double their gross and double their customer pay labor, they're also shocked until we can prove it. It's very tough to go in and tell guys, "Hey, you can double it, and I can help you." They'll be like, yeah, whatever, until they actually see the actual numbers.

Gary: That's scary, right?

Chris: We almost scare people away if we tell them the real numbers we get. They don't believe it. It's too much of a leap.

Hassan: I mean, there's only few people that actually seek you out or seek that person out because they want to know that level and these are very far and few in between.

Chris: Yeah. So I'll tell you a story because I feel like it's very similar, is when I was running Crevier and we were in a 20 group and the quietest guy in the room was a lot like Hassan. His name was Vince Cerone from Brahmin in Palm Beach, and he outperformed everybody. His dealership sold the most cars. I think he was number one in the country at the time, profitable, CSI, he had everything, and he was this gentleman. Like Hassan, very quiet, unassuming, but he was a leader of men and he had a culture. The first thing I did is, I went down there and watched him for a couple days and asked him, like I learned so much, just by watching how he acted and how he talked about things and just basically his basic approach to it. You get way further ahead by being a student than being the expert all the time.

Gary: Yeah. I mean, you were telling me that we were talking about that the other day. We're talking about my cholesterol, first of all. I said, "Well, I don't know, but I'm doing everything I can."

Chris: Well, that was ... let me tell this story.

Hassan: His cholesterol is becoming like a universal, kind of--

Chris: It's terrible Hassan.

Gary: The story.

Chris: Even you can't help him, I don't think.

Hassan: I can't because mine is higher than yours.

Chris: Oh okay. Well, same thing.

Gary: I got a new leader.

Chris: This is to going to apply you. He says, we're in a group of people and he says, "No. I'm doing everything I can," and I go, "Really, everything you can?" He goes, "Yeah, everything I can." I go, "Did you study the greats? Like who do you know that has good cholesterol that you're asking for advice?"

Gary: Yeah.

Chris: He got real quiet.

Hassan: Of course.

Gary: I went back and googled it, and there's a guy, "How I Lowered My Cholesterol."

Chris: He has one. He has a cholesterol of one.

Gary: I found it great, and I was like "Oh my god." Like I missed that step and you're right, like we don't seek out people who have done it because our ego gets in the way. I know what I'm doing. I'm exercising, I'm eating right, I'm taking my vitamins, I'm doing what I'm supposed to do, and so I should be getting there. Why do I need to seek out the advice of somebody else? I know how to handle my health, but the truth is, why not? Why not short cut the system and find somebody that knows what they're doing, and it's just our ego.

Chris: No, that's the thing, like if you wanted to be the best service manager, even if you're performing at a high level, you're crazy not to be in our group because you're going to learn something. Like watching, we both watched the Amy Schumer interview on Charlie Rose, and like who do you think Amy Schumer hangs out with? Hassan, who do you think she hangs out with?

Hassan: She hangs out with regular people actually.

Chris: No. She's hanging out with Jerry Seinfeld, Chris Rock, Louis C.K., and like she's saying "Jerry Seinfeld told me to do this and Louis C.K. told me to do this," and she's studying the greats. Charlie Rose even asked her at one point, "How do you get to be friends with them?" She's like "I just ask, and like I work as hard as they do," and so they appreciate that. She's not looking for shortcuts. She's putting in the work, and so those guys want to help her. Right? Don't you want to help an advisor who's putting in the work over a know-it-all?

Hassan: Absolutely. I mean somebody's putting in a lot of effort into getting better. I kind of get drawn to them automatically and I want to go stand by them and reassure them that, "Hey, I got your back. Whatever you need, ask. I'm not going to impose myself or impose my knowledge on you, but I would like you to find out what you're struggling with and tell me about it. I don't want to go in this entire spiel about you doing this or doing that or doing your walk around. I want to know what you're struggling with to get to the next level and then I might put a plan together in my mind really quick to explain to you from the basics, all the way up to reach that point until you understand it."

Chris: Okay, so let's talk about numbers. What was your record for CP?

Hassan: 105, I think.

Chris: Yeah. Brad tried to break, but nobody's ever broken it that we know of, right?

Hassan: Not that I know of, no.

Chris: In that CP labor in one month, 105, and so we talk about KPIs, whatever that stands for. Does it surprise you that he knows the number?

Gary: No, it doesn't surprise me.

Chris: Do you know what the most you ever wrote in parts and labor total?

Hassan: We're talking about GIP performance indicator?

Chris: It's a keyword. Gary wants to state it. Do you remember what your total parts and labor? Biggest month?

Hassan: The biggest month? I believe it was about 420, or 424, something like that.

Chris: That's crazy.

Gary: That's a big number.

Chris: Then, what's the most you made in a year?

Hassan: Broken down or as a total?

Chris: Total.

Hassan: 421,000.

Chris: Yeah, and so that's more than, you say that number like an advisor that made 421,000, that's more than dealers make, right?

Gary: Yeah. They don't - nobody can match that.

Chris: Nobody can comprehend that and it was not a mistake that he made that. He hustled and he had a system. Let's go through the top few things that you did to perform at that elite level, iconic level, really. The first one that I always notice was control. Do you agree with that?

Hassan: I do.

Chris: Not control with customers only, but control with tax too. How do you feel about that compared to your average or even good advisor. What was the difference in your mindset with control?

Hassan: The main ingredient, we need to be honest with you, is controlling what we do as a person, as an advisor. That comes before controlling the customer or controlling technicians or other advisors on a drive. If you have a process in your mind and that process is scalable, you have to control that process and never deviate from it. Never. Because once you take a step back and realize that you missed two or three or one step in that process, you have failed internally and you feel it. If you can stay the course and then deliver every single time the same way with that process, your customer will feel that as well. Customers can understand, or they can sense, if you're nervous, if you don't know what you're talking about but you're trying too hard. But confidence and process every single time can help you collect those customers and can attract them to you automatically. They can actually, if you have a big service drive like the one we did, or like the one they have where we're at right now, it's very easy for customers to look at you while you're taking control of everybody else, even when his advisor is talking to him and trying to help him. You kind of withdraw their attention from their advisor and they look at you.

Chris: Because they're attracted to leaders and confidence?

Hassan: Right. I'm a little louder, I'm a little assertive and I kind of have my customers at my hip always and I'm giving direction constantly. My customers just agree.

Chris: It makes the customer feel safe.

Hassan: Absolutely. You're taking their decision ability away and you're helping them make that decision. Other people can see you and they can just look at you. Either they give you a thumbs up or be like "Can you help me next time?" and that happened many many many times. Makes you feel good, makes you want to do it even more.

Chris: What about with techs on the flip side, because tax would fight to be on your team. What's the most techs you had on your team, was it nine?

Hassan: Nine that are mine, and there were two or three guys.

Chris: Then you feed the rest of the shop too.

Hassan: Yes, absolutely.

Chris: Techs literally would fight--

Gary: That is all service department.

Chris: You would arrive, you'd been promoted if you got on Hassan's team, because they knew they were going to work. How did you manage the techs? Because you know the thing for you, that I saw many times, is you're calling a customer with an update where you're walking out to write another customer. Like time wasn't something you had an abundance of.

Hassan: Correct. I mean, time is of the essence everywhere you work. You have to manage it correctly in order to perform in that level, in order to maximize your volume. For a couple years I tried so many things with technicians to figure out how can I get them productive or to get them to flag the most amount of hours while they're on that clock. One process worked for me very well is to train them and have like a focus group meeting with them once a week to figure out what the shortcomings are. From me or from parts department or from anybody else on the drive or from porters that are not helping them. We kind of like dial that list down from like five or six concerns, because they're not that many, all the way down to zero. After we figured out all their issues and fixed them, then we had the big meeting with them. I took them all out to dinner and I was like "Listen, there is qualifications to be on my team. You have to qualify to be on my team and it's not easy. Number one, if you're ever under 100% productivity, you will never be on my team and I can get you off that easy. Because I'm not going to waste my time and my effort in presenting and doing my walk around and working that hard for you to waste those tickets away." That's number one. "Number two is your estimates and the way you do your inspections." There's ways of inspecting cars if they're here for a certain problem or certain diagnostic issue, and there's another way to inspect cars if they're here for a quick oil service or a brake check or a light bulb check. There's time limits. I time them and I keep a sheet behind my desk on the wall and I'll mark it the time I give them the RL and how fast he's going to bring it to me. You can tell from their productivity if they're actually doing that or they're not doing that. Many times I kick them off my team and eventually only the top guys in the shop will be like, "Hey, I'm making my numbers, can I be on your team?" You create that aura around you that they can't touch you unless they're perfect, and that's how it works usually.

Chris: What about inspection sheets?

Hassan: Inspection sheets? I am never going to go stand in that parts department or go deal with a parts department. They have to fill it out, time, labor, and leave me the totals at the end so I can break it down the way I want to break it down. After I get it delivered from any technician, it will take me about maybe 10 seconds to just add them up on my calculator and I am dialing that number. I can call customers between my appointments and it'll take me two or three minutes to close a deal.

Chris: Yes, so think about that. Most advisors spend maybe 10 minutes figuring out an estimate. To be on his team, like his new tech orientation to his team was longer than an orientation that a dealership usually does with a new employee. He's like, "This is how it works, this is how you're going to do it, and you're handing me that and I'm dialing, so it better be right."

Gary: Wasn't that like one of the seven habits too? If you touch something once, you deal with it and get it off your desk and you don't keep touching it and moving it. What I'm hearing Hassan say is, don't bring it to me until it's ready, because the minute I touch it, I'm calling the customer and it's sold. Whereas most advisors they look at it and they go, "Okay, I'm going to call that guy later and I'm going to call that guy later," and then the stuff just piles up. They don't get to it.

Chris: Do you think that was a part of why you're closing ratios were so much higher? You watch a lot of advisors now and you've seen the guys that worked around you. Why does the average advisor sell three out of ten things when you were closer to 80% or 90%. It's not one thing, but what are the biggest differences?

Hassan: That's really tough to categorize them, but the one that pops in my head, the most that I see around is mostly product knowledge, right? There's no confidence in presenting that part. Number two is the amount of time it takes to present that part to your client. It should be really fast, really quick, and you've got to expect the customer to ask you a question about that product, or what it does or that part. Your answer should be very short and to the point. When you over explain things, people get uncomfortable, they think you're trying too hard. But a lot of advisors don't invest the time in learning their product. They tell you, "I worked at Honda for like 15 years and now it's a new product for me, so I'm having a hard time with it." It's actually not. I mean, you can You Tube anything nowadays and get a part looked at and the video will show you how it works actually.

Chris: Yeah, a 17-year-old kid will explain it to you on You Tube.

Hassan: Yeah, I mean all parts are the same. There's not much of a difference except when you get into electronics and modules and programming. Every franchise has different programming, modules and others.

Chris: Yeah, that's good. What about CSI? What do you think?

Hassan: CSI, back when I wrote, I mean CSI was not ... the region was not as high as it is right now but still, we had to hit 96% and 97%. CSI is actually something you master and it's really, really simple and people make a big deal out of it. It's super easy because nobody wants to present themselves or present the way they do business and they're not asking customers to rate them. What happened - nobody wants to promise upfront is what I'm trying to convey. Everybody wants to beg for that survey at the end and they haven't put up the work upfront for it. Knowing that if you really promise upfront, you're actually forcing yourself to perform well if you have any pride in your job at all. You promise them up front, you contact them twice a day. It becomes super simple. You didn't even have to finish the sentence during delivery, but can you remember that survey? They're going to tell you "I got you, no problem. You're delivering everything you told me you're going to deliver on."

Chris: Yeah, I agree.

Gary: Good stuff.

Chris: What other keywords do you want to hit Hassan with?

Hassan: I'll go with business for 100.

Gary: Ding, ding, ding. How about goals? We're talking about goals.

Chris: Smart goals.

Gary: Smart goals. We were saying that, well, I've been talking about the fact that I think the high achievers, the best advisors, managers, everybody, technicians, they have a goal when they come in to work. I know, like I would come into the shop when I was a tech and I had a specific number of hours I was going to attain that day, that week, that month, in order to make the money that I wanted to make.

Chris: Let me ask both of you guys who are very similar in your drive. Hassan, do you think about your family when you think about money or do you think about just maximizing the opportunity that you have? What makes you drive and work so hard?

Hassan: I wouldn't say my family is my drive. They're very important to me, of course, and providing for them is like my number one priority, but when it comes into goals and why do I drive that hard is: You go into work every day, you're going to work those 10, 11, 12 hours, sometimes more if you work in the automotive business. There is the company goal and there is my personal goal. There is no way and there's no chance I'm going to go in and work July if I made, let's say, 15 or 20 grand in June. It has to be another 500 or 1000 or 2000 in July. It has to keep going up. The moment you go backward, that's the moment you're losing focus and you're not doing your job the way you're supposed to. There isn't a year that I made less than the other year and that was my personal goal. Regardless of what my manager wanted me to do, I had my own personal goal and there was no way I was going to go back, or backwards on it. That was my driver. Eventually, I knew I was going to get into a point where the pay plan is going to be maxed, and we've done that a couple of times, and they said there was no more up than that, but that still didn't stop me from riding.

Chris: Yeah.

Gary: It's funny that Hassan says that. I felt the same way. Whatever I made that year, the next year I wanted to make more.

Chris: Or it was a failure.

Gary: Yeah, or it was a failure, and so I was always trying to increase my income, but for me, it went a little bit deeper because it was for my family. It was really just a drive to live a better life, like I just wanted to have a better life. I didn't want them to have to struggle. I didn't want my kids to have to feel that way, that we couldn't afford things, have a nice car, nice house, live in a nice neighborhood, they went to a nice school. Like all those things were important to me and you had to have money to do that and so I was constantly driving my income forward to get there. Now that they're gone, it's just all about me.

Chris: Toys.

Gary: Yeah.

Chris: Toys. Do you have any hobbies, Hassan?

Hassan: I do. We used to go racing all the time, car racing in Rancho. Racing will drive for like four or five hours and beat the crap out of those cars. I don't fix them under warranty though, when I come back.

Chris: You fixed them under warranty, I think. That's funny. Driving fast is your hobby?

Hassan: Driving fast, burning some tires. It's always a good hobby. I've always liked it.

Gary: Ice fishing?

Hassan: No, I've never been into fishing. I'm getting into deer hunting, because it's becoming big in our family. We bought a nice piece of land in Northern Michigan. We go hunt all the time.

Gary: Have you bagged one?

Hassan: Few.

Gary: Yeah?

Hassan: Yeah.

Chris: Are you hunting them with a gun or a bow?

Hassan: Bow.

Chris: Bow?

Gary: Wow.

Chris: That's real.

Hassan: I'm not perfect at it yet. It was only a couple times that I went, but I have a brother that's a pro at it and we're trying to learn. I enjoy it now.

Chris: Yeah, that's good. Hassan, I'll pretend like he likes football, and he's a Detroit Lions fan. I never get the feeling he really is.

Hassan: No, I'm a soccer fan. I'm a diehard soccer fan. I mean I love football.

Chris: Who's your favorite soccer team?

Hassan: Barcelona, because it's my son's favorite too, so we got to support.

Gary: That was interesting when Hassan and I were traveling back and forth to Chicago for a while. World Cup was going on and him and his family were dressed up and rooting for Germany, right?

Hassan: Yeah, my wife and my youngest son, they love Germany and Bayern Munich, and me and my oldest son we love Barcelona.

Gary: Barcelona.

Hassan: It has to be a challenge in the house. We can't all vote for the same team or it won't be fun anymore.

Gary: Hassan loves his competition.

Chris: Messi or Ronaldo?

Hassan: Messi all the way.

Chris: Really?

Gary: Messi, of course. Why would you go anywhere else?

Hassan: I mean, we can't discredit Ronaldo though. He's a great player, but to me Messi is a man.

Gary: Messi lost. He missed that kick, right? Wasn't that him? Then he cried, and there wasn't some good stuff.

Hassan: Ronaldo missed a kick too. He missed a penalty too. They're both really good, but I like Messi.

Chris: Yeah. I always just think that's funny, that soccer people don't have an opinion. Either way, they're both great.

Hassan: You like soccer too.

Gary: I know one player.

Chris: I do, but I don't. I mean, I think they're so different. I don't even think you can compare.

Hassan: To what, football?

Chris: No, I don't think Messi and Ronaldo are comparable. They're completely different players.

Hassan: Well, Ronaldo won the Ballon d'Or this year and then Messi won it last year, so they're compatible. It's just a personality thing.

Chris: But their game isn't compatible.

Hassan: No.

Chris: Ronaldo's a straight forward, Messi's all over the field.

Hassan: Right.

Chris: Messi's thing is hustle, Ronaldo's is skill. Like Ronaldo is a pure scorer.

Hassan: He is, definitely.

Chris: Messi changes the game.

Hassan: Messi creates games. He creates the play. I mean, he's a master at it.

Chris: He's an alchemist.

Hassan: Oh, absolutely.

Chris: He doesn't score as much as Ronaldo, really.

Hassan: Yeah, I mean, in some-

Chris: He's not a pure scorer like Ronaldo.

Hassan: Right, in some seasons he did better. Ronaldo is definitely a scorer, but Messi can create games out of nowhere and help his teammates score.

Chris: I think there's a deeper marketing lesson in this. Like most people will say, Messi, but why do you think that is?

Gary: He's more attractive?

Chris: No, Ronaldo is more attractive.

Hassan: I can tell you why.

Chris: Why?

Hassan: Because he's more fun to watch. There's always a trick up his sleeve, to me.

Chris: That might be true, but that's not what I was thinking. The common person relates to him more. Like Ronaldo's untouchable. Messi's a normal guy, like he's a guy you could walk into a bar with. He's a guy that has built his career in hustle and trying out hard. Ronaldo is just gifted.

Gary: Yeah.

Chris: He's a good looking guy and he's a pure scorer, but Messi is like, we all can relate to him. We all look at him and we're like, we could be that. I can't be Ronaldo.

Hassan: I mean, Messi got that by accident. If you read his history and his story, he became a soccer player by accident because his brother got sick and he pulled out of the game and eventually Ronaldo, I'm sorry, Messi had a growing or growth problem and Barcelona adopted him and they paid for his medical attention and then he end up signing with the team. That's how he got it. He had something to prove, I guess.

Chris: He's an underdog, that's why.

Gary: Yeah, that's the other part of it. Right? Yeah, come from behind.

Chris: Because it always amazes me how much people, like vehemently, will say Messi and they don't even, like our trainer won't even consider Ronaldo. Like Ronaldo who? He'll go Ronaldo this or he'll name a bunch of Ronaldo's He's like he's not even the best Ronaldo of all time. It's just such an emotion, it's funny. I don't have a dog in the fight either way. I just think it's a great lesson in human behavior that people relate to the underdog and the guy that is the common man, the blue collar player that did good. Because they're both super talented.

Hassan: Absolutely.

Chris: It's kind of a joke to, like, discredit-

Hassan: Like I said, we don't discredit Ronaldo. I mean he's a great player, but I enjoy watching Messi more often.

Chris: Most mornings we listen to Ronaldo get discredited.

Gary: He hates him.

Chris: Yeah, but it's because he's pretty and like, he's gifted.

Hassan: Yeah, I mean, there's some arrogance with his performance and the way he carries himself, a lot of people don't care for it.

Chris: He's a star.

Hassan: Oh, he is. Yeah, he is.

Chris: Messi, like, he'll walk into a bar and he just has that feel. Right? Look at this guy right here, just gritting his teeth. What do you want to say Lucas?

Lucas: Sorry, but Ronaldo is a diva.

Gary: Ronaldo is a diva.

Lucas: That's what the truth is.

Hassan: Let me guess, Perry Sangerman?

Chris: Lucas said he's a diva, what's that mean?

Lucas: You get tackled and it won't get touched and it won't go down anyway.

Hassan: If you want to talk about divas, you should check out Neymar. He's great at it.

Chris: Okay, now went over my head. Neymar. Who's the greatest of all time? Neymar?

Gary: I only know Messi and Ronaldo from his ...

Chris: Does Pele come up anymore?

Gary: No.

Hassan: No, hardly.

Chris: I'm joking. Cool. Well, anything else we should ask you, Hassan?

Hassan: It's up to you.

Chris: No. You're out there, you see the good and the bad. Is there anything else?

Hassan: I think, I mean, are we addressing advisory only?

Chris: No. You want to talk about the presidency and Trump and Hillary?

Hassan: I'll leave that till later, that's a long conversation. We can't build the walls right now.

Gary: We need some hookah and then we'll talk about that.

Hassan: That sounds good, actually. That might bring up more ideas. We have one in the house, ready to go. To be honest with you, I mean, traveling and watching a lot of advisors trying to do their job or struggling in getting there, you can't help but feel that you want to help everybody. But I don't think everybody is structured in a way where they can actually make a process and follow it. I feel in a lot of businesses that is that case. People think they can just go in and wing it and it can happen. You can do that but you're only going to reach a certain level that's going to make you, maybe, comfortable in life. If you're looking for that extra kick, you really have to organize yourself before you do anything else and create a process that can help you, something you can stick to. As they said back in World War II, you need to have a fox hole. Any time you get beat up, you're going to jump back in the fox hole, you're going to regroup and then jump back out and go in and fight again. A lot of people don't do that. They just keep going until they're worn out without really taking one step forward or maybe reading a book about how to organize yourself, or a sales book or anything like that that can help you get a clear idea of how you should do your things. How you should have one, two, three, four, five, six steps without faltering and breaking down. Because eventually it wears you out, it makes you get sick of the position and you're not going to be productive anymore.

Chris: Yeah, that makes a lot of sense.

Gary: The funny thing about that is we've bumped into people like that where, "Ah, you know, I just can't get a process or system," and they don't want to do it and they push back against it. Everybody in this country, everybody that I've ever bumped into has a process in their life that they worked through. That is getting ready in the morning: they get ready the same way, they take shower, they get dressed, they do their hair, they brush their teeth, in the same order almost every day. Almost everybody does that, they have a system. It's like, if you could do that, then you can take that and apply it to something else. Like that is a system and it is a process that you follow and most people don't deviate from it. It cracks me up that they say, "Oh, I just can't. I can't get that going." It's like "Yes you can."

Chris: When you get to work and your hair is all disheveled, then you change your gel but you're not going to stop putting hair product in.

Gary: Right.

Chris: You just tweak your system and you got a system. Right?

Gary: Yeah. I got it.

Chris: You show up and you have BO, then you change deodorant, but you don't not put on deodorant.

Gary: Right. You don't show up soaking wet, and you go, oh, well, I put my clothes on before I took a shower today. I screwed that up.

Chris: Well, one time I put on deodorant and it didn't work, so now I'm not going to use deodorant.

Hassan: There is some truth to it if you think about it. Think about what you just said: that people get up, they brush their teeth, they put their pants on, they're ready for work, right? What got them to that point? It's a power of habit, right? They know they need to do this and if they're late for work, they get up without an alarm, because they're used to getting up at that time, they're used to brushing their teeth before they take a shower, or after. Some people shave before or shave after. It's a routine and it's a habit and it's their process to get them ready at 6:30, for example. It's the same thing in business. If you create a process and you make it a habit, you can never break it because you automatically watch and see what you missed and it makes you actually a better spectator for other people. You can actually see what they're doing and be like "Hey, you're missing step one, two, three, four if you want my opinion. Or if they ask you for help, you can exactly point out what they're doing because you have that strong routine in your life or strong habits.

Gary: For sure.

Chris: Yeah, consistent. What books would you recommend somebody read?

Hassan: The best two books that changed my life in a really, really good way...

Gary: Oh, this is going to be big.

Hassan: One of them was *Psycho-Cybernetics*.

Gary: Of course.

Hassan: Really good book, and the first book I ever read since I've been doing this job is ... from Chet Holmes.

Gary: *The Sales Machine?*

Hassan: Yeah, *Ultimate Sales Machine.*

Chris: Oh yeah, *Ultimate Sales Machine.* Great book.

Hassan: That *Ultimate Sales Machine* has a lot of processes and lots of ways. I think you brought up some of these examples, the seven habits and touch it once. I think these are from that book and it's a really, really good book. The third book I read was *Change Your Brain, Change Your Life.*

Gary: That's a good one too.

Chris: I haven't read that one.

Hassan: It's really, really good. From Dr. Amen, I believe.

Gary: Yeah, Dr. Amen.

Hassan: *Psycho-Cybernetics* is crazy. It's really a good book. You have to read it two or three times to get it all.

Chris: Yeah, another subject, I was talking to Pratt about Dr. Amen. Would you ever go do that, the scan, like Ben did?

Hassan: With Dr. Pratt?

Chris: No, Dr. Amen.

Hassan: I think we contacted with him about my kid, because of what we talked about, but I haven't done it for myself.

Chris: Did your son do it?

Hassan: Well, we had a consultation on the phone. Yes, so that was good.

Chris: It's cool.

Gary: It's great.

Chris: Good. Well, thank you Hassan. Thanks for-

Hassan: You're welcome.

Gary: The GOAT.

Chris: It's a treat for everybody to see the GOAT.

Gary: Yeah, it's good to have you at the office.

Hassan: Thank you.

Gary: It's been a while.

Hassan: Oh, yeah.

Chris: Remember to put your pants on tomorrow, okay?

Hassan: That's the power of habit, I put them on every morning.

Chris: I want you to brush your teeth, bro. Stop showing up
             naked. It's awkward.

Gary: I never know where I'm going to take a shower.

Hassan: Gary, don't forget you're doing it right in our place.

Chris: You need a system, bro.

Hassan: It might help your cholesterol.

Chris: How high is your cholesterol?

Hassan: You don't want to know.

Gary: I want to know. Give me the number.

Chris: Guys, we got a new person to pick on.

Gary: I know.

Hassan: 337.

Gary: Holy Moses!

Chris: What do they say about that?

Hassan: Hereditary. It runs in the family.

Chris: Dave Anderson would say about that-

Gary: I need Dr. Lau to see his blood.

Hassan: Remember, I don't eat, so I don't know where that comes from.

Gary: I don't either.

Chris: I know you eat really clean.

Hassan: Well, I mean-

Chris: You eat a lot of carbs though.

Hassan: I might eat some bread at night. I mean, not a lot if we're hungry all day but-

Chris: Do they put you on meds?

Hassan: Yeah, I'm taking Crestor right now.

Chris: What about niacin?

Hassan: 10 milligrams. I tried it a couple of times, man. I looked like I was going to ... I looked like I parachuted from a flight, man.

Chris: It takes...you got to do it like for a week. You got to just bear it.

Hassan: Ben has been telling me about it all along. I took a couple of pills and it looked like I just came out of a hell somewhere and my face was all red. It was bad.

Chris: You know, blotchy? Your skin gets itchy.

Hassan: Well, I talked to the pharmacist. He said you should take like a pill of aspirin before you take it, like half an hour before, until your body gets used to the dose and then it'll become okay.

Chris: Are you taking with food too? It helps but you're going to get red. It goes away if you up the dose and then it goes away, but once you stop, you've got to go through that again.

Gary: It's tough, yeah.

Chris: Well, cool. Thanks everybody. We'll see you next time.

Hassan: Thank you.

Gary: Thank you everybody.

Episode #14: The Service Manager's Happy Hour

Chris: I apologize to everybody in advance. Welcome to Service Drive Revolution, where we share the latest strategies and techniques for collecting customers and running a healthy service department. Basically, we're going to undo everything ... Basically everything that will help you get to the next level of performance, from beginner to advanced. But disregard all that, that isn't going to happen this time.

Gary: No, this is going to be a little rough.

Chris: Welcome, G-Man.

Gary: Thank you. Welcome everybody.

Chris: We're happy that there's somebody here with worse cholesterol than you, and so I'm thinking he's going to die before you.

Jair: Oh my god.

Chris: He won't try Niacin.

Mario: Because you guys eat healthy, man.

Gary: I've never been so happy in my whole life. There's a guy in worse health. You could die before me. That's awesome.

Chris: You heard about a guy that could have worse cholesterol than you, but you never met him until now.

Gary: You said, "Find "the Greats." I just found him.

Chris: The wrong way. That's the wrong way.

Ben: It's the first time Hassan's been in last place.

Chris: You guys, Hassan and Gary, I want to tell you guys both something. I want you to really listen to me. Cholesterol is not a race. It's not a race.

Gary: It's a high score?

Chris: It's like golf, the lower the better.

Gary: Oh, god. I'm crying.

Chris: By the way, I'm not a doctor. Okay so, we just came off the Top Dog event, and we had a lot of fun.

Gary: We had a blast.

Chris: But I want to talk about the Top Dog event the year before, when Mario got his wallet stolen by a hooker. But I want Ben to tell the story, not Mario.

Ben: I don't remember the story. Honestly, I don't.

Mario: That's where I'm at too. I don't remember it.

Gary: What? Get out!

Chris: That's convenient.

Gary: You absolutely remember it.

Mario: What's happens in Vegas, stays in Vegas.

Chris: I never believed half of it.

Ben: Hassan you know the story.

Chris: Tell the real story.

Gary: Somebody tell the story. Somebody tell the story.

Chris: Were you there, Jair?

Jair: No.

Chris: No?

Gary: Tell the story Mario. Don't be shy.

Chris: But tell the real story.

Mario: From what I remember ...

Hassan: While he was awake.

Mario: While I was awake? I was awake the entire time, but we were with clients and we were showing them a good time and one thing led to another and somehow I lost my wallet.

Chris: And he chased a hooker down Las Vegas Boulevard-

Mario: That's as much as I can say.

Chris: ...and lost your wallet.

Gary: What? It fell out of your pocket?

Chris: What? There's like, a non-disclosure thing you signed? Like, what?

Mario: Yeah, I don't know.

Chris: You're embarrassed, that's why.

Mario: Yeah, yeah. There is a bit--

Chris: But how? Have you ever had your wallet stolen by a hooker?

Gary: No, no.

Mario: I've been in Vegas and I've never lost my wallet.

Gary: Never had my wallet stolen, ever.

Mario: I mean, people were talking about that, this event. People at this event were talking about, "Hey, you got your wallet?" And I'm double-checking like, "Yeah I do, thank you for the reminder."

Chris: There were no hookers, there were no hookers.

Mario: Yeah, definitely not.

Chris: We screened.

Gary: By the way Mario, we don't entertain clients that way. Just FYI and anybody that's listening, that's not how we do things.

Chris: What are you talking about?

Gary: He was just saying, we were entertaining some clients with some less than ...

Mario: I was chaperoning.

Chris: HR, here Gary? Anyways, moving on...

Mario: Moving on.

Chris: It's a rare treat that we get all these guys in one room, right? This our team.

Gary: It's getting dark.

Chris: We're the island of misfit toys.

Mario: Should we call this Service Drive Revolution happy hour?

Gary: It is happy hour.

Chris: It's always happy hour - that's how we do it. Except for a couple times, we did it without drinking, right? But not very often.

Gary: Not too many.

Chris: Okay, do your Dave Chappelle thing?

Gary: No.

Chris: What was the couch thing? Do the face.

Gary: Do the face? Oh, what did the hand say to the face? Slap!

Ben: Rick James.

Gary: I'm Rick James!

Chris: Behind the curtain, everybody listening or watching, these guys are non-stop Dave Chappelle quotes. Every inappropriate one, too.

Gary: Yes. For sure.

Chris: The funniest one's the Prince, god rest his soul, and the basketball one.

Gary: Oh, Prince and the basketball was hilarious. Those were the best bits ever.

Chris: You couldn't even make that up.

Gary: No.

Chris: That's where truth is funnier than fiction. Hilarious.

Hassan: He also had one on Revolution.

Gary: That's right. He did have a Revolution.

Chris: Prince and the Revolution.

Gary: And he could ball, apparently.

Chris: Evidently.

Gary: Prince is a baller.

Chris: Okay, so we have our secret weapon here, Ben. How many drinks have you had, Ben?

Ben: Maybe three or four.

Chris: And he hasn't had dinner yet. So he's going to tell us a lot of secrets.

Gary: It's truth serum.

Chris: So why do you think Hassan won't take Niacin?

Ben: He likes to be first in everything.

Chris: Competitive. What's your cholesterol, Ben?

Gary: Oh, my god.

Chris: Like, 100.

Ben: 97.

Gary: 97? What? I quit.

Ben: I'm serious. I just took 2,500 milligrams of Niacin, and I'm not red.

Gary: This guy, eats bacon with every meal. I remember the first time Ben, you and I went on the road. We went to Iowa together. We go to this restaurant, and Ben gets like, 9 eggs, and then just like it's egg soup in his plate, and like 72 pieces of bacon, and eats the whole thing. I just don't get it. It's not fair. Life's just not fair.

Mario: Gary, the worst part is, when I go to eat with Ben, and we're eating, he orders 9 eggs, 5 orders of bacon, and then they look at me, and I go, "I'll just have a regular." "Are you sure?" I'm like, "Yeah, I'm okay with the regular serving of it."

Gary: Can I get a small oatmeal, and put a few cranberries in there for me?

Ben: I just don't know what to say.

Mario: 97, though, right?

Gary: 97.

Chris: Is it really 97? That's not a joke? You're not saying that just to ruin Gary's day?

Ben: I take a lot of Niacin, though. It's a secret, but it works. It's a secret weapon.

Chris: But that's the thing, like ... Hassan, honestly, it's not a mystery.

Hassan: Got to work on it.

Chris: I mean, a little red skin, big deal. You've dealt with worse than that in your life, for sure.

Ben: And if you take it for a week, you get through that. But you have to stay consistent.

Chris: Yeah. You got to stick with it.

Ben: But if I don't take it for two days, I'll get red, and it's uncomfortable, but you just got to be consistent.

Chris: Once again, we're not doctors. Consult your doctor.

Gary: Please don't take our advice.

Chris: But the people that we know that are high performers are, they're taking like 3,000 milligrams a day, right?

Ben: Yeah, and every one of the doctors that we see, say that they recommend it, but most patients just don't have the tolerance, or the wherewithal to stick it out until it's not uncomfortable.

Chris: You'd be proud of Gary this week. He was popping those things.

Ben: I saw your candy jar.

Chris: He thought ... Yeah.

Ben: He's got a candy jar filled with like, 3,000 pills of Niacin.

Gary: That's Niacin?

Ben: It is Niacin.

Gary: Niacin. I got one like that on my desk-

Ben: You've got to put that on the table. We have to put that on the table.

Chris: That's one of two jars.

Ben: There's one in the office.

Chris: And he's on continuity.

Ben: Nice.

Chris: Boxes of Niacin just coming every month.

Ben: It just comes.

Chris: So you guys, eat up. It's free. Eat up. You too, Jair.

Jair: Sure.

Gary: I did 1,500 yesterday. It hurt. But I did 1,500 yesterday.

Ben: Take an ibuprofen, or an aspirin.

Gary: Oh, okay.

Ben: Before you do it. It'll help.

Hassan: Hey, Ben, we should take it before our presentation. We will be... all four of us...

Gary: Get all fired up.

Ben: No. Sometimes we're sitting in a meeting with an owner or a general manager, and they're like, "Are you okay?" "I'm not upset. I just took Niacin, I'm sorry."

Ben: No, they're looking like, "Are you okay? Do we need to stop?" Like, "No, we're fine."

Chris: "Yeah, we're good." Everybody is a little giddy, because you guys have put in a bunch of hard work and you're kicking off 2 stores right now, right?

Ben: Yeah.

Chris: Simultaneously, and they're close to each other, so it's fun, because we get to be together. We won't say the name of the stores, but the one today, what was the Effective Labor Rate, Ben? It went from 114...?

Ben: 149?

Chris: To 149.

Gary: Overnight.

Ben: They tripled their daily CP average.

Chris: Not three months, not six months - overnight.

Gary: Overnight.

Chris: Boom. You dropped the bomb.

Ben: One day.

Chris: It's crazy.

Ben: Couple weeks of preparation, but one day.

Chris: Yeah, you loaded the gun, but when it went, it went. It's fun.

Gary: That was a thing I took away from the 50K challenge and the Top Dog event, when all those guys got to present. It's that at some point, each one of those guys made the decision to just do it. I'm just going to go. And it's like, that's-

Chris: It's a leap of faith.

Gary: Yeah, and that's the thing when we come in, and we say this all the time, it's like, "We're not geniuses." We're not any smarter than anybody else that works there, but we have access to a lot more information, and we just don't have an option. We're going to go. It's just going to happen. We're there to fix it, and we're going.

Ben: Yeah, it's funny, I think, that the one thing we hear is that we just won't take no for an answer. They're impressed by that, because they're like, "We'll wear you down eventually." We just don't wear down, and we just keep going, and by the third, fourth, fifth step, we start to see results. But we're not backing down until we get it.

Chris: Yeah, like there's no magic, most of the time. I mean, there's things that we know that work, but like even with, like hiring techs or whatever, we do it. Right?

Ben: Yeah, it's just consistency and execution.

Chris: The one thing, you guys, that I like and we should talk about this internally, is at the event, one thing became very clear to me, and it's a huge win for us, I think. A tribute to what a great job you guys are doing, is that overwhelmingly, over and over and over again, the guys were saying, "You guys aren't consultants, you're my coach." We always talk about how we hate consultants in our industry and we've all been burned by consultants, but that was a huge thing, and we should get rid of the word consultant, and we should brand coach somehow. Because really, we're vested with them, right? A coach, like, is vested with you. You're in it with them, and that's how they feel. They feel like we're in it with them and we care as much. We're not like dropping it and running and making them feel dumb. Ben and I worked with a guy that was like that, where he would isolate them, and like, pick out everybody's flaws, and just spit in plates, instead of just helping. That's the thing that our industry needs right now, is they need help. They need coaches.

Gary: I was talking to the new sales guy we hired, and he was asking me about our business. This is his first day on the job, so he shows up here. I'm explaining to him what we do, and he was saying, "You know, when I hear the word consultant, the first thing I think is that it's probably really hard to get a hold of that person. And so, if I hire a consultant, they come in, and they give me a bunch of advice. And then if I need more help, and I want to reach out to them, I can't get a hold of them. I can't find them. They're off doing something else." I said, "Oh, no. That's not us." I go, "We are so far, you know, in your business." You're just like, "Oh my god, this guy's got his thumb on me, and I can't get out from under it." Because, I mean, we're vested. Like you said, we're there. We're coach. We're on the field, we're playing the game with them, and we're going to make things happen. We're not disappearing and saying, "Here's the game plan. We'll talk to you later."

Chris: What did you say, Hassan?

Hassan: I can't say that. It's just a movie we watched yesterday, something about a thumb up in it so far, and he was like, well, it does feel good, but it's inappropriate. What is that, it feels good?

Chris: Could somebody translate?

Ben: It may fit, but it's not appropriate.

Chris: I don't get it.

Gary: You finally got it, right?

Ben: God and baby Jesus, help us.

Gary: It fits. It fits. It's just not appropriate that it's there.

Chris: Oh.

Ben: Yeah, it may fit, but it's not proper. It was a discussion about the difference between fitting and proper.

Gary: Hey, Lucas, insert drum roll here...

Chris: So, the thing, we've all heard the Bob jokes, right?

Mario: Yep.

Ben: Yeah.

Chris: So, we can overcome that now. Now we got to be the coach. We're going to figure out something for that. I want to talk about that constantly, because it's a ... Even reading those essays for the $50,000 challenge--

Gary: Oh, man.

Chris: Man, these guys. They get so raw and vulnerable, and--

Gary: It was funny. We were just talking about it, because we watched some of the video, the footage from it today. It wasn't the numbers. The numbers are amazing and impressive and everything that they did was unbelievable, but they barely touched the numbers. Like, barely, when they were talking about the experience, and it was just the emotional journey-

Chris: It's way more real.

Gary: Yeah. It was that transformation, and the freedom, and the space to kind of manage their universe. They could control what was going to happen to them, and for them, that was everything. It was more than numbers.

Chris: I mean, how many guys said it was the first time they saw a financial?

Gary: Oh, it was crazy.

Chris: When they had to come to our thing.

Gary: It's crazy.

Chris: Dealers are idiots in our industry, that they don't give their managers the tools to run their departments. Who has a service manager running 50, 75, 100 people, and they don't ever get to see the report card?

Ben: Yeah, they don't train them, either.

Chris: I mean, it's insane. And the poor service manager's just set up for failure.

Gary: In a lot of cases it's a 15, 20, 30 million-dollar business, and they don't see the financial statement.

Chris: Yeah, and they run it like it's a joke.

Gary: Are you kidding me? Like, who else would do that?

Chris: It's crazy. Yeah, well on that note, back to the Dave Chappelle quotes.

Gary: Rick James.

Chris: Hookers.

Gary: Hassan's got one. Hassan, throw one down. What do you got for Rick James?

Hassan: What was that?

Gary: What do you got for a Rick James quote? Charlie Murphy?

Hassan: "Take that one pap."

Chris: What's your favorite movie, Hassan?

Hassan: I like stupid comedy. There's a lot of favorites.

Mario: *Coming to America.*

Jair: Oh, I love that.

Chris: That's a good one, that's a good one.

Hassan: Well, I like *The Waterboy*.

Chris: *Waterboy*? Is that Adam Sandler?

Gary: Adam Sandler.

Hassan: You should watch it. It's really awesome.

Chris: I'm never going to watch it. I'll never watch that.

Hassan: You will never watch it?

Chris: No.

Hassan: It's Adam Sandler. Why wouldn't you watch it?

Chris: Yeah, I watched *Happy Gilmore*. That was enough.

Hassan: Well, I mean, it's almost similar.

Gary: They're all the same.

Hassan: His story is always the same.

Chris: It's funny in *Happy Gilmore* when he fights the guy from the *Price is Right*. I don't remember ...

Gary: Oh, yeah, Bob Barker?

Chris: That's hilarious. That's the best part of that movie.

Gary: "Price is wrong, Bob."

Hassan: But, what does he tell him, when Bob beats him? At the end?

Gary: I don't remember.

Hassan: He said, "The price is right, bitch."

Chris: That's funny. What other little tidbits have you guys picked up from the event?

Hassan: You know, when I went back to ... Maybe I shouldn't be naming names, but you know. I ran into a couple of the managers that were at the event, and they had some of their top advisors that usually don't communicate a lot with their managers. I think the first thing they did, and the GM told me about it, is they walk right to their GM the second day after the event, and they told him the following, and I quote, "I really appreciate you keeping me employed here. I know I haven't been on top of my game lately, but I'm going to earn it for you again."

Gary: Wow.

Chris: Nice.

Hassan: That was a great comment made by a GM and by the advisor to his GM, so.

Chris: What'd you guys think of Jocko?

Ben: He was great.

Chris: He was better than I thought he would be. He was amazing. He's such a great dude.

Gary: Yeah, no, he's awesome.

Chris: He's a pro.

Gary: He's awesome.

Chris: He's there early. Just hung out. Just humble as can be.

Gary: Signed a bunch of books, had lunch with the guys afterwards, it was great.

Chris: What did you guys think about, when you talk about training, like we can't get people to do advisor training. Did you guys hear what he did when he was in charge of training for the SEALS? With going to Hollywood, and getting building sets? My friend Mike, I told him about that, and he did it. He picked it right. Jocko does this scenario, when you walk in a room, and there's the crazy wife screaming, and the dead soldier in front of you, and what was the other scenario? It's was like, three things going on, right?

Jair: The guy got shot. His leg just got amputated.

Chris: That one, the wives and something else?

Jair: Oh, there's people shooting at you, at the same time.

Gary: Oh, yeah, that's it.

Jair: That's it.

Gary: So there's guys shooting at you, there's a wounded soldier, and then the screaming wife. Then he's got to decide-

Chris: So, for everybody listening, because maybe we didn't explain it right, he would go to Hollywood and have them build realistic sets that the SEALS could train in. One of the sets they would build, is they would bust in this door,

393

and then people are firing. There's a soldier, one of their brothers in arms, on the ground with his legs gone, or something, and dying, bleeding out. You bleed out in what, in like 30 seconds?

Gary: Yeah, that's what he said. He's got about 30 seconds to live.

Chris: 30 seconds or he's dead. He's bleeding out, and he's screaming. Then you got women screaming, wives or something. Then there's terrorists in the room or whatever, and what do you do? It's crazy.

Gary: Nah, that's crazy.

Mario: All while they're shooting at you.

Gary: Well, that's the thing-

Chris: It's go time.

Gary: His point was prioritize and execute. He had to decide. So if he went to go save the wounded soldier, the guy's got 30 seconds left, then he's going to get killed and everybody that comes in to do the same thing, that's what's going to happen, so ...

Chris: There'd just be a pile of dead soldiers.

Gary: At some point, somebody's got to take down the bad guys and the guys that are shooting at you, and then deal with the other things afterwards. It's unfortunate, because somebody's going to have to survive, but you don't have a choice. In that moment you've got to decide what the most immediate threat is, and deal with it. That's what he did.

Chris: Yeah, and then Gary really made an impression on you. What did he say? Something about cover?

Gary: Oh, yeah, it's "Cover and move."

Chris: "Cover and move."

Gary: "Cover and move. Cover and move." I think that's critical. It's funny that he said it, and I was sitting in the audience going, "Damn! You have to cover and move. You cannot leave your brothers exposed." I don't care whether you're in the service drive, you're working in the shop, you're here with us in the office. It is what it is. It's cover and move. You've got to support and hold and maintain the front, and cover your brothers when you're in battle.

Chris: He's got the new girl, Sarah, you guys met her, right? When you came in? He's got her better trained. He just screams from up there, "Cover and move."

Ben: I like that.

Chris: She gets him lunch.

Mario: Guys, one of the thing I wanted to bring up, talking about the event and what we got out of it...

Chris: Whoa, whoa, whoa.

Mario: You got something to say, Chris?

Chris: No, go ahead.

Mario: But, what I was going to say is, it was basically, I heard a lot of managers talking about going back, and writing down why they do their processes. How many people have systems and processes, but they don't know why they have them? So their people, naturally, don't know why they're there, so no one follows them. So, just hearing them saying, "I'm going to go back, and I'm going to document why we do a process. I'm going to write down why we present everything up front, or the systems," but they're already thinking about documenting everything. And just in talking with them and communicating, they're opening up their eyes on, "You're right. That's what it does." It was exciting to see their eyes open up to the basic fundamentals, and then going back and creating the why is going to make them a better coach. Like I always tell people, don't be a dictator, don't be that consultant that comes in and dictates how to do it and walks away. We got to be a coach. The coach's responsibility is to motivate, inspire, and push you past your limits. That's the fundamentals of a coach. So, just hearing them, it got me excited that I know they're already going back with a lot of ammunition to be better than they were the year before.

Chris: Who was your favorite speaker? We had Dave Anderson. We had Tim. Then we had Jocko, and then Gus.

Mario: I'm going to go with Jocko. They all enlightened me, they all brought their own presentation, and it was all on performance-base, but there's something about a 20-year-old veteran that's like, protecting and saving my life, for my freedom. I'm rooting for him. I think he impacted me just naturally on who he is.

Chris: How about you, Ben?

Ben: Jocko. Intensity. Focus.

Mario: Control.

Chris: What's the biggest thing you got from him?

Ben: Just consistency. Just having a plan, owning it, accepting responsibility for the people beneath you. No excuses, not reporting the news, the problems, but owning it. Like if they don't know the answer, it's because you didn't tell them. You didn't think about the thing that they might miss, or they might forget, or they might not be focused on. And, being three steps ahead.

Chris: It's crazy. Just owning it.

Ben: Just the intensity is incredible.

Chris: Yeah. And so genuine. How about you, Jair?

Jair: I got to say the same thing. I mean, one thing that stood out, is he mentioned, and I know we've been talking about it, routine. I mean, every morning, he says, I'm up, 4:00. You look at his Instagram, and he takes a picture. He takes a picture of his watch every single morning so that you know, it's like, "I'm in it. I'm ready."

Chris: He's the real deal.

Jair: I'm ready to come out. I'm ready to do this.

Gary: He's got a quote that he puts on his Twitter, and he takes the picture of his watch, says, "Up before the enemy."

Jair: Yeah. It's crazy. He mentioned that. Like, you got to be determined, you got to have your game face on, you got to be ready. He does that, every single day.

Ben: Yeah, I liked how he said, "Respect the enemy." That was powerful. I think respecting the enemy. What you're up against. Not discounting it, not ... You got to be one step ahead. You don't know what they're doing. They're preparing while you're sleeping.

Mario: One of the things, not so much on the event, but in the book when I read it, once we knew he was going to be a speaker, I was reading his book, and one of the most impactful things that he said, is, "There's no bad teams. Only bad leaderships." It was so impactful, and that message, we can go into dealers and really hold the managers accountable, and just tell them that message there, and it opens up their eyes. Because the reality, we're the leaders. We control everything, there's no bad teams, only bad leadership or bad managers.

Chris: Well, isn't there a story in the book about how, when he was testing or he was running it, that they just switched the leader and the other team won?

Ben: Yeah, they would test him.

Gary: That was that boat thing, they were carrying the boat.

Mario: I think catapults or something like that, right?

Gary: I can't remember if they rowed it but they had to carry it.

Ben: They had to fire the leader and put the lowest guy in to see if he could figure it out.

Gary: Yeah, so they had a team that kept losing, losing, losing, and they switched out the leader, and then that team won. Same guys, just a different leader.

Ben: So they would pick, like, the lead guy, I think, because he had the most, he was just the most confident, but sometimes that guy didn't get the best answers. Sometimes the guys that had less confidence but were willing to work as a team.

Gary: He said, the guy who comes out and says, "Well, Mario didn't execute, and Ben didn't do this, and Jair forgot that, and Hassan ..." Then he's like, "Okay, well that guy's not the leader."

Mario: Well, the funny part is, the guy that was losing, all he kept doing is complaining and not figuring out a way to fix it. As he kept going, he goes, "Well, I'll give you the best group," because he kept saying, "It's lucky. You got the best team and I got stuck with these people, and they don't know how to do nothing." So they switch them to give him the best team, and now, the best team becomes the worst, and then the worst becomes the best because of the leadership.

Gary: Right, what does that sound like? That sounds like "my market, my brand, my guys."

Mario: Bunch of excuses.

Gary: "You can't hire techs up in here." It's like, come on...

Jair: It's so funny. You know being in our business you get that. It's the same excuse all the time. "Give me the team. I want the best techs." Or the techs are like, "I want to be with the best advisor." But it's those teams that you form when you have camaraderie and accountability to each other and say, "You know what guys, we're going to put this together and we're going to do it together and we're going to win." I'll bring out a story of myself when I had my team. "Oh, you know, your team it's like a C plus team." I'm like, "Forget that! We're going to kill it." They'd be like, "Oh, you don't have so and so." I remember this one tech, "You don't have Lenny's team," or "You don't have Art's team. Those guys are the killers." I'm like, "Forget all that. We're going to come together." I'll never forget, one month, when I started having that momentum, we were killing them every single month. We annihilated them and I loved it.

Gary: Well that was the same thing on my side. I don't know, I can't even count how many advisors wrote for me. But I was not going to be denied. I don't care, you're going to sell, you're going to move, I'm going to work. You're not going to get in my way. It's the same thing. If you make that, if you have that commitment, you're just going to get it done. That's it.

Chris: Didn't we talk about this not that long ago Ben, about how we were number one in the country, but it was an island of misfit toys? Like nobody individually...

Ben: I don't remember that conversation specifically, what do you mean?

Chris: No just when, at BMW, we were number one in the country but it was ... I mean.

Ben: It wasn't...it didn't look perfect.

Chris: No.

Ben: No, but we had a common goal, a common purpose, a vision. That mattered more than all the other stuff.

Chris: It wasn't that we didn't have a lot of talent, because we had tons of talent, but it just wasn't what you would think on the outside.

Ben: I think there's a correlation between talent and relative degrees of dysfunction.

Chris: What was funny is whenever somebody would hire somebody away from us, they would pay them all the money and they would last 90 days, because it was the group, it was the team.

Gary: We see that all the time. Teams that don't have quite the same talent as another team will win, because they function together as a unit. Then you get a team that's full of super stars, by all rights, spending all the money they should win, and they don't win.

Chris: My grandpa used to say, "There's only one ball". I want to hear Hassan. Who is your favorite speaker?

Ben: Yeah, we need to hear about Hassan's favorite. Hassan is the only other person that's been there.

Chris: Drum roll please.

Mario: Hassan?

Gary: Jair body guards the mic. He won't let it get to Hassan.

Chris: Mario Day, MC. You did a great job Mario.

Gary: He did sing, didn't he?

Hassan: Between being MC and barking I think it was the best. I can't really judge it, because unfortunately, I wasn't fortunate enough to stay and watch Jocko.

Chris: Oh you didn't see Jocko?

Hassan: No, my schedule did not work very well for me. I had a flight that was leaving.

Chris: Oh, so then Tim was your favorite?

Hassan: It's very tough for me. I don't want to judge the guy without listening to him. I read part of his book, but I got to finish it first. But just meeting him and shaking his hand and stuff like that, you can tell he is intense and he's very serious about what he does.

Chris: I thought Tim did a great job. He slipped a couple times on the sales thing, but he did a great job. I love his emotional thing. We have the video of that, and hopefully he'll let us put it out.

Gary: Yeah that thing's-

Chris: I will give it to him. The emotion of a customer on the timeline is so powerful. He's so good. If you haven't seen that, you can go to Tim Kintz on You Tube and watch him do it on a napkin for the sales department, but his analogy applies to anything. He could be selling furniture.

Gary: You can find it on kintznow.com, I think it is. But yeah it's good stuff.

Chris: It's really good stuff. It was fun. We were watching that back today and it's really good. Then uncle Dave is always great. How're we going to top it next year?

Gary: I have no idea. Give me a couple of months to recover.

Chris: That's the thing I was instantly worried about after. I'm like, who's going to be better than Jocko? What's Eddie Murphy's brother? We could get him.

Ben: Charlie Murphy.

Chris: I see him all the time.

Ben: He's really inexpensive.

Chris: Yeah we could get him easy.

Gary: Terry Crews. I see Terry Crews at the gym every day.

Chris: You think Terry Crews does a motivational thing?

Gary: I don't know.

Chris: That guy is so... he's scary.

Gary: Oh my god. He's a giant.

Hassan: Terry Crews was one of my clients.

Gary: Oh really?

Hassan: He came to the dealership all the time.

Chris: It's funny, everybody at the gym bitches because he won't take a selfie with them. I would never ask him at the gym to take a selfie.

Hassan: He took one with me at the Duke's.

Chris: Not at the gym. He's there to workout. Like leave the guy alone, geez.

Gary: That dude's a beast. He's unbelievable.

Chris: He does this thing too, he does this thing where we do cleans. He does cleans and then goes up and jumps. It's just straight up. Like no, that's not natural. It's crazy. We're not talking about like 25s. He's got plates on each side. He played in the NFL right?

Gary: Yeah, he played in the NFL. I think he was a tight end or something like that, or linebacker, he was a linebacker.

Chris: I was going to say he's got to be a linebacker. He's huge.

Gary: Yeah, he ran out of plates. He was doing squats the other day in the gym, he ran out of plates. He couldn't put anymore plates on. I was like, my god...

Hassan: Could've hung on to that bar.

Gary: Yeah, it's ridiculous.

Chris: You don't get around him when he's lifting.

Hassan: Your cholesterol's heavy enough to pull down.

Mario: Yeah.

Gary: Hey bro, who are you talking to?

Chris: Kettle calling the pot black.

Hassan: Hey, I got to be able to rip on somebody with cholesterol, come on.

Chris: You're the winner bro, you're the GOAT.

Gary: I know, my goodness.

Hassan: That doesn't mean that he's not second best.

Ben: I'll give you some Niacin.

Hassan: Niacin. I'm going to start with...

Chris: I can't believe you're scared of Niacin.

Hassan: I'm not scared of it, I mean.

Gary: Well you're not taking it, so you're something of it.

Hassan: I mean I have a prescription drug that I'm taking.

Chris: That's terrible.

Ben: How's that working for you?

Chris: I'd avoid that.

Hassan: I just started that a month ago.

Chris: It'll work, but man that's bad.

Hassan: I'd rather have an ache in my muscle versus getting all red and green.

Chris: Green? That's new. You get green?

Hassan: Well not really.

Chris: Hulking out.

Hassan: It's just a figure of speech.

Chris: That's funny. So how're we going to top it next year? Come on Gary...

Gary: Oh my god. I'm thinking John Gruden, maybe.

Chris: Boo.

Hassan: Can you reveal secrets right now? I mean you can't reveal the secrets.

Gary: I'm just throwing some teasers out. I like sports, maybe-

Chris: We tried Phil Jackson, he wouldn't come.

Mario: Let's make some calls.

Gary:	What about the 49er guy that went to Michigan?
Jair:	Harbaugh?
Gary:	Yeah.
Chris:	He's great.
Gary:	Show off your tattoo Mario. Maybe you can get some play.
Chris:	What are you talking about?
Mario:	They see it, they see it. I don't want to rob the bank.
Chris:	I don't think he does that. He doesn't want to miss any time recruiting. But he's great.
Hassan:	How about Kim Kardashian? I mean she keeps that value going all the time.
Chris:	No. What are we going to learn from her?
Hassan:	She always has attention.
Chris:	Yeah, no. Something related to performance Hassan.
Hassan:	Well, don't even go there.
Chris:	The kind of performance we can do. Something we could do.
Gary:	Really, car business, Hassan.
Mario:	We're in the car business.
Hassan:	Well okay.
Chris:	Hassan's like the agent over there. It's so funny. Kim Kardashian fixing cars?

Gary: Hey, we're in Los Angeles, we got to find something.

Chris: You got the new Kanye album Hassan?

Hassan: Uh, no. It ain't Chipotle.

Chris: What's the deal with that?

Hassan: That's all I remember out of it.

Gary: Oh god.

Hassan: That's the Kanye song. You just asked me if I got the album.

Chris: Chipotle?

Hassan: How's it go Mario?

Mario: It's a Schoolboy Q and Kanye song collaboration. I forget the lyrics, but ... What does it say? Okay, okay, okay, okay, okay, okay. "Beggars can't be choosers. Bitch this ain't Chipotle."

Chris: Mario, everybody just tuned out. It's a video case. I'm out.

Hassan: Drop the mic.

Mario: Something like that. I need the beats. Lucas let's put some beats on. There we go. He got's it. All right, we're going to stick to our day jobs.

Chris: That's funny.

Gary: We fix service departments, not albums people.

Chris: Well everybody watching or listening to this, I apologized in advance, but we had fun. That's what matters sometimes. But we thank you and we will see you very soon. Adios.

Episode #15: The Most Effective Dispatch System

Chris: Welcome everybody to Service Drive Evolution, my handsome co-host, G-Man, how you doing, G-Man?

Gary: Doing well, thank you.

Chris: This podcast is for anybody with a service drive department, if you have techs and advisors, this is for you. We're here to help you we have the best service manager training, I believe, in the universe, and advisor training, for sure, is the best in the universe. And then we have a couple books, *Irreplaceable Service Manager*, and the *Millionaire Service Advisor*. So, this is gonna be a fun one because we're going to answer a question that is kind of about shop loading, and a handsome gentleman Cecil Sims on LinkedIn was bantering with me, and we're gonna help him, we're gonna diagnose his problems.

Gary: Cool, I don't know anything about this.

Chris: Yeah, this is where I'm just gonna ambush you.

Gary: Everybody just out there know that I'm doing my best up here.

Chris: And then G-Man reads a lot of books, and so he was reading a book, what's the book called?

Gary: It's called *Smarter Faster Better*.

Chris: *Smarter Faster Better*. By who?

Gary: Charles Duhigg.

Chris: And Gary's gonna tell you all about that. I was getting confused by that, is it a Kanye song? *Stronger, Faster, Better?*

Gary: Oh yeah.

Chris: If anybody asked me, I said, I meant, *Stronger Faster Better* or something.

Chris: We have a, what would you call it, a guest?

Gary: We have a guest star, Mama Lola.

Chris: Uh huh. Hey mama! She's not into it, she's gonna leave.

Gary: She's getting bored already.

Chris: Cool. So, we've been having some fun?

Gary: Yeah for sure.

Chris: I was in Vegas last week, doing Lithia coaching groups, that was fun, great guys. It was cool though, the one thing that still like blows me away is that variance in ELR's. It's crazy, like you got guys still a little under $70, and then you got guys you know, $130 all in the same room.

Gary: You would think that naturally, you would look across the room and go wow, $100! I'm at $70, $30 an hour, what are you doing over there? Show me what you're doing and I'm gonna do that. But it seems like they just kind of put blinders onto it, you know?

Chris: Yeah.

Gary: It's funny how much it's mental.

Chris: Yeah. I was trying to think of something that maybe we do that's mental. Because, these guys are sweet and they work hard and they're good guys, and they care, they care about their customers, they care, but it's so funny how it's mental. Like can you think of something like that that we do where we get locked up mentally?

Gary: Man!

Chris: I know I get locked up mentally with the Twitter.

Gary: The Tweeter?

Chris: I hate Twitter. I think that we could be really big, we could hit our goals, and we don't need all the social media.

Gary: Ehh.

Chris: Like if we rolled LinkedIn and You tube, we don't need to tweet, nobody cares about Instagram, in our industry, do they?

Gary: Mmm...

Chris: They want to see pictures and...

Gary: It's the new thing though.

Chris: But who wants to see a picture of Gary like what, "I'm eating breakfast"

Gary: They wanna see pictures of what I'm eating. Everybody's asking about what I'm eating.

Chris: Oh, cuz of your cholesterol?

Gary: They all wanna see.

Chris: By the way everybody, pay attention, Gary will be getting a Seahawks tattoo very soon.

Gary: Oh man, it's coming on!

Chris: Where did you say you were gonna get it?

Gary: I was thinking my upper shoulder area.

Chris: Oh, that's gonna be so good. Yeah, his cholesterol, he--

Gary: I just got the notice for my next blood test so...

Chris: When is it?

Gary: I have to schedule it but she just called me today.

Chris: Well we're going to dinner tonight, make sure you order baked potatoes. It's Sylvia's birthday so...

Gary: I kind of fell off the wagon with my anniversary.

Chris: Oh yeah, you're drinking. That's the comment I heard a little bit, I've heard oh, you know, "You guys drink on the Podcast." I thought that was pretty funny. It's the end of the day, that's what we do, we have a drink then we do a podcast. We're working hard here.

Gary: We don't do these that often, so it's not like it's every day.

Chris: It's funny. I mean arguably we give away more content on this thing than people charge for.

Gary: Yeah I just had somebody make that comment to me today on a call with a client, and he was like, "Oh man," he has the training, he's in the coaching group, he came to one of the meetings, and then he was telling me, "I listened to the podcast, and I got this off the one podcast, so I'm gonna do that," and then, I heard this, and I'm gonna go do that."

Chris: Oh nice. That's awesome.

Gary: Yeah that was great.

Chris: First guy that it wasn't about your cholesterol. Somebody's listening.

Gary: That's the first time I've been on a call with like seven guys and nobody asked me about my cholesterol.

Chris: Oh I love this.

Gary: He blew right past it.

Chris: Let me hit you with this. So Cecil, let me see here, "Shop work distribution is a topic I'd like to hear, manual dispatch versus electronic dispatch, also having a dedicated dispatcher, or any version of the team lead technician dispatching." Here's the question: "Depending on the shop size and technician mix, what works best, or at least, which system works best for shop production?" And then I said, "How many techs? How many advisors?' So he has 29 techs, six advisors, one dedicated to express, and five technicians to express. I said, "What are your issues with work distribution?" "The best technician getting the job done with production in mind. We are using simple electronic dispatching and it's just not working." He's writing over a hundred cars a day, and so we got, six advisors doing a hundred cars." First of all, he needs more advisors.

Gary: I was about to say, he's short a couple advisors there.

Chris: Okay so, Cecil, the rule of thumb is, especially for Hi-Line, he's Hi-Line Mercedes"

Gary: He's got lube techs in his Hi-Line?

Chris: Yeah.

Gary: That's weird.

Chris: Do you wanna go into that?

Gary: No, that's another discussion.

Chris: Yeah. I mean we can? But so the rule of thumb Cecil is you wanna be three to one to start. And so each advisor, especially for Mercedes, should be doing over 30,000 in CP labor, and one advisor should be able to keep three guys busy. And so you're five to one on quick lube, that guy's writing too many RO's I can tell you right now.

Gary: Yeah, especially Hi-line, man, that's too many tickets. Anything over ten is--

Chris: Our boys on the front line go as low as eight for Hi-line, and the averages go way up, CSI goes way up, so eight to twelve RO's. And I know eight's gonna sound like a shock, but I'm telling you nowadays, you wanna wow customers. And if you do service advisor pay plans, right, it's all relative to their performance, their commission, so you should think about it that way. And the advisors will actually work less and they'll make more because it will be easier. You're gonna sell more per RO, you're gonna have more time to call, follow up with people if you slow it down.

Gary: Right.

Chris: So your advisor to tech ratio's off. You need more advisors. They need to write less. Can you do that in your head, G-Man? If you write 100 a day, I'm sure that quick lube guy's writing way more than that. Yeah so they're averaging 17.

Gary: Yeah, that's way too much.

Chris: And you know that quick lube advisor's probably writing like 30.

Gary: Yeah, right. He's with the bulk.

Chris: And it's no different with the Mercedes, like a quick lube is, you're not doing $29.95 oil changes in 30 minutes. Or you don't want to, you gotta slow down.

Gary: And the customer doesn't want that, I know that everybody's chasing this faster thing, that they wanna get 'em in and out, and they have this image of a guy rolling in and throwing his keys at you and running to work and then you do his service and he comes back.

Chris: We're gonna talk about quick lube, aren't we?

Gary: Just go into that. So all I wanna say, out of the gate, anybody that's listening, there's a hell of a difference between--

Chris: What if a manufacturer's listening, like somebody from Toyota? They don't care.

Gary: I hope that they are and that they hear me. There's a difference between fast and efficient. People don't want fast. There's a lot of places that are fast, but you would not give McDonald's a five stars because they're fast. It's just food, you're just consuming it, you're just going in and out. You don't give a Motel 6 five stars, it's just a bed, a place to sleep, but I can tell you right now--

Chris: Tell me how you really feel.

Gary: Ritz-Carlton, places like that, they're not ushering you through fast, and that service is good. And so you have to be efficient with people's time, and honor their time, but just speeding 'em through, people don't want that, that's impersonal, you're not making a connection. It just doesn't work. That's how I feel, I'm getting off my soapbox now, I'm done. I'm gonna drop the mic.

Chris: You see Lucas when he said that? No, don't drop the mic. Okay so the theory of that with the quick lube, so we give him a little help here is, you got six advisors standing around and one guy writing the most. Spread it out, slow it down, make friends. It's about retention, you can still get 'em done just as quick, you can figure that out. You know like so, car comes into the drive, and it's a waiter, and you turn on the flashers, it goes right to a stall, but you can spread the work out between advisors. It's too much for one advisor to really touch everybody, really present the work that's needed, check history, all that, so you wanna slow down. Now on the dispatch part."

Gary: Yeah, let's go to his question, we got off on a tangent.

Chris: An electronic dispatch can work, in your situation Cecil, what I would do is I would break your advisors and techs into lateral support. And so I would have a combo of an a 'A' superstar tech that we could call a team leader but you don't have to 'cause the system's gonna dispatch the work. But you want like a superstar tech, some 'B' techs, a 'C' tech, and a couple quick lube techs, and you could do one advisor to three or four, or you could do two advisors to six or seven. Probably in his situation, I would say two advisors to six or seven, and then whatever DMS you're on you can break the dispatch down into those little sections and then it works better because it's concentrated in lateral support groups. You don't call 'em teamsters, they're not gonna show their hours, any of that. So then what we do is we would put a quick lube, or two quick lube technicians in that group, and then when those quick lube technicians weren't doing quick lubes, they do alignments and other things. But they would get mentored, you'd put 'em right next to the 'A' guy, and then the 'A' guy would be inspecting those cars, if it's like over 30,000 miles he would do the inspection with him and check it out. So your quality of inspection and everything is going to go up, but you can do 'em just as quick, you just have those technicians spread out. And then the rule of thumb is, you never have to recruit another A tech because you're growing your own. When you put the quick lube techs next to your best techs they pick up their habits, their skills, and you can even do something where they're incentivized on their production.

Gary: And what are your thoughts around doing just a straight line, one advisor, three, maybe four techs, and just putting a lube tech on the bottom?

Chris: Yeah, you can do that too.

Gary: I just think sometimes with Hi-line, I don't know how many lubes they're doing. I know with Toyota and Chevy.

Chris: That would've been a question, right?

Gary: If they're doing a lot of lubes, then that two advisors, two pronged attack really works well. But the cleanest system is one to the line, from what I have experienced.

Chris: So one to three or four?

Gary: Yeah, and if he's doing a fair amount of oil changes, then you'd have the fourth one would be the lube guy, and you'd have them on the bottom.

Chris: The power of breaking it down like that, Cecil, to one to three, or one to four, and I don't know if you've heard our other podcast, but when we were talking about Hassan the GOAT, he had nine techs. And it really kind of balances out your flow, because if your advisor can't keep three or four techs busy, then you have an issue with the advisor. You can still use electronic dispatch, but the communication is really good, the smaller the team. It's better for the customer, and it's better for the advisor, 'cause they know what they can promise, they know what's going on, and then you're gonna have a better average and a better experience for the customer when that 'A' tech is inspecting all those oil changes.

Gary: That's the question that we always get back, and we just had a boot camp last week and it came up a couple of times. Its "Well, I got this team system going, and what happens if those advisors can't keep that guy busy, or that team busy?" And so the answer to that is really to have a shop foreman, or somebody, the advisor can even do this, to work the repair orders and make sure they overflow the production into a team that's slow. So if you have a team that's busy and a team that's struggling, then you got somebody that can flow those repair orders to the next team, so you got some production flow.

Chris: Yeah, so you wanna know, it's communication. In some shops, we'll have them right on the service manager's window or somewhere that they're out of work, so you know who's out, if you don't have work, come tell us, and then you can pass it around, 'cause it's never perfect.

Gary: It's never gonna be even. And the advisors like that, because when they see that, they go, "Yeah I got a job that's stuck, "My guys can't get to it." They'll pull it and give it to somebody else and then the car gets done.

Chris: Yeah I remember when I was an advisor when I would go to give my team leader, Todd was his name, he was great. He would come to me and he would say, "We're not gonna get these cars done." And I would see, our girl or boy that used to work with us over there and his guys would be standing around, and I'd go over there and go, "Hey can you do this warranty rattle?" 'cause my guys were never gonna give him the good stuff, right?

Gary: Right. That's the thing. "I gotta job for ya." That's a wire harness.

Chris: His team leader's name was Mark. He was a great guy. I remember too, I remember whenever Mark and those guys would touch my cars, they wouldn't inspect them, and I would like make them re-rack them, and they were always mad at me. But I dunno, Todd, my guy, we had a thing - Todd would come over - so this was a weird crazy thing. I don't think I've ever told you this. Are you ready for this? Are you sitting down?

Gary: I'm ready, yep, I'm ready.

Chris: So I've talked about it in the book and I've talked about Communism, the pay plan off."

Gary: Oh yeah, no, that I've heard.

Chris: Okay, well the thing that I've never said is that they paid me on my work eventually. But the thing that they did, is they would put all the oil changes, so we did this thing there, it was a Cadillac dealership, we did this thing where the oil changes were 29 minutes or they're free. And then we had a quick lube, so we had four quick lube techs, right? Literally, like I wrote here, and they were right there, and my team leader Todd would come over and inspect my cars. But the thing that I was gonna say is, all the advisors wrote their oil changes in number 99, and then 99 was split between everybody, and it counted against your hours per oil bonus and everything. Because they thought, there were four advisors there, but people would avoid oil changes, so they didn't want anybody penalized for riding the 29 minutes or it's free, so they pooled 'em. But I mean for me like, it didn't matter. I was flipping 'em out at 99 more than I was leaving them there, because Todd would come over and inspect 'em.

Gary: Yeah if you're converting then you want 'em.

Chris: Yeah, and Todd was great. I lost touch with Todd, but he was great. He was game for anything. Like I would say, "Hey, we're writing a lot of these oil changes," "do you want me to inspect them?" I'm like, "Yeah that'd be great."

Gary: Mmm. (Affirmative)

Chris: He was awesome. But I do remember like whenever we had more work, and the other teams didn't, the RO's that Todd would give me to go give them were. I mean they seemed like good RO's when I handed them to him but then when you gotta go give them to another team, you're like, "Oh wow, this is a pretty terrible RO."

Gary: I would always take one juicy morsel with a couple of jobs that weren't so good."

Chris: Yeah, package.

Gary: Yeah I packaged it together. Little sandwich technique, little bad little good little bad, cuz you gotta give 'em something sweet to take the rest of it, but most times guys, my environment and all the environments I've worked in really, they've been pretty friendly about it and sharing jobs back and forth.

Chris: Yeah, but it's still a thing you know. It's kind of part of it. You're always gonna feel like when you take another advisor's stuff, that you're always gonna analyze it in a negative way, usually, or feel that way, it's funny.

Gary: The other thing that came up too was, okay so you got this team leader now, and all the work's flowing through him, he is gonna have a natural tendency to hog all the gravy, the good work, and give all those guys the bad work.

Chris: Of course, that's what I would do. Our guest Lola is watching. Hey Lola!

Gary: Survival of the fittest. So that does happen, and you have to manage that, and you have to watch it, but the one thing I would say, and the one thing I told those guys in the room is that that team leader really is incentivized to keep his job, that position, because you're in control of your destiny. And I've worked under every dispatch system as a tech and as an advisor and as a manager and as a coach, you can possibly imagine, and I can promise you that having lateral support and at least having some control over what happens to you is better than none. And so these guys wanna keep it.

Chris: So let's walk through that scenario really quick, and we'll talk about how Chris handles it, and this'll give you a good laugh. So let's say we got a couple techs on a lateral support group that aren't flagging any hours. And so we go him and we go, "Gary why aren't you flagging any hours?" and then you're like, "Well because Tom keeps all the good work. He's the team leader and he keeps all the… "Well why don't we get everybody in the office and let's set some goals?" And they're like, "Tom it's weird but, Gary here says that you keep all the work, but Gary's like 50% and you're 140%. How can we get Gary more work?" And then he's like, "Well he doesn't show up until 10 o'clock, and he never inspects cars" and then you're like "Oh okay, well this is good. "Gary, why don't you ever show up until 10 o'clock and inspect?" So you just get it out. Let's just crack the egg, let's talk about it. And then that keeps the team leader a little in check, and then it holds you accountable now, and now there's a conversation and then, in some scenarios, you just have the advisor dispatch.

Gary: Yeah, if gets to be ugly, you can do that. I think in some of our top stories it's 50/50 right?

Chris: We always leave it up to that lateral support group to decide how they wanna dispatch team leader and advisors, and sometimes they'll flip it back and forth, but most of the time I think the better ones the advisors dispatch. But if you have electronic dispatch, that's the fairest way.

Gary: Yeah if you have electronic. The problem with electronic dispatch is just the set-ups, it's gotta be set up right.

Chris: Well you can't let 'em hold three.

Gary: Yeah, you can't hold too many jobs.

Chris: Cap 'em at two?

Gary: Yeah they have one that they're working, and one on hold, that's about it.

Chris: See you know more about this 'cause you were a tech.

Gary: Yeah, I was a tech.

Chris: I've seen guys where that wasn't capped and they had six jobs.

Gary: Oh my god, guys would take the job, they'd go the computer like 10 feet away, they'd put the job on hold, they'd stick it in their rack, and they'd walk up and get another job. And I would just stand there and watch it happen.

Chris: Or the advisor would run back there and go, "Hey, I wrote this really good one."

Gary: There's a kink, you gotta be careful too because of the skill sets, and so he was talking about, how do I divide the job? How does the right job go to the right tech? And there's a lot of skill set functions that are inside the DMS that you set up, so your techs are set up based on skill, your jobs are set up based on skill, and they go to the right guy. But that gets really complicated, and if your advisor writes it up under the wrong type of operation code, and it gets a lower skill, but it's a wire harness, it ends up with a lube guy, and it's kind of a mess, and then you got a guy that's gotta override it.

Chris: Do you think this stuff happens in any other industry? Like do you think there's people in a dental office that do dental cleaning, and they're like, "Oh I can't believe she got that guy with the beard, he's so handsome." "And I got this old lady with the dentures," and they're like...

Gary: Yeah I don't know.

Chris: Is there any other industry like this?

Gary: I could tell you my dentist story is pretty, it's not similar, but the guy's got a comeback that he's gotta take care of, it's pretty bad.

Chris: On yours?

Gary: Oh yeah.

Chris: What happened?

Gary: So I had a really old root canal from when I was like 16.

Chris: Where in the front or the back?

Gary: In the back, back here.

Chris: Yeah?

Gary: And so I broke it. And it broke all the way down to my jaw, and so,

Chris: You're lucky to be alive.

Gary: Right, so they went in and they pulled it and it took the guy, normally they just go in and snap it out, but I've got weird roots.

Chris: Weird roots? What do you mean?

Gary: They splay.

Chris: Do you think that could be the cause of your cholesterol?

Gary: Maybe, I don't know.

Chris: Have you told Dr. Lau?

Gary: I've got weird, weird stuff.

Chris: We know that. So your roots split like a splinter?

Gary: They splay. and so instead of being straight.

Chris: They're like a tree?

Gary: Yeah, they fray or barb like almost like an arrow.

Chris: Is that a weird thing, like one in a million people?

Gary: Yeah, one in a million people. And I gotta tooth back here he said, nothing. "We're gonna protect that tooth, because if anything ever goes wrong, we gotta break your jaw to get it out." That's what he told me. But at any rate, it took him over an hour to get the tooth out, which normally takes him a couple minutes, especially on a dead tooth that's broken already. And he took it out in little, tiny pieces, and then I just went in 'cause they're crafting a replacement, and so I went in and got this MRI scan in 3-D. So I went in to get the - so you can look at it to get ready for the replacement - and there's fragments left inside the hole. And they put a bone graft over the top of it, for an implant, and so...It's a mess. They gotta dig it out again, and he's gotta go back in there. It's a weird thing. But I was laying there on the dentist chair, I was just thinking to myself, "This is a come back. The guy's gotta come back. He did a repair, and he's gotta come back and do it again."

Chris: You know that's what Missy did right?

Gary: No really? Oh yeah that's right.

Chris: She worked in an emergency root canal, so whenever there's like a car wreck or something and they need emergency dental work, that's what she worked in. She could set you up.

Gary: Yeah, I need somebody. And so the funny thing is the dentist that I go to for my cleanings and everything didn't do the surgery. He called in a surgical dentist, he does surgery, and he said, "Well normally I would take care of it, but he did it, so I'm gonna call him back." So now I gotta wait for the tech to come back in town, to do the work on my face. So it's funny, but that part's a little bit - there's some parallels - there to what we do in the service departments.

Chris: Because of the comeback?

Gary: Because of the comeback. And then you know, it's funny because the tech that the job comes back on, other techs don't wanna work on it.

Chris: Oh, of course, nobody wants to touch it. He's gone. Too bad you're not in a loaner.

Gary: Yeah, get a loaner too.

Chris: Do you remember when you were on four tens?

Gary: I remember, yeah.

Chris: And advisors were gone, and customers would be in a loaner for like a week, so crazy. And they're like, "Okay, I'm on a loaner, I don't care." And the advisor's like on a four day weekend in Reno.

Gary: Yeah, just a stack of RO's and cars out on the lot, and nothing was moving. Man, it was so hard. That was a tough, that, you know.

Chris: We're upsetting Lola.

Gary: Yeah right

Chris: She's like, "I want my loaners back!" That's funny. Okay what about that book? When did you read this book?

Gary: I just finished it last week I think. Yeah, last week, maybe the week before.

Gary: I did this one on Audible, I didn't read this one. So I did Audible. I actually just finished a second book.

Chris: Lola wants a little tequila.

Gary: Hey Lola, how are you?

Chris: Come on baby, get back.

Gary: So the book is by Charles Duhigg. He wrote also a book that I think everybody in this office, everybody with us, has read, which is *The Power of Habit*, which is an excellent book, by the way, that everybody could pick up. This one is his new one called *Smarter Faster--*

Chris: Bro, I'm not joking, I was listening to this guy this morning.

Gary: Oh really?

Chris: Yeah so, hold on one second, just let … What's his name?

Gary: Charles Duhigg.

Chris: What's the top thing right there on my…?

Gary: Charles Duhigg, yeah.

Chris: On a podcast for this podcast called *Art in Charm*, or something like that, it's good. Okay sorry, go ahead.

Gary: So the book's really about being productive, and how the top people in this world, this country, how they stay productive and get a lot done. So he tells a lot of stories, and one thing about Charles Duhigg.

Chris: How come he didn't call us? To be in his book? Charles? You're studying the wrong people. We could show you some stuff.

Gary: Yeah, right? He has a tendency to, they tell him, and who did the *Tipping Point*? The guy with the podcast?

Chris: Malcolm Gladwell.

Gary: He and Malcolm Gladwell are very similar. They tell these really long stories to get to their point, and sometimes you're just like, come on please, just get there.

Chris: What's the punchline? I never feel that way with Malcolm. Really, you do sometimes?

Gary: Sometimes, sometimes, yeah.

Chris: Man I'll tell you *Blink*, I had to read that a couple times.

Gary: No but *Blink* I couldn't put down, like I thought it was good.

Chris: I read it twice, right away. Like I finished it, and I read it again.

Gary: That's a fantastic book. But anyway, he pontificates a little bit, but he does get to the point, and the points are really, really good. And the one story that just sticks with me, right out of the gate, is he tells this story about this airliner. It's a French airliner, and they take off, and it's a transcontinental flight, so they're flying really high, and apparently it's a common..."

Chris: Do you they serve French fries in first class?

Gary: They serve French wine, Champagne. But I guess it's a common occurrence that the sensors will freeze, and the instruments will go dead, the whole instrument panel will go dead.

Chris: Like that's happened on a plane I've been on?

Gary: That's what they say, that's what he says in the book. So you might wanna do some fact checking, but that's what I hear. And so he said the protocol is that they dip the nose down a hair, they get down below a certain altitude, they thaw out, and the instruments come back up and everybody's fine.

Chris: This is a really high altitude?

Gary: Yeah, really high altitude. So what happens is, for some reason, they still don't know why, they have the flight recorder to show 'em what happened. The pilot pulled back on the stick just a hair, ever so slightly, just pulled back, and the plane began to rise, and they don't have any instruments so they don't realize that they're climbing.

Chris: It's like the JFK Jr. thing, they have no perception?

Gary: Mmhmm, no perception. And so over the course of an hour or two, they've climbed above the safe altitude?

Chris: They're going into space.

Gary: That the plane can handle, and so the plane stalls, and so it just literally drops out of the sky. But at this point they're still not even really sure if they're going down or up, because they have no perception of what's happening, and then of course as they get below a certain altitude, the sensors thaw and their instruments come up. And so now they know what's happening, right, you can see it.

Chris: But they're a foot from the ground.

Gary: Well no the entire time, they had a chance to save this aircraft, they had a lot of time to save the aircraft, 'cause they were so high, and there's a routine that they should run that'll restart the craft and they'll take off and they would've been fine. And the aircraft was perfectly fine, there's nothing wrong with it. But the entire time, they keep saying, "We have no instruments! We have no instruments! We have no instruments!" Meanwhile, they can tell by the flight recorder that everything's up, it's lit, they could've seen what was going on, and then they come out and they come out of the fog and they look through the windshield and they can see the ocean. And they're like, "That can't be possible!" They had no concept of where they were, they felt like they were going too fast, they were going too slow, it was just crazy. And they ditched the plane in the ocean, and they lost the plane, the crew, all the passengers, everything, in a perfectly good aircraft. And he talks about another flight where literally they had a catastrophe but they were able to save it. And they say that was a Qantas airline or something like that, they had a hydraulic failure, and engines died and it was a real catastrophe. And the difference between the two was the pilot that was in the Qantas airline had flown Cessna's with no instrumentation. And so because he had that, he had built in a story in his head that prepped him for this disaster that was coming, and so he was able to function and fly the plane without the instrumentation because he had already had the scenario in his head. He didn't get confused or lost in what was happening. He was able to take a step back, and say, "Okay I've done this before, I can do this again," and whereas these pilots didn't have that experience and they couldn't focus. And so the purpose of the story is, it talks about focus. And when chaos is happening, even when the answer's right in front of you and it's as simple as possible - there was one gauge literally right in front of them. Had they looked at it they would've known what was going on and they could've saved everybody. But they couldn't see it. They just couldn't. They got spun, it was chaos, they were afraid of what was going to happen, and they locked up and they couldn't see the gauge, and they couldn't save themselves. And I just thought it was fascinating when I read it, and of course I relate it to what we do every day or what we work with. And I think about that in the service drive sometimes when we show up, and everybody says we come in and we say, "Hey you should do this, you should do that." And we show you how to do this, and they're like: "Yeah, I don't understand. I see this everyday, why did I miss that? Why couldn't I see that?" And you're in the fight, you're in the battle, and chaos, and customers coming at you.

Chris: Oh yeah, what's that poster over there, saying you can't read the label of the jar you're in?

Gary: Yep, and they don't have the scenario to say, "Okay when all hell's breaking loose, how do I refocus myself? What is that I do? How do I fly a plane without instrumentation?" They don't have that story that they can run through in their head to try to re-center them and refocus them so they can see what they need to see. And that's what we do, really, honestly by bringing 'em out here and they go to the boot camp, and we just kind of reset and get them focused.

Chris: Yeah but we have a fresh perspective, we don't have their daily stress. Like they're in the fight. We're … what's that analogy Jocko does where you're like up on the mountain watching? It's easy for us. And I think sometimes to us too, it seems so easy, we're like, "Come on, just do it. It'll be fine."

Gary: Yeah, you always tell the story about that engine block, that's like sitting in the drive. Isn't that your story or is that Ben's?

Chris: Oh, that's mine.

Gary: And they're tripping over it and they're going around it, "How are we gonna get all these cars through? We don't know." And meanwhile there's an engine block in the drive. You're like, "Well if you move that engine block, we could probably drive a car through here." And so it's funny 'cause they don't see it, and then they're like oh yeah, that makes a lot of sense. And it seems, like even telling the story…

Chris: How many times do we hear, "Oh I thought of that before."

Gary: Yeah right?

Chris: And I always say, "Well the difference is, "We're just gonna do it." 'Cause you know, it's hard. It's hard when you're… Here's a plug, but it's a legitimate thing: I think that's why our coaching groups are so special to a lot of the guys, is because they get to get out of their store, and they get to step away from it and get re-fed, you know, recharged. 'Cause it's hard.

Gary: It is hard. It's a hard gig. And I could tell you that I think my advice, and what I tell guys to do is, you gotta watch what other businesses are doing, and really give yourself a refresher. Cause when you see things malfunction in a business, like let's say you go to a restaurant, and you wait for too long and then you get sat, and nobody comes back, and they don't fill your water glass, and they don't check on you to make sure you're okay, and you have that experience and you're like, "Man this is terrible I'm never coming back to this restaurant again." But if you looked at it with an open mind and thought, "Okay, do we have any parallels? Is anything that's happened to me right now match what I do to my customers back home?" And if you look at it, now you have a different scenario in your head, and you can start to tell yourself a different story, when you go back, you'll see things in a different way.

Chris: About the worst experience right now is with Apple. The worst with that. So they call me, right, from the Apple business center. And they're like "Hey, do you guys buy a lot of stuff? And we have the new iPhone and we have a special allocation outside of the normal allocation. You want some?" We're like "Yeah, give us some iPhones right?" I was gonna get you one, we were gonna get some iPhones. So I give the lady my address, our address, the office here, and everything's fine and then three days later, I get an email, "Your order blah blah blah..." and the old address from like four years ago. So I call 'em like instantly, yeah. I'm in Vegas, right? And I'm calling 'em like, "Hey this address" and she's like, "Oh that's weird, because we showed the other address." and I'm like, "Well no, it's right here, I can email it to you." "Hold on." They put me on hold. "We're still checking, hold on." And then they're like, "Yeah, it's so weird, the system reverted to an old address." And I'm like "Okay, well cool, well could you fix it?" And they're like, "Yeah we'll call 'em. We'll tell 'em." And then all the sudden I get shipped, and it's to the old address. And so then it goes to the old building, so lucky enough for me, the security there liked me, and whatever, so they called me, and they're like, "Hey you got a package here." So I'm thinking all the phones are there.

Gary: Right, yeah.

Chris: Guess what? - No. The pink one is there. For Missy. So I'm in Vegas and I'm like "Hey honey, can you go pick up the phone there, for you know whatever?" So she goes, and she's like, "Oh, it's only one," and I'm like, "Oh, what?" So then guess what I had to do today?

Gary: You had to set up her pink one?

Chris: No. I had to go get the other one that landed there.

Gary: They're coming one at a time to the old address?

Chris: Yeah, so I call him and I'm like, "Hey can I talk to a supervisor?" So this was Friday I think. I'm like, "Can I talk to a supervisor?" And I get a supervisor. He's like, "I'm gonna look into this, blah blah blah," and then all the sudden like, five minutes later, this girl calls me. "Hi my name's —I'm gonna look into this for you, I'm gonna call them and I'll call you back." Well nobody calls me back, and then I get a another one is shipped notice, so I call there, and she says "Oh I'm sorry, I had a family emergency." I'm like, "Okay, well that's cool, but could we re-route these?" Those people there don't wanna deal with me. I don't live there. "Oh, yeah, yeah, I'll call you back." It's been two days. I sent her an email this morning and I said, "Is there any way we can just cancel the order, like I can get the iPhones now at this point. I don't need you, you're just torturing me one at a time they're landing there."

Gary: Would've been faster to go down and wait in line with all the groupies.

Chris: She hasn't answered me.

Gary: Oh no.

Chris: I'm gonna do a Lucas, I'm gonna write a Yelp.

Gary: That's probably a good idea.

Chris: But I'm gonna give 'em like a 4, and then I'm gonna say but I'm really upset. For everybody listening here, Lucas here bought a car, and he was really upset. He learned a term called bait and switch. He's from England, so it's a new term to him, and he's like, "Well you know, I wrote a Yelp review," or whatever. And then I go on there and read it, he gave 'em a 4? Like it was all very sweet.

Lucas: No for the car I gave them a one.

Chris: Oh you gave 'em a one for the car? Oh no that was the restaurant, that he did that. But he's very sweet, Lucas is very sweet. We're not that sweet here in America, Lucas, you gotta learn.

Gary: Nah, especially not on Yelp.

Chris: Yeah you gotta think like Trump. Swing first, right? Cool, well that was fun, I hope we helped with the dispatch thing, that was good stuff, right? But it seemed like it made sense?

Gary: Yeah, no for sure.

Chris: And I guess the only thing I close with is there's a million ways to skin a cat, and if you have automatic dispatch and it's working for you, and you've put the time into it and it's fine, then that's great if you have a dispatcher. And we still think that the flow is way better with lateral support. Yeah, and the smaller you break it down, at some point, beyond 15 or 16 techs it's hard for a dispatcher, for everything on one guy? It's way better when you break it down into little silos and then manage each silo.

Gary: Yep.

Chris: And if one's running out of work, that's the advisor's fault.

Gary: Yeah, and I think, like I said, I've done it and seen it and worked it and been in every system you can possibly think of. And the best one, from being a tech, to being an advisor, to being a manager, to being a coach and working with other stores has been the lateral support seems to produce the best results overall. So my advice is, you gotta take a really hard look at that, and if you wanna scale out past 15, 20 techs it's the easiest thing to help you scale as well. Well, you need more advisors.

Chris: Yeah, but that's the other thing bro, hire more advisors. Get a good pay plan, turn them into productive people.

Gary: Slow it down. Get more advisors.

Chris: Let 'em write eight to ten a day and then scale from there. Which people are listening to that going we're crazy, but it works, especially nowadays, you gotta take care of people, slow it down.

Gary: Yeah Mercedes.

Chris: Good, thanks everybody we'll see you next time.

Episode #16: Typical Fixed Ops Repair Shop Failures

Chris: Welcome everybody to Service Drive Revolution, hope you're having a good day. This is the only podcast for service drives in the country, and if you have technicians and customers, this is the podcast for you.

Gary: Absolutely.

Chris: And I would like to say, if you enjoy this podcast, please go to our website chriscollinsinc.com, and subscribe to this podcast. Just hit the subscribe whenever we put them out. If you don't want an alert, it'll be right there for you. You'll have Chris and G Man in your pocket.

Gary: Yeah, so I learned something cool about the way they upload them. If you go to the podcast tab and you pick the one you like, and you scroll down, they time stamped some of the stories we have in there. So you can go through and pick the story that you want and get right into it if you want something else. The other thing is, he transcribes it. So if you hear something interesting in the podcast, and you want to go back, and you want to say, "Hey I like that processor, I like what you guys talked about," and you want to put it in place, you can get the transcriptions right there.

Chris: Bro nobody is doing that, they only care about your cholesterol. Please, everybody that's listening to this, like it's crazy, we saw our stats, we get a ton of listens. It blows me away, I almost thought it wasn't real. But please post comments about Gary's cholesterol, don't say anything about "the podcast is good" - you're wasting your time. Just put "I hope Gary doesn't die", put funny comments about his cholesterol.

Gary: So at the end of the month I'm getting my blood test. I will post-

Chris: You will get a Seahawks tattoo.

Gary: I will upload my live blood test results onto the website, they will be there.

Chris: How about those Cowboys?

Gary: I know man, four and one.

Chris: Actually, because we're doing this a little early, it won't be four and one. It'll be five and one or four and two when they watch this. Hopefully five and one.

Gary: We're dating it, we're time stamping.

Chris: So funny. So man, how are you feeling? I'm hitting a wall.

Gary: Oh man, I'm sore bro. Oh my god, I'm sore.

Chris: Why are you sore?

Gary: I feel stiff. Why am I sore? I benched 225 this week, that's like the most I've ever done. My muscles grow really fast. I know you're not accustomed to that, but when you have muscles that grow really fast, they get sore.

Chris: Okay Arnold.

Gary: I have freakishly fast growing muscles.

Chris: You guys go and see Gary at the gym in the mirror, he's pretending he's Arnold, he's staring at the muscle. So funny. We should have cameras follow you at the gym.

Gary: Well they missed it. When I tried to do the big weight, and you walked away and it landed on my chest, and I was suffering.

Chris: That was hilarious. So our trainer, we've since taught him how to be a trainer, but our trainer -Gary was going for, I don't know, whatever the weight was, it was a lot.

Gary: So my goal has been 225 and he's been pushing me to get there, and so I tried it that one day.

Chris: Yeah, and so Gary takes the weight off, and then instantly just goes, "Whoop!" And our trainer is just staring at him.

Gary: I couldn't breathe.

Chris: I almost pushed him aside and did it myself, because he stared so long it was hilarious.

Gary: I was so sore after that, I thought I broke a rib or...

Chris: I know. So funny.

Gary: He's a neanderthal. He said, "You just got to get it off your chest on your own."

Chris: Yeah. "Come on, you wuss."

Gary: I'm like, "I can't man."

Chris: So funny. Today we're going to do a two parter here, but we're going to talk about the reason service departments fail or under perform. We've got some good stuff, It's going to be fun. We've gone on like a two week stretch here. We've been working like crazy for a couple weeks, we need a day off.

Gary: I know. I'm whipped.

Chris: I'm tired. Even the weekends, the whole thing, the flying, oh my god, I'm beat. I'm looking forward to a couple days off here, I'm just going to sleep. Are you going to go do some action adventure at the beach?

Gary: No.

Chris: No?

Gary: No. My mother in law is in town, so my wife is probably going to go show her around, and I'm going to veg on the couch and try to let my brain rest for a little while. It's been pretty taxing.

Chris: Watch... what's that show you like?

Gary: *Westworld.*

Chris: You going to get caught up, or are you caught up?

Gary: I'm caught up, but I'll watch them again, because they're really good.

Chris: Are they an hour or half an hour?

Gary: They're an hour, an hour long.

Chris: I'll never know.

Gary: They're really good. Anybody watched *Westworld* out there, give me a shout out on the comments.

Chris: Nobody wants to do that. What is it, like on Netflix or something?

Gary: No, it's on HBO.

Chris: Oh. Okay.

Gary: Yeah. They do a good job, I'm telling you. It's good, it's really good. But you got to like Sci-Fi, I like Sci-Fi.

Chris: I don't like Sci-Fi. Bomber likes Sci-Fi.

Gary: I know, I should reach out and see what he's up to.

Chris: Yeah. He was into Star Trek.

Gary: Yeah he'd be into this one.

Chris: You don't like Star Trek though?

Gary: No, it's not my thing. The spaceship kind of crosses the line for me, the Sci-Fi. I like it a little bit more, the android, post-apocalyptic kind of stuff is okay, but-

Chris: If I'm going to role play and be stuff like that, it's not going to be space. It's going to be something completely different.

Gary: Yeah, I'm not going up to a convention center dressed like Spock.

Chris: Yeah, there's going to be a maid out there or something.

Gary: No offense Bomber, if you're out there, no offense.

Chris: I don't know, Bomber is into it. Bomber has got the bridge in his garage. That was the best part of his divorce, he was like, he ordered this replica-

Gary: Wow, the set?

Chris: Well it's a replica you can get. I was at a convention with them and they sell it as a replica, it's with the wallpaper, and then-

Gary: And he's got the Captain Kirk chair, and the whole thing?

Chris: Yeah, you know, have you ever seen the picture of Daisy the bulldog?

Gary: Mm-hmm (affirmative).

Chris: He has a outfit for her from Star Trek.

Gary: Oh god.

Chris: It's crazy. He's into it, it's fun.

Gary: That's awesome.

Chris: I mean it's fun when somebody is into something like that.

Gary: Yeah, it is fun.

Chris: So we have one story that's funny, and then we'll get to this, but it applies to customer service. It was your birthday...

Gary: Oh no.

Chris: So you help me if I mess it up. But it was your birthday earlier this week, and you were 32, right?

Gary: Right, 32.

Chris: So your wife was excited, she was going to put together a little party, a little thing, and you wanted to go to this whiskey bar down here, arguably the best whiskey bar on the west coast.

Gary: Yeah.

Chris: Would you call it a whiskey bar?

Gary: Yeah, it's a whiskey bar.

Chris: Whiskey bar? I don't know...I mean they have like four tequilas in there.

Gary: One vodka, four tequilas, and then a wall of bourbon, scotch, rye, you name it.

Chris: So they have this back room that, what is it called, the Stag Room?

Gary: It's called the Jackelope bar.

Chris: Jackelope bar. So you have to make a reservation, and then you have to buy a bottle that they store for you to become a member, to then be able to make a reservation, or some confusing thing, or whatever. So your birthday is on a Monday...

Gary: Right.

Chris: And your wife was emailing, calling, the whole thing. Nothing. So we went to dinner by there, and she ran up to the place and said, "Hey, we want to come into the Jackelope room," or whatever.

Gary: Yup.

Chris: And the bartender was really nice, and he's like, "Yeah okay, well it's Monday, we're not busy. You should be fine." So we ate dinner, and then we go up there, and we ring this bell at the secret door in this bar. It's kind of hard to explain, but the bar is the bar.

Gary: It's a bar, yeah it's a regular bar.

Chris: They got pool tables, they got a deck, you can smoke cigars on the deck, it's very well done, very nice. Bartenders are great, and then down the hall, where you go to the bathroom, there's a little door, and you wouldn't know what it is, but you ring the bell. So we ring the bell, and this girl after a couple minutes comes out all disheveled. Looks like they were fornicating in the back.

Gary: Yeah.

Chris: She comes out, like if you imagine, yeah that's what it looked like.

Gary: She looked very disheveled.

Chris: Yeah. Like, "What! What do you want?" So she pokes her head and she goes, "I'm trying to get organized back here, I'll be with you in just a minute.

Gary: Right. So an important point is they open, the bar is open early, but the Jackelope bar doesn't open til seven, and we were there at about 7:30, 7:30-ish is when we were there, so they had supposedly been open for half an hour.

Chris: Not really.

Gary: No, they weren't.

Chris: So she was getting organized. So she pops her head out and goes back there, fornicates or whatever, for like 20 minutes, we're standing there.

Gary: Yeah, it was...

Chris: I mean, I got to say, if it's not your birthday, there's no way I stand there. No way.

Gary: I could see you were melting.

Chris: There's no way, if I cannot get in, that's cool. They can have their stupid VIP room, I don't care.

Gary: Right. "I'm not feeling very VIP right now."

Chris: Yeah, it was your birthday, so I'm standing there and we're talking, and it's fun, good company. So 20 minutes you'd say?

Gary: It was 20 minutes because it was ten to eight.

Chris: Felt like being on hold for American Express, felt like forever. So then she comes out, and we're like, "Okay, cool." And we haven't had a drink, nothing right? We're just standing there, waiting.

Gary: Just standing there.

Chris: And so she comes out, and she's got her little iPad, her official iPad, like we're doing business right? And she goes, "Okay. What do you guys want?" Meanwhile, we're the only people in the place, she's nothing...crickets everywhere.

Gary: I think she might have actually said, "Do you have an appointment?"

Chris: Yeah, right. So she said that, "Do you have a reservation," we were like, "We tried, but you guys don't answer." Then she says, "How many of you are there?" We're four, and she goes, "Okay, well I might have a couple reservations, I don't know, but I might have two, so give me about 15 or 20 minutes, and I'll text you." And then she confirmed that she had your number, right?

Gary: Mm-hmm (affirmative).

Chris: And right then I'm like, "Okay"-

Gary: This is going bad.

Chris: "Man, if this wasn't Gary's birthday, I'd tell this lady where to stick it." What's funny is I've been out with the owner of that place a couple of times, and he's a super nice guy. Super nice guy, and they care about their thing, but their people suck.

Gary: Yeah.

Chris: Well that lady sucked.

Gary: That lady sucked.

Chris: The bartenders were great.

Gary: But there was a weird line, that's not my zone, that's not my department, I can't help you there, that was a weird thing.

Chris: Let's get to that. That's the "it's not my job" thing that happens. This is so funny. So then we're standing there staring at each other, and I think you said, "Well let's get a drink." So we go to the bar. And then the bartender who, obviously, your wife had talked to earlier, was like, "Hey, are you guys going to go?" and I said, I think he overhead me bitching about it, because I was loudly saying "What a joke." So he was like, he was getting us drinks, and he got us drinks, and then we're sitting there, and then we asked him. I said, "Hey, it's his birthday." So I told him it was your birthday.

Gary: Right.

Chris: I said, "It's his birthday. If I buy a bottle, then can we go in there? Into your secret stupid room that the lady is fornicating in. Can we go back there and watch her fornicate while we drink our bottle?" Right? So he says, "Well you have to buy the bottle back there." Then I was like, "Okay, well here we go." So then we sat there for a half an hour drinking, and then we're like, "Why don't we have a cigar?" So we ordered cigars, we went outside. 9 o'clock, 9 something, so it went from, she, it was like a quarter to when she said it would be 15-20 minutes. Nothing. No text, 9 o'clock, and you can see through the thing, there's nobody over there. Nothing going on.

Gary: Yeah. They have a little fence, if you can visualize, and then you can see on the other side of the fence where the... Yeah we couldn't go there.

Chris: So nothing. So we left.

Gary: Yeah, and we were there till, almost ten I think, before we finally bailed out, and--

Chris: Never got a text.

Gary: Never got a text, nope.

Chris: Terrible customer service.

Gary: So there's a happy ending. So I want to go out on--

Chris: I'm still not going back.

Gary: Yeah. I'm going on my own. So my wife was very upset, because it was my birthday, and she really tried.

Chris: She tried.

Gary: We agreed, I didn't want anything for my birthday this year, and I said, "I really just want to go there."

Chris: So funny, you don't want anything for your birthday, but you kind of do. You secretly do.

Gary: There's stuff, it's just too-

Chris: The girls here in the office decorated Gary's office with happy birthday stuff, and he's like, "I told you not to do anything." But you liked it.

Gary: No, not my thing.

Chris: You liked it.

Gary: Not my thing. Anyway, so she was upset. So she emailed the general manager and she laid out exactly what had happened to us, she called, emailed, she was blowing them up. So he finally got back to her, he wouldn't call her, but he emailed her back. It started out a little rough, there was some excuse in the very top paragraph of it, which I hate when they start with, "Here's how great we are, we're sorry we screwed up." And he got to the bottom and he got to it, he says, "You shouldn't expect that. That's not the level of customer service you should expect when you come here, and to show our appreciation for you at least trying, they're going to give me a free bottle of whiskey and then a free one-year membership for their fancy club.

Chris: A bottle of like the cheapest Jack, like Jack number seven right? Free bottle.

Gary: Well, yeah that'll be interesting to see what the free bottle is. Hopefully they got class and it's not something bottom shelf.

Chris: What was the bottle you wanted?

Gary: I think I was going to get the Four Roses, I think is the one I was looking at. Or no, Angel's Envy.

Chris: Where's that made?

Gary: That one is in Kentucky, if I remember. Kentucky. Nice Kentucky bourbon.

Chris: Bourbon, not whiskey?

Gary: Yeah, bourbon.

Chris: What's the difference?

Gary: I think technically bourbon is whiskey, and rye is whiskey and they're all made in certain regions, and then they name it. Just like scotch is scotch because it's made in Scotland, that's where it's made.

Chris: Well screw them, I'm not going there, I don't care about them and their stupid room, but I like the gift I got you.

Gary: I did like the gift.

Chris: A year long, every month he gets a different bottle of their hand selected bourbon, which is whiskey, but bourbon, they call it bourbon. I'm pretty excited about that.

Gary: I'm pretty excited too, I can't wait!

Chris: You'll have to show me when you get your first one. Okay, so reasons why fixed operations fail or under perform. This is a pretty good list. This is good stuff. So the first one is, most of the time, and this is kind of you in a way, but most of the time, service managers were techs. So technicians become service managers and nobody has ever taught them about the customer side of it, the service side of it. The service writer side of it, the financials, pricing, none of it.

Gary: None of it.

Chris: They were technicians, they were reliable, they were good guys, they were the leaders, they were trustworthy, been there a long time, so they get promoted, but nobody invests in them and trains them. Right?

Gary: Yeah. So when you come out and you go into the business side of things, you have to know how to be a leader, you have to know how to be a communicator, you have to know finances, you need to know marketing. There's so many things that you need to understand.

Chris: It's a real business.

Gary: It's a business, and you are ill equipped. Even though we all feel like it, I remember wanting so bad to be in charge, and wanting to take the ideas that I had always had for all those years, and really put them into action, and I think anybody that's driven and wants to get out in front of it, that's how they feel about it, and then you get out there and you don't know what you don't know. You just have no idea.

Chris: You have to plot a plan for somebody. You have to get them training, and with how you came up, you wrote service for a while. I remember the look on your face when I said you should write service.

Gary: Oh man, it was bad.

Chris: But you did it for six months?

445

Gary: Yeah, six months.

Chris: Yeah, but that's the only way that you can relate and understand. It's a hard job.

Gary: Oh man, god.

Chris: I don't think unless you understand what everybody does and you've walked a day in their shoes, it's hard to manage them, because techs is a hard thing and a whole different thing, advisors, and it's hard. It's not easy.

Gary: Yeah, being a tech, I think it's helped me on the backside. My number one I think, being a tech gear problem solver, so you're really just solving problems and finding different tools. You're not using the swivel socket, you're just finding another tool to fix things. So that really helped me, but also the mindset and being able to understand them, so when I was out in the field helping other dealers, it was interesting to see if they didn't come from the technician side, but they didn't understand how to relate to them. So I was a great bridge in helping them understand, get in their heads and understand what they need and what they want, and it's really kind of worked in my favor.

Chris: Yeah. There's a lot of pieces to it, and a lot of angles. It's ten dimensional.

Gary: Yeah. So we don't know the business, I guess advice I would give to anybody who was an advisor or maybe came from the sales department, when they're managing a service department is get close to techs, your top techs, your leader techs, and then get to know them a little bit, and it'll help you manage them.

Chris: Spend some time back there.

Gary: Yeah. Give you an extra resource, a tool in your toolbox. And if you're looking to groom somebody, like you were saying, have a path. If you're moving on to be a general manager and you're looking for your foreman to take over, you're going to have a hard time. The learning curve is steep. So they got to have some sort of training path where they can learn the basics and understand it.

Chris: I think that we definitely created that path for you, and then I remember, so I remember that conversation, I remember you writing service, and the learning curve in there, but I also remember then when you became the assistant manager. That was a whole other training thing where [inaudible 00:19:06] were taking you to another store, and I remember talking about walking around like a caged tiger behind the advisors, back stopping, making sure customers- and it was a whole different thing right? But you understood it more because you'd written service, you got, one, they're sitting there and a customer isn't getting help, they can. They're just not, like you got the tricks right? You knew the work load, the mindset, the whole thing. It would have been a lot harder, like we have somebody, Adam, who had a hard time because he didn't write, he wouldn't write to me.

Gary: Oh yeah.

Chris: Right? And he did a great job, and he's a leader of men, but it's harder. It's a little harder.

Gary: Yeah, I think when we interviewed him, he was talking, he touched on that a little bit, and said that that was a challenge, and he had to find a different path, a different tool to try to figure out how to work with them.

Chris: But those are guys inside our system, when you talk about the average guy out there, they get nothing. It's like, "Here's your desk, and by the way, your CSI sucks, or by the way, whatever it is, good luck." I mean you can't do that, it's too important.

Gary: Yeah. So I had a friend who worked at the local, at another store in the city, Concord, where I was at, and he was service manager, and so I remember he was going through something, and he asked for my advice, or he just wanted to bounce some stuff off of me, so I went over there to talk with him, and I remember asking him questions, like, "Well, what's your net to gross, where's your,"-

Chris: How much can you bench?

Gary: How much can you bench, what's your CSI, what are your hours, ERO, where's your ELR? I had all these KPIs in my head that I knew were the makers or the markers for a good running service department, and because I was trying to help them just with what I knew, I was still pretty young in the business, and he didn't know any of it. He just didn't know, he never got a financial statement.

Chris: It's not his fault.

Gary: Yeah. It just, he was just adrift without a paddle, and he looked lost, like I just felt bad for the guy. And then he ended up losing his job, and to this day, I still look back on that, and think, "Man, he just got railroaded." Because he was a bright guy, had they given him the proper tools and training, he would still be there, he would still be there helping.

Chris: And I've seen it many times in the dealer world or in the independent shop world, where a guy was a good tech and he opens his own shop, and then struggles. I know a couple guys like that, they think it's easy, and it's not. There's things that happen that you do when you're a tech, when you open your own shop is you diagnose things and give it away, you don't charge enough because you don't value your time enough, so you make a lot of mistakes, and you almost have to separate yourself from the two. The best example I can think about is like when I do my bulldog paintings right? If somebody comes up and is like, "Oh my God, I love that painting," I almost just want to give it to them. The money is irrelevant. To me it's that connection, and did it move them or that they, so I'm the last person you want negotiating a price on a piece of art, that's why you need an

448

agent and a publisher, because they're like, "Oh it's a million dollars," or whatever. The reason why I'm painting is to make people happy, and so the reason why guys fix cars and do that a lot of times is to help people and to take care of them and protect them, and keep them from the shop that's going to oversell them, or whatever, and they don't value their time, and they don't understand that, a lot of times, guys that open their own shops, their own independent shops, make less than they did when they were just techs.

Gary: Yeah, I have a story about that. I know a guy that's just like that, when we moved down here to Marina Del Rey, I had my daughter's car down here, she had an older BMW, and it needed to be fixed, so my wife took it to a local repair shop there, and she met that guy. He was a one guy, he used to be a mechanic, worked at the local BMW dealer, got frustrated, opened up his own shop, it's just him, and he hates it. And he did a ton of work for her for free, and I kept telling her, go down there and give this guy some money, pay him for his time. We're not letting him do this for free, but he did exactly what you're saying. He wanted to help her, and he felt bad, and the car is old, and he didn't think it was worth putting any money into.

Chris: You mean he did it for free?

Gary: Yes, he didn't want to charge us.

Chris: And he's sweet, and his heart is in the right place, but the training and the understanding of the business and how to be successful is in the wrong place, because if you think about it, and I'm a big believer in this, is, and this is in *Bulldog Business*, the book that we're working on right now, is really you help more people when you're successful. So if that guy charged, and people...she would have paid him right?

Gary: Oh yeah.

Chris: She needed the car fixed.

Gary: We were fully prepared to pay.

Chris: Yeah. So if he charged, and fairly, but he ran a profitable business, he could hire more techs and help more people and take care of more people in the right way and serve them from them getting ripped off, if you run a good business. But when you don't run a good business, you help less people, you go away, and you end up working for somebody you don't want to work for.

Gary: Yeah, and that's absolutely true. He could have put some people to work, he could have had some employees.

Chris: And that's the American way, grow, add jobs, help people do it the right way. We need more people in this country doing it the right and running a profitable business than the people doing it the wrong way.

Gary: Yeah. And I want to give him money so then he could go spend it at a local restaurant, and then that restaurant can prosper, and they stay for a while, and they have good food and good quality ingredients, and I can go there and eat. That's the cycle, we have to keep it going, and that's what moves the economy. And I appreciate it, and he did a great job, and he really cared about my wife and my daughter, which I appreciated, but at the same time, take care of them, and then we're willing to pay for that.

Chris: Yeah. I know lots of guys like that, because they'll call and they'll be like, "I'm failing, I opened my own place," and it's crazy.

Gary: Yeah. It's rough.

Chris: And really all they needed to do is just understand how to charge, understand how to sell and what to do, and it's easy.

Gary: Yeah.

Chris: It's all in the education.

Gary: It's a scary thing too, to hire people. When you're at that point where it's just you is pretty easy, but hiring and then--

Chris: The taxes, and it gets complicated.

Gary: Yeah, it becomes really scary if you don't know what you're doing.

Chris: Okay, so the next one that I have on here is that managers don't understand how profitability works, they don't understand how to read a financial, they don't understand pricing strategies, and they don't understand how to hire good people, good techs, good advisors. You can't hire good techs if you don't have the right pricing strategy, because it's harder and harder to hire techs.

Gary: Yeah, I was just thinking about that. Hiring a tech right now is like running a sales ad. So you have to be really good at writing sales copy, and how many of us have written- you're a tech, you're coming out, even a service advisor, service manager, who's written the sales copy?

Chris: You're saying that right now, and everybody listening is going, "What?"

Gary: Yeah, "What's sales copy?"

Chris: "Sales copy?" But it's true, not only do you have to write good sales copy, to write good sales copy, you got to understand what motivates attack.

Gary: Yeah, right.

Chris: Most of these ads are written by the HR department, it's like, "The job description of a technician is to fix cars and be reliable," and it's like what? Nobody is going to answer that ad.

Gary: Yeah, you give me binders, they're like this thick, on how to learn how to write sales copy. People spend hours and years learning it.

Chris: It's a craft.

Gary: Yeah, it's an art. It's another skill gap that needs to be filled.

Chris: Yeah, and just understanding marketing, how to collect emails, and then how to write subject lines and entertain. You can't run or own a service department and write headlines that are like, "Buy three tires, get one free." Nobody is opening that. It's too "salesy", you got to entertain them, you got to know how to write a subject line and things to get people to open it and endear them to you.

Gary: I used to love those ads that we used to run, it was the same thing. You're advertising something that only ten percent of the population needs at that moment, you're just hoping that--

Chris: Ten? Three percent.

Gary: You're just hoping that somebody, and if they know it. Half the time, the people don't even know it.

Chris: "Free, we'll turn your rotors for free with brake pads." You're like, "Well I don't need brakes."

Gary: "What is this turning of the rotors?"

Chris: "Spam." Right? So it's understanding all that stuff.

Gary: Yeah, and it's complicated. I don't want to belittle any of it, because it's complicated for me, today, sitting here. It's complicated when I started, it's--

Chris: But we've got to try. The people that we share ideas and we're testing, and you've got to become part of that tribe.

Gary: And that's a big thing, is having somebody that you can balance ideas off. I remember being lost so many times and being able to pick up the phone and call somebody, and having a friend that knew what was going on. That was huge, you feel like you're on an island, and you just don't know what to do.

Chris: Yeah, so there's that saying. If you average your four closest or five closest friends' income, it's yours. It's kind of the same thing, if you average the profitability of the managers you're hanging out with, it's probably yours or less, right?

Gary: Right.

Chris: So you've got to hang out with some guys that are doing it and have the passion for it and love it, and want to share. Because really there's a lot of guys out there that want to share, they want to be apart of something. It's a lonely deal.

Gary: Yeah, and everybody hungers to learn. There's a lot of entrepreneurial spirit out there in the automotive repair business, and they want to get better and they want to move forward, but finding those resources and access to that has always been the hardest part.

Chris: Just join our group, that's all you got to do, join our coaching group.

Gary: That's definitely a way, that's for sure.

Chris: We have the best looking, most talented service managers in our coaching group. Lest the best looking part. We don't qualify for that, we're not screening for that.

Gary: We don't screen for looks.

Chris: Should we?

Gary: No.

Chris: Does it matter?

Gary: No, it's doesn't matter.

Chris: It would be funny, we never see a service manager who looks like Brad Pitt, nor do you want to.

Gary: Sales guys, that makes bigger difference.

Chris: That's funny. Okay, the next one I have here is, man this is a good one. Most managers manage by feelings and not facts and results.

Gary: Yup.

Chris: I don't know how many times we've had somebody tell us that, unequivocally, "We got to charge $49.95 for an alignment," or whatever it is, and you're like, "Well how do you?" Oil changes too, right?

Gary: Yeah.

Chris: Guys will be doing synthetic oil changes for $19.95 and you're like, "In what world are you in when you can call Jiffy Lube, whatever, and they're charging 100 bucks, 90 bucks, and you're like, "What world do you think a fully synthetic oil change is $19.95?" "Well I feel.." Well, you're wrong.

Gary: Right. That's a good point, when we do the boot camp in here, we do that, exercise that, our labor exercise, and it's always very kind of sobering for most people in the room, because typically, it's a low number or a negative number. So when we get down to the bottom and they see it, my question is how many of these hours do you want to sell? If you're losing money or making a dollar, you don't want to sell. How much work do you want to go through? It's like okay, well you're bringing customers in, but the point of bringing customers in is to be prosperous, right? Is to have a business that thrives, and you have employees, and you're helping people, and they're spending money in the community, and that's how it's supposed to go, but if you're- that's not even a loss leader. That one, you're losing 50 bucks a shot doing a synthetic oil change at $20, you know.

Chris: And it's rare too, in those situations where, I know they're losing 25 bucks on that deal.

Gary: More.

Chris: Because the oil is more than 20 bucks, no matter what.

Gary: The oil, at cost, is more than three dollars a quart.

Chris: Yeah, and so I'll say, "How much are you losing on that?" And they just look at me like, "Why does that matter? What?" It's crazy, and shame on us as an industry that we're not teaching them how to figure that out. They're making decisions on feelings, not facts, because customers don't expect it. You'll drive just as much traffic at $49.95, breaking even at $49.95 than you will at $19.95.

Gary: I remember I was working a store in Pennsylvania, and they were saying that they wanted to have their alignments down, I think it was $39.95 or something like that, because there was a shop up the street that was doing that. They said, "Well that's our competition, and we need to make sure that we're competitive." And I said, "Really?" I go, "That's your competition?" I said, "So have you seen their waiting room, do they have a nice waiting room? Do they have loaner cars, because I think I saw you guys with some loaner cars. Donuts, coffee, leather chairs, big screen TV, wifi, do they have any of that stuff?" They're like, "No."

Chris: It isn't even that, like it's sad to even have to have that conversation, because you're losing 40 bucks.

Gary: Yeah.

Chris: So you're going to lose 40 bucks?

Gary: To get a customer to do what?

Chris: Yeah. You have to have a strategy. If alignments are your strategy to drive traffic and lose money and it's a loss leader, then what are we converting? We got to know what the plan is. Restaurants do that all the time. They'll have two for one drinks, or whatever, but you get in there and they're selling you the handmade guacamole for $14.95. How many of

455

those are we selling, what are we getting out of it if that's what we're doing? We have to have a plan, because we're going to lose 40 bucks. Are we losing 40 bucks and every one of them is a one line RO, or what are we doing?

Gary: And that's something that a lot of those small oil change shops are brilliant at, is that they know. They know how to convert those, you know?

Chris: Yeah, well we had in our coaching group, the guy who ran, I don't know, 100 Jiffy Lubes, and their average was higher than most of the dealers in the room. It's crazy.

Gary: It's crazy, but that's their plan. They know they're going to do those oil changes, so they have a plan for that. What they don't have a plan for is what happens after, but those small repairs and converting those one line into multiple line, couple hundred dollar ROs, they know how to do that very well.

Chris: Yeah, you just got to have a plan. Surround yourself with good looking managers that have plans and still--

Gary: Right. Just don't let them around your wife, I guess.

Chris: What?

Gary: Good looking managers, that's not good.

Chris: I don't know.

Gary: I'm just going to drop the mic, that was my best joke of the day.

Chris: Cool. That concludes this one, and stick around for the next one, and if you liked any of this or want anything more, go to chriscollinsinc.com and subscribe to podcast. Thanks everybody.

Gary: Lots of resources. Bye.

Episode #17: Systematic Service Department Errors

Chris: Welcome, everybody, to Service Drive Revolution, the only podcast ... well, I think the only podcast, but the best podcast for anybody with a service drive, anybody who has technicians and customers. I'm going to give you the best tools, and if you have a service department and you want to learn more, please go to chriscollinsinc.com and subscribe to this podcast. How you doing, G-Man?

Gary: Tired.

Chris: Tired? Okay. We'll get to that, but it's amazing how many ... we've been looking at the downloads.

Gary: Yeah. No, it's been big.

Chris: It's crazier now.

Gary: Yeah, I know.

Chris: The views on You Tube, too.

Gary: Yeah, I know. It's huge.

Chris: It's nuts.

Gary: Yeah, so, thank you if you're tuning into the podcast and listening to us. I appreciate it. If you're caring about my cholesterol, which most people are, and I get a lot of comments.

Chris: Everywhere we go. It's so funny. Even non-car people.

Gary: I know, they're like, "Gary, I'm so glad you're here. I thought you were going to die."

Chris: Right.

Gary: You show up, everybody's surprised.

Chris: It's so funny.

Gary: I do want to give a shout out to George Mijune, and he's out in Florida, if I remember right, forgive me.

Chris: George!

Gary: While I had him on the phone the other day, we were talking with a group and he's got an Honest-1 Franchise and says, "You know, I just want to know, like, are you okay? How's the cholesterol? Let's talk about your health."

Chris: We're worried, bro, that's sweet.

Gary: I want to talk about your business. I'm here to help you.

Chris: We're worried.

Gary: That's fun. It's fun.

Chris: We're going to continue with what we had last time, the top reasons why service departments fail or underperform, is what we're going to talk about today.

Gary: Yeah.

Chris: We got a couple good ones. This is going to be fun. A couple stories, we were at an event we saw Ron.

Gary: Yeah, Ron was there.

Chris: Maybe we'll have him on here.

Gary: Yeah, he was interesting.

Chris: Have him do some marketing stuff. Good guy.

Gary: Yeah, for sure. He's interesting. I had a long conversation with him, and super guy, yeah.

Chris: Yeah. Handsome.

Gary: Handsome devil.

Chris: Funny. Yeah, so, that was fun and Lucas here, he bought a Jeep and he learned ... He's from, would you say England or Britain? Where would you say you're from?

Lucas: Just getting my mic on here. I'd say England.

Chris: England?

Gary: England.

Chris: He's from England and he'd never heard, I guess, the car thing over there's different, but he'd never heard of bait and switch. Never heard that term, but he got a little bait and switch when he got his car. And he's so sweet, like, he should have had one of us there because they messed with him on his trade and all that. Welcome to America, Lucas. Being sweet, which is funny, because the dealership screwed him for like, I don't know, $3,500 bucks or so, was kind of the outcome. In his own way, like how he justified things, he got over it and then he was driving around and his tail light ... your tail light went out?

Lucas: Yeah, just the brake light. Just the back right light.

Chris: He's like, "Oh, I got to get that fixed. I'm going to give the dealership a chance." The same people that did the bait and switch, because you know, we're always talking about service around here, he's got a pretty good idea. Could probably run a service department now, couldn't he? Don't you think?

Lucas: Well, that's what I was thinking. I was thinking, "I've picked so much up working during the podcast and stuff, I'll be able to go in there, buy a Jeep and not ..."

Chris: That'd be a funny TV show. I bet you we could get, of all the TV shows we got offered, that would be a funny one.

Lucas: That would be a funny one.

Chris: Lucas is a service manager just using what he's learned.

Lucas: Yeah.

Gary: What's effective labor, Lucas?

Lucas: Is that amount of hours and profit you're making per hour of labor?

Chris: No.

Gary: It's pretty close.

Chris: You're warm. No, but, close. Good job.

Gary: I tell you, he could get closer than my wife could get. I promise you that.

Chris: Yeah.

Lucas: I'm focusing on the production stuff.

Chris: Well, you know, you still hear it. He just needs a light bulb, right? It's a Jeep, right?

Gary: Oh, god.

Chris: Like, Jeeps are made that you can out the thing on in the middle of the desert, right?

Gary: Yeah.

Chris: And he's got the big ... I don't know, is that a Rubicon or what is it?

Lucas: It's a 2014 Sahara, yeah.

Chris: Sahara, but it's a man's car. You called the service department to make an appointment to get the bulb, which is sweet of you because you should be able to just drive in.

Lucas: Well, you're skipping a little bit. We were driving back from Malibu with the brake light out and we thought, "Let's go down, let's just go get this fixed." I had to have the thing with Ryan, my wife, she was like, "I'm not going back there. We're never going back there. They screwed us on the sale." I did a little-

Chris: Oh yeah. Nothing like that conversation with the wife.

Lucas: I did a little convincing, like, "It's okay. I think they're separate, you know, I think they're ... not completely separate, but they're somewhat."

Chris: And I do feel like working here, you were a little more forgiving to service, right?

Lucas: Yeah, so I thought, "Let's give them a chance." You know? "We haven't even gone to that side of their ..." and it's huge here at this thing in LA. I mean, it's massive, so I thought, "Let's give them a chance." We drive down there and we pull up, but it's a Sunday and that's my immediate shock, was that they were completely closed on a Sunday and that opening hours were 8:00-5:00 or something?

Gary: That's funny.

Lucas: I just thought that was ...

Chris: 8:00-5:00?

Lucas: It was something like that.

Chris: Wow.

Lucas: It was work hours because we then looked at each other and said, "Oh, okay, now we're going to drive around." But it was also the indicator light. I think you call it a blinker light, so it's not just the brake light, so every time we're on the highway and we're going ...

Chris: It's one light, but it has two ... what do you call those Gary, filaments?

Gary: Yeah, dual filaments.

Chris: It has two filaments in it, so it goes both ways.

Gary: Oh, okay.

Lucas: These guys are going to laugh at me.

Chris: I was going to say a bisexual light.

Lucas: I think you call it the blinker?

Chris: A blinker? Yeah, but it's both. It's one and both, yeah. Did you look at the bulb?

Lucas: Yeah.

Chris: There's two filaments.

Lucas: But the issue was we're on the highway and we're-

Chris: You're drinking, you're like, "I don't want to get pulled over."

Lucas: Exactly. We're cutting people off, but we're doing it-

Chris: What?

Lucas: Well, you know how you cut people of where--

Chris: You shouldn't do that.

Lucas: Here you guys cut people off. The way you guys maneuver on the--

Chris: I resent that already, now this is an attack on our driving?

Lucas: Well, let's not go there with that one. We're kind of cutting people off because--

Chris: First of all, we drive on the right side of the road, you drive on the wrong side.

Gary: This is the longest blinker bulb story I've ever heard.

Chris: We're going to fight about this.

Lucas: Let's get back to the story.

Chris: Back to the story. So you're trying to convince your wife, "Let's give them a chance."

Lucas: Yeah.

Chris: Did you call, or just drive down there?

Lucas: The Sunday thing we drove down there, and then they were closed and we had the kind of look at each other like, "Wow they must be losing a lot of money here because it's a Sunday. That's got to be a..."

Chris: It's God's day, it's okay.

Lucas: Yeah, that's fine.

Chris: There's very few service departments that are open on a Sunday.

Lucas: Okay, that's fine.

Gary: I think it's funny though, sorry to interrupt you Lucas, but I think it's funny from the consumer perspective. They're like, "Wait a minute, you're open when I'm at work, you're closed when I'm not at work, and then on a Sunday you're not open." It is retail, you know?

Chris: Well then when would they be open?

Lucas: This is the cultural thing here. In England, everything is closed at 5:00 or 6:00. Your H&Ms, your clothing shops, our versions of the Wal-Mart, they all shut really early. The food shops will stay open a little later because they understand people have got to go to work, but the issue with-

Chris: But they'd be open on Sunday.

Lucas: Yeah.

Chris: Okay.

Lucas: When I got to America, Ryan was like, "No, our shops don't work like that. Everything is open until 10:00."

Chris: I can hear it already, all the techs are going to quit it when we're open on Sunday.

Lucas: We were phoning them up. It was just a random Saturday and we thought, "We've got the day free, so we'll go in and get it done." Then there was the ringing ...

Chris: How many times do you think it rang?

Lucas: Oh, it rang a while, but it was my wife, Ryan, doing it. She was holding ...

Chris: If it's three times it feels like it's forever.

Lucas: Yeah, then she got the phone and then it goes quiet. Then you just hear, "Service!" It took us both by surprise.

Chris: It scared the hell out of you.

Lucas: It just sounded like a twitch or something.

Chris: They've got to be ready, so you've got to be ready.

Lucas: Ryan didn't really know-

Chris: Ryan jumps.

Lucas: Ryan jumps and she says--

Chris: She's already looking at you like, "I knew this was a mistake."

Lucas: I won't say the name of it, but then to clarify she said, "This is the place that I was ringing? I didn't make a mistake on Yelp or something?" Because she wasn't really sure how to react to somebody just shouting, "Service!"

Chris: We know the people that own that dealership. They own a bunch of dealerships. They know we are, they could use the help anytime. All their dealerships are that way, trust me. We talk to them.

Lucas: After we got into the conversation he just said, "It's a brake light? No worries, just come on down and we'll get that switched out." Ryan said, "Do we need an appointment?" "No, no. Just drive on down." "How long is it going to take? Do we need to leave the car and get an Uber into town?" "No, no. Don't worry about it. It's a 25-minute job." We thought, great and we jumped in the car, we drove down to the dealership, pulled into the service. There was a couple of other cars there, it wasn't really that busy.

Chris: What time of day is this?

Lucas: This is like 11:00-12:00 on a Saturday, so maybe what would be considered a busy time, but there wasn't that many people there. We drove in and immediately I had flash backs of all the things that we talk about on the podcasts.

Chris: The bait and switch, the stress, the whole thing.

Lucas: Actually, just walking around. We both got out of the Jeep, it has quite a bit of presence, that car, it's not like it was tucked away in a corner and people are like, "Oh, are they just parking?" We walked up in the service drive, in the middle--

Chris: Were you blasting music or something?

Lucas: No it's just it's a big car. We had the roof off, the usual. We're wandering around, we're just walking around. We were just kind of confused after a while, I was just genuinely surprised by the things we were talking about on the podcast, they were actually true.

Chris: Oh, it's true.

Lucas: I hear you talk about it sometimes.

Chris: It's a big let down. Nobody came out and said hi to you?

Lucas: Right. For the people listening, I am that general Joe dude that's walking up to your dealership, doesn't know that much about cars.

Chris: Yeah, you're a real customer.

Lucas: Yeah, so I'm the customer.

Chris: Because Gary and I, even if it's bad, we know the game.

Gary: Yeah, we're looking forward too, in a lot of cases.

Chris: We know to go right to it.

Lucas: Eventually a guy comes over and I just said to the guy, "We've got a brake light out. How long do you think it's going to be?" He's not making eye contact and not really talking to me. I'm kind of following him as he's carrying folders and doing things with them.

Chris: He was busy bro, he was busy.

Lucas: He was busy, but I just--

Chris: It's like like FedEx commercial. Can't talk now, busy!

Lucas: I said, "We've just got a brake light out." It tells us on the Jeep, it says it on the dash type thing, so I just said, "It says it's the brake light. We see it's not working. How long is it going to be?" He does the, "Mmm, uh, uh ... Actually all of our techs are about to go on lunch, it's going to be three to three-and-a-half- hours."

Chris: Where was Ryan when this is happening?

Lucas: She's right next to me.

Chris: Okay.

Lucas: We just immediately think we're not going to do the fighting thing and say, "Oh we just spoke to someone on the phone," any of that jazz. That was enough for us. We turned around, we were in the Jeep.

Chris: You were having flashbacks of your car buying experience.

Lucas: I just thought, we gave them the chance, we came. It's not their fault they were closed on Sunday. We came on a Sunday, they were closed, that was not a big hurdle. Then the phone call was a little bit wonkers because after the phone call Ryan immediately looked at me and was like, "I'm really surprised at the way that guy just talked to me." She was genuinely shocked.

Gary: That's so funny. That's so sad, but so funny.

Lucas: Then there was that, and then by the time the guy said three hours for a brake light, we were in the Jeep and we drove up to a little independent dude around the corner and he did it in ten minutes, he was a really cool guy and charged us like $8.

Gary: Charged him, good he charged him. Good for you, guy.

Chris: He's losing money by the way.

Gary: $8 is not a lot, but good for you.

Lucas: In terms of customer service and all those things, I was just surprised by the, "They're all going to lunch," or something? I was talking to you earlier and you laughed because I said that's like going into a smoothie shop and saying, "I'll have the raspberry smoothie," and they go, "Aw, Johnny's just gone on his break and ..."

Gary: Not the raspberry. We have bottled water in the refrigerator if you want, but we're not making smoothies. It's going to be a while.

Lucas: Exactly.

Chris: Hey this guy wants a raspberry Smoothie, can you believe this guy? Meanwhile the place is called Raspberry Smoothie.

Lucas: Raspberry smoothie special on the side.

Gary: It's funny, I was listening to this podcast with Daniel Pink, but he was talking about going in and buying a car. It's so funny in our industry how we don't get it, we just don't get it.

Chris: That's crazy, I mean we-

Gary: What is it? It's called the *Art of Charm* is the podcast, and it's the one with Daniel Pink who wrote the book, *To Sell is Human*.

Chris: Yeah.

Gary: He's talking on there about going in and buying a car. Same experience as you, Lucas, with the trade. He has a Prius and he goes in there to a local Toyota store wherever he is, I don't know, and the sales guy comes out and says, "We'll give you this for the Prius," and he's like, "What? Look here on my phone, that's what it says it's worth." He's like, "Well I've got to go talk to my manager," and he's like, "Okay, but it isn't going to change. That's what it says what the car is worth. I want to buy a car, I've got a car." It's the whole, "Well, I've got to go talk to my manager." He's like, "You can talk to your manager, talk to your mom, I don't care, send a Telegram." None of these guys are car guys, we're car guys. We love the car business, we're vested, this is our life. It's what we've grown up in. The guy who does the podcast says, "It's so funny, people in the car business don't understand. They think that they're going to change a couple things, a couple rules in their game and they don't understand that their game doesn't exist anymore. You can't find another way to mess with people. The game doesn't exist anymore.

Chris: Yeah, it's gone.

Gary: The game's over, and you're still thinking, 'Oh, we're just going to tweak a couple things in our game.'"

Lucas: That's one of the things that I was feeling when I was in that environment was that it felt outdated.

Gary: Oh my gosh, it's so terrible.

Chris: That whole thing where they go, "Service!" That's from like 25 years ago.

Gary: I'll tell you a story about another one. Those guys own a bunch of stores, and they own a store, and the general manager will call, I don't know, every year? He'll call in a panic, he has my cell phone, he'll call, "I need your help immediately." Then we'll get on the phone, we'll get his financials, we'll do a strategy session, and then nothing. At the end of it their profitability, all of it, they're the weirdest, they're in a bubble, it's crazy. You're down...I don't know how much we should say about where they're at, but--

Chris: Nothing.

Gary: Just take care of people, just treat them like they're your mom, just be nice. That's it. People will forgive you, but man, ignorance is bliss.

Chris: We were talking at the top of the podcast about how we've been busy lately, and you and I have been running like mad weeks straight. I have a weird low tire warning coming on in my wife's car, so she's been asking me, "You've got to look it, can you fill it up?" I finally told her, I said, "Look babe, we're just slammed. There's no way, I don't have time to deal with it. Just take it to the dealer and have them look at it. I'm sure there's something going on because we put air in it once before." She just looked at the ground, she just kind of looked at the ground. I felt bad. She goes, "I can't go back there. I just can't."

Gary: Where you bought it?

470

Chris: No it wasn't where we bought it. She had it serviced at another place. Where we bought it she didn't go back to. It was a local place, she won't go back there. There's two that we're kind of in between, actually there's three around us, she tried the second one. I said, "Babe, just go to the second one." So she goes to the second one and I called her on the phone a couple of days later. I said, "Hey baby, how did it go? What was going on?" She said, "It was worse than the first one. I just can't go back to these places." I wanted to find the place because I come from the business, I don't want to feed money back into it. I can't.

Gary: Wake up America. It's crazy.

Chris: It's frustrating, it really is. Now my blood pressure is going up. How's your cholesterol and blood pressure?

Gary: I'm sorry Lucas.

Chris: I will tell you this, if you would've told Gary, he could've put the bulb in at the garage downstairs.

Gary: I would've.

Chris: I would've actually, I know how to do that.

Gary: Don't tell my wife because I don't have time to air up her tires, but I'd be out there fixing your tail light.

Chris: I know how to do that. I've done it on a Jeep before.

Lucas: That was the other nice thing, the guy ...

Chris: I can't fix a car like Gary, but I can put a bulb in.

Lucas: He showed me.

Chris: It's just a bulb.

Lucas: He got the screwdriver out, unhinged the thing, and took out the bulb.

Chris: Yeah, what is it? Three screws?

Lucas: He showed me the socket type, and pulled it out, and put it in.

Chris: You shouldn't be doing it, but I could do it for you. I could take care of you. Next time we'll just buy a bulb. Top reasons fixed operations fail and underperform?

Gary: There's one of them.

Chris: This one's good.

Gary: Go ahead.

Chris: This applies to that in a funny way. What's the number one thing?

Gary: Oh, you're putting me on the spot?

Chris: This will be easy, you'll get this in a second. This is no set up.

Gary: Okay.

Chris: How much should you be able to bench press?

Gary: Whatever you can bench press, is how much you should be able to.

Chris: No, there's a rule.

Gary: There's a rule? Oh ...

Chris: That's funny because you're the guy like, "How much can you bench?" and you're like, "How much can you bench?" You're that guy.

Gary: I'm going back to the '80s, bro.

Chris: I like it though, you're that guy and I love that. When you squat-

Gary: It's so bad.

Chris: It's funny, I'll be talking to somebody and Gary will just be sitting there and then he'll go, "What do you squat? What do you bench?" That's the measurement of a man.

Gary: I felt bad enough afterwards, now I feel worse.

Chris: I love it, I think it's great. You've pushed me, I just know plates, I know two plates in a thing. I've never added it up, it's such a headache.

Gary: We were kids back in the day.

Chris: But you should be able to bench what you weigh, right?

Gary: Yeah, bench your weight.

Chris: I can do that.

Gary: At least.

Chris: 300, because I weight 300. No, so what's the number one thing when we get somebody on the phone and they're talking about the performance of their service department, what is the number one thing they say they need in order to perform better?

Gary: Oh, yeah. They need to hire techs.

Chris: No.

Gary: No?

Chris: RO count.

Gary: Oh.

Chris: Right? We need more.

Gary: Techs are number two.

Chris: Yeah. You need more RO's? What?

Gary: See, I blew it. You said it was going to be easy and I blew it. Yeah, RO count.

Chris: Well, it's relative. Techs is a big deal, too.

Gary: Yeah, if we just had more cars.

Chris: If we just had more cars, we could lose more money. If you're losing money on every job you do. I've seen it so many times in Toyota stores where they're writing thousands of RO's, and every RO they write they're losing $10.

Gary: Yeah, it's crazy.

Chris: Because their pricing strategies are wrong. They're chasing volume, and they have no basic foundation of profitability and understanding of how it works. They think, busy, busy, busy, but the most profitable departments we've ever seen, and the most profitable shops we've ever seen, it's like mellow, quiet, easy.

Gary: Yeah, we had a shop that was doing 35 RO's a day, and they were insanely profitable and killing it.

Chris: Making friends, customers loved them. Lucas drives in, they're like ...

Gary: Yeah, "Come on in."

Chris: We inspect your car. You know what you don't understand, Lucas, that's funny to us, is that light bulb is not only an opportunity to make a friend with you and fix your light bulb, but we could inspect your car. I don't know, I'm pretty sure you need a tire or something.

Lucas: I had just taken it off-roading, so I'm pretty sure that somebody--

Chris: Yeah, you broke an axle.

Lucas: Somebody could have taken it to a side and upsold me.

Chris: I guarantee you if we talked to the manager there, he'd be like, "We need more customers." Meanwhile he's shooing them away, right? He's got the anti-customer guard shack.

Gary: We do one of two things. We want to bring customers in, we want more traffic, so we give out a loss leader and we start to drive traffic, but we can't do anything with them. We can't convert, so we just end up with less. Or you have customers who land in your deck like Lucas, just organically, and we don't do anything with them. Then we sit in our office and go, "Man, I wish I had more cars to work on."

Chris: I was in a meeting like three weeks ago and we're calling ... It's the one thing I like to do is take everybody's cell phones and make them put them in the middle of the room so they can't cheat and text back to their dealership, or their place of business, and I call and try to make an appointment. And it's amazing how impossible it is. I just say, "Hey, I'm in town, I'm not from town and my check engine light came on. Can I drive in and can you check it?" "Oh, no, no, we don't do that. Listen, we've got rules. We're three weeks out." I guarantee you if we talk to the manager, because the manager's not the guy answering the phone, "We need more traffic."

Gary: Yeah, they do the "Ooo. I'm not sure we've got time for that one."

Chris: Listen, you need to get a hotel room for two weeks.

Gary: Right. We just had a phone call with somebody not that long ago and we said, "Well what's the number one issue that you're having in your store right now?" He said, "Well if we could just get more cars through the system I think we'd be okay." Then I go, "Oh, really? So, what are you doing about that? Have you run any ads and tried to get more traffic, or what are you working on?" He goes, "No, no, no. We've got plenty of cars, we just can't get them through." I'm like, "Well you don't need more cars through. You need to work on the system."

Chris: Slow down first, right?

Gary: Right, you need less cars and then you can work on them.

Chris: Nobody else out there will understand this analogy but you, but you're trying to learn how to play drums, right? We got a drum set here in the office, so you see me bust out a beat, right? That's the worst thing you can do. What you have to do is slow it way down, and one at a time, one at a time, really slow, painstakingly slow, that's what you have to do. You can't chase RO counts, you've got to slow it down. What are you converting? Are you making a friend? Is that person ever going to come back? In most situations you need more techs and more advisors than you have.

Gary: That's a great analogy because it's true, when I sit down at the drum set I can just see myself just ...

Chris: Playing Journey. What song are you playing in your head, what's that Journey song?

Gary: You know that song that is in my head is that Metallica song with that really strong base drum ...

Chris: Enter Sandman?

Gary: Enter Sandman, yeah. That's a good song. I can see it, but you're right. I have to slow down. In my mind I just want to go, but it sounds terrible and I'm not doing anything, so I've got to slow down and get used to the rhythm. It's the same thing in a service department, really. If you want to get humming you almost have to pull back a little bit, get control of what's happening-

Chris: Get wider. You need more advisors, and then a higher average per, which is the hardest thing because everybody is trying to cut and run it super tight, and you can't have customer service and run it with less people than the customers want to come in.

Gary: You just can't do it.

Chris: You need more people.

Gary: It doesn't work.

Chris: You need one more person than you think you need. That's how you get more traffic is having one more tech than you think you need, and one more advisor.

Gary: Yeah, I think it's scary too, for a general manager, owner of a business, to embrace that because what you're talking about is adding more expense, and they're already losing money. You're like, "Well, you add on another advisor and it's going to help you." There is that dividing line when you cross it, and you have more time to spend with the customer, your sales go up. If they embrace that, their sales will go up, but they're just afraid to cross. It's the fear to take that leap.

Chris: Yeah, but the customers drive everything. You've got to take care of customers.

Gary: Yeah.

Chris: You know the thing I used to do when I ran a dealership, is I would have my wife call and try to make an appointment once a week.

Gary: That's good.

Chris: All the time, because that's the measurement.

Gary: That's good.

Chris: Same thing with any part of any business that you own, you've got to secret shop.

Gary: We just heard that.

Chris: Because you assume, you assume way too much.

Gary: Hey, we were at that event-

Chris: It's embarrassing, it's hard.

Gary: We were at that event and there's a guy, I forget his name, he was talking and he said he hired somebody whose only job was to go out and mystery shop his events. Buy the ticket to the event, go to the event, buy the upsell, and then try to return it and go through the whole process to see how it feels.

Chris: You're talking about the guy that does $200 million a year?

Gary: Yeah, that guy.

Chris: Yeah, that guy. No mistake.

Gary: No mistake. The interesting thing about that, or the genius to me about that, was that he said he wasn't interested in the system as much as how he felt. He said, "I want to know how you feel after you buy." He learned some things, he said, you buy this big package for $15,000 and it's Saturday. You go home on Sunday and you tell your wife, "Oh, I bought this $15,000 package," and she's looking at you like you're nuts. Then Monday, then

Tuesday, then somebody would call Wednesday and they had high returns. All they did is they moved that call up to Sunday. The coaching, "Hey welcome," that whole thing, and reassuring him. The wife would undo it, or the spouse would undo the thing. I think they got to them fast and they realized that that was a gap there, and he said "Okay, then let's get to them and let's solve that and make them feel comfortable." That mindset where he was looking for, he said he's found like 40 opportunities to improve their level of service. He was already very, very successful at the time, and yet found 40 opportunities.

Chris: We should do that. We should do that with someone. Who can we hire to go through our system?

Gary: Yeah, that could tell you.

Chris: That would be cool.

Gary: There's opportunities, no doubt.

Chris: Especially with all the changes we've made lately.

Gary: Lucas, do you want to do it?

Lucas: Yeah, I'll step up.

Chris: We want somebody from America that drives on the right side of the road and doesn't cut people off. Honestly, you're questionable. Your behavior is questionable.

Gary: The English driving style.

Chris: The next one on here, *Outdated Processes.* We have a book here in the office that was written in the 1930s that explains how a service shop runs, and it's exactly how most service shops run today from the creation of the RO, to the dispatching of the RO, to the technician inspecting the car, the whole thing, it's exactly the same. Customers have changed, cars have changed. That would be a funny video, we should do all the things that have happened since 1930, and the one thing that hasn't changed is our industry. There's new stuff, there's new ways to do it, but we're not doing it. The processes are old, and super inefficient.

Gary: It's interesting to me because that exists, even when I was in the parts department. I remember going in there with a fresh mindset because I had never worked in there before, but thinking I wanted to grow the boutique, and I wanted to sell more tires, and I wanted to expand my parts inventory. I hired a consultant to come in and help me about a year or so in, to help me manage my inventory and teach me, I wanted to learn. He told me, "Your boutique inventory is stale and your tires, you've got a problem because you have too many tires on the shelf."

Chris: You weren't selling polo shirts?

Gary: I was selling almost $75,000 a month. You have to have a small, medium ... I don't care nobody buys the small, if nobody buys the XXX, you've got to have them.

Chris: Right, you've got to have it.

Gary: The same thing with tires. You can't have one tire, you've got to have four tires if you want to sell tires.

Chris: You've got to have two rotors.

Gary: You've got to have two rotors.

Chris: Sometimes I've seen that, too. We've got a rotor, but what good does a rotor do you?

Gary: It's the same thing, it's that old mindset where you're managing everything from formulas that were developed when we only sold water pumps, and fuel pumps, and that's all we sold. It's the same thing in the service department. We're just not looking at it with a new consumer mindset and this expanded level of service that we have to deliver. We've got to change and stop looking at ourselves, and start looking at somebody else. I think I learned a heck of a lot more getting out and trying to visit establishments with an open mind, and learn how they do things, and bring that back to the business instead of looking at what we've already done or 50 years, 100 years back. It doesn't help us.

Chris: Meanwhile we're sitting there going, "It's different here." No, it's not. The customers are customers. People want to be treated right and they want it to be easy. You've got to make it easy.

Gary: I mean, Apple serves the entire country. It's not a free... at Apple, but-

Chris: There's not an Apple store in Montana. You forget your power cord to your Apple, good luck in parts of our country.

Gary: Wow, okay.

Chris: To your point though, they're consistent across the board.

Gary: Yeah, the point is that the consumers feel different.

Chris: That's how they killed Microsoft, that's how they killed them. They had a place you could go talk to humans instead of being on hold and transferred.

Gary: My dad was 70 years old and he had an iPad. It crosses generations, they're just not treating people differently, they're ...

Chris: It's intuitive.

Gary: Yeah, but what they're doing though is they're not saying, "He's not going to buy what we've got to sell, or maybe we need to market to him different." No, they're just doing it

481

to everybody. They just make it... they're just moving forward.

Chris: Easy, easy. They make it easy, it's intuitive.

Gary: It is intuitive, you're right.

Chris: We have to stop and think from the customer's point of view. We have a great opportunity. It's a great industry with great people, we just have to change the way that we approach it.

Gary: Yeah, we need a few really, really, aggressive and challenging individuals that want to go out and challenge the status quo, want to push the envelope and do things different. That's what we need.

Chris: Yep, you need to join our coaching group, you need to go to chriscollinscollinsinc.com, and sign up. Email Gary, and get in our coaching group and become a part of the solution, the revolution, the Service Drive Revolution.

Gary: Yeah, but don't email me please, just info--

Chris: Email Gary twice.

Gary: Info@chriscollinsinc.com.

Chris: Who does that go to?

Gary: I'll take ...

Chris: Who does that go to?

Gary: We all get it, well all look at it.

Chris: We need to hire somebody to email info and see how they feel.

Gary: I have Sarah...

Chris: Lucas, email info@chriscollinsinc.com and see how you feel.

Gary: Tell me how it feels.

Chris: How do you feel when you get the response? Is it cold? Are they sending you pictures of donuts? What happens? Will you do that for me?

Lucas: Yeah, I'll step up.

Chris: Anything else in closing?

Gary: No, I guess I've said it all. Why don't I just ...

Chris: We love our industry, we love servicing cars, we bleed it.

Gary: We bleed it. I don't want people to think that we're too hard, but what we're trying to do is really just raise awareness and get people to want to change.

Chris: Change is coming whether we like it or not.

Gary: Yeah, I know. I'd hate to see it go away. The car business has been so good to me, and I've worked in every aspect of it. I worked in small independents, you know.

Chris: Helicopters are going to take over.

Gary: Oh boy. It's given a lot back to me in my life, my kids are in college. So I want to give back and make sure that we keep it around.

Chris: For two kids like me and you with no higher education to do as good as we've done ...

Gary: I could tell you right now there is no bigger opportunity for somebody that's got a lot of hustle, and didn't go to college, and didn't have things handed to them. If you get into that business there's a lot of opportunity there, a lot of opportunity.

Chris: Passion for customers.

Gary: Absolutely, absolutely.

Chris: Good, well thanks everybody for listening. Email us at info@chriscollinsinc.com. Test it, and see, let me know. Please post, if you like this post in the comments on Apple about Gary's cholesterol.

Gary: Check out the podcast, and go into the episodes that you liked. There's transcriptions in there if you want to get more detail. He time stamped them all, so you can go back to the section if you want to hear that. There's a lot of good info in there.

Chris: It's fancy.

Gary: It's really, really, really fancy. I was impressed, you did a good job.

Chris: Cool. Cheers.

Gary: Cheers, thanks everybody.

Episode #18: How To Cultivate A High Performing Service Department

Chris: Welcome everybody to Service Drive Revolution. Good morning, good afternoon, whatever it is, the only podcast for you if you have a service drive technicians and advisors. We wrote some books called *The Irreplaceable Service Manager* and *Millionaire Service Advisor*, because G-Man, people say we don't plug that enough.

Gary: I know. I keep hearing that.

Chris: Today we have a special guest. Dan is here, right?

Gary: Yep. Dan Morris.

Chris: How is your cholesterol Dan?

Dan: It's a little high right now.

Chris: It is?

Dan: Yeah, I heard it's a problem.

Chris: It's genetic bro, don't worry about it.

Dan: I think you're trying to lower it. You're helping me thin my blood a little bit.

Chris: Yeah, you've been sampling some tequila, right? What do you think of that one?

Dan: I think it's awesome.

Chris: That tequila goes good with...

Gary: Yeah, that's a good one. In this office, your cholesterol goes up naturally. That's just how it works here, just so you know. It's an uphill battle.

Dan: No, mine goes down. I'm good. Come on man, work with me. Help me out.

Chris: We're going to talk about the difference between high performers and low performers. The thing that Dan kind of brings to the table is he's been around a lot of shops, he owns a shop. He's part of development for Florida, for one. He's setting guys up for success, so he sees the difference between the winners and losers. He had some fun things, thoughts and ideas on that that I'm excited to talk about. We're doing a coaching group today and tomorrow. It's kind of fun, right?

Dan: Yeah, it's been a blast.

Chris: One hour of labor, exercise. You can see your guys were like, "Ow." They were like, "Ow. Stop."

Dan: They definitely look at the business different than we do, but I'll tell you what, it was very eye-opening. You could see people were not happy with their numbers. They saw the opportunity.

Chris: There's hope.

Dan: Yeah, there is. It was very enlightening.

Chris: You were looking for service training, and you just googled "Service Advisor Training." What did you Google?

Dan: Yeah. I was really frustrated. I actually went to Google.

Chris: Fricking Google.

Dan: My girlfriend Sandy laughs at me all the time because she'll say, "Hey do you ...something?" I'll say, "Well google it. I don't know." I googled "Service Advisor Training" and several people came up. I watched some of the videos and then I came across Chris painting a bulldog picture.

Gary: Makes perfect sense. It lines right up with advisor training, right? The bulldog painter.

Dan: Yeah. I started watching it and I was like, "You know, this is kind of neat." I watched it, I took notes, and it kind of resonated with me. I'm a trainer naturally, I always have been. I took your information, I took notes on it, I got excited and I started watching the other videos. I watched every one of them. Every one I could get, I watched. I don't know, one of them I clicked on and I got to your book series. I ordered both books right away. This was probably a year ago. I got *The Millionaire Service Advisor*, read it from start to finish in one evening. Took a lot of notes, dog-eared a lot of pages, and our name Honest One Auto Care, it's a liability and an asset. People come in all the time and they're like laughing, "I've been driving by you for years, and are you really honest?"

Gary: Yeah, the thing there is when you're talking to an employer, you're interviewing somebody and they're like, "I never lie." You're like, "Okay, he lies." That sort of thing? It's a reverse. They're like, "If you have to tell me you're honest, I don't know." That sort of thing?

Dan: Yeah sometimes because you get all kinds that apply. You never know why they're looking for a job. I'd rather hire, I learned from you, a one or a two. I want to see the results. I didn't do that before. Today now I ask them to bring their numbers. I mean those are the kind of things that I pulled out and said, "You know what? I need to change my interview process. I need to change what kind of people I'm looking for and how I'm attracting them in," because we have a great brand. Our owners want to hire good people. They don't mind paying good money. They just want performance.

Chris: Yeah, it just makes it easier.

Gary: I think today too one of the things I took from it was you got to expect more from yourself and from your people. You just got to have that. You can't allow them to get away with something.

Dan: Yeah. One of the things I liked about today was the fact that everybody we have here wants to be a superstar performer. I mean they're here for a reason.

Chris: Yeah, they're talented.

Dan: They're all from different backgrounds. You don't buy a franchise if you know how to run an automotive business. You buy a franchise because you want the support. As a region developer, that's my job is to find them the resources. We have great resources in our franchise. Just like they do in other businesses, but you got to go out and find the people that that's what they're passionate about. I wanted to find somebody that was passionate about selling service and selling maintenance.

Chris: How many pills a day do you take?

Gary: Me?

Chris: Yeah.

Gary: I think I take three.

Chris: What is this one?

Dan: That's the vegetable one?

Gary: No, that's the anti-gout pill that's got dark cherry juice and everything.

Chris: Oh nice. What's this one? Calcium?

Gary: That is a probiotic.

Chris: Probiotic. This one?

Dan: Viagra?

Gary: That's another gout. You got to take two of those a day, so that's another gout pill right there.

Chris: Doubling up on the gout?

Gary: Doubling up on that.

Chris: What's this funny looking dude? That one looks expensive.

Gary: That is the Nuvigil. That's Nuvigil.

Dan: Oh wow. Let's put all those pills back in there you just touched. That's the B-complex it looks like.

Gary: That's the thing that Lau sent me. Might be B. Might be D. I'm not sure what that one is.

Dan: The yellow one?

Chris: What's the pretty pink one?

Gary: Lau says just take this.

Chris: Show me the pink one.

Gary: Oh that is a generic version of Prilosec.

Chris: What's Prilosec?

Gary: That's for heartburn.

Chris: Heartburn? You take it every day?

Gary: I take it every day. I have heartburn bad.

Chris: Is that normal?

Dan: It's not really good for you to take that stuff. You know it's a synthetic. Have you read the news about it?

Gary: I know. Oh yeah. I got on it because I had frequent heartburn. I can't get off it now.

Chris: What's this one?

Gary: That's a Lisinopril, that's for my blood pressure.

Chris: Wow.

Dan: Yeah let's talk later Gary.

Gary: That's half, by the way. I have the other packet.

Dan: I thought you only got those pill boxes when you were like in your 70's.

Chris: Right? Exactly. Dan you're going to have to carry two or something because there's not a lot of room in there when you get on your cholesterol meds.

Gary: Hey, I just graduated to a bigger one. I had a smaller one, I had to get a bigger one.

Chris: Really? Look at those big letters on the top of the box. When you're doing the cholesterol ones, what do they call them?

Gary: Statins.

Chris: When you're doing the statins, you're going to need a bigger--

Gary: I remember I started, and I was taking let's see, let me pour it out here. I was taking this little guy right here.

Chris: That's it?

Gary: That was it. I went in for my blood pressure, and I couldn't get my blood pressure down. Believe me, I was in amazing shape at the time. He said, "Well take this little blue pill, and then that's all you got to worry about. You're good." I told my wife, I said, "This is a slippery slope because I'm going to be like my grandpa." I remember my grandma saying, "Clarence, take your pill." Now I got this.

Chris: Gary, take your pill.

Gary: Guess who loads this every day?

Chris: The wife?

Gary: Oh yeah. Oh yeah.

Chris: His wife is an angel. You'd be so lucky to have a wife like her.

Dan: That's what I hear. I hear good things about her.

Chris: He abuses her.

Gary: I abuse her?

Dan: He must be. I mean look how hard he worked for her.

Gary: You're fine. I take good care. You're good.

Chris: I remember him in the videos. He couldn't waste time talking on the cell phone. Before we talk about the car thing, you worked with Pizza Hut, you were a partner in 64 Pizza Huts. What commonalities between our industry and Pizza Hut there? Systems and people right?

Dan: Yeah, I think that's a great question. I mean in the restaurant business, you have cost of labor same as we do. You have cost of parts, but it's really food. I mean I have a lot of friends that own Taco Bells, Pizza Huts, KFCs obviously. They call me once and a while and they're looking for other things to do. Market's kind of tapped out somewhat. I'm trying to get them to understand that this business is the same. It's actually easier. You know why it's easier? The guest check is $300, $400, $500, or the repair work. There it's $25.

Chris: They're trying to make it $27.

Dan: Well you know what it takes to run a $1 million Pizza Hut or Taco Bell, how many employees you have? You're talking 40, 50, 60, 70 employees.

Chris: That's crazy.

Dan: It's all the same from a fixed cost standpoint, it's just the nice thing about the auto repair business is your oil, your filters, they don't go bad. They don't expire.

Gary: Yeah, it's not lettuce sitting on the shelf.

Dan: The other thing is you have a few people that are very professional. They take their job seriously. They've invested $30, $40, $50, $60,000 in tools or from a service advisor, service manager position. They've taken years to learn how to build rapport with people and how to sell. Their ability to track the customers is what they need to succeed. The nice thing about it, which was a little bit easier at Pizza Hut, was that you could hire people at an entry level. Here you can't. I tell you what, you only need a few people. You can run a $1 million auto repair store with less than 10 people very easily. You're talking three at the counter and four techs at different varying levels. You can't do that there. No way.

Chris: No. It's a lot more work and a lot more liability in a way, right? You're moving more stuff. Who came up with the idea of the stuffed cheese crust that Gary loves so much?

Dan: I think it was Sam Kennison.

Chris: Sam, oh Sam.

Dan: I think he was the one screaming for it. Yeah, he was screaming for it.

Chris: Nobody likes Sam. It was made for four years. So funny. When's the last time you had a pizza, bro? Yesterday?

Gary: No it wasn't yesterday. It was Saturday. I had pizza on Saturday.

Chris: Might as well have been yesterday.

Gary: I had a slice on Saturday.

Dan: It was Pizza Hut, right?

Gary: No, I was out on Venice Beach. I was hanging out on the Abbot, and there's a place that sells pizza by the slice. It's artisan pizza so it doesn't really count. The calories are different in artisan pizza.

Chris: Really? Never heard that before.

Gary: I'm making this up as I go.

Chris: What would be funny is if you went into that place and asked them to make you a grilled cheese stuffed crust, and they kick you out and beat you up. They're like, "No." Okay. Let's talk about the commonalities that you see between the successful shop owners and managers and the under-performers. The first one you said was the vision, they create vision.

Dan: Yeah, I mean, I think that when you look at Pizza Hut, I mean excuse me, "Honest One," as a general rule the top people, the 20% that just knock it out of the park, they value the marketing. I mean they spend the money. They also find great people. They have a vision.

Chris: They're people collectors.

Dan: Yeah. They know where they want to go. They don't care where they get the experience if they don't have it. A lot of people come in, they don't have experience, but they're good leaders. They were leading people, hey were in marketing, they were in distribution. They have the skills to do it. They understand a PNO. They just want to learn this business, and they got to learn the right metrics. That's the challenge that I had was, "What are the right metrics to get our business to be extremely valuable, extremely profitable," so that people who maybe laughed at the auto repair business... Because nobody, very few people, think about getting in the auto repair business.

Chris: I know, it's crazy, but you can make a really good living, right? For a kid like me or a kid like Gary, no higher education and for us to be able to do what we've done is kind of crazy. There's a weird loyalty to that industry we have that it's like I don't know. It's all about performance. If you perform, you can figure it out.

Dan: That's so true.

Gary: That's the key, if you're driven. You can basically write your own ticket because you're coming into this field where there is a little bit of a vacuum there in terms of people that are driven and want to get results. If you can come in and deliver that, and I don't care if you're an advisor, you're a technician, you're a manager, it just doesn't matter. You're in the parts department, you can figure it out. There's a way to deliver results and make money, you know?

Dan: Well, I can tell you this. One of the reasons I got in this business is because my ex-wife went to, it was an independent, got treated poorly, and it really upset me. I thought about it and I was like, "Man if somebody could do this right... If they could do it right, there's a lot of money in this." It doesn't have to be so difficult. It took me a few years to get in the business and to get out of what I was doing, but I always thought about it. I grew up on a farm in North Dakota and I knew how to use tools and I was into the hot rods. I just always liked it. I like to read self-help books. I remember reading *The Millionaire Next Door*, and it was the businesses nobody wanted. What's the favorite beer of a millionaire? Anything free. Anything free.

Gary: Was that in that book?

Dan: It is, yeah, actually...What's their favorite watch? A Timex. They wanted money in the bank. They had businesses that did asphalt. They did businesses nobody wanted.

Chris: Bro you're not going to be a millionaire because your favorite watch is fancy.

Gary: I know. I like watches.

Chris: Yeah.

Dan: Well you may be.

Chris: What do you drive?

Dan: I drive a 2005 Pontiac GXP.

Chris: Pontiac?

Dan: Yeah.

Chris: What's that say about you?

Dan: It's got a V8 in it.

Chris: No, I get it, but Pontiac? The brand is gone.

Dan: You do what I do. I found this car at the auction. It's one of my hobbies.

Chris: Do you work on it?

Dan: Hell yeah. I've been restoring it, I drive it. I mean I live in Daytona so I'm not driving too far. I'm usually going to Jacksonville, my market, and to Orlando, Gainesville.

Chris: Do you own a motorcycle?

Dan: I don't.

Chris: You don't? I thought you had to, to live there.

Dan: Well I'll tell you what. I was a motocross racer. I actually raced in the San Diego Supercross way back when.

Chris: Oh, you like the adrenaline.

Dan: I did.

Chris: Okay the next one on here is hire great people.

Dan: Yes. You know I'll tell you what, I made a change just probably actually in January, but I knew I needed to make a change once I read through your books. I just wasn't paying the right amount for a strong tech. I went from paying probably about $1,100, $1,200 to paying $1,800 a week plus some incentives. I wanted somebody that was going to stay around. I went through some turnover and I knew that if I could find the right person, which I did find, his name is Scott and the guy is just great. I mean customers love him. He helps sell jobs. He works with people. He develops people. People like to be around him, and that's what I was looking for.

Chris: Where did you find him at?

Dan: You know I put an ad on Craigslist, and I said exactly what I wanted. I wanted someone that could grow possibly into a partner, someone that wanted to move to Daytona, get out of the cold weather. I was looking for someone that could take over more responsibility, so I could do more of my development. Scott called me and to tell you the truth, we kind of hit it off. He came down here for Biketoberfest last year, him and his wife. I got to meet him. I really liked him. He was supposed to start on the 14th of December, but he couldn't sell a couple pieces of equipment. He had a store, and he called me up. He said, "I understand Dan if you want to look for someone else, whatever." He said, "I can't make it down there until probably the middle of January." I was busy. I was like, "Man I really needed the guy back," because the guy I was using was kind of an AB tech. He was working on becoming an A. He's a really good guy, but he couldn't handle the really tough Asian and German diagnostics. I get all the cars.

Chris: That was Gary's specialty was the German diagnostic.

Gary: Oh yeah.

Chris: Run-ability, wire harness. He loved wire harnesses. Have you ever seen a wire harness on a BMW out of a car?

Dan: I think so.

Chris: It's pretty brutal. You'll never forget that.

Dan: Scott's really good at Subarus.

Chris: Oh, Subaru.

Dan: Yeah, he can do anything.

Chris: What happens with a Subaru?

Gary: Oh, Subarus are brutal.

Chris: The only thing I know about Subaru is head gaskets.

Dan: I know the people that run the Subaru in Daytona and they're great people. They'd love to have Scott, but they can't have him.

Gary: Subarus, I don't know it's been a long time since I worked on them, but they would do a wiring run and then about halfway through the car, they'd run out of a certain color wire, so they'd splice in another color. It would be one color on one end of the car and it would be another car on the other end. The wiring diagram was, like it's supposed to be the same color. You'd be trying to figure it out. You just couldn't figure it out. You'd get lost.

Dan: You know a great tech when they can just step in and go, "I've seen this like ten times already in my life. I bet you it's this or that. It's these two things." Sure enough, within a few minutes they're like, "Yep, that's what it is." They can do the work usually if it's a five-hour job, sometimes they can have it done in an hour and a half. They're just like, "I've done this before. Just go sell the job. If you need help, I'll help you." They can talk to the customer and say, "I've done this before. Here's what it takes." They do it with confidence, and that's about having great people. The biggest challenge I had once was finding the right person at the counter. I had a really great manager, but he needed a second person. I just didn't have a training program to take the store where I needed to go. I mean when I started reading your stuff, even though it does slant a little bit at times to a dealership, I didn't care about that because I wanted to move to more of a sales director counter team. I wanted them to have fun. I wanted to see the high-fives that they sold the three-pack or a five-pack.

Chris: What's in a three-pack?

Gary: Three pack.

Chris: What is that?

Gary: Cheese, pepperoni?

Chris: Green peppers?

Gary: Sign me up.

Chris: Is it like coolant, brake...?

Dan: Yeah it's always power steering, brake fluid and then usually a coolant flush.

Chris: That's a three-pack? What's a four-pack?

Dan: Well you add in the transmission flush or you have differentials.

Chris: That's like a four-and-a-half-pack.

Dan: You know you can get that seven-pack. Get both differentials, get power steering, get everything. That's when you take somebody out to eat, when you have some fun and you make a special deal of it. Also the customers, they appreciate it. Nobody brings it up to them. Nobody does. They don't talk about it. It's like, "I've never had anybody take me through a maintenance schedule before."

Gary: I would say over and over and over again, it's like, "Oh my god, a three-pack, a four-pack, you're overselling." You're not overselling.

Chris: If they're due for it, they're due for it.

Gary: Yeah, you're providing maintenance on a customer's car that they need and it's going to cause a problem if they don't get it. Just to me, it's like I at least want to make them aware of it. That's the most important thing is so you're aware of what's due on your car.

Dan: You know what's frustrating for customers out there is it's too late when it gets dirty. You got to keep it clean and fresh. Damage is already done.

Chris: It's crazy, some of the manufacturers, so the tranny thing, right? There was a manufacturer recently that somebody said the reason why they don't recommend tranny services is because they want to replace them. It's crazy! The same thing with power steering. It's crazy on some of these German cars, they replace the rack because they won't recommend the fluid. The fluid literally has so much metal in there. It just burns up. I mean the manufacturers, they make money on it. It's not the best thing for the customer.

Gary: No. They just figure the component is going to fail. Their thing isn't making that component last longer. Their thing is reducing the cost of ownership while it's in the warranty period and the survey period, and then once it gets out ...

Chris: Yeah, it's disposable at 100,000 miles. What I always say is if I would tell my mom to do it, that's the test.

Gary: Or if you'd do it on your own car too.

Dan: The nice thing about your program and what I loved about the book, when you think about Honest One, I really fell in love with the circle of trust. It just resonates with our brand and that's what we want to do. I mean I want to help people keep their car and keep their investment and improve their ROI in that vehicle. Once you get people to understand that you really care about them, they come back. They tell their friends. I mean we have a lot of word of mouth.

Chris: People helping people.

Dan: Sometimes I can't get on the parking lot. Literally I have to go out and move cars all the time. It's like, "Guys, there's no way they can come on the parking lot and get out on the other side. There's too many cars out here. We've got to manage them." It's one of the jobs we have at the counter. We have basically five bays. We'll do $1.1 million this year. I'm sure we'll push it with Chris's help to $1.4 million. That's our goal at the very least, at a five-bay store. That's pretty high bay utilization.

Chris: Yeah. I think you can do better than that.

Dan: Really? Cha-ching.

Chris: We're not really capped at five.

Gary: I'm doing the math in my head. Four bays?

Dan: Five bays.

Chris: Six stalls on a 4-10, you know how many techs you can have?

Dan: No.

Chris: Nine.

Dan: Really?

Chris: Yeah.

Gary: Jesus.

Chris: Yeah, we're not capped.

Gary: I'm thinking $1.8, $1.9 if you didn't do anything crazy and just have five guys in the bay.

Chris: Yeah. Dennis I think so too. We'll get there. It will be fun.

Dan: I like it.

Chris: Maybe more.

Gary: $1.8, $1.9 conservatively.

Chris: Nobody cares about that that's listening though. The other one I had on here was training. Nobody trains. So true. We train here. We've been sending people to all kinds of crazy stuff. We just sent two people to Jocko's leadership thing.

Gary: Yeah down in San Diego, the Muster.

Chris: Yeah. Is that what it was called? Two weekends ago Gary was at a training thing, and I was at a different training thing. We were comparing notes the whole time.

Gary: Yeah, texting. "How cool is your thing?" "I don't know. How cool is yours?"

Chris: I was learning how to make viral videos for Millennials, and Gary's learning how to write copy.

Gary: Yeah, that's right. Copywriting.

Dan: Well you know my background is in training, so I really value it. It's hard to find.

Chris: No it is. We're disappointed a lot too, but it doesn't stop us.

Dan: Part of what I like about the virtual training part and how I train new people when they come in is... I usually give them if they're a service advisor, no matter what at the counter, they read both books. I give them a book, I ask for a two- or three-page summary.

Chris: Like a book report?

Dan: Yeah. I want to know that they've highlighted it, done the things. I try to look and watch what they do. How excited they get about it. If they're not really excited about it, it's kind of a let down because you want people that are really passionate about what they're trying to do, but it's my job as the leader to get them to see what they could do. I mean you can go from being a $10 an hour service advisor just starting out, checking cars in, shuttling customers to making over $100,000 a year if you just would have some passion. People don't know that. You have to let them know, "This is where your job could go." Chris does that in his book.

Chris: That's what it's all about.

Dan: He started as a porter. What did he do?

Chris: Collect customers.

Dan: Once they see that, that's what I like about that, because you've got to get people excited about it. If they invest the time, just like going to college, but here they're getting paid.

Chris: A lot.

Gary: That's a good point.

Dan: I tell you what. If you can become a sales person, what a great career. If you can help people take care of their car or whatever it is that you're selling, it's something you have the rest of your life when you're good. You can go anywhere.

Chris: It's very rewarding to help people. Especially because cars are such an unknown thing. I know as an advisor, I always felt like I was doing them a huge favor.

Gary: Yeah, me too.

Chris: It always felt good. When I wrote service at the Cadillac stores, all the bottles of Crown Royal I was opening at Christmas - I would have boxes of it and I don't drink Crown Royal.

Gary: I was a scotch guy. I used to get a lot of scotch at Christmastime. I miss that a little bit. Bottles and bottles.

Chris: It was fun. Do you get that? Crown Royal?

Dan: No. Black label.

Chris: I don't know why Cadillac customers and Crown Royal?

Dan: I'm more of a Grey Goose.

Chris: Vodka.

Dan: Water.

Chris: We're going to convert you before you leave.

Dan: Yes, you are.

Chris: Yeah, but that's the thing with *The Millionaire Service Advisor* is the whole thing and what I'm trying to get across there. Is that if you stick in one place and you really care about customers and you make friends and you connect, you have this database of customers then you'll have money. You'll always be able to buy a house and be successful because of what you contributed. You've got to give, that's the thing. If you give and you provide and you hustle and have some passion and care about people, this is a fun industry.

Dan: I love that part about "be there next time." I mean, because I'm trying to build retention. The longer you have people with you, people don't like to switch jobs, they stay. If you can say, "Look I want to pay more. I want you to be at the top of your game." That only makes me more money as a business owner.

Chris: Customers hate it when they come in and they see a different face every time. You've got to hire right. You can't mess that up. You can't take a lot of chances because in service, you lose a lot of credibility when every time they come in, there's a different face.

Dan: It's a lot of work for a franchise owner or a business owner because you've got to be up front shaking hands and introducing that person personally. It's a whole strategy about you have to go on Facebook and introduce them. You've got to make up the story why the person left if it wasn't for a good reason. If it was for a good reason, then you do the pictures. You have to think through that whole change. "Hey Tim's leaving. He's moving back to Michigan. He's taking over the family business up there. We've had him for four years, we hate to lose him but it's a good thing for him. Hey, here's a new person, Tiffany." Whoever it may be.

Gary: Right. That was my secret weapon was the "see you next time." When I was writing service, there was a place we used to go to lunch across the street from us, and we'd go in there and the lady every single time, it was a little Korean BBQ place, so we'd walk out and she'd go, "See you tomorrow." Every single time. Didn't matter. She said it to everybody. She framed me, so I was like, "Oh yeah okay I guess I'll see you tomorrow. I guess I'm coming back for lunch." I started doing that in the drive. I'd walk up and say, "Hey thanks for your business, thanks for coming in, and I'll see you next time." I started using that over and over and over again, and yeah the scores go through the roof. Nobody does it. Nobody says those things. It's a surprise.

Chris: I'm trying to remember what my thing was. I had business cards back then, and I would hand them a business card and I would say something to the effect of, "I really appreciate it and if you ever have any questions or any problems with your car, I'm your guy. Don't hesitate to call me any time." Something like that. Yeah, nobody does that. They're always making them do the walk of shame.

Gary: Customers are like, "Yeah, okay yeah see you next time."

Dan: You know the other things customers notice? They notice how you treat your people. It was always important for me.

Gary: You can feel it.

Dan: Oh yeah.

Chris: You can sense it when you walk in a place.

Gary: There's an air of it.

Dan: I always want to shake my employee's hands if they do something I want them to know I know about it. It's important.

Chris: Is it creepy that I hug my employees?

Gary: Kind of, yes.

Chris: I don't, I'm joking.

Gary: When it's the surprise hug that you give me from behind, it's weird.

Chris: That's romance, bro.

Gary: Is that an interview couch back there?

Chris: That's funny. Kind of. Yeah. That's funny. Okay. The next one you had is follow-up.

Dan: Yeah I mean from a customer's perspective, selling service you mean? Or are you talking about something else?

Chris: This was your list.

Dan: Yeah.

Chris: Follow-up. What do you think you were thinking? We had set goals and follow-up.

Dan: Yeah, well if you set a goal or a vision for your team, you got to give them the score. There's four quarters in a year, right? We're in the fourth quarter right now, and we're trying to hit this $1.1 million. We had a hurricane. What does that mean? That means that we might have to work a little harder to win the championship.

Chris: Yeah. It's not going to be as easy.

Dan: Yeah, so we lost about $10,000, $12,000. It was pretty stressful. Trees falling everywhere. Everybody's stepping up, I can tell you that. We beat our number this week by about $4,000. We whittled that down.

Chris: I do love it that you guys are all sitting around talking about your numbers all day. I love that.

Gary: They know what they did that week.

Chris: We did $16,000 today. I love that. You guys are very focused on that.

Gary: I know. That's awesome.

Dan: I've been around, like I said, since really I visited the two stores, they opened their first two stores: the one in Las Vegas and the one in Portland when I was getting involved in the business in 2003.

Chris: I was like 17.

Dan: Yeah. I can tell. Today, we're right around 64 stores. I think there's another 47 in the works and growing. It's exciting. We had the convention here a couple weeks ago in Scottsdale where the home office is. They don't know a lot of the stories from the very beginning days.

Chris: You get up there and tell them?

Dan: Usually around beers later in the night or drinks.

Chris: What's the craziest story that you shouldn't talk about but you're going to?

Dan: I tell you what. How tough it was in 2008. 2008, a lot of us were on the rooftop barely making it. 2009 was tough. I remember I had a really tough time. I lost the house, I lost the business. I kept the business really because nobody wanted it, but I just stayed there. I stuck it out.

Chris: Okay, but what about the hooker story? What's the hooker story?

Dan: Yeah, I can't talk about that.

Chris: Talk about it. Come on. Leave the names out. Just tell us. Paint broad strokes.

Gary: Names are changed to protect the innocent.

Chris: Who has more fun? Pizza Hut guys or car guys?

Dan: Oh, it was probably pretty close.

Chris: Really? I'm finding that very hard believe.

Dan: You know what? This is one of the true stories about Pizza Hut. When they first started out, they could open a store for about $2,500. That's how much it cost to open a Pizza Hut back in the early 70's. They made that money back in two months. Some of these guys that own Pizza Huts today, they own islands, polo teams, jets. They're doing very well.

Chris: You ever wanted to own a polo team?

Gary: I never thought of that, no.

Chris: That's an awkward one. Okay. What's the craziest story?

Dan: Oh they're at one of their Pizza Huts, and they're having a poker game. They got the girls on the table, the waitresses, they're dancing.

Chris: We follow you. Table dancers.

Dan: Oh yeah. One of the guys I know, he's been very successful, has lots of stores. He lost a couple of his Pizza Huts in the game.

Chris: What? I love that.

Dan: Then he won a couple back the next week. They would do this every week. They were just crazy wild.

Chris: Like every week it had a different owner depending on a poker game?

Dan: Oh yeah.

Chris: Oh I love that. I would play poker in that game. I like that.

Gary: Those stakes are high.

Dan: I could tell you all kinds of stories. I was in charge of customer service for a while at WorldWide in my development with the company. You would not believe the complaints, the crazy things that happened. Just crazy.

Chris: Like what? Give us some stories. Like there were razor blades in her pizza?

Dan: No, no, nothing like that. I couldn't tell you that, but just crazy things with male and females that happened in the dining room right next to a Denny's where a whole family is eating.

Chris: Oh, well that happens in our industry too.

Dan: Every business goes through their beginning stage, and they grow and mature. It depends on how you run the business. I mean it's the people you have working for you. If you're involved in your details and you know who you're leading, that kind of crazy stuff only happens at conventions.

Chris: Yeah, that's funny. I'm always the guy back in my room at eight watching Sports Center. We host our West Coach coaching group here, and a lot of the guys they want to go to strip clubs and stuff. It's like, "Oh that sounds so lame." They're all excited. Your guys probably right now are at a strip club.

Dan: You know, they never do that. No way. Most of them are very professional people. We go out and have a few beers.

We have a group of people that I hang with that have been around for a long time. We just have fun and talk about old times. They're all good family people, I can tell you that. Every one of them.

Chris: That's fun. Back to the setting goals thing, you know there's one commonality that I've seen with all the top performing advisors is they're always figuring out what they're tracking to make. Always. The key to that, it's something that we're going to talk about tomorrow is the pay plan has to make sense because if the pay plan isn't easy and they can't figure it out ...

Gary: Yeah, you see it all the time that success is attracted to clarity. When I hear these crazy, complicated rev shares, pay plans, that nobody can figure out--

Chris: that take several pages written by an HR person or a lawyer--

Gary: You're not going to drive results--

Dan: Who's never owned a business before.

Chris: Yeah, trying to bill 100 hours and fill out a pay plan. Well you know one time in Alaska, an advisor sued the dealership. You're like, "What? In Alaska? We got two pages on that?" No. How are we going to pay him? Make it simple.

Gary: What's that?

Chris: Just a percentage. You'll see tomorrow. It's easy. The pay plan has to be simple because the winners do have goals and they're always trying to figure out what they're making and they need to be able to do that daily.

Dan: Yeah, I went through your pay plan module with the bay. One of the things I changed right away is I started spiffing Google reviews. I went from 32 Google reviews to over 75 today.

Chris: What were you spiffing? How much?

Dan: I actually paid I think it was $40 for a four-star and $50 for a five-star. What we did though was this: We had a little form that taught them how to do it because I have a lot of older customers, and they tell me my average customer is 62. They don't use Google that much. I had to teach them how to do it. My next customer has nine Google reviews. I've got 75. When people go and they google "auto repair," it's worth it. Part of my marketing plan is to spiff for four and five. I focus mostly on Google. That's the one that I want. I have over a couple hundred on my website that we've gotten through the e-mail response and things like that, but really the Google reviews to me are the most important.

Chris: That's the driver.

Dan: I tell you what. Probably seven out of ten customers walk in and say, "I saw you had Google reviews." I'm a vacation destination. When people need help, I get the call. Of course, I'm open on Saturdays. We're always busy. I mean it's one of our busiest days.

Chris: What do you think about being open on Sundays?

Dan: I did it for a year and a half.

Chris: And what?

Dan: I just didn't have the team I have today.

Chris: Are you going to do it again?

Dan: You know I'm thinking about it, but I almost want to have somebody that could help us catch up on Sundays that could come in and work ten hours.

Chris: Clean up? That's clean up?

Dan: No, no. I want work done.

Chris: Yeah, clean up. Clean up the ROs.

Dan: I don't even have time to get to my shuttle van. You just ride on the right side, and my shuttle cars need work and we just never can get to it because we're always busy.

Chris: It's funny how many customers on Sunday want to get work done and they can't.

Dan: You know what? It's not a hurry because one of my competitors, and I know all my competitors, and in my area there's no close dealer. The person that's closest to me is a Firestone. The guy that runs it is excellent. He's been there for 20-some years. Down-to-earth great guy.

Gary: Do you believe him?

Dan: No, he is.

Gary: That he's selling his competition right now?

Dan: No, he's just a quality-

Gary: You need to kill him.

Dan: I know that, but he's a quality guy.

Gary: Not kill literally but destroy.

Dan: I am, believe me.

Gary: Is he kind of like on the football field, how after the game, they're like, "Hey nice game bro?"

Chris: Why am I the only one that's super competitive? You're not going to hear me going, "Oh Jeff Cowan." Actually I would hang out with Jeff Cowan. I should hang out with Jeff Cowan. We need to take Jeff Cowan to dinner. He's very nice.

Dan: I never take the time to put down a competitor. I just don't have time for it.

Chris: There's so much business. We were talking to Ron Ipach the other day, and it's like there's enough. Let's just help people. Our industry needs so much help. The more we really together, the better.

Dan: I just hate it.

Chris: If my stuff doesn't provide value, then don't buy it.

Gary: Yeah, there's somebody else's stuff.

Chris: Yeah. Sometimes you're a better match. There are people, believe it or not, there are people that don't relate to our style and that's okay. That's okay. The people that do we're going to give them tons of value and we're going to help them. Also too we like to like our customers. We want to hang out. We want to have a tequila.

Dan: I don't want to waste any time. It's like, you know what I understand totally what's going on and how can we help you?

Gary: If you're not going to execute, that's not good for us either. What we really want is people come in, execute, get great results, which is what we've had over the years. If that's not going to happen, then we're not a fit for you.

Chris: You still kind of want to destroy the Firestone guy in your market.

Dan: I can just tell you this. The competitors around me, and I have four master tech owners right by me within a half a mile, they laughed at me when I came in. They didn't think I would make it. Nobody had made it in that location. Today, all those guys I know I do alignments for them, I know them. We trade tools if we need to. They know we're killing it. They look at me and go, "I don't know how the hell you did it Dan, but you did it." We're not the same business. They have different clientele than we do, but they have an advantage. They don't do any marketing. They can work both sides of the counter. They can fix cars and do it. I have a little bit more nugget to do. I'm a more of a business guy. A franchisee, you're kind of the business. You're wearing many hats. Finance, sales, marketing.

Chris: You want it to be a little more scalable and consistent than that?

Dan: Right. I know we do three times more than they do in sales.

Chris: What's the biggest thing that you picked up today in our craziness that made your guys' heads boom? Could you see that in your guys? There's a point... It's funny when people come to the coaching stuff they're like, "Oh how late are we going to go?" They pretend like they want to work until eight, but literally by lunch you can only take in so much info. They start, you see this thing that happens in their eyes is they start already trying to implement it in their head. Then they get excited and then they're like, "Okay that's enough." It's a lot.

Dan: No, I think that they really understanding the effective labor rate.

Chris: Yeah, the financial part of it because everybody's chasing RO count, hours RO, and it's irrelevant if you don't have the right structure.

Dan: All these guys again, they're executive type people.

Chris: Oh you guys are great. I was really impressed. It's going to be fun. You know what we should do is every time you guys come for a coaching, we do one of these and update the progress.

Gary: It would be cool to see the results.

Chris: Yeah because it's going to be good.

Dan: I tell you, going through those exercises today, and I know they still don't got it down.

Chris: It takes time. It's repetition.

Dan: I can tell you this. They're thinking. You can see the wheels spinning. They're like, "You know I'm not charging the right amount. I'm not leading my team, and it's my fault. We're not profitable."

Chris: Yeah, or our fault they just didn't know. Now that they know, I can tell by the look in their eye they're going to go.

Dan: The reason we're here is because I know when I found and read your book and I went through the *Irreplaceable Service Manager*.

Chris: Irresistibly sexy manager. Irresistibly sexy service manager.

Gary: In my head I'm like, "Is he going to let that go?" Nope, he's not going to let it go.

Dan: No, that's not what I meant. We don't have that.

Chris: That's what you said.

Dan: We don't have that mentality. I mean we really need it. We need to be thinking sales and we need to have the games. We need to be driving like ...

Chris: Yeah, let's have some fun.

Dan: We don't do that. My business went from...I had a tough year last year. I went through a lot of turnover. When you turn people over, you don't grow. What I wanted was stability, so I spent the money to get the right team. What I wanted, and we've pretty much achieved, and that was to get over $1 million, to have a future, to grow it even beyond that, and I don't want to be there every day. I have other business interests. I want that business to make me money and to be proud of the business. When I go to Publix, people know me. I want our brand to be valuable. I tell you what. I went through that. I could see right away that I wasn't leading the business the way I needed to. I was very thankful to stumble across the books, watch the videos, to work with your team. I think I couldn't do it on my own. I took your stuff and I created my own PowerPoint presentation, my own checklist on how to follow up on all the steps. You need to be fully committed and working on this one thing to get it to where you want it to be. I had a lot of other responsibilities as a developer. What I was missing was the video, the virtual training. Then I came back and looked at it. Sylvia called me. She wouldn't let me go. She kept calling.

Chris: Oh, she's a bulldog.

Dan: Every two weeks she'd call and she'd say, "Hey we got a new module." It was Gary's module. I watched that and I was pretty excited. Then I watched the tire sales one because I was working on that as well. The way I look at the investment, we pay every month to be a part of, that is it's like an insurance policy on the dollars I spend on marketing. I've got to have a sales team because I can get the people in the door. Our brand has a good marketing program. Yeah we got a few opportunities, but we drive traffic. We'll probably be over $1 million average unit volumes by the end of 2017 which is outstanding. It really is. It needs to be a lot more than that, but it will. That's what we want from Chris is to really drive our average repair order.

Chris: Yeah, I think you guys are shooting low. You're going to see. That's going to be fun.

Dan: God, I hope so.

Chris: What did you think about the marketing stuff we talked about today?

Dan: You know, I'm a marketing guy. I realize that my business is a marketing business. Really it is. Every business is in the marketing business. It's a little frustrating that when we were looking at some of the marketing pieces today, with how much verbiage is on there and it's so hard to read.

Chris: Yeah, so just for the listeners, we were looking at reminder postcards that were going out.

Dan: Acquisition too.

Chris: Yeah, branding and acquisition. I don't know why in our industry, in the service industry, we're such copycats. How many freaking coupons can you fit on one postcard?

Gary: I know. We love to have multiple offers.

Chris: You have no idea what's going on. It hurts my eyes. It's crazy.

Gary: Give me one reason to come there. One reason to come see you, and I'll come.

Chris: Not only that, but then the thing that we don't do is, because I guess because we don't understand it, is nobody's talking about the success of the piece. We can sit here and debate whether it's good or not, but if you're not pulling 3 or 4%, you got to keep tweaking until you are.

Dan: That's the same thing. One of the things I was thinking about is how do you get this ownership mentality? Many times I talked about the people that help me run my store. It's not the sales that you do. "Hey we did $4,500," or we have days we do $8,000, $9,000, $10,000, $12,000. It's was it a profitable day? I mean if you do an engine job or transmission job or tire jobs, not only do you need to know all the time where you're at, and it's frustrating for me. I'll call up and say, "Where are we at?" "Oh I don't know." I kind of shake my head and go, "That's not the answer." You need to say, "Hey right now we've cashed out $2,300, we've got another $4,000 that's going to cash out before 6:00, and guess what? It's all profitable." That's what I want from somebody that works for me. You got to know what numbers you're looking at.

Chris: Yeah, no, and it's the same with advertising. You send out 30,000. You got to get a return on that.

Dan: What I was going to tell you was my landlord, I remember when I was signing the lease and we were working on the signage, and he paid for some of the upgrades.

Chris: The tenant improvements?

Dan: Yeah, yeah. He did. He said, "Dan, you know what's most important on that pole sign?" I was like, "No." "Auto care. Auto repair." They don't care it says H One. They want to know the biggest thing on that sign should be what you do. Yeah some day you'll be a McDonald's, and H One, people will know what it is. That could be 20 years from now. "Right now," he said, "it's auto repair." I never forgot that. It's the same thing on postcards. It's the same thing. Less with bigger print that has an impact that brings people in so you get a chance to meet them.

Gary: Well, when we went to NADA last year, one of the things we talked about doing was a billboard. I'd never done a billboard before, and so we did a lot of research on what a billboard should look like.

Chris: Have you seen our billboards that we did?

Dan: No I have not. Is it a bulldog?

Chris: One was. One was, right?

Gary: There were five. Oh yeah, there was a bulldog.

Chris: In Vegas, they rotate. They're digital boards and they rotate.

Gary: The things that we learned was more white space.

Chris: Simple.

Gary: You don't want to have this crazy like ...

Chris: "Booth number this and that and we do this and we do that and call our number and here's our website." You can't do that.

Gary: You're driving by at 50 miles an hour, whatever it is. You don't have time to take down all that. You just need white space, a very clear call to action, an image that's striking that makes you go, "What? What was that?" Makes you want to look. You do those things right, and you got a good billboard. Everybody wants to over-complicate it and make them really beautiful and all that. Nobody watches them. Nobody looks at it. Call to action.

Dan: What a great leader does in a business is they do create a marketing calendar, a call to action, whether it's something big every quarter, but they get involved in the community. I mean they drive in things that they're passionate about.

Chris: I'm a great leader because this is what I did is I put a big fat guy in his tighty whitey underwear.

Dan: Is that what it is?

Chris: Yeah. It's a big fat guy with tighty whiteys. Did he have a shirt on? There was a version where he didn't have a shirt on.

Gary: He didn't have a shirt on.

Chris: I'm talking about a fat guy, fat guy.

Dan: What was the message?

Chris: "Is your service department in shape?" Is your service department in shape?

Gary: That's all it said.

Chris: No booth number, nothing, here was that one. Then there was a fat guy in a suit where his gut was hanging out.

Gary: Yeah, trying to zip his pants.

Chris: They were disgusting, but they were funny. That's good leadership right there.

Gary: We had the one where he was on the couch.

Chris: Everybody thought it was crazy.

Dan: It was always a guy? It wasn't a girl?

Gary: It was always a guy. Yeah. Yeah, yeah yeah. Then we had a bulldog.

Dan: On a leash?

Gary: No, it was a big bulldog in front of a food bowl and he was a big bulldog.

Chris: They're food-motivated, those dogs.

Dan: Bulldogs?

Chris: Mine are food-motivated for sure.

Dan: I noticed that at lunch.

Chris: Yeah. Let's recap. Nothing? We have the recap at the end we're doing a total jump.

Gary: Let's work backwards. Number one, ads. Call to action.

Chris: Create vision. Hire good people. Train them. Set goals. Follow up, we forgot. One thing I had on here on my list was talking about hiring techs because that's a funny thing.

Dan: Techs and advisors.

Chris: Techs, the crazy thing is, what's the stat that you were telling me the other day? We're creating this product that is how to hire techs because it seems to be the thing that nobody can figure out that we're really good at.

Gary: I got a lot of good stuff too.

Chris: The two-to-one. Tell me that.

Gary: Yeah, so I'm reading this article on it, and the statistic is that shortly in the next couple of years, we're going to start losing two technicians from this industry for every one that comes in because if you think about it ...

Chris: What do you think about that?

Dan: Well I can tell you this right now. What it reminds me of is in your training, you talk about get good, Gary does, at the things people nobody wants to do or it's tough to do. If you want to succeed at Chris, you've got to help people find techs.

Gary: I'll tell you this right now too. If you're out there listening to me right now and you have mechanical ability, and we were talking about get into a space that nobody's in because that's where the opportunity is. Right now, the opportunity to be a tech is huge, I mean bigger than when I got into the business because they're like gold right now. We want those guys and guys that are good at it can write their own ticket. Two to one, we're going to start losing technicians two to one. The funny thing is that had never even crossed my mind was that when I was a young man, I bought a car. I fixed it up. I had a '67 Camaro, I fixed it up and I used to go cruising and you used to go out on the Boulevard and everything.

Dan: Burn some rubber.

Gary: Yeah, burn some rubber.

Dan: Get in trouble.

Chris: Girls in the backseat.

Dan: Not much room in the back of a '67. Have to do it on the hood.

Chris: Everybody knows that. That's weird.

Gary: The point was, that was our social outlet. Now they don't have that. Now they have Skype, they've got Snapchat, they've got their video games. They're like they don't need to be in the driveway fixing up a car because they're doing these thing online.

Chris: Oh yeah they're not like, "Oh I rebuilt a motor over the summer."

Gary: We're not training kids to get into this industry.

Dan: Well it just came out the other day, Chip Foose came out and said, "You know the problem today is nobody wants to build anything. They want to buy it."

Chris: Wow, that's good.

Gary: That's true.

Chris: Oh boy. Well you can't hire techs. I know that.

Gary: You can, you just have to have the right techniques.

Chris: No you can't. There's no techs.

Dan: That's where the money is, though. I tell you what. When you become a franchisee and you want to build a business, you can either buy it or you can build it. If you can learn how to build it, you can do it over and over and over and over and over again.

Chris: Yeah, it's scalable.

Dan: You could probably go into any dealership and turn it around. You could take it from what it's worth today and probably double it.

Chris: Let me expand on that. We could go into doctors offices. We could go into furniture stores. It's all the same. It's a mindset. Once you have the mindset, it's scalable anywhere.

Gary: It's anything.

Chris: We have a certain checklist of things we do and it works in anything. We've proven it.

Gary: I helped the girl that cut my hair double her revenue just by selling product. Dan what are technicians worth in your space?

Chris: Good question.

Dan: You mean like a master tech really a lead guy?

Gary: Just on average.

Chris: Just a really good looking, like Brad Pitt but he's like a B.

Dan: I'll tell you what. I have no idea. I don't know about Brad Pitt, but I can tell you a great tech gets anywhere from easily $25 an hour flat-rate to $35 easy.

Gary: To you as a business owner monthly in sales, what does he generate for you?

Dan: I would think a strong lead tech probably $50,000, $60,000 a month for me. He's also producing through the other guys. That's the thing that Scott does well, he's an AFC master tech. He's got the experience to say, "Look it's not that tough. Let me get you through AVI," our training program that gets people through the pre-tests and gets them off to class and makes sure they know what they're doing. He sends them to the free stuff or the stuff that we pay for that he wants them to learn whether it's charging systems or AC. He knows where he wants to send them. He builds their confidence and then he says, "Look. You need to become me." In your program Gary where you talked about you got to be hungry. The worst thing a tech can do is be tied to their damn cell phone. Put the damn cell phone in your car.

Chris: You say that?

Gary: I say you got to be hungry. You got to go after it. You can't let yourself get distracted.

Chris: That's what I love about that tech training is it's legit. Gary's one of the best techs ever. Hustle.

Dan: I tell you what. When I see people failing, they don't control themselves. It's like you can't be on your phone all the time. You've got to be on time.

Chris: It's like your cholesterol, bro.

Dan: The whole thing about how much your time is worth.

Chris: You can't eat pizza all the time.

Dan: That doesn't matter. Pizza is good for you.

Chris: It's genetic.

Gary: You can't be at the food truck. You can't be on the tool truck, you can't be hanging out in the parking lot.

Chris: Gary gets this thing on, what night is it that you and the family go to food truck in Santa Monica?

Gary: It's the first Friday of the month.

Chris: They have carne asada fries, which is french fries with cheese and carne asada on top.

Gary: So good. So good. The trailer trash hot dog is the best.

Dan: Does he make it to work on Tuesday? The second Tuesday of the month?

Gary: Some days I miss the workout.

Chris: Listen. Let's talk about that for a second. He missed a couple workouts.

Dan: How many times do you go to the gym?

Chris: We go every day Monday-Friday, and then I'll usually go on Saturday.

Dan: Do you guys walk to the gym here at work?

Chris: Yeah, so it's a couple blocks. We're lifting such heavy weight it's insane.

Gary: This morning though, I thought it was going to break.

Dan: I got something for you I want to talk to you about later.

Chris: What's that? It's not fair to tease the listeners like that.

Dan: Well you know, it's like I always believe that people should have a couple different income streams. I don't think you should have just one. In fact, in the future you're going to need to have two or three that you leverage your incomes. I talk to a lot of business brokers about finding people who want to become Honest One franchisees. There's a large number of people that want to start a business under $10,000.

Chris: What's the bullshit you do? It's not bullshit actually if it works.

Gary: I went to one of those cryo-chambers.

Chris: Have you heard of that?

Dan: Yes.

Chris: Have you tried it?

Dan: I have never tried it, but I've heard of it.

Chris: My best friend did it, and he loves it. Then he did it and so you're covered up, your junk is covered up.

Gary: It's like a spa. You go in, you undress, you have your underwear on.

Chris: Is it a dude helping you or a girl helping you?

Gary: Well I started out with a dude helping me. I went into the locker room, I changed. You put on these big Eskimo booties. You put gloves and you have underwear. You throw your robe on.

Chris: What did this dude do? You look like an Alaskan drag queen coming out? Then there's a girl?

Gary: Then he hands me off to this girl who's very, very cute girl.

Chris: Let me get this straight. You're in furry boots, underwear, are you wearing tighty whiteys? What kind of underwear do you wear?

Gary: I did have the worst pair of underwear in my drawer. They were orange first of all.

Chris: What? Orange? Orange, are they boxers or what are they?

Gary: They were boxer briefs, but they're really high-waisted boxer briefs, so they were bad.

Chris: Then did they tape up your nipples?

Gary: No, no, no.

Chris: Furry boots, orange ...

Gary: Huge, fuzzy Eskimo boots.

Chris: Then orange boxer briefs.

Gary: Then little white gloves.

Chris: Then little white gloves, like Michael Jackson gloves?

Gary: Yep, like Michael Jackson gloves.

Chris: Okay, and then you go in a chamber. This girl, what does the girl say when she sees your orange? Does she go, "Interesting"?

Gary: She says, "All right."

Dan: You have got to walk around with a GoPro helmet on 24/7.

Chris: It's his Halloween costume.

Dan: This ridiculousness. Can you wear the orange underwear when you lay on the mat tomorrow? Can we get that on video?

Chris: We need a picture of that. Put that on the Chris website.

Gary: I'm really comfortable in my skin, by the way.

Chris: You walk out in your orange underwear. Is the first thing the girl says to you like, "Do you work out?"

Dan: Nice six pack.

Gary: There's no six pack. I did feel a little awkward. I did feel awkward because I pulled the robe off in the room. The cryo chamber is weird. You can't get in and take the robe off. You've got to take it off before your crawl in. I take if off, and then she looks at my underwear.

Chris: I can't believe your wife let you wear that.

Gary: She literally looked away.

Chris: You know she was telling her friends later about this guy that came in with orange underwear. Liberace.

Dan: She's like, "I need some extra pay for this."

Gary: I looked so ridiculous.

Chris: That's fun. Cool. Well thanks Dan, this was fun. Did you have fun?

Dan: Yeah, I did. It was a blast.

Chris: You're out of tequila.

Dan: Yeah I am.

Chris: In closing Gary? Between the pills and the orange underwear, you're such a good sport. Oh my god. I'm sorry everybody, I honestly am sorry.

Gary: I don't know, it's just me. I'm just doing what I do.

Chris: This maybe wasn't good.

Gary: I don't know what else to do.

Chris: Just be you, bro. That's it. That's a bromance.

Dan: You got to make this interesting. We need to hear that stuff.

Chris: Yeah, it's a bromance. All right, thanks everybody.

Dan: Thank you. Bye.

Gary: Yep, take care.

Episode #19: Work Ethic Secrets From Master Sommelier DLynn Proctor

Gary: Welcome to Service Drive Revolution. My name is Gary, also known as the G-Man, I'm your co-host. And our host Chris is not here today. So Chris and I have been doing a lot of traveling and we've been all over the place. We just got in from Florida and Chris right now is currently in Phoenix at a Mastermind meeting, so he wasn't able to be here, and we've just been busy, busy, busy. So we haven't had a lot of time to shoot new podcasts, but we got a treat for you today. We want to roll out the interview that we had done with DLynn Proctor. Now, DLynn came to us at one of our elite coaching meetings a while back, and we had a really great time with him, an exceptional individual, and was a great interview. So let me just read a little bit about DLynn. DLynn's been a figure in the wine industry for over ten years. He was named the best Sommelier in America by Wine and Spirits magazine, 2008. He was a finalist at the Best Sommelier in America competition, 2008 and 2009, and he's been featured in *Decanter Wine Spectator*, *Everyday with Rachael Ray*, the Huffington Post, New York Times, and too many other publications to read. But he's also one of the four featured subjects in the internationally acclaimed documentary *Somme*. I've actually seen *Somme*, it's an amazing documentary and if you get a chance it's definitely worth a watch. It follows them, covering a three year journey, on their path to pass this test to become a master Sommelier, it's been called the most difficult test to pass in the world, and it's unbelievable their journey and what they have to go through to get there. There's only been 230 master Sommeliers in existence since they started measuring it back in 1968, so only 230 people since then have passed that test and been given the title master Sommelier. So it's pretty fun stuff, pretty interesting interview, so DLynn's going to talk to us about mindset. To pass a test that's that difficult took a very, very specific mindset to get through there. He's got some pretty amazing customer service experiences and you can probably imagine what it takes, in a restaurant serving very, very expensive bottles of wine, what he's gone through, so he's going to share some of those with us. He also talks about sales, very, very interesting sales topics that are very relatable to what we do on the Service Drive and how he used those in the restaurant business when he was selling wine. So sit back, relax, open a bottle of wine, and enjoy this interview with DLynn.

Chris: So DLynn, welcome to the table. This is my elite group of managers, these guys are the best in the industry in customer satisfaction, profitability, just all around being amazing leaders in their businesses. And we try to give them a little different experience of just not talking about business but experiencing other businesses, because it all comes back around, we can learn something from everybody. So welcome, we thank you for coming, and everybody's watched the documentary, *Somme*, and was blown away. The first question I want to ask you is, I did some research and 5,768 gold medals have been given out for the Olympics and 17,577 medals for the Olympics have been given out. So there's kids that grow up and they say, "I want to win a gold medal." And if you said "I want to win a gold medal," you're dedicating yourself to a life of trying to achieve perfection in something, it's a big commitment that you're going to constantly going to be improving, there's going to be disappointments and victories, but it's a big achievement to say that. And what you've committed yourself to, to say "I'm going to be a master Somme," is even harder than that, because there's only a little over 200 ever, right?

DLynn: About 227.

Gary: Ever! Alive or not with us anymore, right? So wine's something you take on later in life, because you're not 13 saying, "I want to be a Somme," right? So tell us how you came to the conclusion that that was a journey you wanted to go on.

DLynn: Well, let me paint a beautiful picture for you. I grew up in Dallas, Texas amongst the world's finest vineyards, and the world's finest wine-making regions, and-

Chris: (Laughing) The Dallas Cowboys?

DLynn: The world's finest collectors! Not true. I was a guy in a restaurant who worked in simple restaurants in high school, and I was like, well there's got to be something more to it. Why not work in finer restaurants where finer food is served. Where all those people I see walking into that restaurant across the street are going into, and they're all in suits and they're all getting out of nice cars. So at a very, very young age, I was just a gent that always wanted to do more, always wanted to exceed everyone else. I was an athlete, I was a hurdler, I was a relay guy, I ran track, I was a quarterback in football. That stuff was kind of fun, because that's what you did in high school, you were in athletics, but I knew I wanted to do something more because I also enjoyed every Sunday and Monday night and Tuesday night when there wasn't football or track practice, working in the restaurant, because it was always fun. So you fast forward to my adult years, and when I got back into restaurants at a legal age, of actually serving beverage, I was 21 years old and I worked at a restaurant called Humperdincks, which only if you were in Texas you would know exists. So pretty much a fast food but kind of upscale grille, but there was a beautiful

restaurant that was literally across the street, the story I alluded to. And I like, "I want to work there, how do I work there, how can I become a part of that team?" Because I see all these beautiful cars pulling in, beautiful women and men in these fantastic suits, and it looks like luxury. I want to be a part of luxury. So I pulled a few coattails, tapped a couple shoulders, asked some questions. And they said, well, first you have to know cuisine. You have to know preparations. You have to know cuts. You have to know meats. You have to know purveyors. You have to know producers. You have to know states and countries and cities and styles. I said okay, I'll learn it, where do I find a book? And the gent was like, no, you need an entire library. I said okay, where do I find an entire library. And once I did that over the course of a year, guess what restaurant I was working at? That restaurant. Then something very interesting happened. There was a gentleman who was impeccably dressed, beautiful Italian cut suit, a beautiful linen draped around his arm. He would go around the dining room floor, always with a bottle like this, and he'd go to a table and he'd pour, then he'd twist back up, label still facing the guests as he's walking through. Then he'd sit up, then he'd pour, then he'd twist back. His presentation was just absolutely impeccable, and I said, I'm going to be that guy. I have no idea what he's called, what he's doing, that's exactly where I want to be. He was a Sommelier. He literally told me, in the most nice, respectful, not condescending, not anything, he told me, "You will never be a Sommelier." I said, "okay."

Chris: (Laughing) That was a challenge?

DLynn: Yeah. That was 2002. By 2004, I took the first level Sommelier certification, which is called the introductory level certificate. My name was the last name called. I knew I had failed. There were about 30 people in the room that had failed. My name was the last name called. When it was finally called, that meant that I got the highest score in the class. And the only reason I got the highest score in the class is not because I was better than everyone else. Everyone else had already had fine dining experience as a prerequisite, five, six, seven years. Everyone else had already done it. I essentially picked up a book about physics, and memorized the book about physics, and took a test. That's all I did. I still didn't know anything. I picked up a few books, I memorized them without understanding about wine, food, viticulture, I got the highest score in the class. But that meant something to me. What that meant to me was that I could actually do it and take this small success, and hopefully boost further successes. So I started applying for scholarships, I started talking to suppliers like Castello Banfi, and Foster's Wine Estates which was Foster's Beer at the time, and Constellation, and all these big supplier wine companies saying, "Hey, I got a pretty high score on my intro Somme test, if I sell a hundred cases of your wine over the next month, can you send me to Italy? Can you send me here? Can you send me there?" And guess what? They were already doing that type of stuff anyways. I just didn't know. So I found myself on two, three, four 90-day visas throughout France, throughout Spain, throughout Italy. Flights were very cheap from DFW back in the day. I could go from DFW to Charles de Gaulle for $375 roundtrip. But this was also '04, '05, things were much, much cheaper. So what that told me was, is that I had put in the dedication to become something I knew nothing about, but I just knew it looked cool. I knew it looked affluent, I wanted to be affluent, I wanted to be luxurious. Why can't I have what that person has? I don't want what they have, I want to work for it and get it, and work for it and attain it. So that's exactly what I did.

Chris: Do you have a photographic memory?

DLynn: Whether it's photographic or eidetic or whether it's insane, I don't know! But yes.

Chris: So at what point in that journey did you fall in love with ... I understand you were in the business of wine, but when did you fall in love with wine? Because obviously, you have to be in love with it to dedicate as much time-

DLynn: I fell in love with it in 2007, because the wines that I was experiencing were just better and better and better. I was always great at my job, I was always a great salesman like each and every one of you around the table. And because I was a great salesman, that means the affluent that would come into the particular restaurants, they would ingratiate themselves with me. "I only want DLynn waiting on us. I only want DLynn doing the wine service at my table." After I've done 13 wine services for the two of you who come into the restaurant all the time, guess what's going to eventually happen? You're going to say, "Hey DLynn, I'm throwing a party. Got a bunch of CEOs coming over. You know what? You should come by the house, pick anything out of my cellar, talk about it to the guests, pay you some money, have fun, enjoy." And once you do that, you meet, meet, meet, handshake, handshake, handshake, and I'm everybody's best friend because they've got the means, I've got the knowledge, and I've just gave the folks with the means the knowledge! And they've also given me the means.

Speaker 4: Powerful.

DLynn: Yeah.

Chris: How much of your success do you think comes down

to work ethic?

DLynn:	99 percent of it.

Chris:	Yeah. And when you see other guys that get into the industry, what separates you from them when it's work ethic, dedication, what are the biggest differences that you see?

DLynn:	You know, everybody's different. I'll hearken back to years prior to '07, so like '02-3-4-5-6. I remember I was always the guy who wanted to go to the restaurant first and open. I was always the guy who wanted all the tables, all the parties. And I was always the guy who stayed later. So guy, gal, irrelevant, I was always that person. The reason no one ever wanted to come and open the restaurant is because they were hung-over from the night before. The reason they didn't want all of the tables and the reason they didn't get all of the call parties is because they were sluggish doing service because they were hung-over from the night before. And the reason they never closed the restaurant is because of what? They were ready to go drink again! So I made all the money, all the tips, all the bonuses, all the sales goals, because I wanted it more than everybody else. Work ethic. So in turn I made more than everybody else, and money value aside, I gained more than everybody else.

Chris:	Yeah, that's really powerful though, because even in our industry it's the guys that are there early that are getting the night drops and everything else. I mean, I remember doing that and the guys would complain, but ... So you were going to bed when everybody else is going out drinking?

DLynn:	Absolutely, or if I wasn't going to bed I was studying, I was reading. I was on the internet taking notes. I was asking people for their notes so I could copy their notes. And a lot of other Sommeliers would say,

"Why would I give you my notes? I'm not giving you my notes, I worked hard for these notes." I'm like, well I'm still learning what to do. If I take your notes and write them all down, it will give me a reason to go research everything around those notes that I'm taking. But I have to have a starting point. So that's what I would do.

Chris: Wow. Did you ever pay anybody for their notes?

DLynn: Yeah. Oh absolutely.

Chris: What's the most you paid for somebody's notes?

DLynn: 250 bucks. Back then.

Chris: What personal sacrifices have you made in this journey?

DLynn: Sleep, sanity, relationships, probably the big three.

Chris: It's interesting how, we talk about this and I hear about this all the time, when you're so dedicated to something and performing at such a high level, do you believe that work life balances something you're trying to achieve, or is it irrelevant?

DLynn: It's not irrelevant, you try to achieve it, but it's not always possible. Or it's not always possible to the thing that feels it's not as equal as the other things.

Chris: Yeah, I agree with that. So how does the business work? There's two parts of the wine business, one is the wineries, and we'll do that one second. But in a restaurant, we're curious about the presentation of wine, the pricing strategies, and do wineries incentivize you to sell a certain wine, so do you push that one? Or what are the behind the scenes part of that that we don't understand as novices that creates the profitability and the retail end of it? So how do you price it, and then how is it sold to the end user and what's the psychology behind it?

DLynn: When it comes to the restaurants and wineries incentivizing, I would say all of the above. But I guess a great place to start is, you'd rather end with winery, we can end with winery, we'll start with retail. Actually, I want to start with winery just so I can give you a metric, if you will. So if a winery, and this is all truncated, if a winery sells a bottle of wine for five dollars, by the time it goes from the winery to the broker, it's now at ten dollars. When it goes from the broker to the distributor, it's at fifteen dollars, this is just for one bottle. When it goes from the distributor to the retail store it's now from 15 to 20, and when it goes from the retail store to the restaurant it's now from 20 to 50. So that's just pretty much the metric of how the three-tier system, and I also included fourth tier being the broker, works in the United States. Particularly when it comes to restaurants, what's best to run a profitable restaurant on the beverage program, we do it based on the cost of goods just like everyone else and then the cost of sale. So hopefully for us we can run around, for the wine list, around 29 to 33 percent.

Chris: Margin.

DLynn: Margin, yes.

Chris: Now do you ever go direct to a winery and cut everyone else out?

DLynn: You can only do that in the state of California.

Chris: Really?

DLynn: Yes.

Chris:	So in all other states you have to go through all of those other hands?
DLynn:	Now if there are wines that you want to buy in California that are not Californian wine, you have to go through those tiers too. But being a Sommelier at Spago, at Cut, Hotel Bel Air, I'll just name Wolf's restaurants, I used to work for him, I can go direct to the winery and of course buy from the winery.
Chris:	And so then does that increase the margins in those restaurants?
DLynn:	Yes. Because you're getting it at a cheaper cost.
Chris:	So if you're in Dallas you want to achieve a 30 percent margin. But if you're here in Beverly Hills, would they have a 50 or 60 percent margin?
DLynn:	Absolutely.
Gary:	So California has a huge advantage?
DLynn:	Absolutely.
Chris:	Wow, that's interesting. So then, are you graded on ... if you're a Somme in a restaurant and you're in charge, you're ordering the wine and then you're ultimately graded on the margin?
DLynn:	Yes, you are. You're graded on how profitable the wine program is, and if you're the beverage director you're graded on how profitable the beverage program is, which includes beer, spirits, cocktails, shots, Pellegrino, Panna, Coca-Cola, Fever-Tree, a little Fever-Tree, you're graded on all of that. Including wine.
Chris:	So you're picking the water...

DLynn: Everything. Everything that is beverage, you are graded on. And I say graded, yes you're graded on it, because if you're numbers are off and your boss wants you at 25 or 29 or at 33 and you're running 50, there's only so long that that 50's going to go on before you're let go.

Chris: How do you balance the perks from the wineries then? Because there's-

DLynn: And let me backtrack, because I might have confused someone. When I talk about it in this term, I'm talking about the cost of the actual sale. That's what I'm talking about in this term. You'd rather run a 25 percent business, which means my product is very expensive for everyone else because I'm making more money off of it, as opposed to running a 50 percent cost. I'm talking about cost in that aspect, so I should clarify.

Chris: Yeah, it's the reverse. So then you're ... because oftentimes I've ordered a bottle of wine and they will say, "Oh, I was just at this winery." So obviously a big part of the wine industry is to get everybody to come hear your story and taste your wine, so what are the perks on the other side that you're offered to go on trips to go to wineries to convince you that that's the wine you want to serve in your restaurant?

DLynn: I think every young Sommelier or every young beverage professional, when you're young and you're in this industry and the industry is notorious for giving someone a Sommelier title that's 24 years old, but they're giving you this big title and you can go around with your business card and everyone thinks you're cool or important, but you're not making any money. You're making 25, 30 grand a year and maybe a little bit of a percentage of tips or sales. So it's important for the Somme's to be able to take trips, because they can't afford to take those trips. A lot of people just can't afford to take five European trips a year, doesn't matter what you make, there are other things we have to do. So it's important for me to say, I like your wines, your wines, your wines, and your wines, let me do everything I can to sell a lot of them so I can be recognized, or let me ask how I can sell a lot of your wines to be recognized, so that you can take me to Italy, you can take me to France, you can take me to Spain, and you can take me to Napa, and you can take me to Australia. So it's great marketing on the part of the winery who can afford to do it, because they're still getting depletion, but because they've got A and P dollars set aside, they've got those A and P dollars set aside because of what they've depleted, they can bring three people to Australia that have pretty much depleted their Texas and California inventory. So the winery's happy, they've made their revenue, they've tucked some of that into A and P, they're promoting by bringing these folks out and showing them the world, because once I've done that, they never forget. They take that with them for the rest of their lives.

Chris: Then they know the story and they believe in the winery even more, right?

DLynn: Absolutely.

Chris: Because they've experienced it. So then they're balancing the perks with the margins that their boss wants them to achieve, right?

DLynn: Absolutely.

Chris: So early on in your career were there any mistakes that you made?

DLynn: Oh, yes.

Chris: In pricing or ... so what were some of those mistakes?

DLynn: I was opening my second restaurant. I was a bit haggard with my bookkeeping and my sales spreadsheets, I was still learning them. And I had priced a few wines based on six pack quantities as opposed to twelve pack quantities and vice versa, and I was off for about six months. And you just can't turn around a program where you're off drastically on numbers six months. You don't turn it around in two months. You have to slowly adjust pricing so it doesn't look obvious to the guests. You have to slowly cut down on purchases so it's not at the detriment of the restaurant or the program to catch those numbers up. I was fortunate to do so with some donations and with some programs and with some incentives to turn my six months of eff-ups around, turned that around in about four months.

Chris: When you say donations, what do you mean?

DLynn: Well, getting a winery to donate product, to-

Chris: So it helped you recover?

DLynn: Offset, to recover, absolutely.

Chris: And do wineries donate product for you to try and see, but they're giving it to you?

DLynn: Absolutely.

Chris: So that's 100 percent.

DLynn: That's 100 percent.

Chris: Margin.

DLynn: 100 percent margin, 100 percent net revenue.

Chris: That's amazing. What is part of the psychology of presenting the wine and getting the customer in the restaurant to buy the higher priced wine? Like, even to the point of when you look at menus, the way that the wine is laid out price wise on the menu?

DLynn: See, the psychology of it is, when you're in my restaurant and you just had a bad day at the office, you just lost a four- billion-dollar acquisition, something's going on at home, or you're just having a bad day in general, when you come into my restaurant it's my job to take you on a journey. I take you on a journey and I take you away from all the negative that has happened throughout the day or throughout the week or the bad plan ride. And with that I take you on a journey about something that is so close to all of us, even though it's so far from all of us, because we all want to be a part of these types of histories. So when I take you on that journey, I've engaged you to a point of comfort and trust. And when you've engaged an individual to the point of comfort and trust, what usually happens is they usually just say, "Okay, okay, okay." So it's our job to take you on a journey, tell a story, tell you why you should have this with the fillet, or why you should have this with the dish. And then next time you come back, instead of buying the $30 bottle that you would normally buy, I sold you a $52 dollar bottle of wine and you trusted me for that, you'll say, hey DLynn, I want to try something, let's go one ... and a lot of time they just do this ... let's stay under here, instead of saying it out loud to the table, the colleagues, business professionals may be at the table, let's stay under here. It's just gaining trust, but it's also my job not to mess that trust up. It's also my job not to say, "I've actually heard about Chris, every time he goes he drops a $1,000 tip, he orders big wine, his first time in this restaurant, let's get him tonight." It's actually my job to say, "Oh, that's Chris? Hi Chris, how are you? Yes, so you usually drink Harlan when you come in, you know what? I've got a fantastic wine, 2007 vintage, it's about a fourth of the price of Harlan, I believe you'll love it." I automatically gained his trust by doing quite the opposite.

Chris: How do you interact with waiters, and what important role do they play in what they doing?

DLynn: My interaction with a waiter is my same interaction with you and everyone else, because I'm a waiter. I don't care how many Sommelier accreditations I have or Best Sommeliers of the Year, or Best Sommeliers in the World, doesn't matter. I'm a waiter. Waiter to waiter, we drop plates, we pick up plates. We pick up glassware, we pick up forks, knives, and spoons, we help one another. We pour wine, we throw stuff in the bus tub in the back, we roll our sleeves up, they're no different from me. We are all equal. The waiter, the actual bus boy, the captain, the GM, the maÃ®tre d, every single individual in the restaurant is equal, so everyone reacts with each other on the exact same playing field.

Chris But are there things that they can do to set you up?

DLynn: Oh, of course. They set you up for success. They are your QB, they set you up for success. If I'm in the cellar looking for a bottle for table 12, 92, 47, and 31, I want to know that when I get back to that table, the tasting glass is there in front of the host and everyone has their actual glass that they're going to drink from. Whether it's my waiter, whether it's my back waiter, whether it's my assistant Somme. Yes, we all have jobs. We all set each other up for success. But it would be impossible for me to, while I'm looking for four different vintages from five different decades, it would be impossible for me to set all the glassware up on each of these tables that I have to run to, and purposely pour, present, talk, engage, and move to the next one. So they mark the table with silverware, they mark the table with linen, they mark the table with coasters, they mark the table with decanters. They will mark the table by rolling the gueridon next to the particular table that you need to present to. So everybody's job, yes, is imperative, and that's how treat one another, to answer your question. But all equal.

Chris: I get that, but the system is very important to success, right?

DLynn: The French call it mise en place, everything in its place.

Chris: And do you up every table?

DLynn: I'm not sure if I follow?

Chris: Well, I've been in restaurants before, and the Somme doesn't come unless you ask.

DLynn: Oh, I go to every single table.

Chris: And introduce yourself?

DLynn: Oh absolutely. They may not need me, they may. I always go and introduce myself, absolutely.

Chris: And then what is inappropriate to tip? And should you tip separately?

DLynn: Wow, that's a very wonderful question. Everyone within the community says at least $20. I don't care if you make 30 grand a year. You got to go into a restaurant, and if you have a $100 check, you're going to tip $25, $30 bucks. Just because you want that good juju to come back to you.

Chris: Right.

DLynn: Now, if you're making 30 grand a year, you shouldn't be eating a ton of $100 checks, plus tipping 33 percent or 35 percent on top of that? You shouldn't be doing that. But that's how it happens in the industry, I promise you. Outside of the industry, the folks who make us folks in the industry our living, it's more like 12, 15, 17 percent. Which, at the end of the day, you can't frown at, why would you frown at, it's still better than zero. But we have an expectation. And I say we, I'm no longer in the restaurant on the floor, but we have an expectation always of at least 20, because that's what we do to one another.

Chris: Now do you tip the Sommelier separately?

DLynn: There is always, always, always the appreciated handshake, absolutely. It's not mandatory! Restaurants like Spago, yes. Not mandatory, it happens. Restaurants like Spago, and Cut, and Mozza, all the greats around here, yeah. You know, 11 Madison Park, Per Se, French Laundry, Le Bernardin. There's always that handshake. I mean, you could be a Sommelier, you could be the wine director, and I'm just going to throw out a number, you could be the wine director at Le Bernardin who has $115,000 salary, but in handshakes you could make another 50.

Chris: So it is customary, especially if they spend a lot of time and educate you and tell you the story, it is customary to tip separately, right?

DLynn: Indeed. Yes it is.

Chris: Any advice on how the system of when you're down in the cellar and they're setting everything up, is that rehearsed? Is it known? Is it different from restaurant to restaurant who does what?

DLynn: Now, do you mean system of inventory, or system of... ?

Chris:	Well, like in some restaurants, somebody else is bringing the glass and someone's the waiter, some seem way more organized.
DLynn:	Very true. Soâ⃞ ¦
Chris:	In other ones, the wine's there but the glasses aren't-
DLynn:	The hierarchy, yeah, the standard operating procedures, if you will.
Chris:	Is it rehearsed every time?
DLynn:	Everybody's SOPs are totally, totally different. Fine dining pretty much usually adheres to a certain set of core operating procedures, and they're pretty much done the same way at your Per Se's, French Laundry's, Meadowoods, Bottegas, Le Bernardins, etc. So there is a cellar rat, a floor Somme, an assistant Somme, a chef's Somme, and a wine director, and each of them have different roles throughout the night at the restaurant.
Chris:	You said cellar rat?
DLynn:	There's always a cellar rat. I was a cellar rat. There's always a cellar rat.
Chris:	I was a lot lizard, which is a lot-
DLynn:	I guess that's the equivalent rank! Wow!
Chris:	Well I guess every industry has that.
DLynn:	Every industry has it! Cellar rat-
Chris:	When I was washing cars, they would call you the lot lizard.

DLynn: Lot lizard and ... there you are.

Chris: How much of your time is spent preparing for the night compared to working the night? So if you open from six to eleven, right? How much time is spent before that and after that preparing?

DLynn: I'm usually at the restaurant at 9 AM.

Chris: Wow.

DLynn: When I was in restaurants at 9 AM. I'm backing out numbers from the night before. I'm looking at what sold, I'm looking at what sold the most, I'm looking at the frequency of sales, the time of sales, I'm looking at the number of apps sold, the number of desserts sold, the number of American Wagyu steaks sold. I'm looking at all of those things so I can properly prepare for the day that's coming up, and properly prepare for the week and the weekend, etc. Any catering events, any parties, etc. So that usually, let's just say goes from 9 to 11:30, noon. Quick bite from the kitchen, back at your desk, you've got phone calls, suppliers, the guy from Penfolds wants to come and taste you on his wines, you know, the guy from wherever, the want to come by and taste you on their wines. You do that for a couple hours and let's just say it's 2:45, 3:00 now. The rest of the servers and the team, etc., are starting to arrive in the restaurant, and you're looking at all of your reservations, you're looking at, Mr. Chris is coming in, Ms. Sylvia's coming in, Ms. Terry's coming in, you've got all these high rollers coming into your restaurant that night. You see what they have ordered and drank over the number of visits they've had. You see how many times they've actually visited the restaurant.

Chris: You can tell that in the system?

DLynn:	Oh, absolutely.
Chris:	Can you tell how much they tipped?
DLynn:	Not all restaurants are capable of doing that.
Chris:	Wow.
DLynn:	But there is a program that will tell, yes. The table number that they love to sit at, we as a restaurateur, we should all know that. But that's also expensive, there's also programs that do that, and it's very, very expensive. So I would say six or seven hours of prep, A to Z, is spent on the actual two seatings that you're going to have the whole night, or four hours on the floor.
Chris:	That's insane.
DLynn:	But I'm not finished, because your last seating is at 8:30, everyone leaves at 10:45, 11, doesn't mean we're gone. No. You're still taking care of issues that you maybe didn't finish during the day because of every other distraction that happens, and you're still looking at, okay, now it's time to re-inventory the cellar for tomorrow because some of these items that sold tonight, I have to put the order in tonight so that the sales rep or the supplier wakes up with it in their laptop at seven when they start checking orders so they can immediately put it in. Because if I go the restaurant at 8:30 or 9 AM and that cut off has already been missed, I can't get that item hot-shotted today by three. So there's so much work pre than the three to four hours during service, and then the 11 to 2 AM after. And then you go and have a Campari or a nice Belgian beer, then you go home, go to bed. Then you do it again.
Chris:	How many days a week are you doing that?

DLynn: Seven.

Chris: So there's your work-life balance!

DLynn: So at the end of the day when you become a wine
director, it's because you've done all of those things.
You've been a cellar rat who works seven days a week
and made no money. You've been an assistant
Somme who made a little more but no money, seven
days a week. You've been a floor Somme who made a
little more but still no money really, seven days a week
and all these hours, you know, fourteen hour days.
Then you've been the chef's Somme, or AKA lead
Somme, who is doing okay, may get some day off,
totally fine, six days, no big deal. And then you
eventually become the wine director, you've got your
two days off, but you still may check in, you still go
by for an hour or two, you talk to the owner. You
might go talk to Danny [Mara 00:36:54], because
you've got to meet Danny [Mara 00:36:55]. You got to
go talk to Thomas Keller, because he's still ultimately
your boss, or Wolfgang, because he's still ultimately
your boss. So it's your off day, but you still go in for
two hours. But you get two of those, and you get to
pick those two days. So just like every industry, you
work your way up. Just so happens that the wine
director is kind of the CEO of the wine, because wine
doesn't talk back.

Chris: How often do you want to turn your inventory?

DLynn: That's a tricky question, I'll tell you why that's a tricky
question. That's a tricky question because I'm not
looking to turn my inventory on all of the rare bottles
of wine that I have in the cellar.

Chris: Right.

DLynn: If it's a wine by the glass, I'm hoping that I'm doing ten cases a week, or of a particular wine, I'm hoping I'm doing three, four cases a night. So there are some wines you want to turn daily, with five, six case quantities. There's some wines you want to turn ten cases a week. There's some bottles you want to order ... all I need to do is order three bottle pars, and if I sell seven bottles in a week I'll keep my pars at four. So it just really depends on the bottle, the rarity of it, what it costs on your wine list, so that's a moving number, that's moving target always.

Chris: Steve, you can come in an sit on the couch if you want. Do you have a number of how much your inventory can be ... how much you can spend on it?

DLynn: Absolutely.

Chris: What is usually, from a mid level restaurant to the high end of Cut, guesstimate, what are those numbers?

DLynn: And I'll never say Cut's numbers, because I have no idea what Cut's numbers are now.

Chris: Just in general.

DLynn: But a nice bistro might carry an inventory of about 35 grand, and wine ... We'll leave liquor out. A nice bistro might carry a wine inventory of about 35 grand, a nice gastro pub that's a little bit more serious might carry a wine inventory of about 70 grand. A nicer, gets some pretty good ratings from Michael Bower, pretty good reviews, etc., may carry an inventory of about 105, 115, 125 grand.

Chris: Wow.

DLynn: But when you're working at real deal restaurants, real deal steakhouses, whether they're Michelin or not, but highly, highly venerated restaurants, you could carry 253, half a million dollars in inventory. Or you could be like a couple great steakhouses in Texas, my home state, Papa Brothers Steakhouse, grand award winning wine list restaurants, even though Spago has a grand award too, you could carry 1.1 million in inventory.

Chris: So that 1.1 million, the restaurant owns it, or is a lot of it carried by the wineries?

DLynn: No, it's never carried by the winery because by law I've already given that wine to the distributor, and the distributor has already-

Chris: It's too far downstream.

DLynn: Too far downstream. But there are personal owners that are only allowed in some states that have, I give you $250,000 of my inventory to put into your incredibly touted steakhouse, this is what my vig is, this is what I want to make off these wines, but once I get my return it's worth a little bit more, but the restaurant doesn't own it until they sell it, they're just holding it until it's sold.

Chris: So he's coming in checking once a week what's sold, and ...

DLynn: Well he doesn't have to come and check in because we tell him what's sold! Because he wants his check.

Chris: That's interesting. So just like in any industry, there's always variables.

DLynn: Of course.

Chris: Right. So is there ever any gamification used to sell desserts or wine with the waiters, are they ever incentivized to push certain things?

DLynn: The answer to that is always, yes, yes, yes. Because there may be items in the kitchen that chef has to get rid of. There may be items in the kitchen that have thrown off chefs, kind of cost us sales, and he needs to adjust his numbers and ah, that's going to spoil in two days. I know it sounds weird, me saying spoilage in restaurants but it happens. That's going to spoil in two days, I could still make a fantastic merengue out of that tonight with all these great presentations. I need to catch up some dollars here, so I'll put that on the menu for $27 dollars tonight. I'll have the Sommelier get some incredible bottle of wine that a supplier donated that he can sell for $14 a glass tonight, I'll pair those two, and I'll get the whole team around it, we call it pre-shift. During pre-shift we talk about those two items I just talked about. My top salesmen in the room, my top servers who usually make the most, get the most time off, kind of have their way with the restaurant because they do the best, they have their ways and their words of selling those wines and guess what? I say all I need you to sell is 15 tonight. My top three, one, two, three, they're going to sell five each, we're happy.

Chris: But what do they get for doing that?

DLynn: Oh, it could be a $250 gift card, it could be a $75 gift card, it could be-

Chris: It's always changing.

DLynn: It's always something. It could be, if you can sell these 15 items for me tonight, you'll get a new iPad. But the only reason you'll get a new iPad is because at some point a supplier donated that iPad for something that was already done.

Chris: Isn't that hilarious you guys? Same thing, right? The shift meeting too. So I lived across from Church and State here, when Church and State was amazing downtown, and every night at 5:30 they were tasting the desserts, they were tasting the cocktail of the

night, and tasting new wines, because then when the waiters went out, they believed in what they were selling. It was amazing. You'd watch them pass around one plate of the dessert and they would all take a bite of the same plate. But the shift meeting really is the time, like in sports or anything, to really--

DLynn: Hone in on the focus.

Chris: Talk about the plan, yeah.

DLynn: Talk about the plan, talk about the focus for the evening.

Chris: So will you have the crew taste wines in these shift meetings?

DLynn: Absolutely, absolutely. I may say I've got two new wines in on the wine list and these are incredible wines to sell, it's a great opportunity, the owner of Berenger's going to be sitting at one table, the owner of Penfolds' going to be sitting at another, I would like to see you get behind the wines tonight and when you go to the table talk like you know what you're doing. So of course, we would talk about those wines in pre-shift, and everybody would be excited and invigorated to sell them and invigorated to pair them, so there's always an objective for the evening, or several objectives. Always several, never only one.

Chris: Okay. Unhappy customers. What do the successful restaurants do if somebody is unhappy with their bottle of wine or anything, and what are the best policies that you've seen out there in the different restaurants you've worked at?

DLynn: Well I think every successful ... whether it's a restaurant or not, every successful business is going to have loss built into the plan. So it's no different for the restaurant. The customer is always right. If they just ordered a $295 Wimmera Australian Wagyu and they were unhappy with it? Doesn't matter. We cook them another one. If they just ordered a $1,000 bottle of wine and they are unhappy with it? It doesn't matter. I get it off the table, and I get them another one. And by doing that, I tell them they are right without telling them they are right. I succumb to their needs and their fillings and everything without being rude about it. They're always right. So hopefully the restaurant or everyone has that plan of loss built into it because you're going to lose, things in the kitchen are going to spoil. So with the customer always being right, it's my job to put something else on the table that, hopefully, they will. It's my job to say, well, that was a $1,000 bottle of wine that you didn't like. I'm saying to myself, there was nothing wrong with it, but they didn't like it. So it's my job to say, well you know what, I understand that you might not have liked that wine because it had too much tobacco. I might be gaming you right now, it might not be that that wine had too much tobacco, you just didn't like it. So I'll say words like that and say, well you know what, I'm going to find you something that has a little bit more vanilla. And instead of $1,000, I'll get you something that's $250. That way, if you don't like this on, my butt's covered a little bit more, but it still helps you feel better about going from $1,000 to $250, so hopefully I'm gaining your trust back.

Chris: So I'm a firm ... you know, I go around to a lot of different businesses, and the one thing that usually separates the really successful ones from the average performers is mindset.

DLynn: Yeah.

Chris: More than anything, holding themselves to a higher standard, and they have a passion for what they do with that. What do you see in the wine industry and restaurant industry that separates the really special ones like the French Laundry or the really special owners from the average?

DLynn: I love the word passion, I think passion is overused a lot. I actually love the word desire more. Because you can have a passion to do anything, you can have a passion to be a bad person. You're just passionate about being awful. (Laughs) True. Desire, though, desire is something that you live and breathe. Marines desire excellence, that's just what it is. People at their highest ... of whatever they do, they desire excellence. To work at the French Laundry, for example, the only way you're going to get into the French Laundry is by desiring excellence at the level you're going to start at so you can work your way up. There's just a different ethos, a different desire, a different mindset, a different drive. There are only certain individuals that can work in the French Laundry because they have the drive and the desire to do so. That doesn't mean that the great bistro around the corner where the PPA is $32 a person isn't incredible. It doesn't mean those folks aren't as driven or don't have the same amount of desire. But there's also difference between a four-cylinder working as hard as it can, and a twelve-cylinder working as hard as it can. They both have the same amount of desire to put out their most, they both have the same amount of desire to give you the most performance, but at the end of the day, one's a V4, one's a V12. So restaurants of that caliber, every single individual in that establishment, whether it's the contractor, whether it's the bus boy, whether its the maÂitre d, whether it's TK, Thomas Keller, or whether it's the GM. They're all-

Chris:	You're that tight with him, you can call him TK? (Laughs)
DLynn:	TK. They're all working on V12.
Chris:	So you go into restaurant to help a friend that is the Somme at a restaurant, and let's say it's in Beverly Hills and it's a steakhouse, middle to higher end. What should his average be in wine sales per customer?
DLynn:	That's tricky, because just because you're a restaurant in Beverly Hills, you could still be a Bistro. So it really depends because you can't expect to have an $85 PPA and ... you can expect to have an $85 PPA with a $24 by-the-glass, or $24 wine PPA.
Chris:	Now explain what those are, what's a PPA?
DLynn:	Price per person average.
Chris:	Price per person average. So do you track it by bottle and by glass?
DLynn:	You track it by bottle and by glass.
Chris:	So what would be a good number that you would be happy with?
DLynn:	I would prefer to see a third of it, so 30 percent of it.
Chris:	What do you mean by 30 percent?
DLynn:	Of the PPA. So if it's $85 that they spent-
Chris:	I mean average sale per customer, what would be a good number, $85?
DLynn:	The average sale per would be $85 yes, absolutely.
Chris:	So you go in there, your friend's average is $40. Just without even looking at anything what do you think,

what is wrong without even ... I mean, most of the time I can go into a business, and I don't have to look and I kind of already know.

DLynn: Well, inventory and education. That's the problem.

Chris: So they have a bad inventory-

DLynn: They have the wrong inventory, they have the wrong wines in the house, wines that are not recognizable, noticeable, or appealing. You have to know the demographic of your restaurant. If you have the wrong inventory, and the demographic of Brentwood or Beverly Hills says that this is the most sought after or these are the most sold and you don't know that, then you're already shooting yourself in the foot.

Chris: Or you just are putting what you like on there.

DLynn: Or you're what you like, and not your demographic.

Chris: Yeah.

DLynn: And second is the education. You have to have inventory first, you have to have the education second.

Chris: To tell the story.

DLynn: To tell the story. And then you can take that from $40 to $85.

Chris: It's funny, so my bulldogs, I don't know if you saw them running around here-

DLynn: I call them double dogs, of course I saw them!

Chris: They're from a breeder, Cody Sickle. And Cody Sickle, for bulldogs he's won Westminster like 11 times. The numbers are staggering, like nobody's even close to him for bulldogs and winning dog shows. So him and I partnered on a dog, and he was mentoring me, and I asked him, I said ... like Cody, we were at a bulldog dog show and there were like 200 bulldogs and breeders there, and I said, "Cody, you're so far ahead of everybody else. What separates you from everybody else?" And he goes, "I don't fall in love with my breed."

DLynn: Oh wow.

Chris: He goes, "Everybody else falls in love with their breed. And they only breed inside their breed." And he goes, "You see that lady over there? I've bred with her bitch," it's always funny when they call them bitches, "I've bred with her bitch twice and I'm always just looking for the best dog to breed, I'm never in love with my breed." And doesn't that happen in the wine industry? Where a guy loves wine, and he becomes a Somme, and then he wants to serve the wine he loves, but it isn't what the patrons--

DLynn: The guests love.

Chris: Does that happen a lot?

DLynn: It happens all too often, those Sommeliers usually find themselves unemployed. It's not about you, it's about your demographic, it's about your consumer, it's about your customer, it's about your guest. Much the same, I'm sure, for you guys. Yeah, you're right.

Chris: Because I would think in wine it would happen more, because guys get so passionate about it!

DLynn: So excited about ... "I made this wine last year, and I just want everybody to have it!" Well, A, it doesn't go with the cuisine. B, the chef doesn't like it. C, the owner the doesn't like it because he hates the owner of that particular property. And D, it's not your restaurant.

Chris: Yeah, and the customer's coming in want to see the stuff they want.

DLynn: Of course.

Chris: In their price range, and the whole thing. Good job. So any questions you guys?

Speaker 5:   So I look at your wait staff and probably your bartenders very similar to where our service advisors are. They're sales people. So do you have a process acquiring top talent? Do you promote from within, do you go out and get the best of the best, is there a way that you go about getting those people?

DLynn: Great question. That's a fantastic question. Hopefully your restaurant would automatically recruit the top talent because of whatever your establishment is, so all the best would want to work there. But that's not always the case, how do you get a bistro, and I keep picking on bistros, but how do you get a bistro that not a lot of people would know about and not a lot of servers would want to go and work at. Well that's when you actually promote from within. You actually spend the time with those individuals that already work for you, and you groom them. You tell them, I'm teaching you things about where you are now, but I'm also teaching you things about life. I'm teaching you things that you can use going forward. And if you ever choose to leave, guess what? Knowing what you know, you have a friend who you say, "You know what? You've been making this amount of money, or you've been working at this other bistro, I'm actually leaving, you should come work here and get all the great contacts that I have and make a great living and learn some of the things I learned." So, it's a lot of that, but of course nowadays you've also got advertising on Craigslist, you've got advertising on Facebook, advertising on Instagram and Twitter. You've got ways of trying to attract pretty good talent, even if you're not one of the upper echelons of restaurants. But I always love the promoting within, I love that the French Laundry does a lot of promoting within.

Chris:	I know a local chef here that went and worked at the French Laundry for free for six months. He owns three restaurants here in LA now, but just because he learned the systems, the discipline-
DLynn:	The discipline.
Chris:	Everything. He said at French Laundry, there's never a point where anything is not immaculately clean.
DLynn:	You could literally lick the floor.
Chris:	And Keller's there constantly, very involved. And the systems are really tight, really tight.
DLynn:	But see, that's at that level. All the things that you just said are very correct, but that's at that level. How do you go to the bar and grill and expect to ... You're not going to go work at the bar and grill for free for six months, because there's no need for you to do that, it's a bar and grill. So for places like that you still have to have the same type of ethos that the Laundry has and hopefully work toward cultivating and creating and embodying great staff and great talent, etc. And hopefully bringing them up within because as they go and eventually leave your bar and grill and work somewhere else, "You know what? I don't have a spot for you at my new restaurant, but how about you go to my old restaurant where I was for seven years, I think you'll be a great fit there." And guess what? Now that person is cultivated to go somewhere else and do the same thing. So in our industry, everyone pays it forward and pays it back at the same time.
Chris:	Yeah, that's awesome. Give him a round of applause. (Applause)
DLynn:	Oh, no, thank you guys.

Episode #20: The Great Technician Drought Of 2021

Chris: Welcome everybody to Service Drive Revolution. Your podcast or podcast for your service drive. If you have technicians, service advisors, customers, this is the place. Please make sure you subscribe. Hit your subscribe button on iTunes or whatever vehicle you are listening to this on. We appreciate the support. I think like, wouldn't you agree G-Man that we give way more content on this then people charge for?

Gary: Yeah, for sure. Absolutely.

Chris: That's our passion. We want to help you guys. We love the smell of oil in the morning.

Gary: Not me.

Chris: The cholesterol.

Gary: Not me.

Chris: The topic that we have today, it's great. Gary has some amazing stuff. It's called "The Great Technician Drought." You are going to be blown away by some of the stats that he has on this. We'll give you a little light at the end of tunnel after he tells you how bad it is, but "The Great Technician Drought." If you're having a hard time hiring techs, like everybody, we got some ideas and we're going to talk through that today. Should be fun. We're also going talk about a great book that, I think you finished, but I'm going through. But it's amazing. The new Cialdini book.

Gary: Pre-Suasion.

Chris: Pre-Suasion. If you haven't read his books, he wrote, Influence. I think he wrote a book called Ask, but Influence is iconic. If haven't read that book, read it first.

Gary: Yeah.

Chris: But his new one is Pre-Suasion. It's amazing.

Gary: That's a great book.

Chris: We're going to talk about it and how it applies to your service drive because there's some analogies in there that directly apply to what your advisors are doing in the drive.

Gary: Super interesting too. Sometimes you get into a book and you're just like "ugh," they just don't grab you. But this one I got into it and I just couldn't stop. I wanted to listen to the whole thing and then I got the paper copy and started reading it, too, because I enjoyed it so much.

Chris: That's what I love about him, he does so much research and he's got facts. He's a professor. It's facts and it's meat, it's not a lot of fluff. I love that. That's more my style.

Gary: He tells some good stories and he gets to the point fast. Which is one thing I think I was kind of complaining, quasi-complaining about, of the last book I read, the Duhig book. And I love Duhig and I love Malcolm Gladwell. They're both excellent authors and I read all their stuff. But they do circle their point for a little while and they open loops. They'll leave you hanging and they won't give you the answer until like two chapters later.

Chris: Yeah.

Gary: He'll kind of tell the story, give you the answer, and then move on to the next thing.

Chris: No tease.

Gary: Yeah. There's no tease.

Chris: Right to the meat. I love that.

Gary: Right to the point.

Chris: I'd also like to say that if you want to get a little bit better in your business, you want a little help, we have the best advisor training and service manager universities for your pricing strategies, how to set up a shop basically, beginning to end, anything you need to take what you have that's working already and make it even better. You know you're coming up on 2017, so, it's time to get some inspiration and some new fresh ideas and we're famous for having the new stuff. So, if we can help you in any way, please give us a call. The website is chriscollinsinc.com. Chris I-N-C-dot-com. Phone number's on there. E-mail us, call us. Do not write us a snail mail.

Gary: You can write us a letter. We'll get it. Just won't happen fast.

Chris: The questions that everybody's asking ... Nobody cares about the book. Nobody cares about "The Great Technician Drought." So, I gotta set this up because, well, it's kind of like a lot of people in the Trump election. Nobody saw it coming. And I didn't see this cholesterol coming.

Gary: Me either.

Chris: So, I'm not joking. See what we had, if you guys remember, if you can go back a long time in podcasts and listen, Gary volunteers. He says, "If I don't get my cholesterol below 200, I'm gonna get a Seahawks tattoo." And don't I say like, "Where?" Because it could've been a little tramp stamp on your butt or something. But you're like nope, right on my arm. Right?

Gary: Yeah.

Chris: I'm like, "No, that would be crazy. Don't do it." Also, at that time I think we thought the Cowboys were going to suck and they have the best record in the NFL.

Gary: Yeah. No kidding. A couple surprises came out of that one.

Chris: I'm famous for doing impressions. Let me do an impression and you tell me who this is. Okay?

Gary: Okay.

Chris: You ready? Close your eyes. I don't want you to visually I don't want you to ...

Gary: My eyes are closed by the way.

Chris: "I didn't mean to get hurt." Who's that?

Gary: That's Tony Romo.

Chris: What a press conference that was. Oh boy.

Gary: Oh, he was emotional.

Chris: "You don't know how hard...how hard it is to make $24 million and sit on the bench."

Gary: The live stream was pretty funny because everybody was like, "No, Tony. Don't leave. Please stay."

Chris: They live streamed it?

Gary: Yeah, because they did a Facebook Live event for that. When you're in Facebook Live, you can start commenting and everything, so you just see the stream of comments going by. They did it right when I was eating, so I got to sit there and watch the whole thing happen. It was fun.

Chris: So, I read a headline, like "Tony Romo Gets Choked Up" or whatever. I go to the video and I literally ... So, he's got papers, some guy's asking questions, he's like, "I'm gonna answer your questions." Then, whatever. Then he goes, "Well, I'm not gonna answer any questions, but hopefully this answers all your questions. I'm going to read this thing." Then he starts reading it and he gets to that point of where he's like, "I felt like I was letting the team down." And I turned it off. I can't stand Tony Romo.

Gary: Yeah. You know he's been my quarterback for a long time. It's been a lot of frustrating years because he started out really strong and then he just kind of fell and never really recovered from that. He's done some good stuff and some terrible stuff. He's just never really caught his stride. I feel bad for the guy, to be honest with you.

Chris: Enough about Tony Romo.

Gary: Well hold on.

Chris: People are tuning out as we go.

Gary: The way that press conference. He literally got really emotional and then ran off.

Chris: Was he crying at the end?

Gary: It seemed like ... Yeah. Like he was just a rejected beauty show contestant, just crying and running off the stage. It was bizarre behavior to me.

Chris: I'm sure it's hard. I'm sure it's hard to go through rehab and fight through everything and to fight through physically and then, you know. But it's the NFL.

Gary: That's what I'm saying.

Chris: They'll trade him to the Broncos in a second.

Gary: I don't see Brett Favre doing that. I don't see Russell Wilson doing that. I don't see guys ... They're pretty hardened guys, you know?

Chris: Yeah. Nobody was replacing Brett Favre off the bench.

Gary: Yeah. There you go. That's true.

Chris: Also, Brett Favre never missed a game in like 12 years or something?

Gary: Yeah. He had 167 starts, consecutive starts, something like that.

Chris: I mean I know it was a Seahawk, but Avril barely grazed him and he broke his back. He's injury prone, Romo is.

Gary: Yeah. He's fragile. For the NFL he's fragile. I mean, shit, he made it through college, so he did a pretty good job of that.

Chris: What college did he go to? Nobody cares.

Gary: Least of all me.

Chris: Getting back to the cholesterol. The thing is you got this pending tattoo above your head and then all of a sudden we're here in the office one day and I think we're like a week and a half out from your test? I didn't know yet. I'm like, "Hey, it's the end of the day." I'm like, "Yeah you want to have a drink?". You're like, "Nope. I'm not drinking." I'm like, "What?" And then all of a sudden you're eating like lettuce and chicken. So, every day, Gary got less and less fun. He's like, "I got my cholesterol test." So, I'm not joking, by the end he's drinking kale and eating chicken and taking Niacin like crazy.

Gary: Yeah, Niacin like crazy.

Chris: You were taking Niacin like crazy. The night before the blood test, you stopped eating at 4.

Gary: No, I stopped eating at noon the day before.

Chris: Noon. So, the lady's here at the office at what, 7? To take your blood. It's so funny, too, because she takes his blood and I'm teasing. I'm having her come back tomorrow because the second she left he's pouring Cheerios in a bowl. You were eating cereal. It wasn't even Cheerios, it was like Frosted Flakes or something terrible and eating like a breakfast burrito. All day you were binging and the next day would have been great to check your cholesterol. So, you were perfect for a week and a half.

Gary: Well, I was almost perfect for, I mean I did really well for 30 days. I was strong.

Chris: So, we would both agree that there is nothing you could have done different to influence your cholesterol?

Gary: You know I don't know I'm racking my brain. I don't know. I don't know what I could have done differently. I mean honestly. I could have not-

Chris: Can we read it? Can you get a drum-roll.

Gary: I could have ... I could have not eaten.

Chris: I'm gonna find it on here. So this is his--

Gary: Actually Lucas, insert drum-roll here...

Chris: Cholesterol on here.

Gary: Actually, could you do ba-dum-tss? Cause it's a joke.

Chris: Yeah.

Gary: So, right after I got that and then I emailed you and I said, "Depressing."

Chris: Okay. So, this is under "coronary risk." So, his cholesterol last time. So, on 9/1. Man, it's only like a month and a half between.

Gary: So, I was getting my blood test every month.

Chris: Oh, wow.

Gary: Because I wanted to show myself improvement. I wanted to make sure I was making progress. So, every month I was getting my blood checked.

Chris: Okay. So, he was 233 on 7/26. On 9/1 you were 208. And-

Gary: Mm-hmm (affirmative). I had it. I had my arms around it.

Chris: And then being the model citizen, 243.

Gary: Yeah. It went up.

Chris: You've never been under 200 in your life. Well, this life. Right here.

Gary: Yeah. In this life.

Chris: Maybe you were born under 200. So bro, I don't want you to get a tattoo. I know you're like, "I'm a man of my word." And the whole thing. But I would be insulted if you had a Seahawks tattoo.

Gary: It's really more you don't want that on my body because you're a Cowboys fan.

Chris: I'll cry like Romo if you ... Yeah it's not even. I mean it was funny, but no.

Gary: We'll see. We'll see.

Chris: No, there's no way. You gotta promise you're not gonna get a Seahawks tattoo.

Gary: I have to promise? I have promise?

Chris: Yeah, it's stupid.

Gary: I don't know I just feel like I-

Chris: Get a Cowboys tattoo if you want to get a tattoo.

Gary: I wanted to challenge myself. I wanted to paint myself in a corner that I couldn't get out of. And I don't know man. I'm in the corner so I gotta figure it out.

Chris: I go back to the thing that I always said, "You're an anomaly. If you ate Cheetos and dipped them in like, grease, your cholesterol would go down."

Gary: Yeah, probably. Probably.

Chris: Your thing doesn't work. You gotta go the other way. Forget what Jocko and Dave Anderson and everybody said, they're wrong. You need to eat more cheeseburgers-

Gary: I gotta drink more, smoke more and eat more fat and just eat more french fries and I'll be fine.

Chris: Yeah. Totally.

Gary: You know the funny thing is, is coming in off the road and eating all that stuff, the french fries, I mean what was my first test when you started working with me? So, it's coronary risk. I gotta find it here.

Chris: It's right here at the very bottom.

Gary: Oh, the very bottom. There it is. Yeah, so coming in off the road, burgers, I was probably 20 pounds heavier than I am right now? Maybe more. And I was 264.

Chris: Yeah.

Gary: Then being a model citizen I'm 243. Makes no sense.

Chris:	But you almost like ... You were squatting like 260 pounds at the gym this morning.
Gary:	Yeah, I'm telling you I'm working out like fiend.
Chris:	Cholesterol is what it is bro. Maybe they'll put you on some stipends or whatever they call them.
Gary:	I don't want to get on those stupid things. They say they have neurological side effects.
Chris:	You'll be fine. You're old.
Gary:	Please.
Chris:	It'll be fine.
Gary:	I'm gonna get Alzheimer's.
Chris:	Okay, so let's talk about the book. Pre-Suasion.
Gary:	Okay.
Chris:	It's something you talk about a lot. About framing, right? Framing up front. So, the story from Pre-Suasion that sticks out to me the most is the one about the insurance guy who is in England and outsells every insurance guy in the US.
Gary:	Yeah.
Chris:	It reminds me of advisors in the service drive and their process with framing. We let customers come in, worry who's gonna help them. We lose trust every step of the way. And he went exactly the other way, right? Tell everybody what he did to outsell everybody.
Gary:	Yeah, so it's a fascinating story. The way they figured this out. It wasn't Cialdini. Cialdini was telling the story about somebody else, right? If I remember the book right, this guy

was shadowing people who were great in their industry and wanted to find out what they did that made them so great. So, this particular guy who was selling insurance, who outsold everybody in the United States single-handedly, he shadowed him. So, he went to his first appointment with him, they call it a sit, right? He goes to the house, he goes on a sit. He leaves something in his car. Then he plays kind of ... he's a very, very sharp, very smart guy but in the presence of the client, he plays a little bit of the buffoon, right? He's like, "Oh, I can't believe it." He slaps his forehead. And, "I forgot that I gotta go out to my car and go get it." So, he goes out to the car and then comes back in. The guy shadowing him is sitting there going, "Oh, that's strange." And then they go to the next one, and the next one, and the next one and every time he does the same thing. So, now he's really curious. He pulls the guy aside and said, "Okay. Tell me what's going on? Why do you keep doing that? Because you can't forget it all these times." He goes, "No, no, no." He goes, "It's a system." He says, "What I do is, I forget. Number one, it humanizes me, right? And they can relate to me better. Because I'm forgetting, and they're forgetful, and I'm not perfect. So, then they let their guard down." He goes, "But more importantly," he goes, "I have to go out to the car and let myself back in." And he says, "Who lets themselves into your house? Only people that you trust." So, he says, "By telling them, 'Hey, I'm gonna have to go out to my car, is it okay if I let myself back in?' and them agreeing to that, they're establishing trust." Subconsciously, they're establishing trust at a very deep level. Right out of the gate. Before he ever even offers them the product and talks about it. They said sometimes they have to actually give him a key. Because if it's one of those doors where you gotta have a key to get in, to twist the thing, they give him a key. And he says that's gold to him if he has to have a key. Because that's a deep, deep level of trust. The very outset, it's a pattern interrupt, really, for him, right? He's going in, he's interrupting their patterns, what they're expecting. They expecting to sit on the couch, have a guy across from them just pitch to them the entire time. And meanwhile he builds trust with them.

Chris: Yeah, it's a little self-deprecating.

Gary: Yeah.

Chris: But it's humble and nice. But at the same time, who do you let in your house?

Gary: Yeah, family, friends.

Chris: Friends. Who do you have a key in your house to?

Gary: Mm-hmm (affirmative).

Chris: It's a powerful, powerful frame upfront, right?

Gary: Yeah and I was thinking, we talk about that in the service drive. The sale, really, is won or lost at the first interaction with the customer. If the customer rolls in the drive and they stand there and they have to wait, and they get upset, you really kind of lost them right there. If you do a really good job of interacting, build rapport and all that stuff, do the pet the dog, walk around, in the very beginning, that's where the sale is won or lost. It's that frame. You're setting the frame, you're breaking their patterns. That's exactly what he did. The sale for him was won or lost at the minute he got into the sit and he did his exit and re-entry. So, it's pretty genius. Love that story.

Chris: I know this is a little bit of a limited thing because every customer doesn't have it, but there's ways that the supplies in the service drive, that I see all the time advisors mess up, is customer comes in they got a car seat.

Gary: Mm-hmm (affirmative).

Chris: Who would take the car seat out but a friend or-

Gary: A parent for that matter. Yeah.

Chris: Right. It's a trusted thing. So, it always blows me away and advisors aren't jumping on that. What about if a customer's purse or like tote bag or something is on the other side of the car? Getting in and carrying it in for them?

Gary: Yeah.

Chris: All that sort of stuff that is chivalry? I guess? You would say? Is the same sort of thing, is the same sort of frame, where consciously you're becoming a trusted friend.

Gary: Yeah, exactly. It's little things, and we talk about this a lot, we talk a lot about the book The Tipping Point, but it's little things that make a big difference. You gotta find those tipping points. You don't know what that thing's going to be but by doing small, little things like that and understanding ... It's really testing, right? It's testing and being self-aware and constantly changing things and seeing what happens. Because if you get into a really good pattern and you're doing several things when they get there, and you're getting big results, you know it's working for you.

Chris: What's funny is, in order to figure that stuff out, you have to be curious. Most people in our industry just aren't curious.

Gary: Yeah.

Chris: They're like, "Oh, I'm good. I got it. No, that won't work." And I'm sure there's tons of insurance guys, right?

Gary: Oh, yeah.

Chris: Saying the same thing. Eh, well, oh well...

Gary: "Yeah, forgetting a book and letting yourself back in, that's not gonna have an impact."

Chris: Meanwhile they go on sit after sit and they're not closing.

Gary: Right, exactly.

Chris: It's just a waste of their time. Meanwhile, you write up customer, after customer, after customer. You're not collecting them, you're not making a deeper connection, they're not coming back.

Gary: I don't know for sure but I can just imagine that they say, "Okay, well, that guy's in England. He's got a different market. It's a different customer."

Chris: "Houses are different there."

Gary: Yeah, right. Meanwhile, he's outselling the entire United States. I want to get as close to that guy as I can. I want to know what he's doing, you know?

Chris: Yeah, that's funny. It's great stuff, though. But that's a great book. We encourage anybody to read it. You're gonna read it slow, because it's a lot to take in. You're gonna take it in a chunk at a time but, just like Influence it's the kind of book that you go back and read over and over.

Gary: Oh, yeah. No, I love it. One other thing, too, I wanted to mention about the book that I thought was good was those posters that they had. They did that study with the-

Chris: Motivational posters?

Gary: Yeah. So, they have motivational posters on the wall. The common theory is that having those types of images there, of people winning and winning races and stuff like that, wouldn't have any impact on us. But they found out that it does. It does have an impact on us. That kind of goes to the Derren Brown thing, too. When he does that video that he's got online.

Chris: Subliminal advertising?

Gary: Yeah, the subliminal advertising. He talks about that in Persuasion. He calls it "pre-suasion." You're getting predisposed to feel a certain way and the things that you surround yourself around, the things that you talk about, the stuff that's going on in your head, has an impact on what you do. I think by and large we take that for granted, you know? We surround ourselves with negativity. We watch the news in the morning, we read the paper when we get to work. We're thinking disaster and doom and gloom and surrounding ourselves with that. Then we got to go to work and be happy with a client. I think finding a way to surround yourself with that type of imagery, positive imagery, really does have an impact on you. It'll make you better.

Chris: Cool. The Great Tech Drought.

Gary: The Great Technician Drought. Of 2016.

Chris: Hey remember-

Gary: It's been an eight year drought.

Chris: I sent Jeff Callan a text?

Gary: Uh-huh (affirmative).

Chris: To come on the podcast?

Gary: Yep.

Chris: He isn't. He said he would check Monday but I haven't heard back.

Gary: Mm-mm (neutral).

Chris: I'd love to have him on.

Gary: Yeah, no, I think he'll do it. He seemed pretty engaged on Saturday.

Chris: I don't think he'll do it. We'll see.

Gary: Huh.

Chris: Why do you think he would?

Gary: I think for him, he likes to be asked, you know?

Chris: I think he's old school like all those guys. They think that it's a competition, when there's so many people out there we can all help. I don't consider him competition. I don't mean that in a derogatory way. I mean, the more he helps people, the more we help people, the better it is for the industry and there's more to go around.

Gary: Yeah and if you took everybody in our space and just doing what we do for service departments and you put them all together. We don't even make up 25-30% of the market. So, there's 70% left out there for everybody else. There's plenty to go around.

Chris: Yeah and plenty of people buy his stuff and then buy our stuff and back, where it's fine. I think it would be fun to have him on and talk about stuff and joke around. But we'll see.

Gary: Mm-hmm (affirmative).

Chris: I was surprised he didn't text me because I thought it was a pretty good invitation but--

Gary: For me it's interesting...

Chris: What are kids in the industry gonna think with these old guys?

Gary: For me it's interesting to see two different perspectives.

Chris: Well, actually, I'm the kid and you're the old guy.

Gary: Yeah, that's true. You're the old soul though, bro

Chris: Yeah, right?

Gary: I'm still a kid. I'm asking people what they bench, so I'm 12.

Chris: "What do you bench?"

Gary: I'm skateboarding, asking people what they bench.

Chris: Mid-life crisis.

Gary: Oh, it's ridiculous.

Chris: What were you gonna say?

Gary: No, I was gonna say that I bought that copywriting thing from Ray Edwards and we do a lot of stuff with Dan Kennedy in copywriting. I think for me, it's cool to have both perspectives. I don't think one guy is competing with the other guy for my business, I want them both. Because I want to learn from both of them, so for me it's just more material.

Chris: Well, I mean bigger than that, our industry is in a crisis. Nobody wants to talk about it, right? What did that article on the Automotive News say yesterday? Let me find that, dude. I sent it to you right?

Gary: Yeah, god, it said a lot.

Chris: Yeah. So, I've been saying this. A friend sends this to me and he goes, "Oh, wow they're talking about the same thing you've been talking about forever. 'Privately owned dealerships could be a thing of the past.'"

Gary: Yep.

Chris: Is the headline, "Who will be the fleet owners? Uber or Google or a Legacy Manufacturer?" Nobody wants to talk about it but the younger generation isn't buying cars. We think that we can ... it's just gonna change.

Gary: Yeah.

Chris: There's no way around it.

Gary: No, the market's evolving, right? It is.

Chris: The more all of us work together to help our industry get through it and give them all the tools, the better. It's more about saving the industry than our little personal agenda. It's a bigger thing. There's a bigger cause here. There's a lot of great people in the industry and fixing cars. The leaders aren't protecting them. The leaders are gonna let them down. It's gonna be Blockbuster Video.

Gary: I think it's interesting the analogy they use in there with the corner hardware store. How that used to be the place where you would go and now that's gone. I remember that when I used to work with my dad around the house. We'd go try to get supplies and it was really hard to find things. Most of the trades had that stuff locked down. The corner hardware store had nails and some boards and stuff but they didn't really have a lot.

Chris: They didn't have a nail gun.

Gary: Yeah, right? You couldn't get a nail gun.

Chris: Then Home Depot comes, you can buy a nail gun, you can buy-

Gary: Yeah. You can buy an eight foot level.

Chris: A lot. Yeah. Anything.

Gary: You can buy the stuff that the trades had locked down. And that's what's happening in our industry, I think. It's gonna start to evolve in that way and I don't think anybody is really ready for it, to be honest.

Chris: No. Okay, so, I wanted to talk about, on a happier note, "he Great Tech Drought.

Gary: Let's keep poking the pain shall we?

Chris: Yeah. Ow.

Gary: So, there is some good news with The Great Technician Drought. There is some positive things happening. Especially with-

Chris: None of it's on this piece of paper.

Gary: Nothing's on this paper, no. I'm gonna read through these stats. Then I'm gonna talk about some of the good stuff that's going on in our industry, that I think is positive. It has a lot to do with technology. I've been reading a lot, a lot, a lot about techs because we hear that all the time. Constantly.

Chris: And we're working on a product.

Gary: And we're working on a product. So, I've been doing a lot of research and I talked to a dealer just yesterday, as a matter of fact. We asked him what his top concerns are and number one concern is we can't hire enough technicians. We had somebody in our bootcamp not that long ago, they have 50 bays and they had 12 techs. And they have 50 bays. If you were a supermarket, you'd be out of business because they have to maximize every square foot, you know? Somehow in our industry, we find a way around that. So, it is a problem. I'm gonna read some stats that really feed into this. 50% of all technicians right now are over the age of 47. So, that's a pretty interesting stat because they're going to start retiring pretty soon. What they're predicting is, right now we're losing more then we're gaining, in terms of techs. More techs are leaving the business than are coming into the industry. In the next five years, if it stays on this pace, it's gonna be two to one. So, we're gonna lose two for every one. It's a quickly depleting resource. Right now, young people, they're just not interested. You were just alluding to that. It's not a field that they're drawn to. Back in the day I had a 67' Camaro that I fixed up in the driveway and we used to go out cruising. All the guys I knew had old Chevies and we'd do doughnuts and drag race and stupid stuff that kids did. The bottom line was, the car was our social outlet. That's where we went to go hang out. Even guys that didn't have cars would get in our car and go hang out with us. They don't need that anymore. They have video games and online chats and Skype and FaceTime and SnapChat. All that stuff. They just don't interact the same way we did. So, cars are less important to them and this stat really says that. Less than 70% of young people today, they don't even get their license until age 18. After age 18. So, less than 70% of kids age 18, have their license. Is the stat. To me it's crazy-

Chris: Didn't one of Maddie's friends, they didn't get their license until they were 21?

Gary: Yeah. So, one of her really close friends--

Chris: Gary's daughter.

Gary: Yeah my daughter, Madison. Her friend goes to Oregon State and yeah, I think she was a Junior, and she was 21 when she finally got her license.

Chris: She's a Duck?

Gary: She's a O Duck. Yeah

Chris: Wow. Quack.

Gary: So, it's real. They're not interested. I remember my daughter we had to drag her down to DMV. Because she didn't want to get her license.

Chris: You wanted her to babysit.

Gary: Oh, yeah. She had to take Blake to practice.

Chris: Yeah. It's like, "Hey. The whole purpose of having kids is you're gonna work. Get your license."

Gary: Pick us up when we were too drunk to drive home.

Chris: "We're the Daniels. Get to work."

Gary: Yeah so I mean it's-

Chris: We've been counting the days til you can drive yourself.

Gary: That's right. So it's really funny that that exists but that plays into our current drought. Problem solving, also. We don't do a really good job of forcing our kids to problem solve. We coddle them a lot in this generation. That's affecting them because fixing cars is solving problems. If you don't have that skill set.

Chris: "I don't want my kid to have the poor life I had growing up."

Gary: No, yeah. That's, believe me, believe me, that's what we do. The other thing, the other stat I thought was really fascinating, over the last 10 years, technician salary have trailed inflation by 7%.

Chris: Which is in line with what we see in ELR. That's like 65 bucks or 70.

Gary: Yeah, so, if your ELR is low, how you gonna pay a guy? They just don't get the type of wages that they need to stay in this business. Because the entry level to get in, it's $7,000 in tools to enter the industry. That's pretty big.

Chris: That's the first good news, is the key to you being able to hire good techs, is you gotta control your effective labor. You gotta put yourself in a situation where your advisors are good enough, they're not discounting, you're holding a high effective labor rate and you can pay technicians more if you need to. But you're not losing them over ... how many times do we hear, "Oh, somebody stole my tech. They paid em $5 more than I would." You gotta get good at that. That's what we're good at helping you with but you gotta get your effective labor rate up in order to afford that, and weather that storm. More than anything.

Gary: Yeah, I would think about it, too. You're a young person, you're getting out of school. Maybe you did or didn't go to college. Maybe you did a little JC or something like that and you're looking at getting a job somewhere. You look and the average technician right now in the United States of America, or the median, I'm sorry, median is $18.41. So, $18.41 is the middle. Then you have to buy $7,000 in tools to make that happen. I went through all the stats at the last coaching meeting we were at and all the salaries and the funniest one to me was a meter reader makes $18.51. I thought, you can make a dime an hour more.

Chris: Well, techs in other industries like air conditioning and elevators, they make more.

Gary: No, elevator was like $38.88.

Chris: What's it cost an hour to get your elevator fixed? It's like $200.

Gary: Yeah it's ridiculous. It's more.

Chris: What's it cost to get your computer fixed? It's $150 an hour.

Gary: Oh, insane.

Chris: Right?

Gary: Yeah.

Chris: We have to get good at giving customers value and holding effective labor rate in our industry.

Gary: Yeah.

Chris: Which is easy to do but you just need the new stuff.

Gary: Yeah and so think about that. They're not interested, they got this skill set where they're good with their hands and so they're just going elsewhere and they're just going to find work elsewhere. The good part is that right now cars especially, they're on the technological edge. The youth of today, they're attracted to technology. So having players in our space like Apple and Google and Uber and ... The stuff that's happening right now, is raising awareness and getting people interested. They did a survey of 5,000 technicians that had been in the workplace less than two years and what they found was the second biggest reason that they got into the industry was because they liked to work with technology. So, that's good. That's good for us. They're starting to take notice.

Chris: That makes sense.

Gary: Mm-hmm (affirmative). I think right now, especially, there's room for all. So, having those players come into our space, while it is competition, it is interesting to see how the market's going to evolve, it's good because it's attracting people into our industry. Which has been a hard thing. It's been a street fight. Definitely. For sure.

Chris: The other thing I would say, so effective labor is the key. You gotta be able to afford them and afford the best ones. The second thing is you have to have some sort of system for growing. You gotta be able to hire somebody who's a quick lube tech, and move them up. And you have a system for them growing with the company. A path, a career path. Which we don't historically create a career path for techs, we leave it kind of to them but you gotta present that to them. A career path. If I could give you guys a tool, a tool that you could immediately use, is I would go out in the shop and take a couple techs to lunch. Individually. Just two times a week, take a tech to lunch and talk about personal stuff. Get to know them on a person basis and really start to understand how technicians work, how they think, and get close. Become friends with your techs. Don't treat them like a number or just an employee. Because they're the heart and soul of what we're doing.

Gary: Yeah. Most managers we run up against, it's a little bit of a love/hate relationship. They feel like they're prima donnas. I think the analogy I used in the coaching meeting was the head of lettuce in the produce aisle. You go into produce aisle and it's beautiful and everything looks like it's ready to buy and they have the misters that come out and it sounds like rain and they really take care of that inventory and they protect it. They would not leave the head of lettuce out in the sun to wilt and then expect to be able to sell that. That's kind of what we do with our techs. We begrudge them so much and we're not close enough to them and we're not in tight with them. Then so many things go wrong, it just becomes this friction relationship. We're letting our inventory sour. We're letting it spoil. They're not gonna do what we need for them to do, they're not gonna stay long-term. They're not going to want to advance their career. They're not gonna push the envelope and get high efficiency if they don't feel like they're valued. You know? That's the problem.

Chris: Yeah, so stop being such a big shot and take em to lunch. Go out and say, "Hey, tomorrow I want to take you to lunch." Start picking them off. Over a six month time, you could, no matter how big your shop is, you could touch everybody and get to know 'em. Talk about their wife, talk about their kids or their aspirations or whatever it is, but become their friends and start to understand them. Understand how you can, as a leader, help them on their career path and live up to their full potential. Is a big one.

Gary: Yeah and find ... there's always small things in a store, and we've talked about this in prior podcasts, but you gotta take a fresh look at your surroundings too and make sure nothing's in their way. Somebody told me this a long time ago, they said, "Leaders often look at themselves like they're the quarterback. They're sitting back there throwing the game winning touchdown pass." They said, "Real leaders look at themselves as like an offensive lineman that's opening up holes and creating opportunities for your people to score." To me, that was really valuable as a young manager coming up through the ranks because it made me look at things very different. Like I'm looking for things in my people's way. What can I move? What thing, what obstacles can I get out of their way? And we talked about this, again, at the meeting, when I sat down with the techs and said, "Okay, what things are in your way?" We found some simple stuff that didn't cost us anything to fix, that made them really happy and helped us to bond with them. So, my advice would be, take a fresh look at your surroundings, make sure that there is a clear path for them to succeed and nothing standing in their way. Even small stuff like something blocking the tool room. Something that makes it difficult for them to get parts. Clear that path for them and show them that you care. The other thing too is have fun with them. They don't have enough fun. We were joking around saying, "They're out there with their knuckles bleeding and stuff dripping in their hair and snow falling on their back and then we're out front shooting the Jenga tower with a Nerf gun, you know?" They just don't get it. They don't understand it. So, go out and play games with them. I used to do two fun games that I'll give you guys. Two tips for anybody that's listening. I'd love some feedback. Let me know how it works. Dollar bill poker is always fun. What I'll do is, if they have an upsell that comes out or a multi-point that comes out with an upsell on it, I give them a dollar bill for that. Regardless of whether it sold or not, I'll just give them a dollar bill. Then at the end of the day, we'll play dollar bill poker and the winner gets the whole pot of cash. So, it's kind of fun. We get in a big circle and everybody pull out their best dollar and we throw the rest of the dollars in a box and then we hand them out and so it could be $50, $60, $70 sometimes. It's just a fun way to bond with them. It's not a ton of money, but it's fun. Then actual poker with cards. Get a big six deck stack of cards from Costco. Mix them all up and then any time they sell something, give them a card. And every card is worth the face value in terms of dollars. So, if it's a 10, it's $10. Then they play. Best five card hand would win like a, you could have a TV or $100 or some sort of prize.

Chris: But you do that one over time?

Gary: That one I do over about a week, yeah, but they'll collect a lot of cards fast. Because they get really excited about it. But it's a lot of fun.

Chris: Starts momentum, fun, energy.

Gary: Yes. It's just a ton of fun. Yep. They'll love you for it.

Chris: That's your advantage because nobody else is doing that.

Gary: No.

Chris: Everybody else is like, "Oh, we did pull tabs once." But they're not really, constantly engaging them, you know?

Gary: Yeah and then they don't want to leave because they like it there now.

Chris: Cool. Good stuff G-man. Don't get the tattoo bro.

Gary: We'll see. We'll see.

Chris: Your wife would hate me.

Gary: My wife does not want me to get the tattoo. And man she-

Chris: We don't' have like a bunch of tattoos.

Gary: She worked harder than I did to get the cholesterol right. Like that poor woman. She was driving out here from the marina bringing me lunch and food and-

Chris: She still loves you.

Gary: She does.

Chris: It doesn't matter.

Gary: She does. Love doesn't lower cholesterol, by the way.

Chris: Just a recap. Take your technicians to lunch, get close to them. Get our service manager revolution training or get in our coaching groups so you can learn how to get your effective labor rate up. Get the new stuff so you can afford techs. Play a game with them. Get your blood tested for your cholesterol. And read the new book Pre-Suasion by Cialdini. It'll blow you away. I hope everybody has a great week. Thank you so much for listening and please subscribe.

Gary: Yeah and if we don't hear from you-

Chris: We'll automatically get delivered through technology when we post a new one. Boom. It'll appear if you subscribe.

Gary: Right. And have a great Thanksgiving. Thanksgiving's coming up. I love Thanksgiving, it's one of my favorite holidays. I hope everybody has a great one. Go be with your family.

Chris: Is that because the Cowboys play on Thanksgiving?

Gary: No. I just love--

Chris: I didn't mean to--

Gary: I love food. I love turkey.

Chris: Okay, I'm gonna do an impression. Close your eyes.

Gary: I've heard this.

Chris: "I didn't mean to get hurt."

Gary: Oh, man.

Chris: What are chances that he gives some of the money back?

Gary: Oh, there's no chance. There's no chance. Zero.

Chris: The most expensive quarterback sitting on the bench.

Gary: Oh, man.

Chris: Hilarious. Cool. Thanks everybody. Have a good one.

Episode #21: Small Hinges Swing Big Doors

Chris: Welcome everybody to Service Drive Revolution, the only podcast, if not the best podcast, for anybody with a service drive technician, service advisors. We encourage you to subscribe. We love to have you in the family. We pride ourselves on trying to give away better content on this than most people charge for.

Gary: That's right.

Chris: We're trying to start a community here and a family. If you're listening and you're not seeing the video, my bulldog, Lola, she's here on the table. She thinks she's a part of this and she has the worst breath. I don't know what she eats, but her breath-

Gary: High five, yeah.

Chris: Yeah.

Gary: That's not me panting, by the way. That's Lola.

Chris: Welcome, everybody. Today, the topic is, we're going to talk about, "small hinges swing big doors" and how there's a couple of little things you can do in your service department that are going to give you huge results. We're going to talk about a book called *The Like Switch*. Gary is going to give you his book report, his review of that. You got back from coaching in Florida, right?

Gary: Yup.

Chris: What's cool is Gary did the most genius thing there. When we do these coaching groups, we have to rent a hotel, and so he tagged advisor training on the front and sold it out. It was great.

Gary: Yeah.

Chris: We did two days of advisor, in-person advisor training, where we worked with them. Turned out good.

Gary: Yeah, it was great. I mean we sold out both days and Gar and I did it together and the content was awesome. Everybody left there feeling uplifted and we had a lot of comments that it was some of the best training that they've ever been to. It was really, really-

Chris: Of course, it's the best training they've ever been to.

Gary: Yeah, it was awesome. A lot of fun.

Chris: By the way, our online training will be the best training you've ever been to.

Gary: That's right. I've been to a lot of training and we've been in this business long time. Yeah, it was good.

Chris: It's funny. A couple of the managers that were in the coaching the next days, or when I was there, were commenting that their advisors were on fire and all fired up, so good job.

Gary: Yeah, lots of fun. That was fun.

Chris: That was a great idea. You got to do one out here on the west coast now.

Gary: We have one on December 5th if I recall. We have one out here on December 5th, so if anybody's interested, we got that one in Los Angeles.

Chris: Doing the elite meeting on the 5th?

Gary: Yeah, we do, but Ger is doing it.

Chris: You're doubling up?

Gary: Yeah, he's in the conference room doing it.

Chris: Awesome. Yeah, right now as we're doing this, we have a boot camp going on in the conference room. Pretty fun.

Gary: We're busy right now.

Chris: I didn't like having the meeting in Orlando.

Gary: I didn't either.

Chris: I don't like Orlando.

Gary: That was a bust. Nothing against people who live in Orlando, but it just wasn't ...

Chris: We can talk trash about people who live in Orlando. You think we have a big audience in Orlando?

Gary: I think we do. We had a lot of people show up for the training.

Chris: Listen, move out of Orlando. Well the problem with Orlando is that it's just all Disneyland and I don't have kids and it's not for me.

Gary: Yeah, I mean, my thing was -

Chris: You go to Disneyland here? We live very close to Disneyland here in California, and Gary goes all the time. Not me. I won't be caught.

Gary: My family loves Disneyland.

Chris: I don't have kids.

Gary: I just thought it just wasn't us. It didn't feel like us. My hotel room looked like my grandma's house. That just doesn't ... I don't know. Our thing's a little different. I just don't think it was a good fit. Nothing against the city of Orlando, it just doesn't fit us, I think. I don't even think Miami really is a good fit. I think we talked, DC and Boston are probably better. Better fits for what we do.

Chris: Yeah. I know it's cold this time of year, but I like it. I like Boston. New York too. New York's too crazy. Too hard to get in and out.

Gary: New York's hard to get in and out of and very expensive. Boston's really ... Boston's not getting much better, boy, Boston. Geez.

Chris: Let's talk about the life of Gary and Crystal. You went from here to Nashville? You did a boot camp in Nashville and then you spent the weekend there. You took your wife. Went to the Country Music Hall of Fame? Johnny Cash.

Gary: No. Went to Johnny Cash. It's funny, the Country Music Hall of Fame was in our hotel, because we stayed at the Omni right there. Literally, it's in the hotel and we didn't go. We walked and we went to the Johnny Cash. We're not country music fans, so it didn't make sense for us, but I love Johnny Cash. That was a lot of fun.

Chris: Yeah. I love Johnny. Then we met in Florida. So you went to Florida a little bit before me.

Gary: Yeah. So I flew to Florida on Monday morning. Got out there Monday morning and went to work and then we did the training and then you came in Wednesday late afternoon, mid-afternoon.

Chris: I get off the plane Wednesday, and I'm like walking through the airport hearing "Chris. Chris. Chris." It's the beautiful Miss Katia, your wife, and I'm like, "Oh, you're leaving?" She's like, "Yeah. Friends and this." I'm like, "Oh, Katia's social calendar. Gotta get back. Meeting friends." And you were a bachelor for the weekend, right?

Gary: Yeah. Came back and she took her friend to Disneyland that came down and then they came back and left Saturday or Sunday morning they got up and left.

Chris: So it was Gary and Romy, the designer dog.

Gary: That's right. That was it. It was the two of us.

Chris: And the Dallas Cowboys.

Gary: I was afraid for my little designer dog with all the protests going on around here. He's in a difficult spot.

Chris: That's a funny thing, because the protests down here have been crazy. Well, they were crazy. It's over now. They were crazy. It wasn't on the national news. It was weird.

Gary: Yeah, that is weird.

Chris: Weird that they're not showing that, what was really happening down here, because there were a hundred thousand plus people protesting. When they showed it on the news was like, there's a couple thousand and they're standing in the crowd. They don't show the wide shot. It's very weird how they ... It's so different.

Gary: There's so many. That stream of people coming out in front of the building lasted forever. Just didn't seem like it would end.

Chris: Yeah.

Gary: I was fascinated by it.

Chris: That's a hundred thousand plus. Yeah, it's funny, our friend Chris, on social media they were posting pictures. There's pictures people took from the building here, going all the way back, and it's insane, like how far and how long it went.

Gary: People are pissed.

Chris: They'll get over it.

Gary: There was one sign in the crowd that I thought was funny. I think it said, "We survived the dot com crash. We can survive this." Or something like that, which I thought, "That's a realist."

Chris: A little different. Let's see if Trump lowers taxes. That's what I want. Lower my taxes. I pay way too much in taxes.

Gary: I hear that.

Chris: He says he's going to, but we'll see. Those guys, politicians, they always change their mind. They're dealing with stuff that we don't understand, probably. Okay. We met in Florida. We flew back. Then I flew to Arizona for a meeting with this little group called Genius X. That was pretty fun. I learned a lot. In that meeting, we did a mannequin video. Have you heard of those? I'm not the guy to do the trendy stuff, but that was a victim of the company I was with, so it's on Facebook if anybody wants to see it. I'm throwing a paper airplane.

Gary: It's funny. It's funny that those guys in that room, all those millionaires, are doing the mannequin challenge, which is ... It's interesting, but--

Chris: They were in to it?

Gary: Yeah. It's hot.

Chris: I'm like the least ... I'm the poorest guy in the room and I'm the least excited about it. I don't know what that tells you. Maybe I should be more "school spirit?"

Gary: Maybe. I don't know.

Chris: I don't have enough school spirit.

Gary: There's some pretty cool ones out there though. Did you see the Tony Robbins one?

Chris: Yeah. That's the one they showed in the room to get us to do it. I guess Tony Robbins set the world record.

Gary: 2,500 or 5,000 people. I don't know what it was.

Chris: It's like 20,000 people. It's an arena.

Gary: Oh, geez. Leave it to Tony. He doesn't do anything small.

Chris: They did it really well too. Like everybody's holding still.

Gary: Yeah. I saw it. I thought it was manufactured. It was crazy. I saw it on Facebook.

Chris: Then they dropped the beat and everybody starts dancing at the end. It's pretty funny. That's pretty good.

Gary: Man, that Tony's got control. Mass control.

Chris: What are the chances we can get our coaching group tomorrow to do a mannequin video?

Gary: I don't know. I think it's 100%. I think you could get it to happen.

Chris: No way.

Gary: Oh yeah.

Chris: There's a lot of guys in there that are very introverted.

Gary: Oh, I know. But that's perfect. They just have to stand there and do nothing. They would love it.

Chris: It's right up an introvert's alley?

Gary: They don't have to do anything. You don't have to jump around and act like an idiot. You can just stand there and they're fun. Plus I think-

Chris: Should I try it?

Gary: Yeah, I think you have a lot of influence, and they appreciate your help.

Chris: I don't want to misuse my influence.

Gary: Well, I'm not suggesting that either.

Chris: I don't want to abuse it.

Gary: But I think they would do it.

Chris: If I had a choice of what I would rather them do with my influence, I'd rather them go back and do something.

Gary: Execute a pay plan?

Chris: Yeah, do something.

Gary: Create change or get a better pricing strategy.

Chris: Something business-wise.

Gary: Create a leadership system. Etc. Etc. Etc.

Chris: Man, this topic is good, bro, "Small Hinges Swing Big Doors." This makes me think of a story from like 20 years ago where I'm sitting there with the service manager and we've decided we're going to raise the labor rate. And it's like the 20th of the month. We got our menus ready and we've got everything and what do you think that he says? I know you're bad at guessing, but just try.

Gary: Shit. You screw me up when you do that. He says, "I want to wait until the first of the month."

Chris: Yeah.

Gary: Wow.

Chris: See, you're good at guessing. And so, I said, "Oh, okay, good idea. Let's do the math on that." I pulled out, back then it was a calculator. I remember it was a calculator. Could you find a calculator around here now?

Gary: I have one in my office actually.

Chris: You do?

Gary: Yeah, because I got tired of looking for my phone so I bought one, because I'm old school.

Chris: Do you have an MP3 player too? It's on your phone, bro. You got that big fancy new phone.

Gary: I got a Discman up there.

Chris: Anyway, so, you just pull out this little dude, or the calculator in your case, and you just take, I don't know, how many hours you do a month, divided by how many days are left, times five bucks, seven bucks, whatever. So I said, we got the number on the calculator, let's say, I don't know, it's 20 thousand bucks, I don't know. "Why are we waiting until the first again?" Why? "Oh, it just seems logical." It isn't logical. You want to at least do it a week before, because all the ROs, right?

Gary: Yeah. You want to let it catch up. You got a lot of ROs at the old labor rate versus the new.

Chris: It's amazing how sometimes we'll procrastinate and we'll wait to increase things. We'll wait to put in a new menu. We'll wait to change prices.

Gary: What do you suppose his reason was? What is it that was in his head. I don't think convenience is the answer. I'm sure there was something else in his head.

Chris: The truth? The truth is I'm sitting there in his office, he's feeling pressure, he doesn't want to move this fast. It's a lot of change and he's like, "If I say the first then I got time to figure this out." I'm thinking in my head if I let him wait until the first, he won't do it. Right? It's a game and what he was playing was a game of possum.

Gary: You think he would use that time to try to negotiate that.

Chris: I hope I forget or whatever.

Gary: Shit. But he doesn't know you very well. There's no forgetting. It was a lost battle.

Chris: Either way, a lot of times just waiting, procrastinating those little things swing big doors because it's huge money. Then take that a step further. Let's say, the average in our $50,000 service manager challenge increase in ELR was ...

Gary: $17

Chris: $17. Take your average shop time how many hours they do times $17? How much does it cost you to get that extra $17 an hour?

Gary: Nothing really.

Chris: Hypothetically, if you do it right, most of that $17 is going right to the profit. Right?

Gary: Yeah. A few sheets of paper maybe because you've got to print some menus.

Chris: You wait 20 days to do it, right? Now let's say you wait six months to do it. You've got to get your effective labor in, right?

Gary: Yup. Yeah that's always shocking because we hear that a lot. We're doing this. We've got this, and we want to wait. That's one thing we tell them: "Look, if you're waiting, you're losing money every day." To me it's like a sickness. To me it's this life and death. When I hear that, I'm like, "You need our help more than you even know because you can't wait any longer. You just can't wait." I just got a call from one of

598

Honest One guys. He went back and he immediately executed, and he's the only one so far that's actually made it a full swing; he's up 30 bucks.

Chris: He's the only one?

Gary: Out of the gate.

Chris: Those guys were all fired up.

Gary: He's the only one I heard that has implemented everything and is off and running.

Chris: We need to get the those a phone call. What are they waiting for? We'll make them listen to this Podcast.

Gary: They're on a--

Chris: Listen boys, small hinges, big doors, what are you waiting for. Wasn't that like a month ago?

Gary: Yeah. Coming up on a month. I have a scheduled call with them next week.

Chris: The guy that's with the $30 bucks, and all his customer's run away?

Gary: No. He's just ...

Chris: Did he lose a finger?

Gary: No. He's been busier than ever. He's the real deal. He's got a real good system for collecting customers.

Chris: He's going to open another one.

Gary: Yup. That's what he wants to do. He's ready to open up a second one.

Chris: He's going to scam.

Gary: But at 30 bucks? For him it was like night and day. He couldn't believe the difference. I told him, "Bro, it's good. Let's talk about your business." He spent 20 minutes thanking us over and over and over again. I was like, "I get it, but let's go. There's more to do."

Chris: I love that.

Gary: Yeah, it was great. Was a good call.

Chris: The rest of you guys from on this one, "C'mon!" Okay. Let me throw out another one. Waiting to inspect your EROs for missed opportunities. How much does that cost you?

Gary: A lot.

Chris: I heard a great saying yesterday: "Fuzzy targets get missed."

Gary: Yeah that's good. If you don't have time to create revenue, then really what's the time for? What is the time used for?

Chris: Let me give you another one: "I don't have time to train my advisors."

Gary: Yeah.

Chris: Got nothing?

Gary: What's the down side of not training? If you don't train them, then do you have time to deal with the after-math of that, the bad customer service, the customer heat. Then you've got to pay for repairs because we didn't communicate with them properly. We didn't train them up front, so we're dealing with everything down stream. At some point, you've just got to get in front of it. It's hard. We deal with that. It's just hard, but you've got to do it.

Chris: Yeah. Really good leaders don't wait. They go. It was funny at the coaching meeting we were talking about mistakes because in the room, the topic of fear of failure, it's not wanting to make a mistake, came up. Then you and I started listing off all the mistakes we've made in the last year. It was long. The more we thought about it, the more we came up with them. And we're still here. We've got all our fingers.

Gary: You can't run from that. It's funny because my nickname at the dealer was "Ready, fire, aim" because I would just start going, and sometimes I didn't always have the best plan laid out, but we got great results. It costs you more to wait. It costs you more to sit there and wait for the perfect solution and wait for stars to be aligned, and wait for everybody to be happy. It never works out. You're always waiting. If you just go, you're going to screw it up and things are going to happen, but if you're intent on getting to point B from point A, you're going to get there. You're going to have to side-step a little bit, but you'll get there. If you don't ever move, you'll never get there.

Chris: Unless you're Zeke from the Dallas Cowboys and you just turn on the burner. You go straight in.

Gary: Hurdle them.

Chris: Jimmy Graham hurdles them. What other stuff do people wait on? The wait too long.

Gary: Pay plans. Pay plans is a big one.

Chris: Why do people have such a hard time with pay plans?

Gary: It's fear. Everybody will quit.

Chris: That never happens.

Gary: We just don't want other people to not like us. We don't want people to be unhappy that we manage, so we avoid the tough conversations and we avoid the things that have to get done because we don't want to deal with it. The truth is if you manage properly and you manage the numbers and you have a good system for up-selling and conversion and all the things that we do in the drive, you have a really strong menu, by changing the pay plans to match the model, they end up doing okay and making more money in most cases. But you have to be strong.

Chris: It fixes their behavior.

Gary: Yeah. But as a leader, you've got to stand there and stand behind it because it's going to be on your shoulders for a little while to make sure the process sticks. Otherwise, they will go backwards. It's all fear.

Chris: Tell me about this book, *The Light Switch*. Who's it by?

Gary: Dr. Jack Schaeffer wrote the book *The Light Switch*.

Chris: Dr. Jack Schaeffer will see you now...

Gary: Dr. Jack Schaeffer was in the FBI and he was a behavioral analyst.

Chris: So he's not a real doctor. He's a scholastic doctor.

Gary: He's got a PhD in something or other.

Chris: But he went to school so long he became a doctor, but he can't do an exam.

Gary: I'm not sure that he could perform surgery.

Chris: He's no Dr. Lau. He can't fix you're cholesterol.

Gary: He's no doctor.

Chris: He can read literary stuff or whatever.

Gary: Anyways, he's in the FBI as a behavior analyst. His job was to find enemy spies, and then flip them and recruit them, so that they become double agents.

Chris: What?

Gary: That was his thing.

Chris: You'd find a spy. Then you get them to be a spy on the spy?

Gary: Then you flip them. That's why it's called *The Light Switch* because his job was to get them to like him. It's gaining trust and getting on the inside. It's funny because when you watch the movies, you think it's about intimidating them and being the fear.

Chris: Blackmail.

Gary: His whole thing is he would get them. He would turn on the light switch and he would get them to like him. There were things that he would do, patterns that he could repeat over and over again with people, to get them to like him, becomes friends with him. He says the three keys ... I'll share a couple of things I took from the book that I thought were pretty instrumental. One, the three keys to making somebody like you is proximity, frequency, and intensity. You've got to get close often. You've got to have close proximity. You've got to do it often. You have to have a lot of frequency. And you've got to find some intensity in there. It's interesting when you think about people that go through some sort of life-changing event, like a near death experience or a plane crash, and they come out really bonded together. That's because of that. They were very close. They were there for quite a long time, and it was a pretty intense situation. It just glues you together. He duplicates that when he wants to find somebody and flip them, he would go out and find a way to get close to them. Where do they go? Where do they hang out? He'd start hanging out there, and a lot. He'd do it quite often. Then he'd find a way to up the level of intensity, find some sort of subject matter, something about them. If he knew that a family member that had died, he would share that experience with them.

His family died in an intense situation in order to get them to bond with him a little bit. There's a whole section of the book where he talks about body position. One of the things the guy really focused on in our service advisor clinic that we did in Florida was body language of an advisor. He was talking about when you come up to the car, and a lot of advisors put their hands on the window and lean in, and we were saying, "Who does that?"

Chris: Especially with females, they feel trapped.

Gary: The police do that. We feel trapped and threatened, and that's an authority figure. That's not the best way to start a relationship.

Chris: They talk about that in the game too? When you walk up. Side, comfortable, not intimidating.

Gary: Exactly. Open. They need to have an exit.

Chris: They can get away.

Gary: Yeah. They can get away, they can run. You're not trapping them in. Square on is very confrontational in any way, shape, or form, if you're square on with somebody, so you always want to be at an angle. That's what he was saying in this book is he would always position his body in a very specific way to be non-threatening, and to make sure he wasn't doing anything to be a road block to them liking him. The funny thing was the way he held his head. He said, "If you tilt your head a little bit to the side, then people view that as being very friendly and open."

Chris: Like a puppy?

Gary: Like a puppy. I was like, "What??" And I had to read that twice because I couldn't believe it. He said, "Yeah. When you've got to go up, you've got to tilt your head to the side." That changes how people view you. He talked a lot about his face too. If you're forcing a smile, people can figure that out, so he would practice smiling so that it would be natural. When he came up with his head to the side and smiling, he wouldn't look like he was forcing it. It had to feel genuine in order for them to buy in to this whole thing. The whole thing was contrived from the beginning that he was going to make them like him, trust him, then flip them. He built a system out of it. It's this fascinating book. It is fascinating.

Chris: I love that kind of stuff.

Gary: It's genius.

Chris: I love body language and all that. It matters. I was in that meeting ... I don't know if I told you this story. Jason, who's like an internet guru, crazy copy writer guy. He was sitting next to me one day. He's taking notes, and notes, and notes. I filled out a page of notes for every ten, so at a break, I said, "Jason, what are your notes? Can I see?" He's like, "Sure." Super nice. He's was writing down the speech patterns of the people that were talking to help him write copy. He's on a another level. I remember a long time ago sitting in a mastermind meeting, and they're talking about body language. I'm like, "Well how do you notice body language?" Really, you have to slow down mentally. Now I can read body language really well and change the way I mirror people and everything, but back then, maybe my ADD, and I felt that way about saying speech patterns. Because he's like, "You can tell people change different speech patterns." That helps him when he writes copy because he can change the speech pattern in the copy to the emotion he wants people - It's another level like body language - but language. I love that kind of stuff. It's fascinating.

Gary: Pacing and tonality and that kind of stuff has a big impact.

Chris: Then certain words. He was telling me certain words that people say when they're pushing too hard that scare people, so you don't say those words.

Gary: They're forbidden.

Chris: It's unbelievable.

Gary: In this book, he talked about mirroring as well. It was funny. The way he used it is he would come in and start to mirror their posture. His goal was always to get them to mirror him.

Chris: Good ones can do that.

Gary: He'd start working at it, then eventually he would want to make movements to get them to mirror him. Once they did that, he knew he had them. He had control

Chris: You've got to get them to agree with you is a big part of that. You get them agreeing with you. You say things they agree with. You relate to them and then they start following you. You can flip the switch on them. That's crazy. Good stuff.

Gary: I think if you're an advisor or you manage advisors, this book would be great because of some of the tips that you can pick up. You're not necessarily going to flip a spy, or hypnotize a customer. You could, but ...

Chris: Spies have to get their cars serviced too.

Gary: I think you said this a couple of podcasts ago. You said you were always looking for the slight edge. Anything that will give you that slight edge. This book, to me, is one of those things that would you give you a slight edge. If you could figure out how to hold your head and have a comfortable smile and demeanor about you, and have a posture that's open. If you did all those things right, it would give you an edge. It would give you a slight edge.

Chris: Do you know what a slight edge is? It's a little hinge that swings a big open.

Gary: That swings big doors. I should have guessed that one, bro. I'm off now.

Chris: You're not a good guesser.

Gary: I'm off the guessing game.

Chris: Everybody noticed he doesn't have a Seahawks tattoo.

Gary: And high cholesterol still.

Chris: What we learned here ...

Gary: Bro, I've got to tell you this. I was talking with the guy who I was just saying raised the ELR 30 bucks. I was talking with him and he was asking me about my cholesterol. We were talking cholesterol for a little while. I said, "Man, I don't know. I'm just giving up." And he goes, "Well that's great because the joke goes on." I go, "But I'm going to die!"

Chris: Let me see, if you would've fixed it, what's the fun in that?

Gary: It would've been over.

Chris: It's more fun that you're tortured and you can't figure it out. How many people do you think would check if we had it up online and we had ... because you know in the future there will be something we can put in our bloodstream that we can check it live. How many people do you think would check your cholesterol?

Gary: That'd be funny, to have it ticker-tape.

Chris: On our website. Go to chriscollinsinc.com and check out Gary's cholesterol. That'd be hilarious.

Gary: I'm looking for solutions.

Chris: What we learned just to recap. Small hinges swing big doors, so wait to raise your effective labor rate.

Gary: Definitely wait as long as possible.

Chris: Wait to change your pay plan. Cost yourself as much money as you can because you are born rich.

Gary: Wait to hire a tech.

Chris: Wait to hire a tech. Wait, wait, wait. Don't have your coaching meeting in Orlando, Florida. Don't go to the Country Music Hall of Fame, but go to the Johnny Cash Hall of Fame.

Gary: Johnny Cash. I recommend it.

Chris: What did you drink when you were in Nashville?

Gary: Lot's of moonshine. They have those moonshine-

Chris: They serve moonshine? And you just order it?

Gary: Yeah, you just order it.

Chris: What's it taste like?

Gary: They have flavored ones like apple ...

Chris: Okay, bro, it's gone too far if you've got flavored moonshine.

Gary: But they have moonshine that they call White Lightning. It's basically like pure-grain alcohol. It's like Ever-clear.

Chris: You're not in college, bro. Don't you want a nice drink?

Gary: When in Rome, bro, when in Rome.

Chris: That's funny. So funny in the Bible Belt, Nashville, you'd think church on Sunday and they're drinking moonshine.

Gary: Oh my god on Sunday it was packed down there. It was unbelievable.

Chris: Jesus and Nascar.

Gary: It was packed.

Chris: Then we learned how to flip a spy by reading *The Light Switch* by Dr. ...

Gary: Jack Schaeffer.

Chris: Jack Schaeffer.

Gary: Sounds like a spy name.

Chris: It's crazy. It's a good way to get killed.

Gary: He made it. He survived.

Chris: I'm not that brave.

Gary: He wrote a book about it.

Chris: Body language.

Gary: Body language, slight edge.

Chris: Tonality. Good. Thanks everybody. We thank you for listening. Make sure you subscribe to our podcast. Hit the subscribe button. It will automatically get delivered to you when we upload them, so you get them a little bit early sometimes.

Gary: We appreciate the support. We want to raise our score on iTunes. Anybody who wants to support us, we appreciate it.

Chris: A podcast about service drivers is going to rank...

Gary: Let's make the service business number one people. Let's go. I'm a little competitive. I like to be at the top.

Chris: We're not. We'd have to do a podcast on football or something, bro.

Gary: Half of it's football.

Chris: America's team.

Gary: America's team.

Chris: America. Cool. Thanks everybody.

Gary: Thanks.

Chris: Have a great week.

Episode #22: Making 2017 Your Best Year Ever

Chris: Hey, and welcome, everybody, to Service Drive Revolution, where if you have a service drive technician, service advisors and customers, this is the place for to you call home. Hope everything's doing good. We have the top tools and tips for your service drive. We also have books and training, so you should go to chriscollinsinc.com and buy everything.

Gary: Absolutely, yeah.

Chris: How are you doing, G-Man?

Gary: I'm doing good.

Chris: How about them Cowboys?

Gary: Them Cowboys are doing good.

Chris: Okay, I've got a funny letter right off the top.

Gary: This is 2016, by the way, in case you're listening to this.

Chris: We get these all time. We're making a difference, bro, in people's lives.

Gary: Yeah. It's nice.

Chris: We care. We're not consultants, we're coaches.

Gary: Right. Everybody always keeps saying that.

Chris: Which I like, because consultants just kind of come in and waste your time. We got a letter from Matt ... Martiori? It's Italian, obviously.

Gary: Uh-huh, seems like.

Chris: Did I say it right?

Gary: I don't know.

Chris: Sorry, man, if I butchered your name. I'm not going to read the whole thing, I'm just going to read the part that pisses me off.

Gary: The part that pisses you off? There's a part in there that pisses you off?

Chris: Yeah.

Gary: Okay. All right.

Chris: Well, it's a little condescending.

Gary: Okay. I want to hear that.

Chris: It starts off with the best of intentions, like most things in life. "I'm not sure if this email will reach you guys directly, but I just wanted to say thank you. I've read mostly all of your books, and listen to your podcast on my daily hour commute to work. The content and tools you guys provide our industry is second to none. I constantly am looking for ways to grow and better our team at our Toyota store, and passing along to our other 16 dealerships in our family organization. You guys unravel the simplest of concepts, and break it all down so anyone can implement it. I truly enjoy my job every day, and seeing our team grow our metrics is such an awesome thing to watch." Then he goes through his story, moving to Atlanta and the whole thing, and it's all good. Let me see where I can pick this up. "I take every ounce of information I can get and do my best to push those ideas into action in our store and spread the wealth. I've truly appreciated what you guys do and what you guys offer to us. This is nothing short of a long-winded, drawn-out email, so I apologize for that." Not at all, man. "I just wanted to let you know that, for those of us that constantly want to grow our stores and better ourselves or our teams, you guys kick ass. I hope you guys keep rolling with the podcasts and overflow of knowledge for our field. What you guys do is great. I will continue to follow you guys and pass your knowledge on to anyone that will listen to me ramble on and allow me to show them. "P.S." This is where is gets tricky. "Gary, I hope you get your cholesterol down." Doesn't everybody? It's the first thing in Trump's 100 days. Trump's like, "The first 100 days in office, the priority is not the wall."

Gary: Yeah, no.

Chris: It's your cholesterol.

Gary: Yeah. He's got to get it down.

Chris: "No one should deserve to have a Seahawk..."

Gary: Oh, that's the part.

Chris: What's that mean?

Gary: Oh, that's the part.

Chris: Is he a Cowboys fan?

Gary: I don't know.

Chris: Were you in on this?

Gary: I was not in on that, no. Uh-uh.

Chris: You had to have something to do with that.

Gary: I didn't instigate it at all. He just ...

Chris: He lives in ... now he lives in PA, right? What is the ... why you hating on the Seahawks?

Gary: I mean, he's a Steelers fan, obviously.

Chris: Well, they beat us in the Super Bowl, so you've got to love it even more.

Gary: I guess.

Chris: Kick me while I'm down. I'll tell you, watching Ben ... it was Sunday, or maybe it was Thanksgiving.

Gary: Yeah, it was Thanksgiving. Thursday, yeah.

Chris: Dude can throw a pass.

Gary: Yeah.

Chris: Those guys. They're just 50 yards down the field, and he can throw a pass. It's crazy.

Gary: Yeah. He looked pretty good. He looked pretty good yesterday. I mean on Thursday, he played really well. It was good.

Chris: Well, thanks for the kind email, kinda, Matt.

Gary: Kinda. When I forwarded that, I should have deleted the Seahawks reference. You would have got much warmer engagement, but we do appreciate the shout-out. Thank you, and I'm working on the cholesterol unsuccessfully, unfortunately. I was working on it yesterday ...

Chris: You'll probably do better if you give up on it.

Gary: ... with a giant cheeseburger-bacon thing, monstrosity.

Chris: It's always the better thing. I didn't talk about our topic. I got right to that, but today we're going to talk about making 2017 your best year ever. We've got a bunch of tools for you on that, that I think could be fun. Yeah, make 2017 your best year ever. You have your notes and I have mine, so just jump in whenever you want, G-Man, if I lose it. The first thing that you need to do is you need to get clarity. If you really want to make a running start at 2017, you need to sit down with your numbers and come up with goals. You were kind of saying that everybody should increase 10 percent. I don't know. Everybody should double their sales from ... anybody who isn't in our coaching group probably can double their sales.

Gary: Well, I think what I hear a lot of times guys just say, they just don't know where to start. I want to create a forecast for 2017. How do I start building a forecast? What's real?

Chris: Just double, times two. Greg Cardoni says 10x. "We're shooting low."

Gary: Well, I think if you just wanted to start at the baseline, what's the bottom line that you should be shooting for, the Consumer Price Index typically is 2 to 3 percent, depending upon the year, so let's just call 3 percent being the minimum standard. You've got to grow with the Consumer Price Index. That's what everybody else is doing.

Chris: Do you really think there's people out there thinking that way? That is sad.

Gary: I'm trying to get them to a point where, okay, this is the minimum acceptable level. In my mind it's 10 percent. Three percent is just keeping your head above water. Ten percent, you're breathing fresh ... fresh oxygen.

Chris: What?

Gary: Fresh oxygen. Then from there, I think you've got to push. I agree with you. I think you've got to put a goal up there that's pretty scary and you've got to go after it, but there's got to be a place where in your head you're like, "Okay, I have to grow." We see so many companies that are just flat-lined, year after year, month after month after month, and they're like, "Well, hey, I'm doing okay," but man, you've got to grow. Especially in this competitive marketplace that we're in right now, you have to start growing your business.

Chris: Yeah. Let's just talk about some specific numbers they should be looking at when they're doing their goals. The first one would be net, net-to-gross. If you don't see a financial or you don't understand that, you should make 2017 the year that you learn that.

Gary: Yep, for sure.

Chris: A tip that you could do to learn that is, if you work somewhere where you don't have access to it, buy a coffee or a mocha or something for the office manager and make an appointment, and say, "Hey, will you explain it to me?" Make them like your mentor and teacher, not like you're an inconvenience and trying to interrupt them. Make an appointment, be respectful, but ask them to teach and you help you understand expenses, sales, gross. All that would be a good one, or get into a coaching group that will help you. You've got to understand the financials, so the first one would be net-to-gross, because really the two things I think that matter the most are net-to-gross and either your retention numbers, how many customers you're retaining, the satisfaction numbers, however you measure that, but how happy your customers and are what profit you're making. The long-term, are you collecting customers, making friends and they love you, and then just money to the bottom line. Then what drives money to the bottom line is your gross profit percentage, effective labor rate, parts gross margin, that sort of stuff, cost of labor, all that. You should take a morning with a cup of coffee and look at all that. Then I don't care what kind of shop you have or where you're at in the country, a hundred bucks is the minimum for an effective labor rate. You're not even trying. You don't have a pricing strategy and you're not trying if you're under a hundred bucks.

Gary: Yeah, I agree. It's got to be a hundred bucks, yep. You've got your two bottom-line drivers are going to be the customers that you're retaining, how happy they are, and then the net profit, and then in my mind you've got to work your way back up that food chain, back up that ladder, because everything else is going to play into that, starting with your gross. You know, what's your percentage of gross to sales? Is it a healthy gross? Are you, at minimum, above 70 percent, and then you work your way down. You know, what are your expenses as a percentage of gross? You taught me this when I first came out of the shop, and you just start going through each column all the way down and make sure that everything's in line. If it's not, you've got to go back and take a look at it.

Chris: You know, I would say to the guys out there that have been in the industry for a long time, so you've been running the shop for a long time and you don't know all this, it's okay you don't know it, but let's get you knowing it.

Gary: Yeah.

Chris: Let's give you those tools so you're managing from a position of authority, not from behind, you know?

Gary: Right.

Chris: In a lot of ways, if you don't know all that, you're kind of like the guy that never learned how to read, and you're illiterate but you're pretending that you can, you know. That's no situation.

Gary: Right.

Chris: We've got to teach you up on that. The first thing is clarity. Get to know your numbers and then what you want to do, and then I would say whether we say 3% or 10%, you should try to live up to your full potential. Figure out what you should be doing per ticket, hours per ticket, effective labor rate, how much you're going to increase your car count, and then come up with a nice number. I would say let's shoot big, make a goal that'll scare you a little bit. We have it right now, right? We've got a board. You can't see it, but it says we're only $101.6 million away from our goal monthly, so we've got big goals. Monthly.

Gary: Yeah, monthly.

Chris: Yeah, so make some big goals, and then that's got to trickle down to your troops. Then once you have that established, you need to sit down, and whatever your production for your technicians, whatever your advisors' goals are, should add up to that, so keep that in mind. You should sit with them, and I would do it in December, long before January, and say, "Hey, it's coming up, what did you think of this year?" and ask some questions. Spend one-on-one with everybody, spend a little time. Have some small talk and then get into the numbers, and say, "What could we have done better," and get their feedback and really involve them in the cause.

Gary: They'll have ideas too, and I know a lot of times we stray away from that because we just don't need any more, anybody else's opinions, and we're like ... but the truth is if you stop and you open your mind a little bit, they can give you some good ideas. They've got their boots on the ground. They can provide you some valuable insights, but you have to separate yourself from ... I think personally you've got to get out away from the daily stresses of wherever you're at. We had this conference room back at my store, upstairs and it was kind of away from everything, so when we'd go to do something, that's where we'd go. Lock away and spend some time, kind of really with deep focus, trying to figure out what we wanted to do. If somebody's coming in and out of your office, you're just ... all you want to do is rush through it and be done with it, but I think it's too important to set yourself up for success in

2017. I agree if you spend some time in December, get your people, get them rallied around what you want to do, have them have input and buy-in, you're going to be a lot better off. You'll start with some momentum; you know?

Chris: Yeah. There's nothing more powerful than a team that feels like they're in on it, you know, they're a part of it. They want to help at that point.

Gary: Yeah, exactly.

Chris: Involve them. That's kind of the first one. Then the next one is you need to write it down. Everybody needs to have those goals in writing. It's powerful to write them down every day, but you need to post it everywhere. Every advisor should have their goals. You know, the good advisors, they'll even have them on a sticky on their computer, just on a sticky note, but everybody needs to know exactly what they are. Break them down by the month, week and day. Here's a little trick. You know you have 52 weeks in the year, you're going to take two weeks off for vacation maybe, so 50 weeks. Take the total number, divide it by that, then by how many working days in that month, and that'll give you your daily goal. That's important. Then you just know if you won or lost every day. Another thing I put in here is this is a good time to update minimum requirements and pay plans. I like to go in and do it in January, the beginning of the year, just once. "This is your pay plan for the year, let's go kids," kind of a thing.

Gary: Yep; plus it sets a precedent, too. If you do it every year in January, then they expect it. That way, if something gets out of control on you, you can rein in back in and it's expected, because you're going to do a pay plan review in January anyways, so they'll know what to do.

Chris: Yeah, they know. Then it's out of their head and they're ready to go.

Gary: Yeah.

Chris: Make sure too, with your techs, that you're sitting down with your technicians and going over production and really looking at that, because that's the heart and soul of your business, is techs, parts. Take a deep, deep dive into all that.

Gary: They're a hard group to get engaged, just because in a lot of cases they outnumber everybody three-to-one. I know for most managers that I've talked with, that becomes a stressor because it's just a much larger group. Getting them off the line costs you money, so the minute you take them off the line and take them upstairs to have the chat, you're just burning through dollars. Dollars are just lighting on fire, so it becomes a stressful thing. However, I think that it's so important to get those guys involved, and you have this shot to kind of really get things set, set the frame for 2017, that I would overlook all that and spend as much time as you had to do get them involved in it.

Chris: Yeah, and be organized with it. Have an appointment and let them know, "I've got 30 minutes for you, I've got all your numbers here." Be organized, but if you have that one guy that likes to talk a long time, "Clock's running out. We've only got ten minutes left, because I've got somebody else coming in right after you." Just hold it. In 30 minutes, you should be able to have this conversation, I would think. Then the next one is, you know, what are you going to do to get better next year? What personal things are you going to do to get better? Get in training, surround yourself with some people that are winning and kicking butt in what you want to be better at, read some books. How many books do you think you read this year?

Gary: It's more than 40.

Chris: Gary was a machine this year.

Gary: Yeah. I just knocked out a couple more, and I'm just wrapping up this other one. I'm on the tail end of it, so ...

Chris: What is it?

Gary: I might hit 50. It's called *Deep Work*, is what it's called.

Chris: *Deep Work*? What's it about?

Gary: It's about the benefits of having deep focus on the problem that you want to solve, and uninterrupted times in your day, in your week, that are planned, where you can literally lock yourself away for hours on a time and focus on a problem. It's pretty interesting. It talks about how that really affects the physical construction of your brain and how your brain functions, by focusing deeply. It's a fascinating book. I'm almost done with it.

Chris: I saw this thing that they were studying kids and focus, and it's crazy. It's on that show "Nova," but they wanted to see ... the study is more about kids from poorer areas and more affluent areas and their education, and that basically kids in poorer areas get a worse education because they don't have all the stuff. They don't have all the extracurricular activities, they don't have the best teachers, they don't have the best environment. Then they were saying a big part of it is the parents. If you come to school in the morning and you're all stressed out, you're going to be less likely to learn and retain than if you're happy and you're in a happy environment, and the parents are complimenting you before you go, like, "Hey, little Johnny, you're so handsome, you're going to be great today at school." Just that little thing sets you up for success. What they were doing in these low-income areas is they were meeting with the parents once a week and teaching the parents how to set the kids up for a positive day. Just little things like giving them stickers when they brush their teeth. They were gamifying them, honestly. The kids have these boards and they're gamifying them for brushing their teeth, being up on time or whatever. The kids are super-into it, and then because they went to school already with positive things they'd accomplished, then at school they retained more. Here's the part that fascinated me, is they put these headphones on this kid. This kid's in a room with the psychologist and there's a screen, and they have two speakers. Out of the right speaker they start telling a story, and so it's a story about a rat or something, and it's on the screen so it's a cartoon, kind of animated, narrated story about a rat. Then at one point they go, "Okay, don't pay attention to the left speaker," and they start playing another story in the left one. Then they play a third one, so they have three stories going on in this room. It's maddening, and the kids, the smart ones that are the high achievers, can just listen to the one.

Gary: No kidding?

Chris: They can block it out.

Gary: They can tune it all out.

Chris: They have these crazy hats on them and they're reading their brain waves, so they can tell if they have that deep focus or ... and so what they find is that when they're distracting them, they get that deep focus more than anything else, because they have to. You would think it would be the opposite, but they get more focused because they're just locked onto that, and so then they retain more. It's weird. Kind of the obstacle is the way. The fact that it's more difficult and you have to concentrate makes you retain it more. Does that make sense?

Gary: Yeah. It makes you pay attention.

Chris: It's fascinating.

Gary: Your mind can't wander, because it's got to focus. It has no choice, right? If you have all these distractions, your mind can't wander. If you have one thing, then your mind would have a tendency to wander.

Chris: Why I was watching this was to get ideas for us for training, so retention and how could we change up our training programs and that sort of thing, and I think we should start doing that in the boot camp. We should start playing three different things and just mess with them, right?

Gary: I don't know that that works for everybody.

Chris: "Just pay attention. Just pay attention to the right speaker." It's pretty funny. It's good stuff.

Gary: I know my daughter does that. She's got Netflix playing in a little screen on her computer, she's listening to music and she's writing a paper, all at the same time, and that's how she's able to get through. She always had a challenge focusing when she was a young child, and that's how she gets through, by having distractions so that it focuses her on what she's supposed to do. It's kind of interesting. For me, I have to have music or something like that, but I couldn't function that way. My son is that way.

Chris: I have to have music, but that's it. That's funny. Okay, so update your pay plans, your minimum requirements. Yeah, what training are you going to, so make some goals for reading books, getting into some classes. Train up your advisors, train up your techs. Read some good books. Obviously every podcast or every other, we're trying to give you some good book ideas, so we'll help you with that. What else did you have on your list?

Gary: That's pretty much it. I would say you want to look at your opportunity too from a facility standpoint. I know we've been talking a lot with dealers as they come through here, and they just have so much opportunity, lifts that aren't spoken for. They've got guys ... you know, their entire team, everybody's got two lifts. If you've got a facility where there's opportunity there, that's another opportunity to scale and grow in the next year. You know, hire some people and fill those spots, and do it systematically, but a lot of guys overlook that. They just think that it's ... I don't know, like mentally you get capped. "This is what we've got and we're doing the best we can." I think if you think creatively about it, you can start to add in bodies and grow your department.

Chris: Nobody's ever capped. We've never found it, never. In I don't know how many years we've been doing this, nobody's ever capped. They're mentally capped, but they're not capped.

Gary: Yeah. Even if you've got a place where you've got 12 bays and 12 techs, there's creative ways to schedule where you can add in more bodies and create more production. Oh, that's one thing I wanted to add. I was talking with a dealer on the phone not that long ago, and they were talking about wanting to scale and open up on a Saturday. We were trying to build a model for them that would make sense, and the one trap that everybody falls into is they say, "Okay, we're going to open up Saturday, we're going to extend our hours, we're going to have this," but they don't add any productive staff. If you have the capability of producing 300 hours a week, and you add on a Saturday but you don't add any more bodies in there, you're going to be capable of producing 300 hours a week, you're just going to do it over six days. I just thought that was interesting, because for me, I would think that's what we would do, but a lot of guys don't think of that immediately. They think, "Okay, if I expand hours, I'll have more opportunity," but the goal is if you're going to expand productive hours, you're going to go to a night shift, you're going to go to a Saturday ... expand productive staff.

Chris: Yeah. You know, I didn't think of this, but that made me think of the fact that if you're going to have some pretty big goals, you're going to have to add techs.

Gary: Oh, yeah. For sure.

Chris: You're not going to get 20% more out of what you have.

Gary: Uh-uh.

Chris: You're going to get to about June and realize you're on the same track as last year. You know, Ted and Tom ran at 100 percent, and they're running at 100%. That's not going to go to 150. If you want to add production, you need to add techs. Whatever your numbers are, you need to figure that out. You're not going to do much more with what you have, most of the time. I mean, there's always an exception to that rule, but you're not the exception.

Gary: No.

Chris: Yeah. Another cool idea is to do a book report with your crew, so have your techs and advisors ... give them a book, and then assign everybody a chapter or every two people a chapter, and then have a meeting like a lunch, buy them lunch, and talk about the book. The idea being that if, you know, two guys get together and they do a book report on their chapter, by the end of it, everybody has kind of gone through the book, and hopefully it inspires them to read the whole thing. By the end, if they do a good book report, then everybody has heard what the whole book is about.

Gary: Yeah, that's good. You know, that collective consciousness and that team energy to get the book done. Everybody doesn't want to have to read the thing from front to back. I know reading is time-consuming sometimes, and so like you said, it would help them put the chapters together and maybe not have to go through the whole thing.

Chris: Yeah. Just read one chapter. That's good. Okay, and so just kind of to recap, you need to ... I'd sit down for a morning with a cup of coffee and go through your numbers, go through your profitability, effective labor rates, your gross profits, parts percentage, everything. Go through it all and then make some goals, and make some lofty goals and then do the same thing with your troops. Update your pay plans, update your minimum requirements. Make a plan for training and getting better this year, improving. Find new friends, find friends that are doing what you want to do. There's that old saying, if you average the income of your five closest friends, that's your income, so go find some new friends. The book report idea, and then once again we thank Matt.

Gary: Then I'll just leave you with this thought. You know, it's a common thing that we have a lot of knowledge and we all know a lot of stuff, but really to make 2017 your best year, you've got to execute. Everybody knows how to lose weight, it's just doing it, right? Everybody knows how to get rich, but it's having the discipline to do it. You've got to execute and have the discipline to then follow up with your goals. That's why it helps to write then down every day, refocus, have clarity on them, because it gets a lot easier when you're not chasing a bunch of different stuff.

Chris: Yeah, because you want to really focus on them and make execution your goal in 2017, more than anything. Less ideas, less talk, and more execution, is the goal.

Gary: Uh-huh.

Chris: That's good.

Gary: Thanks, everybody.

Chris: Thank you.

Episode #23: It's Time To Get Uncomfortable

Chris: Welcome, everybody, to Service Drive Revolution, the podcast for you if you have a service drive, technicians, advisors and customers.

Gary: Yep.

Chris: We have the tools and training, books, everything to help you increase your retention, profitability and have more fun, honestly. Right, G-man?

Gary: That's right.

Chris: How are you doing?

Gary: Honestly, if you work on yachts, motorcycles-

Chris: Everything.

Gary: Everything.

Chris: Restaurants.

Gary: Restaurants, yeah.

Chris: Yeah, we've given Millionaire Service Advisor to people in other industries, and they liked it. We could repurpose that book, actually. We have a great podcast for you today. This is going to be a lot of fun. We're going to talk about how making yourself uncomfortable is the key to success. We have a book report on a book by Dr. Pratt, *Code to Joy*.

Gary: The great Dr. Pratt.

Chris: The great Dr. Pratt. We'll talk about that. I'll tell my story about that. I'm going to do a little shout out to Joe Mac.

Everybody in our group knows who Joe Mac is, and the legend. I had the idea the other day that we should sell posters of him with darts and do a limited edition run of 25 of them and sell them. I wouldn't want him... it's a tribute. It's not to offend him. It's meant in the nicest way.

Gary: Being at the top, that's what happens. We're coming after you.

Chris: For everybody that doesn't know what we're talking about, Joe Mac is consistently winning our American group as advisors - if it's just one person, should it be 'an advisor?' His team outperforms everybody, usually, in that group. He's really hard to beat. There are different categories in that. We have this software that ranks them. Guys try to beat him, and they can't, so they want to throw darts at him.

Gary: Manager of the Year, this is going to be his fourth year, right?

Chris: I think so, yeah.

Gary: Four years in a row? Yeah. Four years in a row, Manager of the Year.

Chris: We love you, Joe Mac. Hope you're doing good. Hope you're looking-

Gary: It's a juggernaut. It's a dynasty.

Chris: Which one do you want to talk about first, G-man? Making yourself uncomfortable or the *Code to Joy*? Let's talk about *Code to Joy* first. I ask you, and then I-

Gary: Let's walk into that one. I have not read that book, actually. I have two copies of it he sent me. I haven't read it.

Chris: He sent it to you?

Gary: Yeah.

Chris: Wow. He didn't send it to me. I had to buy it, big sock over there. Let's talk about Dr. Pratt for a second. Beyond the book, Dr. Pratt is an angel from heaven, honestly.

Gary: Yeah.

Chris: He's the Head of Psychiatry at Scripps in San Diego, right?

Gary: Mm-hmm (affirmative).

Chris: He's probably, he's a performance guy more than anything, I think. I know a lot of NFL and NASCAR guys, golf guys go to him. It's funny. I was on an airplane from Chicago to L.A., sitting next to Common. You know the rapper, Common?

Gary: Oh, yeah. Mm-hmm (affirmative).

Chris: Can you spit a Common verse?

Gary: No, but I like Common.

Chris: Me neither. He was nice. I was sitting next to him. I said, because I had seen his name in something with Dr. Pratt, I said, "Dr. Pratt." "Oh, man, that boy." I know we talked about him forever. I think one of the things that I learned from Dr. Pratt is how powerful it is when you get rid of all the old stuff. It's like you have a new lease on life, a little bit. My story is, when I was going through my divorce, it was pretty intense. Every time I would drive by my exit for my old house that I lost in the divorce, I would get choked up. I had to drive there all the time, because I was going to San Diego all the time. I'd drive from L.A. to San Diego. It was in Orange County. I had to drive by it. I would get choked up. A friend told me, "You should talk to Pratt." I was like, "Whatever," but I did it. I had a session with him, and I couldn't, once I was done, I couldn't feel it. It's weird. It's like magic. It was like a million pounds had been lifted off of me. In that moment, I'd try to be the tough guy all the time. In that moment, I realized how vulnerable, really, we all are, in a way. Does that make sense?

Gary: You think you can push it down. We've been taught that as men, we can just shove it down there and not deal with it, but it's in there. It's boiling. It's like a cancer.

Chris: I'm pretty tough. It's funny. I couldn't cry at my grandpa's funeral, who I loved to death. My grandpa was like my father, and I couldn't cry at his funeral, but I could cry when my dog died, which is weird, so I'm probably more messed up than most. I'm not a super-emotional guy, but the stuff that he teaches really works. The one thing I would say in here, because he goes through the trifecta in here. He has this thing called the trifecta that you do every morning. It's comparable to meditating. In fact, we do it before we meditate.

Gary: It's like mini-meditating, almost. It's like a meditating hors d'oeuvres.

Chris: It's three things that you do. It's in the book. It would be impossible for me to explain it.

Gary: Yeah.

Chris: It's a breathing thing, and a rubbing thing in a special spot, saying a special thing.

Gary: It sounds really weird.

Chris: It's not weird at all.

Gary: It's not weird?

Chris: No. It's programming your subconscious to perform is what it is. Your subconscious is dumb. I've learned more about my subconscious. I've had sessions with Dr. Pratt where I just sit and talk about how the subconscious works so I understand it. I've had experiences where I feel like I understand it way more than I ever did, but he gets it. He said to me early on, "You know your subconscious is two million times stronger than your conscious mind." I was like, "What? Get out of here." It ends up.

Gary: He's right.

Chris: He knows what he's talking about.

Gary: It's funny. You have a base layer of understanding of the mind and how it works, I think, going through life. It's just there, and things happen the way they happen.

Chris: You get in a habit.

Gary: You think that's it. You start to get into reading this stuff and understanding and getting around guys like Pratt and really understanding how it works. Things make a lot more sense to you. Over the weekend, I was having lunch with my son, and asking him how things are going in college. He was out there by himself and everything. He said that sometimes, he's having a hard time sleeping. I said, "What's going on?" He goes, "I don't know. My mind's racing and things jump into my mind." He goes, "What I've got to do tomorrow, my homework, my major, what's going to happen to me, my life, everything." Then he said, "My car accident." I said, "Your car accident?" He got into a pretty nasty car wreck junior year in high school, which is four years ago, almost. He said-

Chris: He has PTSD from it?

Gary: Yeah. He says sometimes that memory will drop into his conscious thought and he'll feel anxiety and stress around it, and fear, really. I thought that was weird, but that's just subconscious screwing with you. It's your subconscious, because it's so childlike in the way it operates, and it doesn't have a sense of time. It gives you things back, like it happened yesterday, when you don't want them. Understanding that path and that's what it's doing to you because we haven't programmed it to do something else, to me, it was cool to have that clarity, because I could try to help him with it. It's funny. We go through life, and that stuff happens to us. We just think it's just how it is.

Chris: You should have Pratt wipe that out.

Gary: Yeah, he needs help with that, for sure.

Chris: That's interesting.

Gary: It's funny to hear stuff like that, because you just don't think about it.

Chris: You take it for granted, and you just get in this routine. You don't understand until it's gone or until you confront it how much things like a divorce or a car wreck or a business failure, getting fired, anything like that. You hold onto that, and it affects. You're using that as a lens to see everything, but when you get rid of that lens, then you can see things clearly. The best way I've heard it described is that when you're in tune with this and you're in tune with your subconscious and you have a routine and you're meditating and that sort of thing, you're turning down the stuff that doesn't matter. You're turning up the focus on the stuff that does. All the noise of the stuff that doesn't matter goes away. That's a good way to describe it.

Gary: For sure.

Chris: You're turning down the noise and the stuff that's killing your time management, killing your focus and all that, and you're just turning up the focus on the stuff that matters, because you're getting clarity. You don't have all these conflicting things going on, because you've told it what to do. You've got to train it. It's dumb.

Gary: That's the other thing...

Chris: It's really dumb.

Gary: It's powerful and smart and dumb at the same time, because it's dumb, because it doesn't understand what to do with all that information. That's why I say it's childlike. A lot of the stuff that I read, that's how they describe it. It's funny, because that's how it operates. It wants to give you the bad stuff. That's why we all do that. We get some weird memory of some time when we were uncomfortable or embarrassed. It throws it at us. Then your heart rate increases, and you feel like it's happening to you right then. Meanwhile, it happened years ago. You've just got to get control of it. I was an automotive technician. I worked with my hands. That's how I lived my life. Sitting here talking about the brain and the subconscious, to me, I wouldn't have expected myself to be here, but I tell you honestly, I'm glad I learned those lessons. I always looked at that stuff as being hokum and BS, but understanding how your mind works and getting control of that is powerful, regardless of what you're doing in life.

Chris: Yeah. I don't know. You're not serious about performance if you're not looking into that, because there's a reason. I was telling you, it was crazy. I didn't know Arnold Schwarzenegger did TM.

Gary: Yeah, that's cool.

Chris: He said that's what helped him separate his body from his mind when he was lifting so hard.

Gary: It's crazy.

Chris: In the 70's, bro, he was doing TM. In the 70's.

Gary: That's nuts, but that makes sense. I've read a lot of stuff about him. The things he was able to accomplish, he had to have been doing TM, especially to transcend body-building. Everybody looked at him like he was a lunkhead. He could barely speak English.

Chris: He was anything but a lunkhead, that guy.

Gary: He became governor of the state!

Chris: He said what happened to him was that he had so many things going on. He's trying to be Mr. Olympia. He's got a movie career. He's trying to buy apartment buildings and get loans, and all this stuff. He felt like he had a tremendous opportunity in front of him, but he was messing it up. He's like, "I go to work out." He was telling the story, "I go to work out at Gold's in Venice. Everywhere I go, they're creating a documentary. They're changing the battery on the belt while I'm doing squats." He's like, "I could never quite get it right. Then it quieted. It turned down the noise, and turned it up." I know that we have a tendency to be old-school and scared of performance and talking about the mind and all that sort of stuff, but I'll tell you what. There is nothing clearer than we are over-stimulated.

Gary: Oh, yeah.

Chris: You have to have some sort of option. There's no way. You're texting, Facebooking, TV, ads, everywhere.

Gary: Email, yeah. Everything's coming at you.

Chris: We're not built for that. That's a new thing that technology is outpacing our ability to process.

Gary: We've been talking a lot about technicians and their, how to retain top techs and how to understand them and their mindset. One of the subjects that came up was, how is it that a technician that's been great for 15 years and is your top tech starts making mistakes, and then gets into this downward spiral where he can't get out of it, and he makes mistakes after mistake, and then you eventually have to fire him? All along before that, he was a great tech. We were saying that you get in your head, it's like an athlete. He just is in his head too much, like a golf swing. When you're thinking about the mechanics of it too much, you can't hit the ball. That's what happens to techs. They make a mistake. They're like, "I'm a bad tech." You get this thing swirling in your head, this doubt. You can't focus. You've got all this other distraction going on, I can't even imagine, because they didn't have that when I was out there. Then you get into this thing. Understanding what's happening to you and your mind is playing tricks on you, and that you can get control over that, your subconscious, and have it stop trying to make you fail, really would help break them out of it, would help break you out of it.

Chris: There's a couple comparables to that, I think. If you're driving on the freeway and you're just looking at the white line right in front of you and you're not looking at the horizon, you're going to start correcting too much. You're not going to stop on time. You're going to run into a car. You're going to make all kinds of mistakes, but when you're looking at the horizon and it's very clear, these motor skills just become automatic, because you're just holding still and you're headed in one straight line instead of constantly. It's not any different than if you balance a bottle or a ball on your head. If you're concentrating on that and you're looking up, it's going to fall off, but if you walk straight and you're on the horizon, you can balance it. It just becomes a part of your general purpose of what you're doing. I think we've all experienced that in one way or another, but if your head is down and you're not looking up at the horizon and the full picture, you're going to make mistakes. You have to train your mind to do that. It's more relevant now than ever. That's our gift to you, but anything by Dr. Pratt, any of his videos on You Tube, he's an angel.

Gary: I think if you just did two things, let's call it three things. One is you read the book *Code to Joy*, and I think if you watched some of his videos on You Tube and then did the three-part harmony, his Trifecta, you would feel improvement right out of the gate, just doing those things.

Chris: Oh, yeah. It's like a mini-meditation, but you're going to have clarity.

Gary: Yep, and I recommend it too, I don't care what you're doing. I'm telling you, I highly recommend. If I had that as a tool when I was in the shop, that would have been indispensable, because it's a hard job, and it's hard to keep your head right. That would make a huge benefit.

Chris: Making yourself uncomfortable is the key to success. I don't know what analogies you have for this, but I have the analogy of being 29, taking over a dealership as a general manager, knowing nothing really about the sales department except for I had fixed a couple of internet sales departments, but that's it. I had sold cars when I was really young, but barely. I was an advisor selling cars, so I got the process. I remember my first, it was actually the week before I was announced as the general manager. I don't know, we had 300 and something employees, big dealership. The general sales manager pulled me into the office. We were in Santa Ana, California. If you drop a bomb on that dealership, you don't kill too many BMW customers. It's not a great area, but what is great about it is all the freeways. You've got the 22, the 5, the 405. They're all right there. It's convenient, freeway-wise, but it's not the greatest market, not the greatest zip code, I guess. The dealership, I think, was built in the 90's, the building. The general sales manager calls me in, closes the door. He says, "You know, I know it's coming. I know you're going to be announced as the general manager. I'm really happy for you and I think you're great for the job." He and I had a good relationship. Said, "But..."

Gary: But! The infamous but!

Chris: Here we go.

Gary: You're really handsome, but!

Chris: At the time, our competition down the street had just built a $30 million building. They were where the 405 and the 5 meet. They were beating us by ten cars a month at that point, and it all could be traced to the facility and our mindset. He says, "Nobody thinks luxury cars when they think Santa Ana. Our building's old. We just need to," basically just said, "We need to accept the fact that we're going to be number two in the Western region and number five in the country, and that's a good place to be. There's nothing wrong with being number five."

Gary: A lot of guys would like to be number five.

Chris: A lot of guys would like to be number five.

Gary: You're ahead of the game. Don't rock the boat. Don't come in with any crazy ideas.

Chris: I think at the end of it, if I had to remember and guess what I would have said, "You know that this isn't going to have any effect on me right?" I wouldn't argue every point with him, because I just would let him get it all out, but I would say, "You know that you're wasting your flipping time."

Gary: Right. This is washing over me.

Chris: You know that my goals are going to be a lot higher than number five. Tell me again how we should be okay being number five. Explain that to me one more time. No. That was a lonely moment, saying, "No. I want to be number one. I want to be number one in the country." It's a weird thing. It was very uncomfortable.

Gary: Yeah, putting yourself out there like that and having a goal that you share with people that most people say you can't hit, it's hard to push past that. Everybody wants to rein you in and have you become more practical. Come on, Chris, Leo. What if we got to number four? Let's start there. Let's be number four in the country. They all want to be reasonable. We were just talking earlier, too, people love goals that they can hit.

Chris: Oh, yeah.

Gary: Let's check it off the list.

Chris: We love easy. Here's the way that I would explain that is that in order to perform at a high level, you're going to have to learn new tools. It's going to be uncomfortable. I remember going to a Mastermind meeting. My buddy Mike was there. They were all talking about, what a great thing he did at their, they used to have these meetings where there'd be a couple hundred entrepreneurs there. Mike did a thing on tear sheets. They're like, "What a great thing he did on tear sheets." I'm sitting across the table from him. It's a conference table. I go, "Tear sheets, bro?" I said, "I thought you were in the fertilizer/weed thing. What?" He goes, "I just did it to practice public speaking." I'm like, "What?" I go, "I hate public speaking." I was deathly afraid to go up in front of a crowd and talk. I hated it. I would get sick, whatever. I told him that. I said, "Oh, man. I get sick. I hate public speaking. I'm the quiet guy in the back of the room," the whole thing. He said, just looked at me and then he goes, "You'd better get over that. I've never seen anybody be successful that didn't learn how to do public speaking. Yeah, it sucks. It's uncomfortable, but picture them in their underwear, whatever you want to do, but you'd better get over it." At that moment, I was like, "I'm just going to get over it."

Gary: I love that about Mike, too. He's just so matter of fact, "Better get over it."

Chris: How's that going to work? He's so funny.

Gary: He's not like, "Let's talk about it, Chris. Let me help you."

Chris: Same guy that we're just sitting there, and randomly goes, "You know what I decided? I want to be a billionaire."

Gary: I have a story about being uncomfortable and growing. I was working at the dealer, Concord. You came in and brought me out. I was learning the business and trying to find my way through. Very uncomfortable, because I was a technician my whole life. Cars don't talk back to you. You don't have to interact with them. You don't have to schmooze them like you do a client as a service advisor. I was struggling, really, with the personal interaction, not just with clients, but also with employees. I was not a good leader. I was a terrible leader. I was stressed out all the time. There were a lot of things that were going on, but it was going badly. I decided I needed to do something drastic. I signed up for this class on 'How to Speak with Tact and Finesse.' They had one that was in my local area. I said, "Nope." I got in my car, and I drove to San Francisco, which was 45 minutes from me.

Chris: Why?

Gary: Because I didn't want to do it in my backyard. I wanted to get away.

Chris: You thought you were going to know somebody?

Gary: No, I didn't think I'd know anybody, but I just-

Chris: Just change of environment?

Gary: I knew the area. I grew up there my whole life. I knew everything. I just said, "I've got to get out of this."

Chris: Interesting.

Gary: "I've got to break something." I had no clue what I was doing, but I knew that somehow I had to crack my environment. I go to San Francisco. I go to this class, and they make you public speak, which, of course, I hated, too. I was deathly afraid of that.

Chris: It's the best thing for you.

Gary: They had this crazy eye contact exercise where you had to sit across from somebody and stare at them without giving them an expression while they spoke to you.

Chris: You got the prettiest girl in the room.

Gary: She was really cute.

Chris: Really? I thought you were going to say it was some dude with glasses.

Gary: No. She was really cute. I felt like such an idiot. I didn't know what I was doing, but going there, getting outside of my comfort zone, staying in the city. It was a two-day class. I met this group of people from Bank of America. I've told this story a couple of times. I'm not sure if on the podcast, I have. I met this group from B of A. They took me under their wing. It was just interesting to meet people outside of my industry and get outside of my comfort zone, try to grow a little bit. I came back much stronger, and knew that there was a path and that if I could go through that, I could fix this and I could figure it out. That started me down the road of self-improvement and trying to learn how to communicate better, how to become a better leader, how to become a better steward of my customers, and really got me on the path. Without that being uncomfortable, I don't know that I would have gotten it.

Chris: Yeah. I've never signed up for this sort of stuff, but there's a method to the madness. These big guys like Tony Robbins, they'll take guys swimming with sharks and just stuff that, jumping out of a plane, to me is scary, but once you do it, then it's like, "I did that, so big deal changing a pay plan." That's really the effect it has on people. You can create that for yourself without skydiving. The way to do it is, you've got to come up with the big goal or the big scary thing. You've got to start telling people. Then you're hooked. Then you're jumping. It's like you're on the plane, going skydiving. You've got to jump. Once you commit, that's the first step, everybody, in this. Maybe even write that down. To be uncomfortable, you've got to commit to a big goal. Once you commit to that big goal, you've got to tell people. Once you start telling people, then you're really committed. Then you've put it out there into the world, and the world is going to start helping you figure that out, if you really believe it, if you're serious about it. Back to my analogy about fifth place wasn't enough. I wanted to be number one, and I started saying that. It wasn't easy. It wasn't easy. Everybody tried to convince me I was a service guy; I didn't know what I was doing. I just, the thing that it makes you do is it makes you try harder at everything. My marketing had to be better. My system for customers coming in on the floor had to be better. My managers had to be better. I had to get new managers on the desk. The whole thing, it forced me to make decisions quick, because I wasn't going to sit there with a guy who wasn't going to sell cars. I wasn't going to waste my time. I wasn't going to change him. I tried, but it just wasn't. It makes you move faster. People are either on or off. Once you share the goal and you tell everybody where you're headed and try to enlist them, you know right away who's on your side and who isn't. You can tell them, "I get it that you want to be fifth, but I couldn't sleep at night if I wanted to be fifth, so we're going to figure out another way." He ended up coming around and loved being number one, obviously.

Gary: Of course. Everybody loves being on a winning team.

Chris: Yeah. It required me taking some big risks and not being afraid of failure. You're going to make mistakes. That's okay, but the biggest mistake would be not to make a big goal and to be sitting there on your death bed when you're 80, looking back on your life. You might as well have worked at the post office. You're just doing the same thing every day. Come on. Let's increase our O's. Let's have the biggest net we could ever have. Let's have really happy customers. Let's really shoot for it. Let's do something great.

Gary: Yeah. Let's go out there and go get it. That's sound advice, and I've been giving that to my kids a lot lately. You've got to put something out there in the universe. Just go out there and go get it. You can't just accept less, because it feels right or it's easier. You've got to go. I think with anything, putting that big hairy, scary goal out there and like you said, writing it down and sharing it with the world, it almost becomes the dogs on the sled. You crack it. They just take off running. They're dragging you behind. You're just going over obstacles, trying to get there. It's what you've got to do. Otherwise, you shoot too low, maybe even shoot low and hit it. You're like, "What if I would have said I want to do more?" Then it becomes, it's regret. It's not something that you want to live with.

Chris: It's good. Also, make sure that your spouse and family is involved in it. My girlfriend, bless the Lord, she knows the goal. She wakes up and says it before I do. It's like a race for us to say it every morning. Get your spouse and your family, because that's a big part of it. You want them to understand why you're paying the price, if you have to work late a little bit or if you're a little stressed. They need to understand what you're doing. That communication is key. Then they're behind you and supporting you instead of going, "What's wrong with you? Why are you being so moody?" or whatever happens.

Gary: They understand the why. They've got to be part of the why, for sure.

Chris: Go skydiving. Go swimming with the sharks, whatever it is.

Gary: Walk around on hot coals.

Chris: The key to success is, you're going to have to be uncomfortable. As soon as you set that big goal, the next thing you should establish in your mind right away and just accept is that it's not going to be easy. Things are going to go wrong. Things are going to go wrong, so just accept it right then. Then it's like, "It's no surprise." Nothing's going to get you off track.

Gary: The failures are just lessons along the way, just teaching you each step of the way where you've got to detour a little bit to get to the goal. They're all there.

Chris: The thing I would say to you listening to this is, if you want to get better and you want to get uncomfortable, make a list. Sit down and make a list of, excuse me, the things that you need to get better at, whether it's leadership, public speaking, pricing, whatever it is. Then go out and find something and get better at it. It's uncomfortable. I see it a lot of times in guys coming here for the boot camp or the coaching meeting. They're super uncomfortable. There's guys that have come out here. We're in L.A. We're downtown L.A. There's guys from the Midwest. Bless them, they're the sweetest guys. One of the guys is a guy who won the $50,000 challenge last year. They come to L.A., which isn't an easy place to come if you've never been on a plane. You land at LAX. Then you're in all this traffic. This is the big city. Beyond New York, there isn't anything busier than here. They're way outside their comfort zone, but man. They never regret it. They're like, "I'm here to learn. I'm committed." It means so much more because they're paying attention. They're paying a price to be here. They're outside their comfort zone.

Gary: That journey has value.

Chris: I always love that. That always really means a lot to me when guys do that, because there's literally been guys that have never been on a plane, flown across the country before. All the sudden, they're doing it to learn how to run their department better. It's huge.

Gary: One of the guys that was there, it was his second time ever to have been on an airplane. He's here.

Chris: And first time in LA.

Gary: Yeah, and his first time in LA. That's a shocker. It's definitely, it's outside your comfort zone.

Chris: It's uncomfortable. That would be our thing to really think about. Make a list. What is it? Then go get it. Making yourself uncomfortable is a key to success. Recapping our shout out to Joe Mac, we should make those posters and darts, Gary. Throwing darts at, we'll give all the proceeds to charity.

Gary: There you go.

Chris: *Code to Joy* or any video or anything with Dr. George Pratt. He's an angel. You need to train your subconscious and turn down the noise and turn up the focus more than anything. It's harder and harder. We're overwhelmed with things going on constantly.

Gary: Absolutely.

Chris: What do they call that? There's a word for it, where you are constantly going to your email, constantly.

Gary: I don't know what that is. It's an addiction.

Chris: A reflex or something... it's crazy. That's it. Thanks, everybody. We'll see you next time.

Gary: Thank you.

Episode #24: Service Advisors: Should You Hire A Veteran Or A Newbie?

Chris: Welcome everybody to Service Drive Revolution where if you have customers at Service Drive and technicians this is the place, your home, where we also offer the best service advisor training, service manager training on profitability, customer retention, customer collecting, and just overall having more fun which you're allowed to do. How you doing, G-Man?

Gary: I'm good.

Chris: Good, good, good. The topic today is fun and this is going to be ...

Gary: Fun and consequences?

Chris: This could end up being a two-parter because we could go ... Talking about this. The topic of this is a question. The question is: "Service advisor, what's better? To train your own newbies or hire a wile veteran."

Gary: Wow.

Chris: Don't.

Gary: Don't say it yet?

Chris: We're not there yet. We're not there yet.

Gary: No? Okay. All right.

Chris: What's better?

Gary: I'm itching to throw out my opinions.

Chris: Me too. What's better? To train your own newbie, green pea, or hire a wiley seasoned veteran. Okay. People care about you Gary.

Gary: I guess so.

Chris: How does it feel to have people care about you so much?

Gary: It feels pretty good. It feels pretty good.

Chris: People are worried about you. Just randomly called in, Todd Sylvester, called in the switchboard here at the big office.

Gary: Yup.

Chris: The big switchboard. Ring, a ring, a ring. "I just would like to give Gary some advice that there's a book he should get." You read a lot of books.

Gary: I know.

Chris: Add this one to your list.

Gary: Yup.

Chris: *Cholesterol Clarity.*

Gary: Yup.

Chris: Thanks Todd Sylvester for sending that out.

Gary: I appreciate the positive thoughts. I'm going to pick the book up and read it.

Chris: I guarantee we won't learn anything from *Cholesterol Clarity* that we don't already know, but get it.

Gary: Eat right, exercise.

Chris: Everybody wants to reinvent it.

Gary: Stop drinking.

Chris: Yeah.

Gary: You know.

Chris: The cholesterol fad diet. How are you doing? I know you blew it yesterday.

Gary: Yeah. Dude, I was a mess.

Chris: You were eating terrible.

Gary: This whole weekend has been ... I shot myself.

Chris: You're almost suicidal the way you eat. It's terrible.

Gary: Yeah.

Chris: Okay. There's a couple fun things that happened. You got roofied. Right?

Gary: We don't know. We're speculating.

Chris: Listen to this story. You fill in the blanks, but I, being the detective that I am, I know who roofied him which nobody else probably would have figured this out.

Gary: Okay.

Chris: In your building that you live in they had a little Christmas party, right?

Gary: Yup.

Chris: How may drinks did you have, do you think?

Gary: I probably had three glasses of wine and then-

Chris: Which is nothing.

Gary: Yeah.

Chris: You're a pro, right? Nothing.

Gary: Over the course of like three hours, plus we ate dinner there because it had been catered.

Chris: Yeah, it wasn't like you were on an empty ...

Gary: Right.

Chris: He's not on an empty stomach, he built a foundation, he's drinking wine which is no big deal and your wife blacked out. She didn't remember what happened.

Gary: Yeah.

Chris: Which was an opportunity for you to make up a bunch of stuff. I was telling him when I was hearing the story I'm like-

Gary: Unfortunately, my memory is a little hazy too.

Chris: Because his wife wakes up and she's like, "What happened last night?" I'm like, "Oh, Gary, you could have said, 'Well, I don't know, honey. When the cops came and you were on the bar taking off your clo'" ... You could have said anything.

Gary: Anything. Yeah.

Chris: She would have believed you. That would have been so funny but you're too sweet. You're too nice.

Gary: I worry about her. I was worried about her.

Chris: Okay, so you're in this bar and you guys are having wine or whatever and then she ends up getting sick, right?

Gary: Yeah. We were actually at ... My building has a promenade that goes all the way around it and it backs up to the marina or the channel and the boats were going by. They serve food and wine. That's where we were. We were at that event and we were eating food, and drinking wine, watching the boats.

Chris: Just in context so everybody knows, Gary's wife is like supermom, straight, like probably the last time she got sick from drinking was 20 years ago.

Gary: Yeah. She doesn't drink a lot.

Chris: She's a supermom. She's not a party-

Gary: No.

Chris: She's doing crossfit and ...

Gary: Yeah. What happened is, we met some people there at the promenade, and we were chatting with them, and they wanted to show us their apartment so we went upstairs with them and their apartment is directly across from ours. We went up and they poured us a drink so we shifted from wine and I got a bourbon, so he poured me half a glass of bourbon with a big rock in it.

Chris: Still nothing.

Gary: Then my wife had vodka soda with a little twist inside of it. Again, they were the short glasses. We didn't even finish that because we were just kind of sipping there, looking at their apartment, they walked over to ours and then we went back down to the marina ...

Chris: At this point everybody feels fine.

Gary: Everybody's fine. Yup, we're fine. We went to the marina and then there was a bunch of people out on the docks next to their boats and they were having a big party right there on the dock. That's where we went and a couple of people that we know in the building know people that have boats and so we went out there and we're hanging out out there for a little while.

Chris: Then when did she get sick?

Gary: She got sick, I would say, about ten minutes after we got there, but apparently the timeline is not quite clean.

Chris: You think that you got there at nine?

Gary: Yes.

Chris: You were there for ten minutes but you didn't get home until midnight?

Gary: After midnight. It was about 12:30 when we walked in the door.

Chris: Yeah. Classic roofie situation. Okay.

Gary: I lost a lot of time.

Chris: Then she's in the bathroom throwing up.

Gary: Yup.

Chris: You're there talking to those people at the apartment or who are you talking to?

Gary: Yeah, so we-

Chris: Is it like a hallway? Or what is it?

Gary: No, no, it's a long pier and there's boats off to either side. You know, all the slips that the boats are in so there's probably a dozen, maybe a little more than a dozen boats there and we're down the center.

Chris: How many times did you leave your drink unattended do you think?

Gary: As far as I can remember I never had a drink in my hand.

Chris: Okay. What point did you punch the guy? Tell that story.

Gary: I didn't officially punch anybody. Katya disappears to the bathroom and then her friend gets worried and says she's going to go check on her, which makes me worried because I don't really ... The passage of time at this point, I'm not really 100 percent.

Chris: Yeah, you're roofied.

Gary: I go and I can barely stand. That's one thing that I'm recognizing is that I'm having a hard time standing.

Chris: Which never happens.

Gary: No.

Chris: I've never seen that happen to you.

Gary: No. It was weird. I walk down to the bathroom and her friend is there with another friend and then there's this guy and so Kat is in the bathroom getting sick and I'm outside the bathroom and the friend is having a conversation with this guy basically saying-

Chris: Suspect number one.

Gary: "Leave us alone." I walk up to him and I said, "What's going on?" He's like, 'Hey, just looking for the bathroom." I said, "Well, the men's room is right over there," and I point at it. I said, "It's over there," and he wouldn't leave. Then he was like walking in one to walk in the bathroom, like looking in the bathroom. Here I start to get a little overprotective of my wife. She's in a very vulnerable situation.

Chris: You should. Yeah.

Gary: I got pretty upset.

Chris: You're feeling a little like, "I want to go because I'm feeling a little rocky."

Gary: Yeah. I'm ready to leave.

Chris: Yeah.

Gary: I know she's ready to leave. I want to get out of there. Then this guy just wouldn't leave, wouldn't leave and-

Chris: He's just standing there, right?

Gary: Just standing there.

Chris: He's the one that roofied you guys.

Gary: Hovering.

Chris: He's waiting for you guys to pass out so he can take you to his boat and rape you. I'm not joking. That's what he's doing. Why else would somebody just stand there?

Gary: I don't know, he's an odd-

Chris: Especially if you told him to get lost.

Gary: He's an odd dude. Eventually I threw him to the ground and tossed him down the dock. He still came back. He still came back after us which was weird. It was a weird thing. That was a weird night, bro.

Chris: See. He roofied you.

Gary: Weird night.

Chris: That was the guy. Why else would you hang out?

Gary: I don't know. I don't know.

Chris: Guarantee you're going to read about that guy getting arrested for roofying ...

Gary: Yeah. It could be.

Chris: People.

Gary: Yeah. We must have had drinks at the ... That's the thing that I don't remember.

Chris: When was the last time you got in a fight with somebody?

Gary: God, it's been forever, man. It's been years. Years. More than years.

Chris: Hilarious.

Gary: Before I had kids probably. Because he started talking to me after I threw him down and we were trying to leave. He was talking to me as we were walking and I just kind of flipped a gasket and went after him.

Chris: Have you ever seen that guy before?

Gary: I couldn't tell you what he looked like right now. When I think about and I remember what happened that night it's very fuzzy, he doesn't have a face. It's so weird. I don't remember anything. I could barely see my wife's friend. I could barely make her out in my memory that she was actually there. It was bizarre, man, I'm telling you, it was like...

Chris: That's nuts.

Gary: Yeah.

Chris: That's never happened to me.

Gary: Yeah.

Chris: That's scary.

Gary: Her friend texts us the next morning and says, "Oh, we had such a good time with your guys last night. We're so glad you could make it." I don't even remember talking to them. I don't remember having a conversation. I don't even remember ... Like I said, I felt like we were there for five minutes. I remember talking to this one guy, our neighbor across the way that we walked in with, and having a conversation with him a little bit about his business and then that's it. I don't remember anything after that. I don't know. Then, like I said, we were drinking something at the dock because there was solo cups in our house which we don't have. There were red solo cups in the house and Katya is like, "Where did this come from?" "I don't know."

Chris: I'm telling you, you got roofied. Wait, you don't remember leaving your drink unattended but then you woke up with solo cups that you don't remember having.

Gary: Exactly.

Chris: Which means your drinks weren't attended.

Gary: Exactly.

Chris: Right.

Gary: Yeah. Yeah.

Chris: Somebody slipped something in your drink, bro.

Gary: I think so.

Chris: It was that guy, but now you don't know what he looks like.

Gary: No.

Chris: Do any of the people that saw you get in a fight with him know what he looks like?

Gary: Yeah. They must.

Chris: Can we backtrack?

Gary: I texted her friend and a couple other people we know and told them I felt like an ass. I never really hang out with these people who have boats and this was the first time.

Chris: They're like, "This scary guy. Be careful. He likes to fight."

Gary: Yeah. Here comes this douche-bag that wants to fight everybody asking everybody in the party how much you bench, you know?

Chris: "How much do you bench?"

Gary: "What do you bench?"

Chris: How old is my mom? 50, 60 ... She's going to be 66. My mom is 66 and I think she's listened to the podcast or something because she goes ... No, I sent her the video of us doing the dead lifts, you know?

Gary: Yeah, yeah, yeah.

Chris: She goes, "Oh, honey, how much can you bench?" Right there with you. "How much can you bench?"

Gary: It's from that era.

Chris: I'm like, "Mom, with my MMA fighting I don't bench."

Gary: That's right. I don't look at it that way.

Chris: Yeah.

Gary: That screws up my whole ...

Chris: Yeah.

Gary: I don't want to.

Chris: Funny. Okay. That's great.

Gary: We survived, so everybody knows.

Chris: Lucky you didn't get raped.

Gary: Yeah. My wife survived and I survived. We weren't feeling too good yesterday and then today she still feels a little rough, but I think we'll be all right. We'll survive it.

Chris: Get new friends. That little place you live down there is like the party/date rape craziness.

Gary: God, it is a party capital, that place I live.

Chris: You need to be careful.

Gary: It's nuts. A bunch of 40-somethings want to have a good time. That's for sure.

Chris: Another little fun thing is I got to see Roberto. I like to call him Roberto but it's Robert Cialdini.

Gary: Yeah, yeah, yeah.

Chris: I flew to Phoenix. He did this thing. He talked and then he did a Q and A and it was amazing, probably one of the best.

The thing that I love about him, and I know you read that book already, so his latest book is *Pre-Suasion*, right?

Gary: Yup.

Chris: You read it.

Gary: Yup. *Pre-Suasion*.

Chris: The thing I love about him with influence and with this book is, it's just science.

Gary: Yeah.

Chris: It's not feelings, it's not hypotheticals, it's just science. It's so easy to understand because they try things a bunch of times this way, a bunch of times that way, and the whole thing.

Gary: It's all testing and reporting and they test it ... Like you said, they test it one way, and they test it another, and the stats are the stats. It just is what it is.

Chris: He said one thing. I was trying to figure out how we could incorporate this in advisor training but he was saying ... If I said, "Gary, do you want to buy this slightly drank glass of tequila?" Maybe a water bottle would be better, but if I had a water bottle, I'm like, "Gary, do you want to buy this water bottle?" Your first reaction would be, "Well, how much?"

Gary: Right.

Chris: If I said, "Gary, what's the distance between the Earth and the Sun?"

Gary: Three million miles. Something like that.

Chris: Is it?

Gary: I don't know.

Chris: You're just guessing.

Gary: I'm guessing, yeah.

Chris: Then I said-

Gary: It's a big number.

Chris: Yeah. Then I said, "Hey, do you want to buy this?" Your mind would be off price.

Gary: Yeah.

Chris: Because you said that big number and you tried to figure it out, or think about it, or ...

Gary: Yup.

Chris: That's kind of an interesting deal with that I though. Man, I took four pages of notes.

Gary: I know. I'm looking at your notes. Very small writing.

Chris: Honestly, a lot of this I can't reveal because it's his thing but let me get a couple highlights here. Yeah, so *Pre-Suasion* is established science. Yeah, some of this stuff I don't know. It's good but I don't know that it applies to service.

Gary: Did he talk about the Pepsi can? That they use to put ...

Chris: No.

Gary: In the book he talks about how on TV, you know how they do product placement? He was saying they put the product right out in front and it was really prominent and they didn't get a spike in sales. There was no impact from it. What they found out was that it was too contrived. People knew it was a setup, like you're being set up to look at Pepsi. Then they way they did it the next time was they put it in the background. Then when they put it in the background kind of just off to the side just so you could see it, but it's not really very prominent, they noticed that people immediately - there was a spike in sales and that they realized that having it kind of-

Chris: Yeah.

Gary: Off to the side and not as much of a focused attention, that it had a bigger impact which I thought was fascinating.

Chris: Yeah. Yeah. It does make sense.

Gary: I love the studies that he does.

Chris: Yeah.

Gary: It's crazy.

Chris: Okay, so the one ... Actually, I was painting motivational posters all weekend so I think I showed you the one that I did, but motivational posters work and you told me this before, actually, from reading the book. The study is that they took a poster of a runner crossing a finish line and the tape, you know, that you break at the end of a race and it said, "Finish," on it. The tape did. They put that up in phone rooms, so call centers, and, no joke, having that poster up increased donations, or closing ratios, or whatever it was depending on what the phone room was doing by 60 percent.

Gary: Yeah. That's crazy.

Chris: Because the image of finish was up on the wall everywhere.

Gary: Yeah.

Chris: Then they did another study and this teacher had a stack of cards and he would put different ones posted up in the room, he would drop the cards, and then they would track to see how many people helped. It's another motivational poster. Gary, get ready, because we're coming out with bulldog motivational posters.

Gary: They're coming?

Chris: Because this is crazy. They're coming. They did a poster of just a guy up on the wall and when they put that poster up it increased the amount - 20 percent of the students helped the teacher when he dropped his stuff. Then they did one of two people side by side and same thing, only 20 percent of the classroom helped the teacher when he dropped his cards. There was one poster that it actually went to 60 percent, so tripled, 60 percent of the students helped the teacher and it was motivational posters of guys arms in arm, like their arms as a team. It tripled just by having the poster up. Is that crazy?

Gary: That's crazy.

Chris: We're very visual. He was giving all these stats about how you can kind of hijack the subconscious.

Gary: Yup.

Chris: Visual and music, so pictures and music are the strongest. That's not the craziest part of that study. The craziest part of that study is the students were 18 month old babies.

Gary: 18...?

Chris: We are pre-wired from the time we're born to be apart of a tribe.

Gary: Geez. 18 month old?

Chris: Yeah.

Gary: 18 month old. Geez.

Chris: Isn't that crazy? Went and helped.

Gary: That's nuts, man.

Chris: I know. He said when read that in the study he fell backwards. He was like in crazy shock. You can tell he puts his heart and soul into these books.

Gary: Yeah, for sure.

Chris: One thing that got me like ... You know, his wife was there and she was telling a story about how to write this book for, I don't know, seven or eight years, seven days a week. He said, "You know, I knew I had a problem with this books when ..." He said he was in a city somewhere and he went to step off of the curb and he got buzzed by a car. He almost got hit. You know, it was like a life or death, like that shock. His first thought wasn't, "Hey, I'm glad I lived." His first thought was, "Okay, good. I get to finish that book." That's commitment.

Gary: God forbid that's left undone.

Chris: You got to imagine how many studies does he read?

Gary: Oh my god, just study, after study, after study.

Chris: It's crazy. Yeah. He just stacks it.

Gary: Yeah.

Chris: It's insane. It's fun though. He was great, sweet guy. I got my picture with him.

Gary: I think that the persuasion or "pre-suasion", as he puts it, that's in the periphery, like the motivational posters, the Pepsi example of it being off to the side. It's just funny how susceptible we are to that. Study after study is proving it out that it's not the direct persuasion that happens. It's the stuff that's off in the distance that's around you that makes you act a certain way.

Chris: I'm going to open up a loop for everybody and I'm not going to close it. We'll close it on another one. He gave the science behind why customer satisfaction surveys don't work. There's a new trend in that that does work and we should talk about that on the podcast.

Gary: Okay.

Chris: Why CSI doesn't work.

Gary: Okay.

Chris: It makes total sense too. It's crazy. A little tease for everybody just to irritate you.

Gary: I'm interested. Yeah. The loop is open on my end.

Chris: Let's recap so far: Gary is a badass, he beats people up, he was like date raped with a drug.

Gary: I'm dying from cholesterol poisoning. I'm not beating anybody up.

Chris: *Pre-Suasion.* Come on, bro. You're like a tank. You can dead lift as much as I can.

Gary: That was fun this morning.

Chris: You're catching me. Not even catching. We're even on the dead lifts.

Gary: Yeah.

Chris: Don't underplay your strength. You're like a tank.

Gary: Okay. All right.

Chris: I got like 100 pounds on you and you're dead lifting ... How much do you weigh?

Gary: Probably 200.

Chris: How much do you bench?

Gary: Yeah. More than my body weight.

Chris: Okay. I don't have you by 100 pounds if you're 200. You should lose some weight, bro.

Gary: Yeah.

Chris: Everybody should get *Pre-Suasion*.

Gary: Yup. Absolutely. I highly recommend it.

Chris: You're buying the book *Cholesterol Clarity* that Todd Sylvester suggested.

Gary: That's the next one on my list.

Chris: Okay. Let's get to our topic. Do you want to go first or do you want me to go first because I have a pretty strong feeling about this.

Gary: I know you do. I have a feeling it's contrary to mine. I'm going to go first and then I'll let you ...

Chris: Do it.

Gary: Come in with the ...

Chris: The question is, Gary, what's better? To hire a wiley veteran or grow your own newbie?

Gary: Okay. I have experience with this because I've done both. I remember having a team of veterans that we hired and I remember not wanting to go to work. I remember not wanting to get up in the morning and go into the office because I hated my team so much. It was just a miserable group of people. Then I remember sitting back going, "Hey, wait a minute, I'm in charge of this. Why do I feel this way?" We cleaned the slate, and started over, and I brought in some newbies.

Chris: They were green?

Gary: They were green.

Chris: Never written service.

Gary: Never written service but they had worked in the restaurant industry and so I converted them from being in the restaurant industry to being in the car business and it worked out great. We had a great team, much, much happier.

Chris: How many of the veterans did you get rid of?

Gary: Four. Four.

Chris: You got rid of half of them? You had eight on that side?

Gary: Yeah. We had eight advisors and we ended up getting rid of four. We were going to do three and the fourth one left on his own. We thought we could turn him but ...

Chris: No.

Gary: He wouldn't be turned. No. That was my experience. I have seen it both ways but if I had to go back and do it again I think my preference would be to probably get somebody a little green and teach them so that way they played by my set of rules and they didn't come in with their own habits.

Chris: Yeah. Okay. That's a cute...

Gary: I'm waiting. There's an awkward silence here. I'm waiting for the shoe to drop.

Chris: There's two ways to answer this question.

Gary: Okay.

Chris: You'll agree with this. There's the straight up answer that everybody wants and then there's the truth. Right? The truth is if you want to change numbers really quick, if you're turning something around, you got to go with the wiley veterans. You don't have time to train.

Gary: Yeah.

Chris: Then you want to do what you did then you can flip on the culture, and the numbers, and the expectations, but if I'm interviewing an advisor and they bring their numbers and I see like, "Hey, this guys putting up crazy numbers," and I hire him, he's going to put up crazy numbers, right?

Gary: Yeah.

Chris: It's kind of like you're betting on a racehorse that you know - even if their attitude isn't the greatest - you know that they're going to be able to put up numbers. If they connect with customers, they're customer collectors, and they can put up numbers, if you're trying to turn something around you're way better doing that than trying to train a green, because a green pea usually takes like a year. They go through--

Gary: Yeah.

Chris: They go through these different stages of realizing what the job really is because it's hard.

Gary: Yeah.

Chris: There's the beginning, and then there's the drop off, and then you got to put them back. It's very rare that a green pea can get up and going really without your help in six months.

Gary: Yeah.

Chris: Right?

Gary: I think in our scenario we had two things working for us.

Chris: Strong culture.

Gary: Number one, we had a very strong culture.

Chris: Great manager.

Gary: We had the economy of scale. We had eight advisors and so we had four of them doing very well and bringing in four green peas. I mean, our sales went down, definitely, and it took a long time to get them back up but we were able to survive because we had four strong veterans that could help get us through. We definitely had that going for us and we had time on our side, there's no doubt. In the capacity of coming in and trying to turn a business around and working as a coach in coming into a dealership and trying to do that, I would not have made that same decision because I wouldn't have time. By the time I got it done it'd be on my way.

Chris: Yeah. You don't have time for green peas.

Gary: No. No, no.

Chris: You have time after.

Gary: Yes.

Chris: Once the momentum is going.

Gary: Yeah.

Chris: That's the real answer is it depends on where you're at. Are you trying to turn it around or do you have a strong culture?

Gary: Yeah.

Chris: You have a couple veterans that can teach them that you know they're going to see or is everybody...? If everybody is underperforming, you should get yourself a hotshot, set the bar high, and then, because you know the green peas coming in, they're only going to aspire to what their example is.

Gary: Yeah.

Chris: You can tell them all day like, "Hey, you should be doing this," but if everybody around them isn't it's going to be hard. They're spending more time with those other advisors then they are with you.

Gary: Yeah.

Chris: No matter what.

Gary: Yeah. Our bar was pretty high.

Chris: Yeah.

Gary: We had to bring in some pretty top end service advisors on the top side of it. Yeah, that did help us.

Chris: Kind of to the other lesson with that is, once momentum is going, it's hard to stop and then you can pull green peas in once you have momentum.

Gary: Yeah.

Chris: Right?

Gary: Yeah.

Chris: You had momentum.

Gary: Yeah, no. Yeah. There's no doubt.

Chris: Even then your numbers dropped a little?

Gary: Yeah. We went backwards and it took us a little while to come back but it wasn't far enough. We were still profitable.

Chris: You loved to come into work so that's important.

Gary: I did like coming to work.

Chris: Would you sit in your car in the parking lot and not want to get out?

Gary: Yeah, god, I just ... I did.

Chris: You did?

Gary: I did not want to go in there. Yeah, it was just miserable. You don't want to work around people like that. The gang mentality took over so those guys all worked together on one shift and they would just commiserate with each other and it just got worse. It just got worse, and worse, and worse. You know, we wanted to create a fun environment, we wanted everybody to make a good living, and have a good time at work, and spend some time together and build a team. They were pushing against that.

Chris: They were entitled.

Gary: They were entitled, very much so, and they felt like they could do it better, right? They got better ideas, they could do it better, meanwhile we had a really good thing going. We're profitable, and you know...

Chris: It was a great place to work.

Gary: Yeah. Absolutely.

Chris: There's nothing better.

Gary: To hell with them.

Chris: We agree on this, right? Kind of?

Gary: I think so. Yeah. I thought we were going to be at odds but I think we definitely - I think -

Chris: In context of, like you know, from going in when you were doing our done-for-yous and you're going in and fixing stores you don't have time.

Gary: Yeah. No.

Chris: It just depends on where you're at. If you're listening to this and you're broken and you need to turn it around, go out and spend the time and find yourself a veteran and ask them to see their numbers, and make sure that their numbers are good, and go that way. But if you have a strong culture and you have good advisors then plug in a green pea and, you know ... That's always a great thing too because people don't understand how much money you could make-

Gary: Right.

Chris: In service. If you get some guy in a vocational thing learning to be a plumber and all of the sudden he's an advisor making twice as much and, you know-

Gary: Yeah.

Chris: Having a good living.

Gary: I know. It's a great way to make a living if you-

Chris: Yeah. No, it's fun.

Gary: You're good at it.

Chris: I mean, look at us. it changes.

Gary: Yeah. For sure.

Chris: You started in the shop but you wrote service too. It's crazy. Just take care of customers and it all works out.

Gary: Yeah, exactly, the work just comes your way. Obviously, it's the only sales game as far as I know in the world, that the customers are being manufactured out front and they just come in on a conveyor belt. They're just coming at you.

Chris: Yeah. You just have to be consistent and smile.

Gary: Yeah. Treat them right, take care of them, offer them the things, the services that they're due for.

Chris: Don't roofie.

Gary: Don't roofie them.

Chris: Don't fight them. Don't push them.

Gary: There's no reason to roofie them.

Chris: Did you hit the guy or did you push him?

Gary: I pushed him a couple times and then I picked him up and kind of threw him down.

Chris: Was it like the stupid high school push or was it like, "It's on like Donkey Kong," push?

Gary: I gave him a couple of pretty good shoves, I guess. I don't know.

Chris: Were you worried?

Gary: It's hard for me to remember. No.

Chris: No?

Gary: No.

Chris: Bro, you could hurt somebody. You weren't worried about going to jail or anything?

Gary: No.

Chris: Man.

Gary: I thought about it the next day.

Chris: Not in the moment?

Gary: Meanwhile my brain was not functioning at normal capacity. I was not thinking at all as you know.

Chris: When I saw you guys the next day you guys were in a fog.

Gary: Man.

Chris: Something was slipped into your drink.

Gary: Yeah.

Chris: It's crazy. You got to be careful.

Gary: Yeah. Thank god, too, some guy grabbed me and talked some sense into me.

Chris: All those times your wife goes out, like down there, you got to be careful.

Gary: I know.

Chris: What if you're working and she's out, you know, her social calendar. You got to be careful.

Gary: Yeah. That's scary because she's got a lot of friends there and so you think that she's okay, and safe, and I'm not there as often as I'd like to be so I got to ... Yeah, she's got to be a little bit more careful. She's got to stick a little closer to home, I think.

Chris: Meanwhile, everybody, Gary will be starting his anger management classes tomorrow.

Gary: The good news is nobody got hurt, nobody went to jail. I went home and went to bed so everybody was fine; a little sickness but that's it.

Chris: Wasn't it over 30 new members to the family last week, right? You did a cyber ... What is it?

Gary: Cyber Monday.

Chris: Cyber Monday which is a crazy ... It's funny that's even a thing.

Gary: They made up a holiday so you could sell stuff. That's what they did.

Chris: Yeah. You did it.

Gary: They invented.

Chris: We did this thing for the first time ever, we offered the advisor training separate from everything else which we've never done, right?

Gary: Yeah.

Chris: We just broke it off. It was good.

Gary: Yeah.

Chris: We have a lot of new people in the family.

Gary: Yeah. It was awesome.

Chris: Hopefully they move up to coaching and we escalate them along their journey, but fun.

Gary: Yeah. They're excited. We got them all on and we've been kind of conversing with them back and forth.

Chris: They got the new stuff too.

Gary: Yup.

Chris: The new stuff that we recorded, so our advisor training has been all updated. Really the difference is my beard.

Gary: Right. Right. We updated the content.

Chris: Updated content.

Gary: Yeah.

Chris: Yeah, but it looked better.

Gary: You went through and modernized.

Chris: I don't look like a baby's butt. When I look at pictures of me without the beard I'm like, "Who is that guy?" That wasn't that long ago.

Gary: No.

Chris: Four years ago.

Gary: I had a conversation with my old service manager on Saturday and she was saying that she missed the baby face. She likes the baby face.

Chris: Yeah.

Gary: Yeah. She said, "I don't know if I can get use to the beard."

Chris: She's no road map. She can't get use to the beard? That's funny. I love you Bickster, but no, the beard is staying.

Gary: The beard stays on.

Chris: Even when it's not a trend anymore.

Gary: Yeah. That was exciting. We gave away the tech training as a bonus in there too, so they got some pretty good stuff for a really good price.

Chris: Don't they get to send an advisor to a live...?

Gary: Yup. We did two tickets to live advisor training, east coast or west coast, so they get to send them to that too. That was the other bonus that we threw in on the backend.

Chris: Yeah, I mean, you gave them ...It was just to get them in the family basically.

Gary: Yeah.

Chris: Because they got way more bang for their buck than ...

Gary: Yeah.

Chris: We got buck for the bang.

Gary: Yeah.

Chris: Is that a way to say it?

Gary: We wanted them to get a big hit off of it so we want them to come in and train their advisors. Then they go back and really knock it dead, and they could just see what we have to offer because I think ... Like you say all the time, it's the best advisor training on the market and we say it, but it's the truth.

Chris: Yeah.

Gary: It really is.

Chris: The advisors will love it.

Gary: Yeah, if you follow the system you can just hit the ball out of the park so we want them to hit the ball out of the park.

Chris: Cool. If you're listening to this you missed the Cyber ... If you didn't buy it you missed the Cyber ... Is it Cyber Monday?

Gary: Cyber Monday. Yeah.

Chris: You missed it so you're screwed, but we love you anyways.

Gary: We'll do maybe Easter. They'll be an Easter special.

Chris: Thank you.

Gary: Keep your eye on your inbox.

Chris: We'll keep you posted on Gary's cholesterol, his getting roofied. Why isn't my life as exciting as yours? Getting in fights. Man.

Gary: I'm getting frozen in my orange underwear, I'm getting in fights.

Chris: That's another ... Should we save that story for another one? Your wife?

Gary: We told that one. No, we're not telling that story.

Chris: No, we got to tell that story. Man. Okay.

Gary: That one is taboo. We're not telling that story.

Chris: That's not taboo. Come on. We'll bring that up. That's funny.

Gary: We'll see. We'll see.

Chris: Okay. Thanks everybody and we hope you have a good week.

Gary: All right. Thanks.

Episode #25: How To Improve Focus And Time Management In Your Service Department

Chris: Welcome, everybody, to Service Drive Revolution, where if you have a service drive, if you have advisors, technicians and customers, this is your home. Where we give you the latest tools, tips and the new stuff that's working in service drives, really, frankly, could be all over the world, but definitely in North America. Thank you so much for joining us. How you doing, G-Man?

Gary: Doing good.

Chris: How was your day today?

Gary: My day was good, actually. A really good day.

Chris: Yeah?

Gary: Very productive.

Chris: Yes.

Gary: Winding down.

Chris: It is winding down, yeah. This is our 25th podcast episode.

Gary: 25.

Chris: 25.

Gary: Man.

Chris: How long have you been married?

Gary: 20 ... Wow. 23 years. 23 years.

Chris: We've done more podcasts than the years you've been married.

Gary: I know, it's crazy, right?

Chris: Is that crazy? Should we hang it up at 25?

Gary: No. I don't think so. I think we keep it going.

Chris: Really?

Gary: Until I fix my cholesterol, I'm not sure we can end this thing.

Chris: Oh, brother.

Gary: Until it gets fixed.

Chris: Let's not hinge it on that. I'm the greatest gift giver ever.

Gary: Yes.

Chris: For your birthday-

Gary: Yes.

Chris: I got you...

Gary: The greatest gift giver ever.

Chris: A year's worth of monthly bourbon.

Gary: Yup.

Chris: This little company hand picks bourbon.

Gary: Mm-hmm (affirmative).

Chris: You got it in the mail today.

Gary: Yep. I got my new bottle and we can open it today.

Chris: Celebration of the 25th podcast.

Gary: That's right.

Chris: We're going to drink bourbon.

Gary: I don't know what's in this bottle, but I do know the last bottle I got was very, very good.

Chris: It went quick.

Gary: Shared ... Yeah. Shared a bunch around the office and people liked it. I'm going to open it.

Chris: By the way, everybody listening to this: We don't drink during the day. This is night. We do this - we're so busy during the day - we do the podcast after work. This is extra credit. I know I've had comments before that, "Oh, those guys drink ..." It's extra credit.

Gary: Not every day.

Chris: Look at this.

Gary: Not every day.

Chris: Look at this stuff.

Gary: Man.

Chris: You can't see this because you're listening. It's called Jack's Dirt.

Gary: Black Dirt.

Chris: Black Dirt.

Gary: Black Dirt.

Chris: Single barrel bourbon, New York. Made in New York, wow.

Gary: New York straight bourbon whiskey, instead of Kentucky.

Chris: Looks like they made that label on a Kinko's. That's some boutique stuff right there.

Gary: Yeah. It's written. It's hand numbered. Barrel number.

Chris: What barrel number was it?

Gary: Let's get the barrel number. HC72914-1.

Chris: Jay, you're just trying to sneak in here.

Gary: Jay's got his cup. Jay ...

Chris: Bourbon for the poor?

Gary: Those of you who can't see, Jay here slid a cup in, because he wants a taste.

Chris: I'll slide the ice across for you there, Jay. Just come on in, it's fine. They see the back of your head. Jay here is in here trying to ...

Gary: Jay is Bogarting, or trying to sip on my whiskey.

Chris: Fun, though.

Gary: Yeah, it's awesome. Thank you, thank you very much.

Chris: What's your favorite, in retrospect? You were just saying a minute ago, before we went live here. You were watching some old podcasts. We literaly have come a long way.

Gary: It has come a long way.

Chris: Can I try that, Ger? Could you hand it to me? I'm wired up. Sorry.

Gary: Yeah.

Chris: Everybody's probably like, "Hey, what are you going to teach us today?" Right?

Gary: I know, right?

Chris: Oh, my gosh. That tastes straight out of an oak barrel.

Gary: That's good.

Chris: That's good.

Gary: It's a little hot. Good. Thank you for that, by the way.

Chris: We're going to talk about ...

Gary: It's the gift that keeps giving all year long. I'm going to be excited.

Chris: That thing won't last a week. We're going to New York, and we'll come back, then it'll be gone.

Gary: It'll be gone. Right. That's cool, I like this.

Chris: What we're going to-

Gary: Cool bottle.

Chris: Talk about today, G-Man? We're going to talk about new time management stuff.

Gary: Yeah.

Chris: It is new, it's not the old, hashed time management stuff.

Gary: Right.

Chris: It's inspired by the book *Deep Work*, by Cal Newport, right?

Gary: Yep. Cal Newport.

Chris: You read that, you liked it.

Gary: I love this book, actually.

Chris: You've taken a bunch of notes and you're going to give some tools. I'm going to be the sidekick. I have not read the book, although I do know some stuff about time management. What we'll do is I'll be like Chrisworth and you'll be Hal Michaels. Everybody will want to kill me. The worst announcer in the NFL. Thank god it was the Cowboys. Chrisworth, there we go.

Gary: You got to say, if you want to save time, you got to protect your time. Then, you'll have more time.

Chris: The key to winning is you got to score points.

Gary: That's right.

Chris: You got to score more points than the other one. The quarterback's got to throw the ball.

Gary: Yeah. What this offense does-

Chris: You're runningback's gotta run.

Gary: .Is it throws the ball, and they catch the ball. When they throw the ball, catch the ball.

Chris: Jackass. How does that guy get a job on network TV?

Gary: I don't know. I honestly don't know.

Chris: Hal Michaels is so good, but it's almost like he doesn't care anymore.

Gary: I know.

Chris: He's like, "Okay, they put me with him. I give up."

Gary: It's almost unwatchable at this point.

Chris: You go from Madden to him.

Gary: It really spoils it for me.

Chris: I'd rather have Dennis Miller back, honestly. That would be better. It would. I like Dennis Miller.

Gary: I think you took it too far.

Chris: I like Dennis Miller.

Gary: Man, that was a disaster when they did that for Monday Night Football. It was terrible.

Chris: No, it was, because there was three of them. There are too many people talking. It wasn't a disaster. If it was just Al and Dennis-

Gary: It might work, that might work.

Chris: I would much rather hear Dennis talk about his right wing politics than Chrisworth talk about Russel Wilson in any capacity whatsoever. How many times can he bring up the play?

Gary: Yeah.

Chris: He's always like, "The play, the play." We know, we know. We lost in the last minutes of the Superbowl. We know, Chris. We got it.

Gary: Yeah.

Chris: It's been two years, let it go.

Gary: Yeah. That's all the information he's got. He's gotta draw on that. I don't know.

Chris: All right.

Gary: Half the stuff he says is wrong.

Chris: I was asking you what your favorite podcast was. Do you have a favorite one?

Gary: Wow. I think, I don't know... The one that I laugh the most at, and I'm laughing at myself, I guess, I'm self deprecating, is the one that we talked about the frozen thing. Your drawing that story out of me. I was telling about how I went in. I thought, that one just made me laugh. That's probably the funniest one that I can think--

Chris: The frozen thing? What is the frozen thing?

Gary: I don't want to go through that story again.

Chris: What is it, though? I don't know.

Gary: It's where I went to that freezing chamber and then I wasn't expecting ...

Chris: Underwear.

Gary: To be in the room with anybody, and wearing orange underwear.

Chris: You like, get into your underwear, we found that out. Right? I teased at the end of the last one. This is funny.

Gary: I don't know why I brought this up. I stepped right into it.

Chris: You walked right into it, because I forgot. We teased at the last one that--

Gary: I'm turning red.

Chris: I have some dirt on you that your wife shared with me.

Gary: Yep.

Chris: Evidently, when Gary comes home every night after a long day ... I don't know, most of the time it's 8:00 or 9:00 at night, probably, you're getting home, right?

Gary: Yep.

Chris: Because you don't live down the street from the office.

Gary: Right, exactly.

Chris: Gary lives in this - I gotta give context here - Gary lives in this community in by the beach and a marina. It's a marina, so you're on the beach, kind of. There's two buildings that are very similar. The pool is in between them, but they're big, huge floor to ceiling windows. You can see across. You can see. When we were over there the other day, we could watch one of the football games on a guy across the pool's TV.

Gary: Yeah. We could see.

Chris: He had a huge, amazing TV that I wish I had.

Gary: You could almost see the score from across the pool.

Chris: You could see the score. Evidently, when Gary gets home every ... Okay, the other thing. Wait, more context. Gary's bedroom is on a floor below where you come in and where the living room is. It's one of those--

Gary: It's on the third floor.

Chris: It's like a townhouse type thing, but you're one the, what? Sixth story, seventh story?

Gary: Four. No, it's four.

Chris: Four?

Gary: Yeah. The roof's five.

Chris: Wow. It seems higher than that.

Gary: Yeah, four. Yeah. The garage is another level below it. Technically, it would be another story. It's probably six all together, six stories.

Chris: It felt like six. He's on the sixth story, but his bedroom is on the fifth. Fifth, or the fourth?

Gary: Fourth.

Chris: It's two down from your living room and kitchen.

Gary: Yeah.

Chris: You walk into his house. Evidently, the windows are wide open, blinds are open. Evidently, his wife disclosed that what drives her crazy about your marriage, frankly ... this is a problem in your marriage.

Gary: She's got bigger problems with me than this, believe me.

Chris: No, this is a problem. That's the problem, is this is a problem, you know? She's crying out for help and you're just ignoring her, taking her for granted. She's crying out for help. Evidently, what Gary does after a long day is he walks in the front door and then, right in front of the windows and the whole world, he just drops trou and undresses; Which makes no logical sense to undress right there. Your hamper isn't there. Nothing is there. Evidently, you get down to your underwear and then you walk over to the couch and you're like, "Honey, I'm home." She's fully clothed. It's weird. Isn't that weird?

Gary: I don't think it's that weird. I think ... To provide context, is I come home and I'm wearing a suit, maybe, or something like that. I don't want to wrinkle my clothes and sit on the couch. I don't want to go downstairs to change. I take my suit and everything off, and I lay it on the chair. Then, I go and I lay down on the couch with her. The windows ... I'm pretty far away from the ... It's not like I'm right up against the windows. It's ... She is dramatizing it. It's not that, it's not as weird as it sounds.

Chris: Okay, Gary.

Gary: It's not as weird as it sounds.

Chris: Can we see ... Can we see the color of the eyes of your neighbors across the way?

Gary: Yeah, we could see ...

Chris: What makes you think, coming the other way, they can't see the color of your underwear?

Gary: I don't know, man. I don't think anybody's looking in my windows.

Chris: See, you think nobody's looking?

Gary: I don't think anybody cares.

Chris: But that's not an excuse. You're going to be walking around your neighborhood and they're going to be like, "That guy, that's the guy with ... That's the guy in his underwear. That's the guy."

Gary: I'm really frustrated with my wife for telling that story, by the way. I had to go on record last night. I went home and, fully clothed, got on the couch because I was wearing jeans. I wasn't worried about it.

Chris: Good.

Gary: She says it happens every night? It happens every once in a while. I just don't--

Chris: Poor wife.

Gary: I'm tired. I don't want to go up and down the stairs. I just want to relax for an extra--

Chris: Your poor wife.

Gary: Minute before I go to bed, you know? I think everybody can relate. I'm sure there are people out there that can relate. If you want to post a comment, I'd love to hear from you.

Chris: No, no.

Gary: I'm sure--

Chris: No comments about Gary's underwear.

Gary: I'm betting, I'm betting people agree with me.

Chris: Nobody does. There's nobody listening to this podcast that has big floor to ceiling windows that comes home and drops trou in front of their windows. There's nobody, trust me.

Gary: Man, I got to re-examine my life.

Chris: If there is, unsubscribe.

Gary: I gotta examine my life.

Chris: You need to talk to...

Gary: I'm getting in too--

Chris: You need to talk to a doctor.

Gary: I'm getting in too many awkward situations. I think something's wrong.

Chris: You need a shrink. I can just see you sitting on a couch with a shrink like, "Okay, Chris and Katya think it's weird, but it's not weird, right?" He's like, "No, it's weird. There's actually a clinical term for that. It's called "drop-trou-itis-something." They'll have a name for it. It's exhibitionism.

Gary: "Drop-trou-itis."

Chris: You're an exhibitionist. That's what you are.

Gary: I absolutely am not.

Chris: You're an exhibitionist.

Gary: No. I'm not an exhibitionist.

Chris: You're so proud of that body. You're like, "Look at me."

Gary: No way.

Chris: "Me, Arnold Schwarzenegger."

Gary: No way. I'm the old guy that just doesn't give a shit anymore. I'm that guy.

Chris: No. That's not true.

Gary: Like a grandpa who shows up in his underwear, you know? I'm that guy. I'm getting to that age, where I just don't care anymore. Whatever, to hell with it. I'm going to be comfortable.

Chris: That's too good. Your poor wife...

Gary: Shall we get into content now? Shall we talk about the book and get off this subject?

Chris: Yeah, really can't get that image. I just want to go on record that if you're listening to this and you agree with Gary--

Gary: Oh, man.

Chris: Unsubscribe. Just quit. Nobody's going to agree with you.

Gary: Unsubscribe.

Chris: Yeah, if you're an exhibitionist like ...

Gary: That's crazy.

Chris: You're in your underwear in a big, huge ...

Gary: Oh, man.

Chris: Those windows. Really, you know what those windows are? They're picture frames.

Gary: Oh my god.

Chris: They are picture frames. Did you see how much your neighbors spend, how much they care about the way their apartments look?

Gary: Yeah. No, they're very nice.

Chris: Why is that, do you think? Because people are constantly looking in.

Gary: Because they know they've got an audience?

Chris: Yeah. There's no blinds. I didn't see any. Do you have blinds?

Gary: Oh, yeah. There's blinds.

Chris: I didn't see--

Gary: There's a shade that comes down, yeah.

Chris: I didn't see any blinds.

Gary: Yeah. There's a shade, there's a shade.

Chris: Come to think of it, a couple of them had blinds closed.

Gary: That's the other thing. I don't want to bother with the shades. They're a pain in the ass to put up and down.

Chris: Do it for your neighbors.

Gary: Tall windows. They just got to look away, just look away.

Chris: Yeah, there you go.

Gary: Just look away.

Chris: That's fair.

Gary: Hey, to your point, you said I overlook the pool. My place overlooks the pool. There's a lot worse things happening down at the pool than what I'm wearing in my apartment, believe me.

Chris: Yeah, but it's not eye level.

Gary: There's guys down there in speedos.

Chris: You have to walk up to the edge and look down. You're framed in a perfect window.

Gary: Hallelujah.

Chris: Oh, man.

Gary: All right, content, content, content. Let's move. *Deep Work?*

Chris: You're Allen Michaels. I'm Collinsworth.

Gary: Here we go, I'm going to move it.

Chris: What you need to do to have better time management is spend your time better.

Gary: You need more time.

Chris: You need more time.

Gary: You need ...

Chris: Is that what Collinsworth would say?

Gary: If you had 25 hours in a day, you'd have more time.

Chris: Stop wasting your time.

Gary: That's right. All right, I want to talk about this book. I read a book just recently. I wrapped it up a couple weeks ago, and it's called *Deep Work*. Chris mentioned the author. The author is Cal Newport. Really, really good book. I'm going to show it for the camera if anybody is watching. I'm just going to put it up, *Deep Work*. Great book. It talked about really focusing your mind and how your mind works. Deep work, or being able to think deeply/focus deeply on a problem is a muscle. That in order for you to be able to do that effectively on a consistent basis, you have to exercise it like you would any other muscle if you want to be strong. He goes into a lot of different techniques and tactics, what a lot of other people have done, a lot of famous people, a lot of the thought leaders in our country, have done to train their mind to think deeply about it. There's a couple things, I wanted to talk about a couple of stories in the book. Then, I wanted to give couple of techniques that you could use almost right away, that would help you think deeply. It's pretty interesting. He tells this story about this social media CEO that he doesn't name, but took a plane to Tokyo because he found that he because he was on a plane and he had nothing else to do, he could focus very deeply at that time. He had a book that he had to write. He had to finish it, and so he took a plane from here to Tokyo. Turned around, got on a plane from Tokyo back, and he wrote an entire book in that amount of time. 30 hours or something like that, on a plane.

Chris: Makes sense, uninterrupted.

Gary: Yeah, uninterrupted time. One of the things he goes into in the book are, Marissa Mayer, the CEO of Yahoo, she banned working from home. People weren't logging into the servers enough. She wanted people to log in. What ended up happening was that really the only thing effective that happened from them logging onto the server was they got email. Email was one of the most distracting things. He talked a lot about social media.

Chris: Did production go down?

Gary: Production goes down. Absolutely.

Chris: That's hilarious.

Gary: Yeah. You get what you ask for.

Chris: Right.

Gary: We all ...

Chris: Email is like an addiction. What was the thing Jerry was talking about, About how you get endorphins when you're checking email?

Gary: Yep.

Chris: It's like a drug. You get addicted to it, right?

Gary: Yeah. We get accustomed to it, so we're constantly checking our Facebook, constantly checking our email.

Chris: You're getting nothing done.

Gary: Right. Those distractions prevent your mind from getting deep and focusing deep into the problem. Because we think so shallow and we allow that to come into our lives, then we don't have the ability to focus deep when we actually need to. You think about your computer screen all the time. You're trying to work on a problem, you're trying to come up with a new idea. Maybe you're working on a marketing campaign. Then, a little email thing/window is popping into the top of your screen, at the upper right. It says, "Hey, somebody just posted on your Facebook." You're like, "What did they say?" You want to go check it out, and it won't allow you to get to that point. We think that we can adjust. We have the opinion of ourselves that we can just take a quick look at that and then I'm going to go back. What they find is that your productivity drops dramatically, sometimes by 80%, by just what they call 'task switching'. Taking your attention, momentarily, off of the project that you're focused on, looking at something and then coming back.

Chris: That's the term for it? Task switching?

Gary: Your brain has to reset. Task switching, yeah.

Chris: Yeah. Does he talk in there about how long it takes you to get back on task? Didn't Microsoft do a thing where it's 20 minutes?

Gary: Yeah.

Chris: Between ... If you check your email and go back, it takes you 20 minutes to get back in the flow.

Gary: Yeah, to get your brain to refocus and get back on the task. Each time you're losing 20 minutes every time you look away and stop, it takes you 20 minutes to get back. It doesn't feel that way. That the thing we get into. It just doesn't feel that way. I think about how this applies to the service drive and service managers. You and I have worked in a lot of drives. I just remember sitting in manager's offices all the time trying to have a conversation or make a plan. Go through financials and talk about what we're going to do. There's this constant interruption. Like you say, the 'got a minute?' meetings; Where they're coming in all the time saying, "Hey boss, you got a minute? You got a minute?" Then, they're asking some question about some problem that doesn't even really matter.

Chris: Yeah.

Gary: It's not relevant.

Chris: One of me favorite things to do. Somebody just did it for Joe Mack, one of our guys that runs a big dealer group in Carolina, went down and watched Joe Mack.

Gary: Mm-hmm (affirmative).

Chris: He was like, "Yeah." He stayed there all day, nobody interrupted. Two-hour lunch, went and played golf.

Gary: Yeah.

Chris: When we tell people coming into the program, we're like, "That's how it should be. You're a leader. You should be out in front, thinking strategy and all that. Not in the soup." People are like, "Well, I only have three advisors." It's like, it's the same. It doesn't matter. That's all. There's systems in place. When people see it, it's like, "Oh, I want that."

Gary: Mm-hmm (affirmative).

Chris: Because you're not getting dragged around by the tail all day.

Gary: Yeah. It changes your life when you can stop and actually focus in on a problem. I remember somebody asked me this a long time ago, when I was still working up in the service department up in the bay. They said, "If you're sitting down at your desk and you're thinking about your business, are you working?" I thought about that for a minute and I said, "Yeah, of course. Right?" I think when we come from, especially me, I come from this background where I'm a tech, and the revenue and success is measured by motion, right? If you're going to turn hours, you have to move fast. You're constantly moving. When you're in motion, things are happening. Then, you go to this other place where now you're a manager and you're sitting behind a desk. Actually, revenue is produced by not moving. Right? By being able to sit and be still for a while. Being able to focus on your business is really what's going to produce the maximum benefit, for you and for everybody. Then, allowing yourself to get distracted by things that just don't matter. Customer problems that we've heard a million times over that the advisors know how to solve. They get lost in the weeds and they get in the soup, like you say. It just drags them down.

Chris: Yeah. Lost in the weeds, maybe. To give the Chrisworth on that, a lot of times, they're just lazy.

Gary: Yeah.

Chris: It's easier to drop it on the manager's lap instead of owning it one more step.

Gary: Yeah, or it's an attention-getter. They want that attention.

Chris: They want their attention, because their manager never pays attention.

Gary: Yeah.

Chris: Yeah, that, too.

Gary: They come in, "Hey boss, remember me? Remember me? Look at me." My advice is: You gotta stop that. That's the first thing. You have to be able to get control over how many people come in and bug you. Empower them to solve customer problems, empower them to solve problems with production. Give them leeway so that they don't have to come in and bug you every five minutes. Because you're going to tell them, the answer is going to be the same almost every time. You got to let them, you got to give them some leeway. You got to buy yourself some uninterrupted moments. In the book, one of the things he talks about is scheduling blocks of time. It doesn't have to be every day and it doesn't have to be an entire day. He even suggests that deep work, really, in maybe five to six-hours max is what you can really focus your mind like that on. What he-

Chris: The interruptions?

Gary: What's that?

Chris: Then you need "goner minutes?"

Gary: You need to separate from what you got. I don't think I could do five hours. One of the things he was suggesting was, do an hour. A couple of times a week, three times a week.

Chris: It's crazy how much you can get done.

Gary: Schedule yourself an hour.

Chris: Just, how many times, when you worked in a store, did you go in on a Saturday?

Gary: Yeah.

Chris: On a Sunday.

Gary: I used to go in on Sunday.

Chris: Yep. I would get, "I'm going to be here a while." In two hours, I was done. My desk was clean, I was done, because nobody was there to bug me.

Gary: Yeah.

Chris: It's crazy.

Gary: Sometimes, I'd just stay late at night, too. Just work through the evening, because again, it's just quiet, it's dark. There's nobody there. There's no salespeople, there's nobody. Then, you can just get a ton done. It shouldn't have to be that way. I think if you can find yourself blocks of time. I think we all have it. We have a hard time finding it because we're still in the fight. We're in the battle. With people coming in all the time, you're having to try to refocus. You can't find the time because you got that 20-minute lag where you're trying to get back to task. It's just too hard. You feel like you don't have the time. If you scheduled it, you locked your door, you went for an hour/hour and a half, you would. It would be amazing how much you could get done.

Chris: Now, when you would go into your office on Sundays, would you strip down to your underwear?

Gary: No.

Chris: I mean, wouldn't you have been more comfortable if you would have? There were no sales people there.

Gary: I'm guessing I would have been more ...

Chris: Exhibitionist.

Gary: I would have been more comfortable, but I'm not an exhibitionist, which I why I chose not to--

Chris: Let me be the one diagnosing--

Gary: Take my clothes off.

Chris: What you are. You're not allowed to diagnose yourself.

Gary: To quote:

Chris: Let Doctor Chris diagnose. You have been diagnosed as an exhibitionist.

Gary: Talk about task switching. You got me task switching. I'm going to quote my friend Jocko:

Chris: You're fine, you got notes.

Gary: Back to the book.

Chris: You didn't ask me what my favorite podcast was, that we've done.

Gary: I didn't. Yeah, what is your favorite podcast?

Chris: The Jocko one. It really was a learning experience. We learned a ton.

Gary: Man.

Chris: We got our ass kicked.

Gary: Yeah.

Chris: I was so bummed.

Gary: That was a rough one. That was a rough interview. I caught a lot--

Chris: Had so many good ones up until then.

Gary: I caught a lot of hell for that.

Chris: Then, smack. Yeah.

Gary: The funny thing is I was just trying to engage them. It just ... Yeah.

Chris: He's a ... Hey, we learned.

Gary: Yeah.

Chris: It was good.

Gary: We learned.

Chris: We'll use it. At some point, that'll come in handy.

Gary: This pain, at some point, will become useful. I was talking about this CEO. The productivity went down. Let's see, let me look at my notes here. Microsoft ...

Chris: See, it took you 10 minutes to get back.

Gary: I know, to get back on task.

Chris: That's all the proof you guys need. I'm like email to Gary.

Gary: Bill Gates used to do what he called 'think weeks'. He'd disappear, and he only did it a couple of times a year. He literally would go off grid. You couldn't get him.

Chris: I want to do that.

Gary: No email, no social media.

Chris: I want to do that.

Gary: No cell phone, no texting, nothing. Off grid, which I think it's genius. If you think about it, two weeks a year, that's not that much time.

Chris: Yeah.

Gary: It gives him the opportunity. What did he come out with? If you look at how successful he was, you have to look at that and say, "Man, that's something there I want to try." What if you just did two days?

Chris: Mm-hmm (affirmative).

Gary: Disconnected yourself. Being able to separate yourself from all that noise really helped him learn how to focus deeply, really go in and create some really cool stuff. There's a lot to it. My recommendation is to get the book, first of all. I highly recommend you reading it. He tells stories about people who have done, some pretty great people have done some great stuff, the techniques they used. Then, puts it into practical terms, and gives you some techniques that you can try and use on your own. There's five, six. different styles of focusing and performing deep work in a different way. You just got to find whatever fits you, your schedule, your job. Whatever would fit your lifestyle and the way you want to work, right? Not everybody - I can't - I don't know that I could disappear for an entire day and focus deeply. I definitely think an hour or two here or there would be a great way to start and help me get there, for sure.

Chris: I did that when I did the *Gamification* book. I rented a house in Malibu. It was off season, it was winter. The prices were good. I rented it for eight days. It ends up, no joke, when

701

we get there, my whole goal was to finish the *Gamification* book. I can't get anything done here.

Gary: Yeah.

Chris: I get interrupted non-stop, right? I get there and the lady tells me, "This is where Steven Spielberg wrote ET." It was his old house. It was a little house in Malibu, up on a cliff. It wasn't on the beach, but it was up on a cliff.

Gary: Mm-hmm (affirmative).

Chris: The whole time I'm writing *Gamification*, I'm thinking I'm channeling Steven Spielberg and ET. There's no connection really, between the two. What I did do is there was a library in that house. I left *Irreplaceable Service Manager* in the books. I think I put it in there. There were a bunch of great books. I'm like, "They'll probably throw it away." It'll mean something to me. I want that book to be here with all these books. It was pretty funny. I did, I got a ton done.

Gary: Yeah.

Chris: Still had time to relax, barbecue and have fun. Seriously, the phones didn't work out there.

Gary: Yeah.

Chris: There was nothing you could do.

Gary: I think that's the point, too. At some point, you've got to quiet the noise down. There's just so much of it. In this day and age now ...

Chris: It's crazy. I'm not a big fan of social media, but--

Gary: Oh, man.

Chris: We don't know anybody who's successful that does their own social media.

Gary: No.

Chris: All these guys that are successful, somebody else is doing it. They're not on their Instagram or--

Gary: Yeah, they're farming it out.

Chris: Yeah. It's such a distraction.

Gary: Yeah.

Chris: Same thing with email.

Gary: There's a story in the book about that, about a writer who was a New York Times columnist. All the writers at the time are tweeting. They build, basically, their career and their following by tweeting and being out there. It was a distraction for her. She didn't want to do it. They were like, "You got to have a Twitter."

Chris: You got to tweet.

Gary: "All the cool kids have a Twitter. You got to go do it." She's being forced into this routine where it doesn't really fit her. It's not creating a following, because then her work suffers. Now, okay, yeah. People are looking at her Twitter, but then the stuff she's writing isn't as good because she can't focus on it. It's funny. We're all being forced into that gap. It's not for everybody.

Chris: Yeah. Every time we get a social media guy, they're like, "You got to have a Twitter." If you look at our Twitter, if you can find it, I think we've tweeted three times. I hated every time. I'm just not into--

Gary: I thought that was pretty funny.

Chris: Facebook's enough.

Gary: You're like, "I'm not getting a Twitter."

Chris: Even a Facebook is too much. No, it's so true, though. We do. We're constantly switching. We never get to really focus on the big levers that move the numbers, you know?

Gary: Think about it, too. Right now, when you're waiting in line, you're waiting in line somewhere, what do you do? You got your phone out and you're thumbing through something. Any time you have any time to sit anywhere, you're like, "I'm going to check my phone. I'm going to go look at my ..."

Chris: Seahawks.

Gary: "Let me check my Facebook, let me see the Seahawks. Let me look at the last--"

Chris: It's funny, too, because--

Gary: "Press conference."

Chris: The NFL is 365 days a year now.

Gary: Yeah.

Chris: There's always news. There's always something.

Gary: It just draws out attention right in. We don't even get to quiet the noise down at that moment. We're just always on, always on, all the time. He was saying in the book that your brain is a muscle. I talked about this earlier. Physically, your brain will change by you focusing deeply. It'll physically change the composition of your brain. It literally is a muscle - you have to exercise it. We don't get there, we're doing this all the time, you're never going to get a chance.

Chris: Wow.

Gary: It's a great book, a great book.

Chris: How much can your brain bench?

Gary: My brain?

Chris: Does your brain get fatter? What happens?

Gary: My brain? My brain does not bench as much as I do, that's for sure.

Chris: That's funny. That's good stuff.

Gary: Yeah. *Deep Work*, Cal Newport. I recommend it. Go out and get it. I listened to it, I'm reading it right now. I'm probably going to go through it a few times because, again, I love books that have content and lessons in them that I can highlight, that I can actually apply to my life. This one and the book *Pitch Anything* are probably my two favorite books so far this year. They both had lessons in them.

Chris: Yeah. I'll tell you, if you, in your service drive, do your deep work or your thing that you should be doing every day; locking the doors, going through repair orders, missed opportunities, that's where the leverage is.

Gary: Yeah.

Chris: Everyone's like, "I don't have time." You're like, "Well, you have time to be on Facebook or whatever else." This is life or death.

Gary: Mm-hmm (affirmative). Yeah. The number one thing you can do in your drive is look at your repair orders. See what they're doing. What are your advisors doing? Are they offering-

Chris: Inspections?

Gary: Are they missing stuff? Are they doing inspections? If you think that it's happening every time, and you got some really good advisors, you're sadly mistaken. Even the best advisors are missing stuff all the time. You got to coach them. There's a reason why - we talk football a lot -but there's a reason why these football players are making millions and millions of dollars and they still have a coach. They need somebody to remind them: put your foot here, step here. They forget. They've got to run the same drills that we ran in Pop Warner, they're still doing in the NFL.

Chris: It's all about the basis.

Gary: It's all about the basics.

Chris: Tackling is all about basics. It's funny how some teams can tackle and some can't.

Gary: Yep.

Chris: It's just fundamentals.

Gary: Yeah, it's just fundamentals.

Chris: They start thinking they don't need it, and then they, all of the sudden, they can't tackle.

Gary: Yeah, they're trying trick pays. I think that's what we do in service departments all the time. I was talking to a manager about this the other day. When things are working, we start to layer and we start to layer processes on top of processes. We don't go back to the basics. It's all blocking and tackling. That's what they've got to do. That ability to shut the door and focus deeply for an hour or so. Get into your business and look really deeply into your business and what's happening. That changes everything. That would fix 90% of people's problems, I tell you.

Chris: Yeah.

Gary: They just could do that.

Chris: It's good. To wrap it up, G-Man, what we're talking about here is time management. The key to it, the new stuff for time management is avoiding the new stuff, which is email, social media. Closing off your door.

Gary: That's funny, bro.

Chris: It is.

Gary: The new stuff is avoiding the new stuff.

Chris: Yeah, it is. Get away from your social media and your email all day. You don't have to have Twitch and be checking it. If it's an emergency, they'll call you. It'll be fine. Somebody will get ahold of you.

Gary: Mm-hmm (affirmative).

Chris: It can wait. You can check email twice a day. You can do Facebook once a day. You don't need to know about some dog that has a cute video or whatever on there.

Gary: Right.

Chris: It'll be okay. Focus on the big levers, the big stuff; Like going through repair orders, one on ones with your people. Get out in the shop, get out in the drive. Call a couple customers and say, "How was it?"

Gary: Right.

Chris: Call a couple customers that declined work and ask them why they declined it.

Gary: Try to make an appointment--

Chris: They need the work.

Gary: In your service drive.

Chris: Yeah, try to make an appointment. Get out in front of it and don't be distracted, don't be like, "Squirrel, squirrel."

Gary: Right.

Chris: With everything. That just takes some discipline and focus, but the results are huge. Huge leverage.

Gary: Yeah.

Chris: That's the key to time management. Don't do it in your underwear. You don't have to do it in your underwear.

Gary: That's right.

Chris: Wear underwear, but don't have that be the only thing you're wearing.

Gary: Make sure they're not orange, then you're okay.

Chris: You might go to jail. Man, I don't know how you've avoided jail.

Gary: No.

Chris: You're walking around in your underwear, you're getting in fights. That's crazy. You're out of control.

Gary: Oh, man. I'm not out of control.

Chris: You're having a midlife crisis.

Gary: These are simple stories.

Chris: Next thing you know, you're going to be driving a fast conver-- Oh, you have a fast convertible. Oh my gosh, everybody pray for Gary.

Gary: Hey, I'm an empty-nester. Things are ... We're having a good time.

Chris: It's Tuesday. I know it's Tuesday, but on Sunday, pray for Gary. He's having a hard time.

Gary: Man.

Chris: That was 25. Thanks, everybody, for listening. We love you for subscribing.

Gary: Keep downloading. We appreciate the support. Moving up iTunes. I know Chris doesn't think so.

Chris: Manage--

Gary: I think we can be number one.

Chris: No.

Gary: Service Manager Podcast, number one.

Chris: Manage your time. Thanks, everybody. Bye.

Gary: Bye.

Made in the USA
Middletown, DE
20 September 2024

61136123R00398